PROMOTERS, PLANTERS, AND PIONEERS

THE WEST SERIES

Aritha van Herk, Series Editor

ISSN 1922-6519

This series focuses on creative non-fiction that explores our sense of place in the West - how we define ourselves as Westerners and what impact we have on the world around us. Essays, biographies, memoirs, and insights into Western Canadian life and experience are highlighted.

UNIVERSITY OF
CALGARY
PRESS

PROMOTERS, PLANTERS, AND PIONEERS

The Course and Context of Belgian Settlement in Western Canada

CORNELIUS J. JAENEN

THE WEST SERIES

ISSN 1922-6519

University of Calgary Press
2500 University Drive NW
Calgary, Alberta
Canada T2N 1N4
www.uofcpress.com

LIBRARY AND ARCHIVES CANADA CATALOGUING IN PUBLICATION

Jaenen, Cornelius J., 1927-
          Promoters, planters, and pioneers : the course and context of Belgian settlement in Western Canada / Cornelius J. Jaenen.

(The West series, ISSN 1922-6519 ; 4)
Includes bibliographical references and index.
Also issued in electronic formats.
ISBN 978-1-55238-258-5

          1. Belgians—Canada, Western—History. 2. Belgian Canadians—Canada, Western—History. 3. Immigrants—Canada, Western—History. 4. Canada, Western—Emigration and immigration. 5. Belgium—Emigration and immigration. I. Title. II. Series: West series (Calgary, Alta.) ; 4

FC106.B2J33 2011   971.2'0043932   C2011-902288-5

The University of Calgary Press acknowledges the support of the Alberta Foundation for the Arts for our publications. We acknowledge the financial support of the Government of Canada through the Canada Book Fund for our publishing activities. We acknowledge the financial support of the Canada Council for the Arts for our publishing program.

Cover design, page design, and typesetting by Melina Cusano

TABLE OF CONTENTS

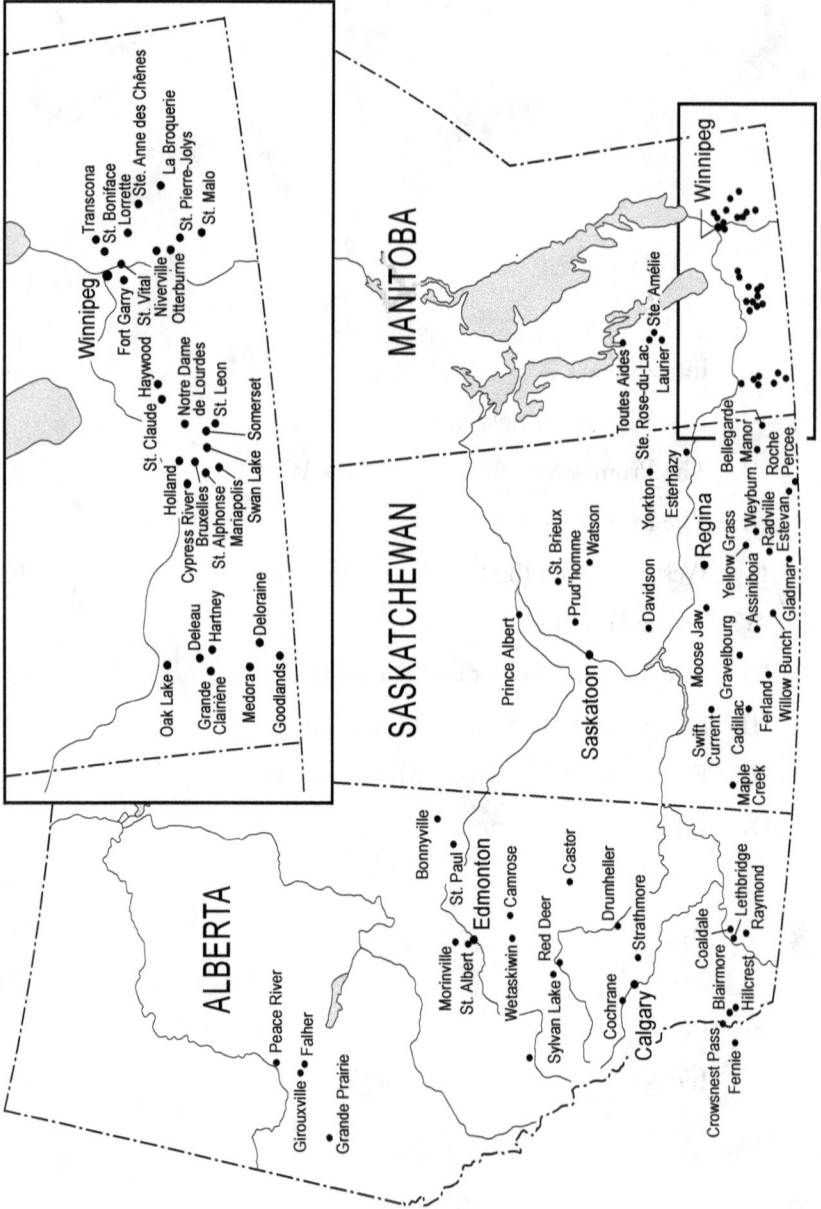

ALBERTA

Peace River
Girouxville • Falher
Grande Prairie

Bonnyville
St. Paul
Morinville
St. Albert
Edmonton
Wetaskiwin • Camrose
Sylvan Lake • Red Deer
Castor
Drumheller
Cochrane • Strathmore
Calgary
Coaldale
Blairmore
Crowsnest Pass
Fernie • Hillcrest
Lethbridge
Raymond

SASKATCHEWAN

Prince Albert

St. Brieux
Prud'homme
Watson

Saskatoon

Davidson

Moose Jaw
Swift Current
Cadillac
Maple Creek
Ferland
Willow Bunch
Gravelbourg
Yellow Grass
Assiniboia
Gladmar
Regina
Weyburn
Radville
Estevan
Bellegarde
Manor
Roche Percée
Esterhazy
Yorkton
Ste. Rose-du-Lac
Laurier
Ste. Amélie
Toutes Aides

MANITOBA

Winnipeg

Winnipeg
Transcona
St. Boniface
Lorette
Ste. Anne des Chênes
La Broquerie
Niverville
St. Pierre-Jolys
Otterburne
St. Malo
St. Vital
Fort Garry
St. Claude Haywood
Notre Dame de Lourdes
St. Leon
Somerset
Holland
Cypress River
Bruxelles
St. Alphonse
Manipolis
Swan Lake
Oak Lake
Grande Clairière
Deleau
Hartney
Medora
Deloraine
Goodlands

INTRODUCTION

L'oubli de ses origines ou l'ignorance de ses traditions repré-
sente pour toute société un appauvrissement regrettable. Mais
une mémoire vivante enracinée solidement dans une histoire
pleinement appréciée enrichit notablement la culture d'un
peuple. Le rappel de ses expériences historiques établit son iden-
tité, clarifie sa vision, et assure la vitalité de ses projets d'avenir.

– Remi J. De Roo, Bishop of Victoria, 1987.

The motivation for writing about the Belgian experience in Western
Canada is identified with a number of factors. A project conceived in the
cadre of the Generation Series of Canadian ethnic histories, as a collabor-
ative work with Professor André Vermeirre of the Université de Montréal,
proved to be stillborn. When I returned to the project, encouraged by
some colleagues and diplomats following an international colloquium on
the Belgian Presence in Canada at the University of Ottawa in October
1999, I came to realize the deep attachment I had to such an undertaking.

First, I am the child of Belgian immigrants – a Flemish father and a
Walloon mother – and all my grandparents came to Saskatchewan after
World War I. In fact, at one point I held a Belgian passport that also
meant that I was subject to military service in the land of my ancestors. As
a young child, I spoke French, Flemish, and a Walloon dialect. According
to my extended family, I was somewhat of a Belgian nationalist, although
I am uncertain of the nature of such a designation in my pre-school years.

A second influence was the public school where I learned English, the language in which I now write most effectively. That one-room country school, taught by highly skilled and dedicated teachers who could manage eight grades of more than thirty pupils, was designed as more than a place of learning. It was an experiment in acculturation and socialization, intended to "civilize and Christianize" immigrant children, as I learned much later in university. The curriculum, with its varied extra-curricular activities, patriotic exercises and community activities, followed the precepts set out by J.T.M. Anderson (teacher/inspector/Minister of Education/Premier) in his *The Education of the New Canadian* (1919). This process, designed to cleanse me of traits and habits of Belgianness and Catholicism that did not coincide with the anglo-celtic model, failed to take into account the strength of counter-educational forces. My family, for example, did not feel inferior culturally or socially to the dominant group, and in some respects harboured some attitudes of superiority. Thus, an important emotional attachment to my ancestral roots remained while feeling quite integrated into the community. These resurfaced decades later when the present project began to take shape. As the product of an innovative and effective educational program, I came to understand better the immigrant experience in the context of attempts at nation building in the context of a difficult environment, during years of economic instability in a multicultural milieu.

The third influence in the shaping of this book was the physical and socio-economic environment of rural Saskatchewan in the inter-war years. I grew up in years of drought and depression, saw topsoil drift into banks like snow and hordes of grasshoppers obscure the view of the blazing sun. I witnessed at first hand the enormous and discouraging challenges people faced. Some surmounted terrible odds but others turned to internal migration to more attractive regions to begin again. Thus, it was that my father followed the advice of a compatriot in the Red River valley and we moved close to the main centre of Belgian settlement in Western Canada. In Winnipeg, I began my college and university studies that eventually determined my career, and indirectly this study.

Finally, my career as a teacher – at all levels of education ranging from a one-room elementary school, high school, independent boys' school, university to post-graduate studies – took me from British Columbia to Newfoundland. Throughout this further broadening of my perspectives, I was involved with many ethno cultural issues and projects as well as relevant historical societies. This enabled me to appreciate the diversity of experiences immigrants faced over time and in different locations. Within each ethnic group, there is a wide range of attitudes and objectives. All this caused me to reflect on my own role within the community when I was invited to sit as a representative on the Canadian Consultative Committee on Multiculturalism, the Manitoba Advisory Committee on Bilingualism and Biculturalism, and the Manitoba delegation to the Etats-Généraux du Canada Français. There were lessons to be learned as I observed the interaction between ethno cultural groups and their fragments in national, regional, and local contexts.

The conception of this history differs from that of most so-called ethnic histories by beginning with a documented consideration of the process of emigration in its material and psychological aspects, not merely of push/pull factors as related to immigration. Moreover, the major source of information for this segment of Western Canadian history has been the Belgian archives. The settlement process, which is the major thrust of the study, is examined with three contexts in mind. Firstly, there is the question of space. The flow of emigrants was to a distant western region of a huge continent, followed in many cases by an additional westward movement from a St. Boniface / Winnipeg port of entry onto three significantly different prairie steppes to the barrier of the Rockies. Settlement along the Pacific Rim did not reflect the same spatial movement but was one of implantation on Vancouver Island and interior continental valleys. Secondly, there is the element of time. Geographic regions assumed different qualities and importance with the exploitation and development of natural resources, the evolution of the economy, and the social, political, and cultural character of each era. Landscapes in which Belgians settled could appear quite different over time because settlement itself altered the environment, as did climatic fluctuations, the opening to world markets, improved transportation, and other human interventions. Time and space constitute the context of our study. Thirdly, there is the human element, never mechanical and sometimes unpredictable, that remains prominent in the economic, institutional, and socio-intellectual paradigms employed to characterize the settlement process. Individuals and families made decisions that resulted in responses to challenges that we characterize as adaptation, accommodation, integration, and resistance. In the absence of over-arching Belgian ethnic institutions, particular religious and "national" cultural bodies, or internal ethnolinguistic homogeneity, the role of the individuals and small groups assumed a primary importance in the story we recount.

I am convinced that this personal journey has influenced the manner in which I have approached this project. I owe a great debt to many individuals, institutions and publications. Unlike most ethnic historians, I have decided to identify individuals and events, sometimes of less than national importance, because that is what makes history a living record. A number of personal and family experiences across Western Canada are included, not as a filiopietistic desire to sing the praises of particular pioneers but to illustrate the complexity of the immigrant experience. Some individuals have been honoured publicly, such as a dairy farmer in Saskatoon remembered in the naming of Brevoort Park, but many remain unknown. Men and women identified in this study are not singled out to the exclusion of others because they are pre-eminently notable. They are illustrative of the process of emigration, immigration, settlement, integration, innovation and adaptation. It is necessary to put a human face to what would otherwise be only academic analysis, theoretical speculation and demographic reduction. Biographical details are sometimes useful in revealing the events in the life of an individual or family and especially the meaning attached to these events. The hopes, fears, fantasies, emotions, achievements and discouragements of these individuals, families and communities are their living history. Without doubt, there are others we have failed to identify but research can only uncover a small portion of the historical panorama.

This is a history of an elusive yet identifiable group, initially deemed by politicians to rank among the "preferred," yet scarcely mentioned in studies of Canadian ethnicity and multiculturalism. What distinguished Belgians from many other newcomers was the perception they were in a "preferred" category because of their attributed resourcefulness and adaptability, their identification with both the English and French socio-cultural communities, and the image of a brave, independent, democratic, civilized Belgium that emerged from foreign occupation during two world wars. Although they are a comparatively small national group in the ethnic mosaic of the West, they were portrayed as successful promoters, planters and pioneers. They promoted market gardening, dairying and the orchard industry. Although Belgium was a small nation, its capitalists were prominent promoters, generous in securing capital in launching and encouraging financial, industrial and commercial enterprises in the region. They were planters, or early settlers, as were many others, who distinguished themselves in promoting the cultivation of chicory, tobacco and sugar beets and who proved to be accomplished marketgardeners. They were pioneers, as were all first colonists, who prepared the way for others not just as "rude sons of toil" but also men and women of thought. They were true pioneers in mining operations, unionization, education and missionary work. In other words, the measure of their participation in the development of Western Canadian culture, economy and ideology was not dependent on their numerical strength, their political power, or their corporate life. Instead, they participated, contributed and innovated as individuals, as family units, then as workers, community members and Christians. Belgians differed from the larger immigrant groups inasmuch as they were not recruited by important immigration societies and they did not settle in ethnic blocs. Belgian nationality was a diplomatic and political creation of the Great Powers in the early nineteenth century. Belgian identity, however, was rooted since mediaeval times in the independence, commerce, industry and higher learning associated with Bruges, Antwerp, Liege and Louvain. Not surprisingly, Belgian settlement in Western Canada was associated with adaptability and individuality rather than primarily with nationality or ethnicity.

As this account of the settlement and integration of Belgian nationals in Western Canada unfolds, it becomes evident that the Belgian bi-ethnic experience is instructive, even unique, in the context of and in comparison to the experience of a large number of other ethnic groups in the region. Belgians came from a bilingual milieu into a Canadian region where the French language was under siege. Both Flemings and the less numerous Walloons were nominally Catholic, the former generally characterized as conservative agrarians and the latter as more liberal, sometimes anticlerical. The miners were generally radical, socialistic and anticlerical, a source of concern for the Canadian clergy but not for the Belgian authorities that distrusted clerical emigration projects. Flemings were more likely able to speak French than the Walloons to speak Flemish or Dutch. Catholic immigration agents sought out Belgians, especially when recruitment in France brought meagre results. The Walloons recruited by these clerics were culturally Catholic, so they assimilated into the French-Canadian communities in Western Canada where they were settled. Nevertheless, they displayed marked "old country" nonconformist attitudes in what was essentially an ultramontane local environment. Many took up the cause of Catholic schooling associated with French language rights and they supported the francophone press, radio, drama and literature. Enclosed, or *encadré*, in the defensive francophone community in Western Canada, the Walloons failed to produce significant Walloon institutions. Flemings, on the other hand, generally settled in clusters in anglophone communities, integrated readily into the dominant anglo-celtic host society, but sacrificed neither their Catholicism nor their bilingualism.

We have tried to incorporate relevant concepts and evidence from all the disciplines of the humanities and social sciences. It seemed important in this study to focus on the substantive questions concerning migration, integration, social conflict, self-image and group solidarity in a rapidly evolving Canadian pluralistic society. My hope is that the tale I tell is somewhat comprehensible and relevant to the readers, regardless of their own background and perspective.

Cornelius J. Jaenen

View of a Trapper's Cabin, Kananaskis, AB, 1911. (Glenbow NA-2158)
Reception of a Belgian official investigating immigration conditions.

THE VIEW FROM BELGIUM

Belgian emigration to Canada has been unobtrusive and somewhat in-conspicuous in terms of world migratory movements. The concept of emi-gration for Belgians usually meant relocating, either temporarily or long-term, in a neighbouring European region, especially in northern France and the Paris region. Furthermore, in the decade preceding the outbreak of World War I, and in the period from the 1920s to the 1970s, immigrants settling in Belgium exceeded nationals who emigrated.[1] Emigration to Canada depended not only on local economic and social conditions in Belgium but also on the image of Canada, if any, in official and popular sectors. Investors, commercial entrepreneurs, speculators, missionaries and professional people were more likely to have some knowledge of op-portunities and conditions in Canada than were farmers, artisans and labourers. When confronted with attractive prospects for a better stan-dard of living emanating from a variety of foreign propaganda approach-es, there remained the dual problems of choosing the best foreign venture and of weighing the impact of leaving one's familiar milieu.

Belgians had a discouraging experience with colonization companies. The classic example was the Santo-Tomas project in Guatemala in 1845–50. All government assistance to expatriation thereafter ceased. In 1856 the Ministry of Foreign Affairs announced an official policy: "The policy of the government is to leave complete freedom to emigration, not to pro-mote it, and not to protect it." The Senate repeated the same approach in 1889: "The attitude of the government must be passive, in the sense that the government must neither desire nor encourage emigration.… It is ne-cessary that each one be free to act as he wishes."[2]

Canada as a desirable place to settle had to compete with a number of seemingly more attractive localities. This foreign attraction resulted in several emigration experiences, referred to in Belgium as "emigration fevers."[3] The most important waves of emigration were directed to Wisconsin, U.S.A. (1855–56), Brazil (1885), and Argentina (1888–89). In the 1880s, Flemish immigrants settled in Moline and Rock Island, Illinois, and around Detroit, Michigan. Walloons from Hainaut went to the mines and industrial centres of Pennsylvania. One must not exaggerate the impact of these waves. Tiny Luxembourg, with a population 5 per cent that of Belgium, sent almost as many emigrants to the United States in the late nineteenth century as did Belgium. In other words, Belgians were not as enthusiastic about emigration as many western Europeans, notably the Scandinavians, Dutch and Swiss. If there was no great enthusiasm for a future in the United States, there would be even less for prospects in Canada. Jules Leclercq, in comparing life in Canada and the United States, found Canadians to be less energetic, less enterprising and less confident of success than Americans.[4] Forty years later, Henri de Man, who saw Canada too anchored to the past[5] expressed the same sentiment.

How overcome the proverbial parochialism of the common people, their inexperience with and distrust of rupturing ties with their traditional community? The provincial governor of Luxembourg opined:

> In general, the Luxembourgeois does not emigrate because he is content with his lot. When he does leave to go far away, it is not usually to find a means of making a living but motivated by the desire to make a fortune. Even then, he rarely leaves his native soil without the thought of coming back.[6]

In the Flanders region the sentiments were no different from those in Wallonia because the inhabitants had "a parochial attitude pushed to the extreme, so that they would abandon their native soil only at the last extremity." Gustaaf Vekeman, who had left Flanders for Canada, found it difficult to convince his compatriots to follow his example:

> All who listened to me [lecturing] were Flemings, like me, and the Flemish, almost without exception, are not ripe for emigration. This is beginning, however, and it will go well in a few years from now, that is to say when it will be too late....

Give the small farmer or Flemish labourer the strict necessities, that is to say somewhat better than dry bread, and for nothing in the world will he leave his native village or the unhealthy rowhouse he lives in – along with other families – in some dead-end street of a large city. What!? No longer see his neighbour Jean-Pierre and his neighbour Theresa, no longer play his game of lawn-bowling, no longer drink his pint of old beer at the corner cabaret, no longer compete in pole archery, no longer attend the village kermesse![7]

Octave Laurent tried to reassure his compatriots in 1894 that a trip to the Niagara region and Ottawa was for his generation no longer a voyage of exploration but it was a holiday trip.[8] There were no sponsored projects. Canada would need to project an alluring image. Belgian authorities were concerned about the welfare of those who elected to emigrate. The government set standards for port facilities, steamship accommodation, and recruitment procedures. It also intervened to protect emigrants from fraud and irregularities. Moreover, it sent fact-finding missions to Western Canada to verify settlement conditions and corroborate consular reports. The assumption of responsibility for the welfare of Belgians abroad included diplomatic intervention and repatriation provisions.

Image of Canada

What was the image of Canada at the popular level and at the elitist level of administrators, clergy and professional classes? Was it the undeveloped northern frontier of the United States, a wilderness inhabited mostly by warlike Indians and dangerous animals? The more informed had reason to worry about agricultural prospects on the semi-arid prairies and the extent of Indian and Métis unrest. The Flemish parish priests and the episcopacy, like their Dutch Catholic counterparts, were generally unenthusiastic about emigration to Canada, regarding it as a danger to the survival of the faith in a perceivable hostile and aggressive materialistic Protestant environment. In other words, apart from Catholic Quebec, the Canadian provinces and territories gave the impression of being similar to the United States, although economic prospects appeared much better in the American republic than in Canada.

Early reports indicated that Western Canada might be attractive to agriculturalists, especially as settlement began beyond the Red River valley in the 1880s. Colonizing clergy were anxious to maintain a strong francophone Catholic presence in the West but few Belgians emigrated for religious reasons. Georges Kaiser in *Au Canada* (1887) indicated that undue clerical influence as seen in Quebec did not promote the same progress seen among the anglophone population. Eugène Goblet d'Alviella, Octave Laurent and Léon Brabant held similar views.[9] In the end, economic prospects would prove more important factors in emigration than cultural and religious considerations. This may well explain why more Flemings than Walloons came to Western Canada before World War II.

Consul E. H. Edouard Sève, visiting the United States and Canada in 1868, cautioned that farmers should come to Canada only if they possessed at least 5,000 francs (a substantial amount) and a "strong dose of energy and perseverance." As for day labourers, skilled workers and clerks there was little opportunity for them. He warned that it was easy to be misled by seemingly high wages, but the cost of living was very high, working conditions differed from those in Europe, and many jobs were seasonal because of the severe winters. As for business opportunities, it would be wise to come to study conditions before making any permanent plans.[10]

A widely read travel book published in Paris in 1888 evoked the emptiness of the Canadian West. It was still a land inhabited only by a few Indians and Métis, wild game, a scattering of small farms along a solitary railway line:

> Always more grass taking on a green colour and in this grass posts pounded in by the surveyors at the borders of the concessions. Without this indicator no one would suspect that civilized man has profaned the ancient sanctuary of the buffalo and elk.[11]

Georges Kaiser had little sympathy for the First Nations, finding them extremely ugly and lazy.[12] Consul Ketels thought they posed a serious impediment to the development of the country. Moreover, he thought Chinese immigrant labourers constituted an 'invasion' of people belonging to 'another race, another civilization, another ideal' that posed a danger to civil order. He believed that the railways that recruited these immigrants would come to regret their efforts.[13]

Louis Strauss thought Manitoba's climate closely resembled that of Belgium. Therefore, it was an attractive place to settle.[14] Baron Hulot conceded that in Belgium an hectare produced eighteen hectolitres of wheat, while in Manitoba in 1882 an hectare produced twenty-eight hectolitres. However, the numerous disadvantages included early fall frosts, severe winters, occasional grasshopper plagues, prairies fires, the lack of building materials, the high cost of machinery, and the high wages of hired help. His was not an encouraging inventory.[15]

On the other hand, there were some positive opinions. By 1911, an anonymous and entertaining traveller, who had learned about opportunities in Canada at the International Exposition in Brussels in 1910, visited an old friend in Boissevain, Manitoba. In this somewhat fanciful work based on an actual trip, he stated:

> ... in Canada there are gold mines awaiting only men of goodwill to dip into their treasures.... Here one can buy farmland at very modest prices; these are splendid opportunities for farmers who have a little capital and who possess some scientific knowledge.[16]

In addition to this vision of fields of 'prairie gold' there was the prospect of finding real gold. Three articles in *Le Bien Public* extolled the mineral resources of the country, indicating interesting possibilities for prospectors.[17]

The agricultural potential of the West was reaffirmed by a Belgian farmer who came to Forget then went on to file a homestead in Willow Bunch:

> If I may give advice to Belgian farmers, this is what I would say: instead of farming for the benefit of a landowner, instead of simply existing during your lifetime, working hard and paying high rent, would it not be better for you to come to Canada and become a landowner yourself, earning more money and experiencing less hardship than in the old country?[18]

Willow Bunch in southwestern Saskatchewan was recommendable as a promising place to settle because three railways were soon to service the region, the soil was fertile, and there were still homesteads available in a region where French was the dominant language of the many Belgian, French and French Canadian settlers.

Nevertheless, O. De Meulenaere, warned that the immigration brochures and pamphlets with testimonials sent to Belgium were a form of propaganda designed to populate a largely uninhabited expanse of a 'new nation' still in its formative stage.[19]

Push factors

Of great weight in the decision to migrate were the push factors in Belgium, deprived immediately after its independence in 1830 of markets in the southern Netherlands and the Dutch colonies. In spite of the important economic boost afforded by an extensive program of railroad and canal construction, the government set up a commission in 1843 to examine the condition of the working classes. The report was most disconcerting as it documented widespread poverty, rising alcoholism and rampant child labour.[20] During the next decade, conditions worsened as a typhus epidemic struck, and a shortage of basic staples resulted from a blight that destroyed about 90 per cent of the potato crop and rust that damaged half the rye crop. Massive imports of grain from Russia and the United States intended to meet the crisis resulted in a collapse of domestic prices so that by 1880 peasants refused to sow their fields. Small tenant farmers, who comprised 72 per cent of the all farmers, found it difficult to survive on their small holdings.[21] Between 1880 and 1890 the number of people engaged in agriculture decreased by 258,493 and not all of these could be absorbed by industry, commerce, or the liberal professions within the realm.[22] G. Lennox addressed the concerns of agricultural failure and soil depletion in Flanders in pamphlets prepared in 1885–86, in order to underscore the supposedly ideal conditions in the Prairies and British Columbia.[23]

Victor Van Tighem wrote to his brother, Leonard, at Coalbanks [Lethbridge]:

> Dear brother, the situation in Belgium is even more miserable than it was and the persecution is slowly on the increase. We expect much from the coming elections, but not without fear, because many people have neither religion nor morals left. Corruption is widespread....[24]

In addition to desperate economic conditions, Van Tighem referred to 'persecution' in Flanders from liberal politicians who had suppressed many Catholic elementary schools, including the institution operated by his Van Dale congregation in Kortryk. The Van Humbeek Act, 1879, instituted one official state school in each commune, appointed state-licensed teachers, and cut off grants to church-supported 'free schools.'[25] His worst fears were unfounded because the Catholic Party won the election in 1884. It would appear that he, and probably most of his compatriots, ignored the fact that in Western Canada the Catholic Church was waging a losing battle for linguistic and school privileges.

Furthermore, there was a crisis in the textile industry and social unrest in the Walloon mining sector. Mechanization in the textile industry, especially lace-making, resulted in high unemployment rates in several cities.[26] Added to this was the fact that the population increased by 76.1 per cent between 1830 and 1900. Nevertheless, during the nineteenth century most Belgians who migrated went no farther than northern France.[27]

Why did Belgians who sought a better standard of living or some occupational advantage think of "America" as limited largely to the United States? Lack of communication with Canada was a factor. Foreign affairs were handled through Great Britain, and Belgian consular officials were attached to the embassy in London. Canadians dealt with Belgium through the High Commission in London. Direct steamship connection was limited. In 1883–84, two vessels registered as Belgian from Antwerp foundered on the way to a Canadian port. All the transatlantic steamship companies had an agent in Antwerp but most used Liverpool as their port of departure. It was only in 1904 that the Canadian Pacific Steamship Lines began sailing out of Antwerp for Canada.

The consul in Quebec reported in 1885 that a contingent of eighty-five persons had arrived in Winnipeg, a small contingent compared to the thousands coming from Eastern Europe. There was also the problem of opposition to non-agricultural immigration:

> Work having become scarce, Canadian artisans and skilled labourers do not look kindly on immigrants from Europe who arrive to compete with them; they want to prevent the competition of all European labour just like they want to place hurdles on Chinese immigration in British Columbia.[28]

Shipping was restricted also because of the lack of significant trade. An 1882 consular report remarked that Belgian exports to Canada consisted largely of gin and window glass.

These difficulties were further highlighted in 1891 when Paul Watelet, immigration agent in Charleroi for the Canadian government, came to Canada. A sum of 20,000 francs was designated for the repatriation of Belgian nationals who, wishing to return to Belgium, had insufficient funds to do so. In 1905 the caution money for repatriation of individuals was doubled to 40,000 francs.[29] The contingent of emigrants that arrived in 1893 had actually been destined for South America, but the agent for Brazil and Argentina for some undisclosed reason diverted this "illegal operation" to Canada.[30]

Port authorities in Antwerp, point of departure for central and eastern Europeans bound for America, kept emigration statistics, but these are not always reliable in tracing the final destination of those departing. Belgians emigrated in greater numbers than official statistics would seem to indicate. Some left from other ports, especially the wealthier classes, professionals and missionaries. For the period 1901 to 1912, departures from Antwerp were 68 per cent Flemish and 25 per cent Walloons. Canada was listed as the final destination of 12 per cent of those leaving Hainaut and West Flanders and 5 per cent from East Flanders, according to the most reliable calculations. Manitoba accounted for 84 per cent of those from the Flemish regions and 57 per cent from Hainaut.[31]

The First World War was followed by deepening crises in Belgium which stimulated a second wave of emigration to Canada. In the postwar decades there was large-scale unemployment, inflation, lockouts and strikes in industry, and the problems associated with rebuilding devastated regions. There was also a volatile political situation embittered by ethnic and regional strife and right-wing agitation. Emigration resumed in 1919 with the departure of 649 war brides. The desperate situation of some individuals seeking to emigrate is evident in private advertisements placed in journals such as *Belgique-Canada*.[32] By 1929, it was clear that Canada was no longer an ideal destination. The Canadian Pacific Railway underscored the depression and drought in Western Canada by announcing that it would no longer engage in the recruitment of farmers. The Belgian government responded by forbidding departures of all agricultural workers and farmhands to Canada.[33]

The post-World War II emigration was in many ways the most important in terms of numbers but not in terms of creating identifiable communities. Economic, social and linguistic conditions were very different from those prevailing at the beginning of the century. The Flemish population surpassed the Walloons and their regions were quickly becoming the prosperous centres of the new industries, whereas the coal, steel and glass industries of Wallonia were in chaos. There was continuous political instability of successive coalition governments, ethno-linguistic confrontations, labour unrest, and the loss of the Congo in 1960 with its attendant financial repercussions. From 1945 to 1967, 55 per cent of Belgian emigrants were francophones from the old manufacturing centres of Brussels, Liège and the Borinage region of Hainaut. Between 1945 and 1975, 38,500 left for Canada. The provincial Agricultural Committee of West Flanders investigated prospects in Western Canada and concluded that it was still a favourable region to send farmers. Nevertheless, the typical emigrants, especially by the 1990s, were individuals rather than families, young, single, well-educated, urban and more often Walloon than Flemish. One survey for 1991–95 found that almost a quarter of the emigrants were twenty or younger, 28 per cent were university graduates, and the majority came from the urban areas of Brussels and Liège.[34]

Government Regulation

In 1843, the Belgian railways began offering free baggage allowances to Antwerp for German emigrants bound for North America. In 1857 consular agents abroad were asked to inform the Ministry of Foreign Affairs in Brussels of economic prospects in their jurisdictions. In 1872, Walter Warnotte prepared a report for the Ministry on emigration services, or lack thereof, at the port of Antwerp compared to the situations in Le Havre, Bremen and Hamburg. In 1873 the government appointed a Commissioner for Emigration, responsible to the Minister of Foreign Affairs, not only to monitor conditions but also in conjunction with the Governor of the province of Antwerp to stimulate European emigration in general through the port of Antwerp. After the failure of several colonization schemes in Ethiopia, Tunisia and Guatemala, authorities closely scrutinized the activities of foreign immigration agencies, steamship lines, manufacturers, and freelance recruiters.

This approach coincided with a period of agricultural crisis in Flanders, and there was much discussion about emigration as a safety valve. The clergy opposed all emigration on religious and nationalistic grounds. Internal migration was still preferred over transatlantic migration. In 1874 the Ministry of Foreign Affairs still recommended agents in the emigration services "to abstain carefully from encouraging the emigration of Belgians to transatlantic countries."[35]

A fierce political debate ensued in 1886 as the proponents of free trade and extensive out-migration challenged the conservatives who based their hopes for better economic conditions on internal public works projects. Encouraged by early favourable reports from Belgian settlers in Manitoba, the *Journal de Bruxelles* proclaimed:

> If our workers emigrated in greater numbers, the salaries of those who would remain would increase and our trade would increase in intensity. Each emigrant is a commercial agent abroad. In fact, if it were possible, we would even advise the Government to favour not only the emigration of workers, but also of merchants and industrialists.[36]

Another right-wing newspaper advised the government to "search out somewhere, far away, a territory where we could deport all our rogues."[37] It was not a view that received enthusiastic support in the Ministry of Foreign Affairs. It published its own brochure in 1888 outlining the policy of the Beernaert cabinet:

> ... of course it is not the intention of the Government to promote the emigration of Belgians. On the other hand, the Government fulfills its duty to protect its nationals by enlightening them concerning the resources offered by countries open to colonization.[38]

Information offices opened in each province verified and adjusted solicitations of navigation companies and recruiting agents, but these produced few positive results:

> As for the information concerning the economic situation of the countries and the resources which they offer, the emigrants

apparently trust the information supplied by recruiting agents of companies, since they scarcely, if ever, show themselves in my office to find out anything. This service, by all accounts, has not been working at all in 1890.[39]

Mobility was marked at both the beginning and end by train stations, docks, immigrant sheds, quarantine and health inspection sites. They fulfilled a certain functional arrangement, but the new train station opened in Antwerp in 1905 was a veritable architectural cathedral. Through Antwerp passed thousands of emigrants seeking a new life abroad, the result of an experiment in May 1835 when the first train on the continent steamed from Brussels to Mechelen. Railways introduced modernity with industrialization and factories. They also brought emigrants from Central and Eastern Europe directly from Cologne to Antwerp, the terminus of the railway but also the point of departure of the steamships.[40]

Information derived from various sources convinced the Belgian government to place the protection of emigrants above the commercial interests of the shipping companies. The Royal Decree of 1876 touched all aspects of ocean passages. It stipulated the surface area required for each passenger, the minimum size of the bunk beds, the minimum weekly rations and the store of food aboard. Each ship had to be equipped with a sick bay and ships carrying more than 125 passengers had to have a doctor aboard. Penalties were provided for infringements and non-compliance.[41] Article 17 defined who was an *emigrant*: "Will be deemed an emigrant any passenger who does not eat at the table of the captain or officers and who pays the price of his passage, meals included, the sum of less than 30 francs per week on a sailing vessel and less than 50 francs on a steamship".[42] First class passengers were not classified as 'emigrants' under this regulation and were not included in the enumeration.

In 1884, an information service for prospective emigrants was organized. Agents were required, according to the Circular of 27 December 1884, to fill out questionnaires concerning the possible countries of emigration indicating "the standard of living, climate and produce, categories of jobs available, and chances of success and the future for emigrants."[43] But it was not until 1890 that an emigration service office was established in Antwerp under the direction of Eugène Venesoen. His commission was to supervise the activities of both shipping companies and emigration agents. Legislation ensued regulating safety equipment and ventilation on board vessels (1891), fixing the rates for ocean fares (1892), inspection of water supplies (1895), and forbidding the acceptance of offers of free passages (1897).[44] Officials drafted a formal list of all the registered agents and sub-agents. In 1894 there were no fewer than ninety-one registered names, including Hacault of Uccle, Bruneau of Marcinelle, Watelet of Charleroi and Destrée of Namur for emigrants destined for Western Canada. By 1894 the only steamship company that had not conformed to the ministerial regulations regarding the registration of sub-agents was the Red Star Line.[45]

These regulations remained substantially unchanged until an update in February 1924. The rules stipulated more clearly that all agents had to be certified by their home government – in this case, the government of Canada. Moreover, no one could undertake the transport of emigrants without the consent of the Ministry of Foreign Affairs in Brussels. In August 1926, the Belgian commissioner of emigration in Antwerp decided to interview all emigrants destined for Canada to be certain they had not been recruited illegally, or deceived by false promises. Canadian agents sometimes interpreted this as an attempt to control the flux of emigrants. By 1928 the Commissioner reported on "the difficult settlement and existence of our farmers in most Canadian regions." He singled out the Canadian Pacific Railway and the steamship companies for "scandalously exaggerating in their publicity the rapid and lasting advantages that Canadian soil offers for agriculture."[46] Belgian authorities were concerned not only about emigration but also about the welfare of its nationals who settled abroad.

Irregularities and Fraud

To protect emigrants from false promises and fraud both at the recruitment end in Belgium and at the employment end in Canada, the Ministry of Foreign Affairs established a special commission in Antwerp in 1873. The Ministry also created a special information bureau at the Musée Commercial de l'Etat in Brussels with eight provincial branches in Antwerp, Arlon, Bruges, Ghent, Hasselt, Liège, Mons, and Namur. It did not promote emigration. Rather, the objective was "to acquit itself strictly of the duty of protection which behooves it when it permits citizens to inform themselves on the resources offered by different countries open to colonization."[47] In 1905, the Ministry published a pamphlet titled *Emigration Canada*, to keep readers informed of the situation abroad.

Problems did occur with individuals and companies: agents, sub-agents, overzealous self-styled recruiters, swindlers and circumventors. Some may have been well-intentioned, but they operated outside normal channels and in violation of emigration regulations. In 1897, for example, one Charles Van Brabant, a farmer in St. Alphonse, wrote articles for newspapers in Ghent urging people to use his services to acquire land in Manitoba. He posed as an official agent for the Manitoba government, asserting that there were over five hundred Belgian farm families around St. Alphonse, when in fact there were about fifty. The clergy called his bluff when the Société Saint-Raphaël said that he had no ties with them. The provincial governor of Antwerp further confused matters when he said he had received at least seventeen letters from Van Brabant, posing as local land agent, in which he recounted the hardships experienced by many farmers in Manitoba. The case was closed when the would-be agent allegedly served a jail term for theft.[48]

Organizations were as liable as individuals to violate proper proced-ures. The Ministry of Foreign Affairs contacted the Canadian immigra-tion agent, Tréau de Coeli, to protest that large posters had been printed and small handbills distributed with the headline "Why remain slaves in your country when you can be free and independent?" Tréau de Coeli distanced himself from this offensive approach by affirming that either return men, "farmer delegates," or sub-agents of transportation compan-ies with Liberal party connections, who were paid one hundred dollars a month and expenses, were responsible. Agents and sub-agents had their own problems. The paper *Le Canada* reported that when workers reached Western Canada they often found that the companies that had hired them failed to honour their contract terms, even reneging on agreed wages to be paid.[49]

Just how common such misrepresentations were can be gauged from the thick files of Belgian Ministry of Justice investigations turned over to Foreign Affairs in Brussels. The motivation in two cases, for example, remains unclear. An agent's activities in Charleroi were contested by a large firm for whom he had previously worked when he was accredited by another company. Another agent who had successfully helped sixty-one immigrants between 1904 and 1907 suddenly found his license renewal application denied in 1908 on grounds of unspecified "bad behaviour."[50] Clarence de Sola in Montreal complained that the consulate "has been crowded with indigent Belgians seeking employment, many of them in a state of starvation." He added that many were immigrants "induced to come here by alluring promises held out to them by Steamship and Immigration agents."[51] There does appear to have been some consistency in judicial pursuit. An applicant in La Louvière was refused a licence to work for the firm of Fédor Berns in 1905 because previously he had been "in the employ of several emigration firms and had been dismissed by them for incorrect actions." Another agent convicted of illicit emigration work in 1907 was identified and denied a licence when he reapplied in 1913. Yet another was apprehended when one of his clients deserted and he tried to sue him.[52]

The appointment of agents was limited also. In 1914, a public servant at Passchendaele was told he could not be licensed as an agent for Red Star Line because of his government position. An individual from Montignies-sur-Sambre was informed by the Ministry of Foreign Affairs that he could be accredited only as a company and he would have to provide 40,000 francs security. This drew an outraged response:

> Lex and lex, all Belgians are equal before the law, consequently all the agencies which I have cited in my letter of 25 February last, did they deposit the said caution-money?

In 1920, a Belgian employed as a translator at the American embassy in Brussels, who used his position to recruit emigrants, asked for an "open license" to carry on recruitment. He was told he would have to act through an accredited firm.[53]

Pursuits for alleged fraudulent practices increased in the 1920s. In 1924, the firm Aimé Gyselbrecht & Frères of Ghent, which circulated information for the Union Ticket Office, Red Star Line, White Star Line, Canadian Pacific Steamships and United States Line, was subject to questioning about one of its agents:

> The continuous acceptance by them of travellers brought by this person, without his being provided with their regular authorization confirmed by you [Foreign Affairs], constitutes a transgression of Article 14 of the Regulation of 25 February 1924, formerly Article 16 of the Regulation of 2 December 1905.

In the papers seized by Justice officials was found a telegram from a M. Martin in Redvers, Saskatchewan, requesting that men be sent out, this in contravention of emigration regulations.[54]

The lines of communication were sometimes complex. A licensed agent of Cunard Lines hired sub-agents to help him recruit. Although this was not a direct infringement of any law or regulation, he was dismissed in 1926 on the orders of a provincial governor. The following year, an agent of Canadian Pacific Railways was dismissed for recruiting in another agent's territory. The railway company's activities were thwarted in another area when its candidate was refused permission "as long as he remains a tavern-keeper." More serious was the dismissal of another of their agents for delivering "in return for handsome payment, false work contracts for Canada." The White Star Line was no more fortunate when its agent in Ghent for emigrants bound for Canada was tried and convicted of infraction of the regulations and swindling.[55] The Belgian Ministries of Justice and Foreign Affairs were vigilant in their efforts to protect their nationals.

Another scam that came to light was the creation of clubs and companies to promote clandestine emigration. In 1919, a Société Belge de Colonisation tried to lure Belgians in Western Canada to sunny Florida. The consul in Calgary personally knew of two settlers who had been deceived and had returned penniless. He warned a prospective client: "Inform yourself first of all if this society is really Belgian. Then, who are the people heading up this company. It is not sufficient for an organization to have a Belgian name but to be assured it is also necessary that the directors be not only honourable people but also people with first hand knowledge of the country and have business experience."[56] In 1926 it became known that Italian, Polish and other nationals in Belgium had paid sums of up to two hundred francs "on the false promise of acquiring jobs as miners or farm workers in Canada on two year contracts" through the good offices of the Teaching Club of one Oscar Van Slype. The Canadian Immigration Office in Antwerp informed the authorities that it had no relations with this club or its owner. Van Slype was convicted in Brussels in May 1927 of having defrauded at least 737 persons.[57] At the same time, two directors of the Belgian Express International Travel Office were arrested on charges of arranging the fraudulent entry of emigrants from Canada into the United States. They avoided conviction on the legal technicality that "they had not sent persons to a transatlantic country in second and third class who settled without hope of returning."[58] It was reaffirmed that emigration officials did not exercise any control over first class passengers.

Letters of inquiry about attractive job offers in Canada circulated by the Butterfly Publicity Company came from several Walloon towns. The *Journal de Charleroi* carried several of its public announcements, indicating that the costs for a passport and ocean passage would be paid by writing to Charles Linder in Montreal. A circular letter boasted:

> We have the pleasure of announcing that you have been chosen to come to work in Canada ... in Canada, French is spoken, life is beautiful, cost of living is cheap, salaries are high. the hours of work are short. – *Yves Perrin, Director Charles Duval, President*

In 1929 the Commissioner for Emigration in Antwerp advised the Minister of Foreign Affairs that "it is important to put an end to these shifty transactions of the said swindler." But one of the agents of the Butterfly Publicity scheme, Albert Desterbecq, was not completely deterred from his 'despicable ways.' In April 1932 he was convicted of false representation and illegally sending eleven workers to Canada.[59]

Reputable companies could also become caught up in emigration scandals. Several sub-agents of the Red Star Line were suspected of organizing a fraudulent emigration from Canada into the United States. The Commissioner for Emigration in Antwerp was advised that it was necessary to "show ourselves very prudent in our dealings with the American authorities" for some unstated reason. However, Canadian companies were not immune to criticism:

> On the other hand, I was able to conclude that the majority of Belgians who left fraudulently for the United States of America were carriers of cards of introduction from the CNR. You will want in future to show yourself particularly severe towards emigrants carrying the said cards which it seems to me are too readily provided. You must draw to the attention of the Red Star Line the responsibility it bears in this matter, the CNR not being authorized to sign on and transport emigrants in Belgium.

The issue had developed in 1924 out of allegations concerning the operations of a company operated by Van den Abeele and the suit Louis Van Ouidenhoven brought in its defence against the Commissioner of Emigration. By 1927 the investigation focussed on Maurice Wallecan of the Red Star Line. None of these proceedings did much to enhance the image of Canadian recruiters.[60]

Société Saint-Raphaël

In 1888 a group of Catholic lay persons organized the Société Belge de l'Archange Raphaël, based on the German *Raphaëls-Verein*,[61] to direct devout emigrants to established parishes in North and South America. Count Frédéric Louis Walbott de Bassenheim, as secretary, was a leading architect of this project for Catholic *encadrement* of emigrants. He wrote to the rector of St. Boniface College to have a local representative named for Western Canada.[62] Father Allard, the Grand Vicar of the archdiocese, informed T. A. Bernier, mayor of St. Boniface and Superintendent of Catholic public schools in Manitoba, who was seeking support for the schooling of the deaf and dumb, that there was a Belgian society "whose objective is to direct a current of Catholic emigration our way." Bernier speculated about the possibility of combining his project with the Belgian outreach.

> It seems to me that the matter is not impossible, and if this meeting of forces took place would it not become easy to open new parishes in order to occupy new zones, where we could develop our community? Would it not be possible to offer as a first nucleus for these new colonies this orphanage which might at the same time be an agricultural and industrial institution to which we would join an establishment for the deaf and dumb.[63]

Negotiations were slow so, in the meantime, Taché had Bernier appointed on a federal mission to Europe. His appointment to the Senate followed shortly thereafter..

The Société Saint-Raphaël asked for and received complete access to the port of Antwerp for its agents who booked emigrants into reputable hotels and assisted them with their transport and baggage. However, it did not provide travel loans or recruit colonists or clergy. As a charitable association, the Société Saint-Raphaël was exempt from government regulations governing emigration. Its task was limited to "enlightening the emigrant, protecting him and furnishing him with all the information it disposed of and which could be useful in his settling abroad." The response to the Red Star Line accusation that the society competed with it in the emigration business, was that the society acted "as a committee of vigilance ... inspired solely by charity."[64] There is some evidence that the society was so thorough in warning about the difficulties, deceptions and hardships that might be encountered that as many as three-quarters of those seeking information were discouraged from emigrating.[65]

Another aspect of the society's work was emigrant reception in Montreal. Father Léon Jean Dehon, founder of the order of the Priests of the Sacred Heart, opened a committee for the assistance of Belgian emigrants in Montreal in April 1896. The Société Saint-Raphaël took charge of this work. This followed the visit to Manitoba by Louis Hacault in 1892, sponsored by the society to which he reported. An information booklet was prepared for distribution.[66] An office was opened in Le Havre. Father Frédéric D'Heurter acted as agent in Liverpool and was in contact with the agents of the German Raphaëls-Verein in Hamburg, Bremen, Rotterdam and Amsterdam.

Ferdinand Van Bruyssel informed the Ministry of Foreign Affairs that the society was not the proper vehicle for the diffusion of information to emigrants:

> It acts in conjunction with the clergy whose tendencies in the recruiting of colonists as also in the manner of regrouping them at their destination deviates completely from the rules that should inspire public agencies.[67]

In the 1920s the Belgian branch of the Société Saint-Raphaël was re-organized by the congregation of Josephites of Grammont under the patronage of Cardinal Mercier and Bishop Seghers of Ghent. By this time, official government agencies had taken over most of the supervision of emigration. Future criticisms would not be directed so much at clerical intervention as to civic inequities. Unlike the French, Belgians abroad could not vote and they did not receive their pensions abroad. Moreover, the children of emigrants were called up for military service and if they did not respond they were deemed deserters.[68]

Fact-Finding Missions

There were agencies in Belgium interested in the economic prospects for emigrants.[69] The initial fact-finders were the consular staff, part of an overseas network reporting back to Brussels on social and economic prospects for investment, trade and settlement.[70] Jesse Joseph, who had commercial connections in London and who had participated in a committee exploring the economic prospects of the St. Lawrence waterway, became honorary consul at Montreal on 14 November 1850.[71] At the time, the British Government conducted the external affairs of the British North American colonies. The consul in Montreal reported in 1856:

> The emigrants who are factory workers can find a job upon arrival and work is also abundant during the summer months. Bricklayers, brickmakers, carpenters, smiths, painters, tinsmiths, gas workers, farmers, etc. are in demand as is also the case for most professions....
>
> Emigrants arriving by way of the St. Lawrence River are not exposed to the problems, deceptions and the misleading information so common at New York and along the inland routes leading from that port to the West.[72]

In September 1885, the Belgian government named Ferdinand Van Bruyssel its chief of mission, with the title of consul general, to promote economic ties with Canada.[73] The network of consulates spread into Western Canada thereafter with the initial offices opening in Calgary in 1888 and Vancouver in 1897. Consuls were appointed at Winnipeg in 1901, at Prince Albert in 1906, and Regina and Edmonton in 1908. To promote settlement in southern Saskatchewan, a consular office operated at Forget from 1908 to 1915, when it was transferred to Manor, where it functioned until 1921.

On the basis of consular reports, the Belgian government constantly warned prospective emigrants of the hardships, deceptions, financial costs and uncertain future they might face in leaving their homeland.

In 1887 the *Société d'immigration française* sent its secretary, August Bodard, accompanied by Georges Kaiser, a Belgian engineer and Professor of Industrial Geography at the University of Louvain, on an investigative tour of Western Canada. Bodard stated that the objective of his society was to change the demography of the region so that Manitoba would once again become "a great French-speaking country." He projected a bloc settlement of four hundred Belgian families near La Broquerie, east of the fertile Red River valley. Kaiser, who published his impressions in *Au Canada* (Bruxelles, 1897), found the soil conditions fertile and winters not too terrifying, but he observed that there were natural disasters such as droughts and early and late frosts to contend with from time to time. He expressed his complete faith in Bodard's project, especially his devotion "to the Catholic faith and the colonisation of Manitoba by immigrants of Latin race." In Belgium, meanwhile, Paul Watelet of Charleroi, who was the delegate of the company, expressed serious doubts that two hundred settlers could be recruited.[74] Watelet, who was under investigation for using letterheads suggesting he was paid by the Canadian government and steamship companies to recruit immigrants, personally accompanied five groups of emigrants as far as Liverpool. In 1891 he gave up his position with the *Société d'immigration française* and left for the United States.[75]

Francophone Catholic immigration was also an objective of Archbishop Taché of St. Boniface. He attempted to interest the Countess de Bruges de Gerpinnes, without success, to sponsor a bloc settlement. When he contacted the Société Saint-Rapaël in Bruges, Count Louis Walbott de Bassenheim, its secretary, informed the archdiocese that such a project would require as sponsor a priest fluent in both Flemish and French.[76] Shortly thereafter, Quebec's famed colonizing priest, the abbé Antoine Labelle, visited Belgium and met with members of the society and also with a conservative Catholic journalist of the *Courrier de Bruxelles*, Louis Hacault. Labelle convinced Hacault to visit Western Canada. Hacault was favourably impressed by the small Belgian communities already implanted in southern Manitoba; also he was deeply moved by the apparent need for Catholic francophone settlers in the province to redress in some measure the religiolinguistic imbalance. In 1892 he brought his family to the farming community of Bruxelles in the hill country of southern Manitoba reminiscent of the Belgian Ardennes. Here he took up his pen in defence of francophone Catholic rights and aspirations. His *Notes de Voyage au Canada en 1890* became a powerful propaganda piece and was widely distributed in his homeland. He made an attempt through another pamphlet to interest the Count Walbott de Bassenheim to launch a colonization project.[77]

In 1897 the consul general in Montreal decided to visit the Belgian settlements in southern Manitoba to report first hand on their progress and on the prospects for future immigrants. His report laid particular stress on soil conditions.

> In general, the soil in Manitoba is of unusual fertility.... It is, moreover, very easy to cultivate; serious colonists at Bruxelles and St. Alphonse have declared to me that a man alone can seed and harvest 50 acres of land without undue labour. He will only require help during about ten days at harvest time.[78]

This information, combined with the fact that homesteads were still available, would be attractive to Flemish farmers on their small tenant holdings which could barely support their usually large families.

When Archbishop Langevin of St. Boniface attended the general chapter of the Oblates in Belgium in 1898, he met a certain Abbé C. Delouche who was in touch with businessmen interested in emigration and agricultural settlement. In fact, it was a group of Antwerp financiers, headed by a certain J. Wégimont, who organized a Compagnie d'exploitations coloniales et industrielles in February 1899 to explore further possibilities in Western Canada. They planned to buy up tracts of land in Manitoba on which to settle farmers who could there "preserve their faith and find at all times and everywhere an assured support to sustain their material and spiritual needs."[79] Archbishop Langevin made the necessary overtures to the Minister of the Interior in Ottawa and to officials of the Canadian Pacific Railway Company in Montreal, while Abbé Delouche devoted himself to a reception centre for emigrants in transit through Antwerp and the publication of *L'Oeuvre des Emigrants à Anvers. Projet. Rapport* (1901).[80]

In 1900 a contingent headed by Louis Bareel, an agricultural engineer, accompanied by R. A. Demmé, who had spent fifteen years in Canada, visited the West with a view to assessing prospects for the Société agricole et industrielle du Manitoba being organized in Antwerp by the aforementioned group of financiers. The Oblate missionaries were to act as recruiting agents, the cardinal-archbishop of Malines gave the scheme his blessing, and state approval was assured by the conservative Catholic Minister of State, Auguste Beernaert. However, the consul general warned that the plan was doomed to failure so long as the clergy were involved because, in the context of appeals for federal remedial legislation in the

Manitoba School Question, the investors "had less chance than ever of obtaining Canadian government subsidies because for a long time religious corporations had mounted a systematic opposition to the government."[81]

The Commissioner for Immigration in Winnipeg assigned Léon Roy as guide and interpreter for this group and convinced them to tour the northern parklands as far as Prince Albert and Edmonton in the North-West Territories. Roy later reported that the scouts had been impressed but they also appeared to have interests other than settlement in mind.

> They found all the Belgian settlers very prosperous and I had the assurance from them that they would strongly recommend this country to their people as a proper place for immigration. They also told me that it was the intention to form a strong syndicate who would invest money in land in order to encourage cheese and butter-making and to facilitate generally the progress of settlers.[82]

The Bareel group did report favourably on its return to Europe and Tréau de Coeli, the Canadian immigration agent in Antwerp, was convinced that some emigration to Argentina and Brazil at the time would be diverted to Western Canada. However, the Antwerp businessmen for whom Bareel had been acting were more interested in land speculation than in a colonization project.[83]

Our most important informant, however, was the Vice-Consul in Ottawa, E. Robert De Vos, who had also joined the expedition, gathered his own information, not just about agriculture but also on mining and investment possibilities. He interviewed settlers and the consular agents A.J.H. Dubuc in Winnipeg, J. M. Whitehead in Vancouver, and T. R. Smith in Victoria. In a detailed closely written 149-page manuscript report, De Vos made some pertinent financial observations:

> One can conclude from the preceding remarks that in Canada it is as possible for those who possess nothing as well as for those who have brought some capital to succeed. It is generally said that the settlers who did not have the means to buy a farm immediately and who had to gather up dollar by dollar the necessary amount to this end were those who succeeded best. This does not imply evidently that money by its nature prevented

success, but simply proves that the person who did not possess it upon arrival, had to pass through a hard period of preparation before being able to think of establishing himself, and that by working for someone else he familiarized himself with the usages and customs and the characteristics of the country and consequently had the advantage of investing his own money only after he had learned in what manner one could produce the best results.

A good deal depends on how one uses one's money. The settler usually finds advantage, if the sum is more or less substantial, to deposit it in a bank and start off quite modestly. In that case life will be a little less comfortable than when he starts in a big way, but the first two years must be considered as a transition period, an apprenticeship, which often occurs at the settler's expense and in which the latter risks seeing all his small fortune founder if he does not proceed with calm and prudence.[84]

It is evident that the consul general was impressed by the De Vos report. He wrote:

Our compatriots who desire to emigrate to Canada will find numerous practical and useful pieces of information on colonization [settlement] as organized in the Dominion, on the location and respective value of different agricultural regions in the west, on their crops, cattle raising, industries, etc.[85]

All vice-consuls were asked henceforth to send regular reports on agriculture, mining, business and investment prospects on a regular basis.

In 1904, R. A. Demmé accompanied three bankers – Joseph Brunner of Brussels, E. Jacobs of Antwerp and P. G. West representing several French banks – on an inspection tour of the West in the interests of a newly organized Syndicat d'études canadien. They were favourably impressed by the fact that relatively poor emigrants "have managed to become owners of large farms" and "appear prosperous." It was significant that one of the bankers represented the Antwerp investment firm Maison Frederik Jacobs et Fils, that would became an important player in future developments. The syndicate entered into negotiations with the Canadian government for the acquisition of 200,000 acres along the

Alberta-Saskatchewan territorial boundary. The project never matured when it became clear that officials in Ottawa expected the Belgians to establish "model farms for practical instruction in agricultural procedures and to organize in Belgium and France propaganda centres to make known the great advantages of these vast and fertile regions," to build churches and schools, and even to recruit "medical doctors who speak French."[86] The syndicate proceeded to organize the Alberta Company which bought up 130,000 acres of land and then turned its attention to mortgaging and industrial investment.[87]

In the 1920s the Belgian authorities again became curious about actual economic prospects and the situation of its emigrants as demands for workers for the sugar beet industry, dairying and market gardening increased. In 1929, on the eve of the stock market crash and the Great Depression that followed, the Minister of Foreign Affairs entrusted Louis Varlez, professor at the University of Ghent and former head of the Service des Migrations at the International Labour Office, and his nephew Lucien Brunin with the mission of "visiting certain Belgian centres and studying the conditions of immigration and colonization in Canada."[88] In the West their expenses were paid by the provincial governments, all of which had an interest in attracting qualified immigrants with some capital, and the Canadian Pacific Railway Company, much troubled by allegations of false representations made to potential immigrants. Their report added little new information but served to reassure the authorities in Brussels. A typical section read:

> The Belgian farmer who emigrates to Canada usually knows what region of the country interests him, and where he wants to settle. This is because the propaganda service of the Canadian government, like that of the Canadian Pacific and other companies with land for sale, is very well organized. In Europe, the emigrant will usually have received a descriptive atlas of the various Canadian provinces indicating their special crops, lifestyle, climate and opportunities. The only reproach that can be levelled at this abundant and basically useful literature is that it depicts only the bright side of things and by well-turned phrases stirs the imagination of the rather unsophisticated and unprepared reader. But the Belgian emigrant, especially the Flemish peasant, is usually not satisfied with such mere vague

promises. He will come only if he has precise information from a brother, a relative, or another inhabitant from the same village. Only then will he decide to leave and usually with the intention of settling near the place where his friend has established himself successfully. The result is that one encounters veritable Belgian centres in Canada, and it is in these areas that our compatriots experience the best success. The emigrant who does not know where to go to settle will find, moreover, a whole group of organizations ready to provide him with information concerning the region's potential and the properties that are available.[89]

It was all that could be expected from a carefully orchestrated tour of the chief centres with Belgian settlers. They had no opportunity to visit the more isolated farmsteads, prairie villages, coal mines, bush camps, and ranches. The Great Depression and the terrible drought that soon ravaged the prairies made for little optimism and, as one family reported to the consul, "if it wasn't for the Atlantic, we'd come crawling back to Belgium on our knees."[90]

Belgian consulates in the major centres remained sources of information and direction for prospective emigrants. Two examples taken from the consular files for Calgary are illuminating. A Belgian doctor in China, who wanted to know what his chances of success were in Western Canada in 1917 was told that there did not appear to be any shortage of medical practitioners in the major cities, although a skilful surgeon could always expect to be well remunerated. Then the consul added an encouraging note: "A Belgian doctor would have a better chance than another because he would have the sympathy and confidence of the public, but he evidently would have to justify this sympathy and this confidence. It is quite necessary to speak English perfectly."[91] On the other hand, a teacher with a wife and children who desired to leave Belgium in 1919 was not encouraged to emigrate, even if the salaries were supposedly better in Canada. He was told that farmers and labourers had good chances of success but teachers needed to keep two facts in mind. Firstly, "the cost of living, even in normal times, is considerably more expensive." Secondly, a good command of English is indispensable.[92] Such advice could lead to successful implantation and to averting disappointment, even disaster.

Overview

In the late nineteenth century, Belgians received mixed messages concerning emigration to Canada. The usual push factors stimulating individual and family migration existed prior to 1914 and in the decade immediately following World War I, especially in Flanders. In the post-World War II years, young urban professional Walloons found Canada attractive but not the rural western regions. Government policy never encouraged emigration but regulations were enacted to protect the individuals and families who chose to venture abroad from dangerous and unsanitary travel conditions, over-zealous recruiting agents and misleading contractual arrangements. Even so, the authorities found it necessary to control advertising, clandestine operations and fraudulent schemes. The Société Saint-Raphaël sought to direct and protect emigrants in the port cities but the Belgian government preferred secular agencies to religious organizations. In addition to the consular service that reported to the Ministry of Foreign Affairs in Brussels through the embassy in London, eight fact-finding missions visited Western Canada to ascertain the prospects for further emigration and the requisites for successful settlement, also to assess the extent of integration of Belgian nationals in a new environment.

Coal mine at Estevan, SK, 1912. (Western Development Museum, Saskatoon)
Early settlers on the Prairies exploited lignire seams for fuel.

II

THE PROMISE AND CHALLENGE
OF THE WEST

In implementing the first federal Immigration Act (1869), agents appear to have assumed that Belgium was among the "preferred countries" for recruitment. Government policy for the settlement of Western Canada favoured British Isles immigrants, ethnic bloc settlements and colonization companies. Canada had no diplomatic ties with Belgium until well into the twentieth century, so immigration agents operated through the High Commission office in London. Western Canada consisted of the provinces of Manitoba (1870) and British Columbia (1871), and a vast North-West Territories out of which the provinces of Alberta and Saskatchewan were created in 1905. Immigration in the Canadian federal system was a shared federal and provincial jurisdiction; therefore the Dominion, Manitoba, and British Columbia governments could appoint their own immigration agents. The railway companies, churches and land speculators financed their own settlement schemes.

Four federal actions had set the stage for western settlement: the survey system in 1871; the Dominion Lands Act, 1872, providing for homesteads; the Immigration and Colonization Act, 1872, providing for overseas immigration agencies; and the creation of the North West Mounted Police to ensure peace in contrast to American frontier violence. The "opening" of this Canadian West was the result of three related forces: first, a market-driven capitalist economy to inventory the resources and commodify and develop the soil and its products; secondly, industrial innovations in production, transportation, and communication; thirdly, centralized government in Central and Eastern Canada capable of asserting ownership of land and resources, subsidizing enterprise and transportation, and promoting immigration.[1]

In general, immigrants were welcomed as a means of developing the regional economy, consolidating the institutional framework, and affirming Canadian sovereignty. However, as we have seen, Belgians voiced cautious optimism as to a future in the new West. Flemings and Walloons, like many European immigrants who went to Western Canada, came first as farmers and miners. A few also came as tradesmen, land speculators and missionaries. Miners from Hainaut who were disappointed and disillusioned with working conditions in Atlantic Canada and Pennsylvania were lured by prospects on Vancouver Island and the Crows Nest region. Canada was imagined as a place where hard work would bring its rewards. Some thought it to be a classless society, a country of European origins with an established Catholic community.

Belgian immigration took place in three waves or periods that economists have related to the operation of the staple or export-led model of growth. The first period of Belgian immigration from the 1890s to 1914, with about sixteen thousand arrivals that constituted less than 1 per cent of the massive influx of immigrants, coincided with frontier expansion, railroad building and the expanded production of wheat. In 1893, for example, just under four thousand Belgians left Antwerp bound for North America, 35 per cent of whom came to Canada. The second period from 1919 to 1939, with another fourteen thousand new arrivals, was one of export expansion centred on wheat, minerals and lumber. The third period from 1945 to the 1980s, with over thirty-five thousand newcomers, was a post-war boom period of "expansion in oil, iron ore and pulpwood exports, with an attendant expansion in transportation services."[2] In a 1996 census, 123,595 respondents claimed Belgian origin, of whom 42 per cent resided in Western Canada. This Belgian immigration was essentially the movement of individuals, extended families and small communities.

Challenges to Settlement

The flow of immigrants to Western Canada began as a trickle because of an awareness of a number of handicaps that could retard successful implantation. Biographies of Belgian settlers in local and district jubilee volumes record these challenges. First of all, there was the problem of transatlantic connections because until 1872 the only direct link between

Antwerp and Canada was by Hamburg-American Line from Liverpool to New York, and then by train to Quebec for 120 francs in third class.[3] In 1873, the Red Star Line, founded by the International Navigation Company of Philadelphia (1871) and the Société Anonyme de Navigation Belgo-Américaine (1872) opened large emigration sheds in Antwerp to house those going to New York. Those destined for Canada were under pressure to change their plans and settle in the United States.

Steamship service to Canada would require subsidization. In the spring of 1883, Messrs, Steinman and Ludwig of Antwerp obtained a Canadian government subsidy of $5,000 per voyage for redirecting vessels of the White Cross Line to Quebec and Montreal (Halifax in winter), but within three years the company had run up a deficit so the contract was passed over to a German line, the Dampfschiff Rhederi Hansa. In 1888, Bossières Frères opened a service from Le Havre to Quebec and Montreal subsidized by the Montreal Chamber of Commerce. From 1894 to 1896 a Belgian company, the Columba (reportedly subsidized, although this was denied by Prime Minister Mackenzie Bowell) introduced direct service from Antwerp to Quebec with no better results.[4] In 1905 Allan Steamship Line signed a contract with subsidies for eighteen voyages per year between France and Canada. Government subsidies were an incentive because statistics for the number of passengers leaving Antwerp destined for Canada indicate that in the period 1900–15, 5,023 (34.8%) went by direct line and 9,391 (65.2%) went by indirect line, but in the period 1919–31, 12,073 (74.8%) went by direct line and only 4,068 (25.2%) went by indirect line.[5]

An official report to Belgian authorities in 1929 indicated that finally tremendous improvements encouraged emigrants to choose the direct route to their destination:

> The Belgian, Dutch and English emigrants enjoyed greater comfort and occupied the rear cabins and decks. They had their own dining room, parlour, smoking room and bridge. The Slavic emigrants and those from eastern Europe were located in front and enjoyed a little less comfort. This difference is intended especially to satisfy those governments with stricter regulations, and results in separating the cleaner emigrants from those with more rudimentary manners. We frequently went down [to third class] to talk to the Belgian emigrants at

different times of the day and at different meals.... All appear to be full of enthusiasm and courage about the future. All those we questioned knew already the exact place where they were going, having received information from relatives or friends already settled in Canada. They assured us they were satisfied with the food and accommodations on board and they had nothing to complain about.[6]

This had obviously not been the experience of those who arrived before World War I.

Secondly, there was the geographical barrier of the Great Lakes and Canadian Shield that separated the West from central Canada. The American route through Chicago and St. Paul, Minnesota, tempted travellers to remain in Illinois and Wisconsin. This difficulty was partially overcome by the construction of the Canadian Pacific Railway and the arrival of the first transcontinental train in Winnipeg in 1886. Rail travel could be hazardous at the turn of the century and the decades following. "Colonist coaches" from eastern Canada were crowded with immigrants who ate and slept on the wooden benches. Outright dangerous were the trestle bridges, many of which collapsed under the weight of freight and passenger trains. In addition to derailments, frontal and rear-end collisions took a toll as trains lurched along with a full head of steam and neither brakes nor signals provided absolute security. Immigrants rarely forgot their introduction to Canadian travel. Immigration propaganda distributed at Antwerp was often silent on these matters.[7]

This geographical isolation was accentuated by official preoccupation with eastern Canadian affairs. The *Manitoba Free Press* seconded the decision of the Winnipeg city council to undertake its own publicity campaign:

Up to the present time of all the immigration agents sent to Europe no one has had more than a theoretical knowledge of Manitoba.... Nothing more, surely, need be urged than to make a good demand upon Canada to select at least one resident of Manitoba to represent our case in Europe.[8]

The geographical barrier was also interpreted in some quarters as the border between civilization and frontier disorganization, even barbarism.

Thirdly, there was the problem of the negative image of Canada in Europe. Prime Minister Laurier, introducing the Autonomy Bills in 1905, observed that for many Europeans, "frontier civilization was with them a byword for lawlessness."[9] For Canadians, however, the acquisition of the North-West was an extension of the cherished values of a peaceful, orderly and law-abiding community into a "new" region in contrast to the alleged lawlessness of American westward expansion associated with civil war, Fenian raids, whisky traders and Indian wars. Europeans also knew that three epidemics had swept the country in the decades following Confederation. The early missionary reports stressed its untamed vastness, severe climate, and the hardships of evangelizing the Aboriginal peoples. The Red River resistance of the Métis, followed in 1885 by the North-West rebellion had required the intervention of the North-West Mounted Police and Canadian militia. The efforts to impose law and order on a frontier society were interpreted by a few as indicative of British colonial exploitation and domination. The dumping of orphans, unfortunates, and unemployed by Britain on the Dominion also reinforced a negative perception.

Little wonder that European immigrants, usually aware of the stereotypes of the American Wild West, on arrival in this strange new environment were often terrified of wild animals, dreaded the blizzards and prairie fires, and even expected to be attacked by marauding Indians. Charles Croonenbergh, who visited the West when the North-West Rebellion was still important news, underscored the cruelty of the "Redskins." The Chevalier de Hesse Wartegg also stressed their cruelty in war, especially their scalping of victims.[10]

Much of nineteenth-century travel literature portrayed Canada as barely industrialized, traditional in its ways, and lacking the drive and modernity of the United States. In 1909 there appeared a sensational expose of the so-called "Canadian legend." The European belief that Canada was a land of liberty, of great opportunity, of easy living, of phenomenal fertility, of low prices and high wages, of great investment opportunities was completely false.[11] With 111 documents, press releases mostly from Quebec and a few from Western Canada, the author described what he called the realities of Canadian life. Two arguments caused particular concern: there was a strong anti-French sentiment in many regions and the clergy were too dominating in Catholic areas. Two years later, Léon Brabant challenged the Canadian emigration agent's assertions in a series of articles in *Le Peuple*, warning people not to believe promises of easy success and prosperity in Canada.[12]

Fourthly, the region was so vast and made up of such diverse environments that immigrants could become quite perplexed when they arrived at their destination. Henry Youle Hind's expedition in 1857 and John Palliser's report for the British government in 1862 had identified a fertile north-easterly belt on the western plains, running from the Red River valley to the Peace River valley but had also warned against intensive farming in a dry south-westerly belt known subsequently as "Palliser's triangle." Palliser's conclusions had been influenced by the Scottish geologist James Hector and the French naturalist M.E. Bourgeau. In fact, the region would later suffer depopulation as its native vegetation and sparse rainfall were suitable only for ranching.

Fifthly, the survey pattern and homestead regulations created some problems for newcomers. The Torrens system of land registration, devised in Australia, was adopted in Manitoba in 1885 and in the North-West Territories in 1886. The rectangular system of survey based on astronomical observation, copying the square-mile system of the western United States facilitated the surveying of homesteads and the organization of local government and school districts on a grid system. The grid survey by numbered sections (640 acres), with a ninety-nine-foot road allowance between all sections, and townships of thirty-six sections numbered north from the American boundary, provided a convenient basis for land description. But the system ignored natural boundaries with consistent soil patterns. Besides, the homestead regulations did not permit contiguous grants of land, thereby forcing scattered settlement patterns. In many districts Belgians found that they required more than the initial 160-acre plot in order to farm profitably. In the Palliser triangle, very large tracts of land had to be laid out for grazing. Beginning in 1873, provision was made for ethnic bloc settlements but Belgians never organized, like Icelanders, Mennonites and Doukhobors, to obtain such a reserved bloc of land, perhaps because the colonization projects previously launched in Quebec by Belgian entrepreneurs had not proven viable.[13]

Sixthly, immigration regulations could prove to be counter-productive. In 1874 the federal government assumed responsibility for all immigration through the Department of Agriculture, transferred to the Department of the Interior in 1892, but the provinces remained in charge of colonization. This bureaucratic reorganization did not result in much more efficiency.

The Department of Agriculture, for example, reported large numbers of immigrants for which the Department of the Interior could not account.[14] Not until 1917 was a Department of Immigration established which continued to function under a number of different names suggestive of a diversity of concerns such as citizenship, manpower and employment.

Seventhly, there was the problem of inadequate reception facilities for many newcomers, especially those who did not arrive as part of a large contingent with interpreters and travel agents. A popular historian made the damning observation that those who were enticed into coming arrived "to a land where not a single constructive step had been taken by anyone to prepare their arrival."[15] As early as 1872 there was an immigration shed in Winnipeg where immigrants could obtain free shelter for a period not exceeding seven days. A report in 1892 described a building without a foundation or weeping drains, often flooded to the main floor level, unheated bathrooms rendered useless in winter. "During the last year the constantly crowded state of the sheds has caused much inconvenience and hardship and no doubt illness."[16] In fact, there were thirteen deaths in forty days at these sheds attributed to inadequate medical inspection of new arrivals and overcrowded unsanitary accommodations.[17] Only in 1905 was a satisfactory immigration hall constructed near the Canadian Pacific Railway station, by which time the Belgians had established their own network for directing compatriots.

Joseph Van Hove, who was an interpreter at the Cosmopolitan Hotel in Winnipeg, drew the attention of the consul "to the strange and quite extraordinary situation" in 1900 that not a single immigration officer spoke Flemish. He cited the case of a woman who was questioned for three hours merely to produce a travel voucher, could not obtain information as to how to rejoin her husband so returned to her hotel, and the following day was obliged "to put her purse on the table so that they could take the price of her room, since no official could explain to her how much she had to pay."[18] The Canadian Immigration Commissioner investigated and promised to call on Van Hove to interpret whenever necessary. However, Van Hone was not given a permanent appointment and in 1904 he again charged that "of all the European nations (even Galicians, Doukhobors and Icelanders) the Flemings are the only ones not to have an interpreter." At this point, the Ministry of Foreign Affairs became aware that neither their consul nor vice-consul spoke Flemish.[19]

Newcomers were unprepared also because immigration propaganda distributed in Europe exaggerated the attractiveness and potentialities of Western Canada to the point that it has been described as "by all odds the richest, purplest fiction ever written about the Canadian West." On climate, for example, one pamphlet claimed it to be "the finest climate on earth for constitutionally healthy people." A CPR pamphlet forecast that eventually wheat production would be so great that "the output cannot fail to run into figures both of quantity and money that imagination can hardly reach."[20]

Finally, there were local environmental challenges. With experience, the immigrants became well acquainted with certain drawbacks to prairie agriculture. Initially dazzled by the promise of a homestead that could become one's very own property, immigrants soon found the costs for equipment and supplies high and the labour involved in breaking land and erecting essential outbuildings and a house, often only a sod-house at first but later a modest frame structure, both slow and strenuous. Drought, hail, grasshoppers, frost, rust, and prairie fires sometimes dashed all hopes of reaping any return on one's investment and work. During the early decades of pioneering, the lack of social amenities and of basic medical, educational, and religious services could take its toll. Isolation was an especially heavy cross for pioneer women to bear. There were environmental annoyances, lack of good roads, scarcity of good water, and lack of sufficient wood on the open prairies with which to contend. All goods brought in from the eastern provinces were expensive, including the coal oil, binder twine, barbed wire, machinery, furniture, and clothing on which they were dependent.

The hardships faced by many Belgian immigrants can be gleaned from the family histories published privately or in jubilee volumes. We learn, for example, that a family in Bruxelles, in southwestern Manitoba, first lived in a mud and frame "shack" with mud floors and a straw roof that was unable to withstand heavy rains and on at least one occasion caved in and ruined a year's supply of flour. They cut their first crop by scythe and tied the sheaves by hand, which were then threshed by a compatriot who owned a steam engine and threshing machine. The huge steam engine cut deep ruts as it lumbered along to a suitable threshing floor, burning prodigious amounts of wood to get up a sufficient head of steam. More than once, the sparks issuing from its tall smokestack set straw stacks and surrounding fields alight.

New Optimism

There were reasons, on the other hand, to be optimistic. John Macoun, a self-taught botanist and staunch supporter of the Conservative party, was dispatched by the Macdonald government to reinvestigate the agricultural potential of the southern Prairie region. His report affirmed that the extension of the American desert "is proved to have no such existence." Macoun's *Manitoba and the Great Northwest: The Field for Investment* (London, 1883) questioned the Palliser, Hind, and Dawson theses of the unsuitability of the southwestern triangle of the Prairies for intensive agriculture.[21] Also, Louis Riel's dream of a sovereign Métis nation had evaporated, as had the fears of a general Indian rising on the frontier. The new optimism, and the desire to forestall American influences in the region, were reflected in the choice in 1881 of a southern route for the transcontinental railway and the move of the capital of the North-West Territories from Battleford to Regina. Belgians were inclined to settle in the southern regions, rather than in the more fertile northern belt, because several technological advances made settlement on the open plains less formidable. These changes included the introduction of the hay mower, binder, and threshing machine, improvements in milling and meat preservation, and the introduction of barbed wire for fencing large areas.

Secondly, provision was in place to establish law and order in the West. The federal government organized the North-West Mounted Police along the lines and with the ideology of the Royal Irish Constabulary. The North-West was to be an orderly British environment in which immigrants could settle, averting open hostilities with Aboriginal peoples. There was no apprehension that Belgian immigration would disturb the *status quo*.[22]

Thirdly, on the administrative level, the North-West Territories won federal representation, proceeded to upgrade its judicial system, and obtained authority to incorporate land companies and to levy direct taxation. The stage appeared set for attracting immigrants to what the colonizing priest, the abbé Jean Gaire, called "the limits of the human desert." The authorities in Ottawa were willing to envisage bloc ethnic settlements, although there was some public apprehension in Manitoba:

> So far as this province is concerned there can be no room for
> any further colonization reserves, unless the area of Manitoba

is increased by enlargement of her boundaries; and we protest against any such reserves being granted in future without the concurrence of the Provincial Government. In the vast regions of the North West Territories there is land enough to spare.[23]

Belgians did not arrive in sufficient numbers to envisage a bloc settlement. Upon the creation of the provinces of Alberta and Saskatchewan in 1905 out of the North-West Territories, there arose an acrimonious debate about denominational schools that were frequented by Belgian children. Clifford Sifton, who had directed immigration policy, parted ways with Prime Minister Laurier on the issue. His successor, Frank Oliver, clamped down on railway and colonization companies and opened the southern dry belt to settlement.

Why did Western Canada appear more attractive after 1890? Prime American farmland had been settled and so Canada seemed a northern extension of the fertile virgin lands. Also wheat prices had begun to climb by this time and the cost of its transport had begun to decline. Economists noted that labour and capital flows became mobile. Dryland farming techniques such as summer fallowing were developed and new faster maturing strains of wheat such as Red Fife and Marquis became available. This was the period when Belgian immigrants began taking up farms in the West.

Immigration Policy

The British North America Act, 1867, provided for shared federal and provincial jurisdiction in matters of immigration. On 30 October 1868 competition and duplication were avoided through a compromise whereby the federal government would set up an immigration office in London and another on the European continent. The provinces could name immigration agents accredited by Ottawa in Europe. By 1875 most provinces were so involved in railway construction that they were willing to leave immigration matters entirely in federal hands.

The first Immigration Act, 1869, provided for an entry tax and for quarantine of all vessels transporting ill passengers. The entry tax went into a fund destined to the care of sick and indigent immigrants as well as the cost of their travel to their final destination. Upon arriving at a port of entry, the ship's captain was required to provide a passenger list indicating the total number of persons, names of heads of families and unmarried and/or unaccompanied persons, their country of origin and destination. Moreover, he had to declare if there were "any mentally ill, idiots, deaf and dumb, blind, or infirm, and if they were accompanied by relatives able to care for them." The concept of exclusion of certain classes of persons was initiated by the clause that forbade landed status to "indigents or poor unless the captain offered provisional assistance to these immigrants to transport them to their destination."[24]

The implementation of immigration legislation was discriminatory, emphases being placed on "preferred countries," notably the British Isles, and on agricultural pursuits. Ministers in charge of the portfolio were invariably Anglo-Canadians. In 1891, only 6 per cent of immigrants came from outside the British Isles. This imbalance was still 22 per cent non-British in 1901.[25] Race theories and public prejudice at the bureaucratic level account for this slow development of more open door practices. In 1875, during a brief Liberal administration, there was only limited seasonal employment on the railways and canals. Conditions were not improved by the fact that the Allan Steamship Line continued dumping crowds of destitutes from the British Isles.[26]

Not all bureaucrats were in agreement with government policy. In 1892 the Department of Agriculture discontinued the practice of sending agents to Europe on the recommendation of Sir Charles Tupper. M. Lowe in Agriculture agreed with the policy but A.M. Burgess, Deputy Minister of the Interior, did not agree. In 1896, Clifford Sifton took charge of immigration and he "simplified the homestead procedures, promoted vast irrigation schemes in the arid areas of southern Alberta, eliminated the so-called land-lock by forcing the railways to select and patent their grants, and imparted new life to the immigration branch."[27] He also provided a larger budget for advertising, agents, subsidies and tours of visiting journalists and dignitaries. He believed different "races" had different characteristics and some, including Belgians, were more inclined to farming than others. By 1903 it was concluded that the High Commissioner in London was doing little to promote immigration, so a separate office dealing with immigration was set up in London with W.T.R. Preston in charge.

Edmontonian Frank Oliver, who succeeded Sifton in 1905, was more inclined to disregard the narrow agricultural bias and to broaden the occupational background of acceptable immigrants, while introducing a more rigorous system of selection. Revisions to the Immigration Act excluded not only the medically and morally unfit but also those likely to become public charges and political agitators. "Alien navvies" and strike breakers were quite welcome as labour-intensive resource industries, transportation companies and businessmen were consulted in determining needs for national economic development. When he was accused of filling the West with "foreigners," Oliver still felt it necessary in 1910 to affirm "in carrying out this policy we use due endeavour to secure the additions to our population from the people of our own blood ... the people of our own race."[28]

How did Belgians fare in these racio-cultural assessments? The French complained that unsuccessful Francophone settlers were called French, but when successful they were called Belgians.[29] John Smart reported in 1907 that Belgian farmers "are among the best we can bring to Canada," while J. Obed Smith in Winnipeg found them "very industrious and they succeed well." His successor, J. Bruce Walker, two years later, commented that "they are from a very good class." He ranked them above Germans and Scandinavians as "above the average" and possessing "a pronounced discernment for agriculture." They were "preferred immigrants."[30]

The consul general's report to Brussels in March 1908 echoed the same sentiments with pride concerning his compatriots:

> Our compatriots are generally very appreciated and often succeed. I heard speak of them with praise; they are found to be hard working, thrifty, resourceful; they combine the main qualities of the English and French races; they have the tenacity of the former and the initiative of the latter. In short, Belgians are well regarded here; if they are Flemish, they have no problem learning English, which is useful, if not indispensable in Canada.[31]

The amended Immigration Act, 1919, provided for a literacy test but also left a significant loophole that permitted illiterates "otherwise desirable and admissible" from certain "preferred nations," including Belgium, who were "bona fide farmers, farm labourers, or female domestic servants" to be accepted.[32] Immigration resumed in the 1920s, but when the drought and economic depression struck an order-in-council of 21 March 1931 limited immigration to Commonwealth subjects and dependents of Canadian residents with sufficient capital to establish themselves immediately. There was also the restriction to provinces that had "not signified its disapproval of such immigration."[33] After 1934, even the $1,000 settlement capital was an insufficient qualification for entry. In 1937 the doors opened slightly but the outbreak of World War II late in 1939 nullified any great influx.

In the years after World War II, the Mackenzie King government responded to pressure from business interests that wanted a labour supply and from ethnic communities concerned about relatives and friends in Europe with a more expansive policy. The policy still contained the codicil "without altering the fundamental character of the Canadian nation." In 1947 it was stated explicitly that the administration intended "to ensure the careful selection and permanent settlement of such numbers of immigrants as can advantageously be absorbed in our national economy." The prime minister opined that "the people of Canada do not wish, as a result of mass immigration, to make a fundamental alteration in the character of our population."[34] These restrictions of "existing character" and "absorptive capacity" did not discourage Belgian immigration. In 1950, an order-in-council classified Belgians on the same basis as British subjects and in 1953 accommodation was made for flood victims. The newcomers were now better educated, urbanite and less family-oriented than the two earlier waves of immigrants. The new technologies and business ventures were of more concern than agriculture and manual trades to which earlier immigrants had gravitated. Also, the church no longer played a predominant role in the social life of the recent arrivals.

The Conservative government of John Diefenbaker announced a shift in policy in 1962 from national origins to individual skills and education. Immigration was now a "technical issue," although still tied to "absorptive capacity," favouring the well-educated and professional admissible directly to the middle class. Statisticians stopped compiling figures on ethnic origin in order to concentrate on citizenship and country of residence.[35] The Liberal government in 1966 continued the policy direction by divorcing citizenship from immigration and combining immigration with manpower and branches of the Department of Labour. Sponsorship was controlled in order to avoid bringing in too many unskilled labourers. The Quebec government decided to take up its constitutional right to exercise full jurisdiction in immigration because from 1945 to 1965 only 3 per cent of immigrants admitted were Francophone.[36] This was a significant revelation because it was now the Francophone Walloons who were more interested in coming to Canada than the Flemish who tended to gravitate to English-speaking regions.

Migration Patterns

Migration has been studied in terms of chain migration and bloc settlement. Sojourners and scouts were the usual initiators of chain migration. These individuals, typically a head of a family or unmarried sons, sought employment near a region of possible settlement in order to ascertain the likelihood of success were they to remain permanently. In the case of a favourable impression, members of the family, then the extended family, and finally friends and neighbours were induced to come. Chain migration was a transatlantic movement of linked individuals coming a few at a time to a common destination. Bloc migration, on the other hand, involved larger numbers coming more or less together. Chain migration could develop into bloc migration, although in the case of the Belgians there were only small bloc movements. It was the means by which communities in St. Alphonse, Bruxelles, and Manor developed. The St. Raphaël Society in Antwerp had in fact nursed the thought in 1891 of a Belgian Catholic bloc settlement:

> There [Western Canada] in the measure that its influence increases, the St. Raphaël society will be able to realize at the same time as its charitable objective a patriotic aim dear to it: group Belgians together, in a manner that far from melting with foreign nationalities, they form small cores remaining in contact with Belgium and not be lost for religion and motherland.[37]

Chain migration developed its own "highway" as newcomers touched base first with compatriots at St. Boniface, then moved on to Deloraine and Forget, before moving out beyond to new homestead locations.

There is also the phenomenon of internal migration, as people moved from one region to another within the same political jurisdiction. Manitoba and the North-West Territories sought settlers not only from overseas but also from central Canada. In 1888, for example, Manitoba appointed A.J. McMillan its Emigration Commissioner in Ontario. The province mounted agricultural exhibits at fifty-three fall fairs in central Canada and arranged for farmers' excursions to the West with the assistance of the Canadian Pacific Railway and the Grand Trunk Railway. The railway companies were interested in having their blocs of land settled too. During the inter-war years when drought and grasshopper plagues struck the southern prairies, there was a movement of farmers and service people to the more northerly parklands region. After World War II, economic prospects in Alberta and British Columbia stimulated another inter-provincial migration from Manitoba and Saskatchewan. These internal migratory movements are reflected in the census returns for Belgians.

Sometimes people moved across an international boundary only to return later to a different region of their original land of adoption. For example, Clement De Pape came to Manitoba from Lembeke in 1894, at the age of twenty. For several winters, with his brothers August and Charles, he hauled wood to Cypress River and Holland to buy essential household provisions. In 1897, he and August went to Moline, Illinois, to work in the John Deere factory. The following year, he married Marie Hutlet, who had emigrated with her family from Halenzy. They moved to Red Deer, Alberta, in 1905, then on to the Queen Charlotte Islands to operate a hotel. Their life-style became almost nomadic with brief periods of residence in Prince Rupert, Denman Island, and back to Alberta in 1921. They returned briefly to southern Manitoba before settling finally on Hornby Island, B.C.[38] Miners who came to Vancouver Island and southern Alberta had in some cases originally come to Nova Scotia, moved on to Pennsylvania, only to return to Western Canada in search of better working conditions. This kind of migration was common for a number of Belgians, as an official Canadian inquiry in 1911–12 discovered:

> The bulk of Belgian emigration at the present moment directs its steps towards the north of France. It is reckoned that every year more than one hundred thousand Belgians cross the frontier to work all the harvest in the French provinces, but thousands of them remain in France, in departments where not only the price of land is higher than anywhere in Canada, except in the immediate vicinity of large cities and towns, but where the attachment to the land being stronger than here, it is more difficult, even at a higher price to acquire a large domain.[39]

A few Belgian agricultural and factory workers who came to Ontario moved to Indiana and Michigan and later relocated in the Dakotas and southern Manitoba.[40] The Mauws and Cherlet families that had originally emigrated to Ghent, Minnesota, moved to Swan Lake in 1920, a move that represented a decision to change country of allegiance but also to remain within a Belgian environment. The Catholic clergy launched several projects to induce Quebeckers to settle in Western Canada and Franco-Americans to return from the New England states to the West, and when these projects were not very successful they turned to Francophone areas such as southern Belgium in search of Catholic settlers.[41] By 1912, the Catholic Immigration Association of Canada, an organization of clergy and laity, directed newcomers to communities with an established parish and school regardless of ethnic or national origin. A "key map" of acceptable communities was prepared for settlement purposes. Clearly, the Catholic community was not perceived by this organization as necessarily ethnic or Francophone.[42] Although reliable statistics are not available for the movement of peoples between Canada and the United States, there is reason to believe Canada was a net loser in this process as in certain periods more people left Canada for the United States than arrived from Europe. There does not appear to have been a significant movement of Belgian immigrants out of Western Canada into the American Midwest. In more recent decades, of course, employment opportunities and retirement have accounted for a significant exodus to areas such as California and Arizona.

Immigrants who came in the inter-war years were looking for economic security in a land free of foreign invasion that held out hope of economic and social betterment. War brides formed a link between the New and Old World. Most who came had minimal education. A few single men were part of the annual trip to southwestern Ontario to work during the summer in the beet and tobacco fields. Some of these so-called "swallows" took up residence in Canada, including the western provinces. It was not unusual for a number of established farmers to return to Belgium to visit relatives and friends and encourage others to accompany them back to Canada. A few retired in Belgium leaving their farms to their sons.

In the last quarter of the twentieth century, industrialization and urbanization, while creating new employment opportunities, resulted in rural depopulation in Western Canada. Small towns such as Deleau, Manitoba, and Wauchope, Saskatchewan, disappeared quickly while others, such as Manor and Forget in Saskatchewan, held out longer. The cities were more attractive than the rural areas, although employment could still be found in the beet fields of southern Alberta and in dairying in the Fraser valley. Eastern Canada absorbed most of the newcomers until the 1990s; nevertheless, the "oil patch" had its attractions too. The growth of Calgary, Vancouver and Edmonton made these centres attractive to those coming with better educational qualifications and specialized skills. Young Belgians were often graduates of such institutions as the Microelectronics Centre of Leuven, the Human Genetics Centre in Leuven, Space Research of the University of Liège, and the Institute of Interface Science in Namur. Industrial giants such as Pertrofina, Solvay, Cockerill Sambre and Bekaert launched young men and women on careers in Canada.

Recruitment Propaganda

It has been asserted that of all the means employed to encourage immigration "the most conspicuous and the least useful" was the appointment of agents abroad.[43] The Quebec government named Edouard Barnard its agent in Europe in 1871. On his return he was appointed on the same mission by the Dominion government. John Lowe warned Joseph Marmette, Barnard's successor, not to make exaggerated claims and not to favour one province above another.[44] When Sir Hector Langevin suggested that Jules Boon be named agent in Belgium, the minister opined that "such an appointment could not be made."[45]

The distinction between a government agent and a booking agent for a steamship line was not always clearly delineated. An immigrant office worker complained that M. Berns, supposedly a Canadian agent, profited from his position because each person had to pay an additional 47,50 francs to make up the difference between what was paid the Allen Steamship Line and the 160 francs allotted to M. Berns. The complainant wondered whether Berns had a monopoly and whether he represented the Canadian government or the steamship company. A complaint addressed to the governor-general alleged that the letter of introduction he had been given to show to the agent in Halifax, which would entitle him to a voucher for a stay at a hotel in Quebec or Montreal until a suitable job was found for him, was taken from him and no voucher given in return. There is no record how such a complaint was investigated or rectified.[46]

There ensued a brief period of activity. In 1891, abbé J.B. Morin was appointed government agent for the North-West to encourage him in the colonizing work he had already undertaken. Father Gabriel Cloutier in Manitoba was sent to Belgium to recruit at the time Auguste Bodard of the Société d'immigration catholique was named government agent. Mayor T.A. Bernier of St. Boniface was also commissioned to try to recruit workers for a manufacturing base for his community in 1884. The government of Sir Charles Tupper was opposed to any continuation of this practice; nevertheless, the curé Antoine Labelle, celebrated Quebec colonizing priest, was sent on mission to recruit settlers for Western Canada in 1885. In 1901, the journalist Henri d'Hellencourt, who had emigrated to Manitoba and had become editor of *L'Echo du Manitoba* in 1898, spent three months recruiting settlers with the support of the minister, Clifford Sifton.[47]

A Canadian Emigration Library was established in the Commercial Museum in Brussels in 1892 and a permanent immigration office was opened in Antwerp in 1898, on the recommendation of Henri Bourassa, Rudolph Lemieux, and consul general F. Van Bruyssel. The library was to house all Dominion and provincial statutes, all available descriptive publications concerning Canada, documents and tariffs regarding transportation facilities, photos of agricultural life, blue books of the Labour Commission, relevant maps, catalogues, and samples of grain, tools and implements. The consul general pointed out that the Homestead Act, however, posed a problem because settlers could only obtain definite title by becoming naturalized British subjects, an obligation many Belgians resisted.[48]

Désiré Tréau de Coeli, a prosperous trilingual Belgian living in Hull, was appointed immigration officer in Antwerp under the direction of the High Commission in London, with an annual salary of $1,200.[49] Before taking up his posting, Tréau de Coeli investigated the circumstances of Belgian settlers in the West in order to better inform prospective emigrants in northern Flemish areas, where he concentrated his efforts, on what to expect. He consulted Msgr. Langevin in St. Boniface to obtain a list of useful overseas contacts. He also wrote to the Belgian government "so that my mission at least avoid any opposition."[50]

The first problem he encountered was the invasion of his assigned territory of Belgium and Holland by Paul Wiallard, the agent in France to which Belgium had once been attached: "I would not like to be commanded by a newcomer who would reap the benefit of my work," he observed.[51] He busied himself giving about twenty lectures with lantern slides each winter and distributing geography textbooks in over twenty schools. When Léon Brabant stirred up opposition to this intrusion into the schools, the Ministry of Foreign Affairs decided to publish its own *Emigration Canada*, with annual updates to at least 1908.[52]

It was important therefore to have some positive publications in circulation. The earliest propaganda brochure drawing attention to unlimited opportunities in the West was abbé Pascal-Joseph Verbist's *Les Belges au Canada* (*De Belgen in Canada*, in Dutch), although his chief interest was in Quebec.[53] His compatriot, Gustaaf Vekeman, a farmer who had settled in the Eastern Townships of Quebec, was paid $400 for the translation and printing of twenty thousand pamphlets in Flemish "for special distribution in Belgium." He was also charged with the distribution of pamphlets in French "which were printed in 1873, on the subject of Manitoba and the North-West, he having written a Preface to adapt this edition to the present time."[54] He relayed information about "The Great Canadian West" as an appendix to his *Le Canada, ou Notes d'un Colon* (Sherbrooke, 1884). After describing the geographical situation of Manitoba, the climate, its products, and cattle-raising, he offered some advice to newcomers:

> There is advice of very great importance that we must offer emigrants, that is to be very attentive to adopt the practices whose wisdom and advantages have been demonstrated from experience, and not to waste their time wanting to implant in a new country the customs and usages of their mother country. For example, for what concerns ploughing on the prairies, the method followed in Manitoba is very different from other countries. The prairies are covered by a very tough grass that must be destroyed to render the land suitable for farming. Experience has proved that the best way is to plough only to a depth of two inches and to turn over a furrow from 12 to 14 inches wide.[55]

He proceeded to explain that settlers should arrive in July to September to choose their farmland, that they would need to break ground the following spring using oxen in preference to horses, and sow only oats, flax, or potatoes before mid-June the first year. He understood that the best source of emigrants would be the Flemish regions, therefore his brochure was published in two separate Flemish booklets, *Eene Reis in Canada of Nattige Raadgevingen aan de Belgische Landverhuizers* (Sherbrooke, 1882) and *Canada. Het Groote Noord-Westen* (Ottawa, 1882). In 1885, Vekeman was paid an additional $500 for two thousand copies of *Lettres d'un Emigrant*, to which he would add a dozen new letters.[56]

Vekeman also laid great stress on the lack of compulsory military service, which until 1909 in Belgium weighed especially on the lower classes to fill the required ranks by lottery, the rich having purchased exemptions for their sons. He also believed Canada was a very tolerant country with little evidence of either religious or linguistic conflicts. This may have been true of the Eastern Townships at the time, but it hardly represented the political climate of Western Canada in the settlement period. In 1887, Vekeman had prepared the *Almanach des Emigrants*, with a Flemish translation, and felt justified in applying for a subsidy to recruit emigrants in Limbourg and Luxembourg provinces.[57] In 1890 he was still negotiating with *Het Land* and *La Liberté* to publish on a regular basis articles about Canada, for which he wanted a $200 honorarium annually. He rendered good service but he also expected to be rewarded accordingly.[58]

In 1885–86 there appeared two pamphlets in the *Guide universel de l'émigrant*, the first dealing with Manitoba and the second with British Columbia. These brochures attempted to promote immigration by drawing unfavourable assessments of life and prospects in Belgium compared to Canada. It invoked soil exhaustion after centuries of cultivation, overpopulation, burdensome taxes, military service and social inequities, while studiously avoiding any mention of possible inconveniences immigrants might face in Canada.[59] This negative approach, likely to arouse Belgian authorities and the press, drew the directive from Ottawa that "it is not thought advisable to have anything further to do with Mr. Lennox" in Brussels.[60]

The following year, Stanislaus Drapeau published an official brochure entitled *Canada, le guide officiel du colon français, belge, suisse, etc.* which continued the comparison of Canada with Europe. Drapeau commented specifically on educational opportunities: "One can cite thousands of cases where the children of immigrants, who came from countries with few or no resources, received an excellent education." It was a misleading statement for much of the Prairie region at the time, where, apart from the Winnipeg and Brandon regions, a school system was barely in place yet.[61]

Alfred Bernier, who was commissioned to act as an immigration agent in Europe, published a pamphlet, *Le Manitoba, champ d'immigration*, destined for any group that might be interested in his province, hoping to divert attention from the eastern provinces.[62] Bernier's appeal was seconded by Auguste Bodard of the Montreal headquarters of the Société d'immigration française. He prepared two booklets, *Guide du colon. La laiterie, l'élévage, la culture et les mines dans le Grand Ouest du Canada* (1891) and *Emigration en Canada. Description du Pays. Les Colonies Françaises, Belges et Suisses* (1892), which reproduced responses to questions he had put to immigrants concerning their satisfaction and success. No indication was given about the selection process of published replies.

Louis Hacault followed up with *Les Colonies belges et françaises du Manitoba*, an account of his exploratory journey to Manitoba in the interests of the Société Saint-Raphaël and right-wing Catholics, along with a number of testimonials that had been received for a British inquiry regarding pioneer conditions. He also published these letters in *Le Courrier de Bruxelles*, with which he was associated. A Flemish translation appeared in 1893.[63] It was not until 1890 that the province of Manitoba decided to avail itself of the constitutional provision for shared jurisdiction with the federal government over immigration by opening its own Immigration Office in Winnipeg. The Manitoba government also opened an office in Liverpool to prepare and distribute literature and posters destined for the British Isles and northern Europe.[64]

The Dominion government requested the abbé Gustaaf Willems, a priest serving several communities in southern Manitoba, to gather testimonial letters from successful farmers. These letters were to convey a message of economic opportunity, social equality, and just rewards for hard work in a land where Catholicism was respected. The resulting booklet, *Les Belges au Manitoba. Lettres authentiques* (1894), eventually published also in Flemish, while urging compatriots to "choose Canada in preference to all other countries," hinted at some challenges in this new environment. One farmer observed that income from his mixed farming operation required supplementing in winter through cutting timber. Another warned that any who came with little capital and expected immediate success would be sadly disappointed. Yet another admitted he had been fortunate to have adult children who brought in supplementary earnings to enable the family to become established sooner than otherwise possible. Most commented on the importance of family and community ties, and one bachelor lamented: "it would be good to send out a regiment of girls because there are far too many single men."[65]

The most active propagandist was undoubtedly Désiré Tréau de Coeli. In 1899 he delivered dozens of brochures to the Minister of Foreign Affairs in Brussels. Among them were: *A travers les grandes terres de blé du Nord-Ouest canadien* (1893), *Kanada – ein schliesslich des Kanadischen Nordwestens: Manitoba, Alberta et al.* (1897), *The Winnipeg District: The City and Farm Lands Adjacent* (1898), and *Guide officiel du Klondike, le grand champ d'or du Canada* (1898).[66] He also contacted over four thousand teachers and placed many copies of an excellent geography textbook, *Géographie du Canada et Atlas de l'Ouest canadien*, in many schools.[67] Furthermore, he distributed widely an information bulletin, *Le Canada occidental* (*Canada West* in Dutch), bearing the motto "good crops, sunny climate, low taxes, free education." It also took on the United States, the great rival in attracting immigrants:

> What clearer and more conclusive proof of the advantages offered by Canada than the annual growth of American emigration. There are farmers living in one of the most beautiful countries in the world who leave their farms to come to settle in Canada, the neighbouring country they know and prefer to the great American republic.[68]

In 1907 the Privy Council of Canada decided to call Tréau de Coeli Canadian Information Agent, rather than Canadian Government Agent for Emigration, because the Belgian government was very sensitive to the designation and privileges of emigration agents and it did not encourage emigration.

The Canadian Pacific Railway also published attractive brochures and posters to attract travellers and settlers, beginning in 1883 from its office in Amsterdam. In *Etablissez-vous au Canada* (1913), the railway attempted to overcome the popular image of "a few arpents of snow" with the assurance the winters "resemble much the winters in certain parts of Switzerland which each year attract thousands of Belgian tourists." It offered established farms on land it owned as well as loans. In *Manitoba et le Canadien Nord-Ouest*, the Canadian Pacific Railway Company asserted that, whereas in the United States jobs were at a premium, in Canada "there are many openings for a person who wants to work." Railway coaches were described as luxurious, with the added "it is now no more complicated to leave Belgium for Canada than to move from Flanders to Luxembourg."[69] Ernest J. Chambers produced *The Unexploited West* (Ottawa, 1914) for the Railways Lands Branch.

Another approach was to draw attention to agricultural advances on the Prairies at international exhibitions. At first, only a small agricultural display was mounted at the Musée Commercial de Bruxelles with opportunity for verbal or written inquiries. The limited interest can be gauged from the fact that in 1889, for example, there were only seventeen verbal inquiries and twenty written inquiries concerning Canada.[70] In 1885, it was decided to send an exhibition to the International Exhibition in Antwerp, but not to provide militiamen to act as security officers. The Massey implement company was anxious to show its new farm implements and so the Canadian government allocated the sum of twenty thousand dollars in expenditures.[71] Richard Berns reported that the objective had been attained:

> Belgian merchants, manufacturers, and capitalists are convinced that our [Belgian] overcrowded population can find in Canada the resources which are wanting here, that is to say, occupations for the labouring class, good holdings for farmers, and excellent investment for capital. And Canadian manufacturers have learnt that through Antwerp they can establish a new opening to the Continent of Europe for Canadian products.[72]

Berns made several recommendations. He believed Canada should establish a Canadian Agency in Belgium, should suppress all relations with the journal *L'Emigration* and support the *Journal Populaire* and a similar Flemish paper. The Minister of Agriculture did not favour a regular agency in Belgium, "apart from the question of merits, he sees difficulty at the present time."[73] The commissioner in London, undoubtedly, wished to retain control over continental operations. Also, it was felt that space was too expensive for participation in the 1895 exhibition in Antwerp because no such charges had ever been exacted in other international exhibitions.[74]

In 1905, the government decided to erect a pavilion at the exhibition in Liège, an important manufacturing centre. Tréau de Coeli was satisfied this venture succeeded in bringing "the agricultural and mineral products" to the attention of the public.

But the cost had been enormous, compared to previous experiences with international fairs.[75] He had distributed thirty thousand copies of a pamphlet "The World's Best Wheat Fields" and extended all-expenses-paid invitations to several prominent farm experts to visit Canada. An important publication was associated with Canada's participation: *Le Canada. Son histoire; ses productions et ses ressources naturelles* (Ottawa: Ministère de l'Agriculture, 1905). His office in Antwerp featured displays of grains, stuffed fowls and photographs of agricultural activities.

At the Brussels International Exhibition in 1910, the CPR employed Henri and Charles Van Heden, the latter becoming a permanent employee in Canada. An observer thought that the Canadian government exhibits gave visitors "a precise idea of Canada as one of the world's granaries and possessor of the richest mineral deposits on the globe." The assessment given later in the House of Commons was no less optimistic:

> Thanks to the ministry of Agriculture, our pavilion in Bruxelles was the feature of the latest universal exhibition. Hundreds of thousands of Belgians were able to read our circulars, the atlases and the information published in the French and Flemish languages, describing the riches and beauties of our country. I am persuaded that this exhibition will attract for us several thousand Belgian settlers. It is easier to carry out propaganda through these exhibitions than through agents.[76]

Immigration Assistance

The Canadian government followed through on its propaganda efforts by offering assistance to immigrants. This took several forms. The first approach was through free inland passes to certain classes of immigrants from the port of entry to their destination. The system was prone to abuse because shipping agents in Europe booked people for inland destinations telling them to plead poverty and ask for passes upon landing. In 1872, the Dominion government signed an agreement with the Grand Trunk Railway fixing the third class fare at three cents per mile.

The practice was terminated in 1888 and replaced by a bonus system. The bonus paid to each head of family and to each single male in possession of proof of settlement in the North-West within six months of arrival was ten dollars. To the wife and children over twelve years, a bonus of five dollars was paid. This practice was abandoned in March 1894.[77]

A passenger warrant system was instituted to meet competition from foreign countries and to establish an absolute differential in favour of the St. Lawrence and Maritime seaports as against New York. Fares were reduced by a maximum of one-third for approved immigrants, the reduction being shared equally by the government and the steamship lines. In practice, fares were reduced by five dollars only on tickets to Manitoba and the North-West into the early 1900s.

These approaches were all related to the commissions paid to booking agents of the steamship lines. The recognized practice was to allow them to deduct 5 per cent from the gross amount of the passage money, charged from the point of departure to that of destination. At first, only agents of the Allan Line were eligible, this in recognition of their efforts to populate the West. The commission was extended to the Anchor Line and the Dominion & Temperley Line, and finally any line using the St. Lawrence entry. Agents were paid for Belgians coming to Winnipeg in 1882 as farmers or mechanics. The five dollar commission was paid for immigrants to the Canadian West even if they came via New York and the American railways before the introduction of the Canadian Pacific transcontinental service. In 1907 it was decided to pay the bonus only to a few select booking agents in six "preferred countries," who were "native of the country in which the booking agent is operating." In Belgium, five agencies were recognized: Raydt & Bryunseels, Frendberg, Berns, Caron, and Schyn. All claims from continental steamship booking agents were to be processed in London to avoid any conflict with European emigration restrictions.[78]

There was also assistance given to so-called "return men," i.e., established immigrants who returned to their country of origin to lure friends and acquaintances to join them in Canada.

These men normally received financial support and free transportation from the government, the railway, and steamship companies. There was the problem that some zealous recruiters operated independently, sometimes offending Belgian authorities, and others made false claims of accreditation. A certain T. Metternet posed as an important person in Manitoba working for the Transoceania Society, for example, and was pursued by Ministry of Justice officials.[79] Similarly, Edmond Fasseaux of Grande Clairière, while visiting his father in Binche, placed an advertisement in *La Belgique* saying he was "officially charged by the Canadian government to inform and to guide free of charge those who would like to accompany him on his return to Manitoba." He did not ask for compensation for his services, but he had no official status and therefore was prohibited from recruiting publicly.[80]

By 1894, officials in the Department of the Interior had come to the conclusion that, in spite of the number of return men that had been subsidized, "they had not been successful in producing any compensating effect on the flow of emigration to Canada." As a consequence, the government, along with the railway and steamship companies, decided to place the practice "on a more business-like footing and give greater assurance of results commensurate with the expenditure involved than the old method had done." Following a consultative conference, a new policy was set out:

> Under the plan adopted these have received free transportation one way only together with a small pecuniary advance and their return passage, and further compensation is made to depend entirely on the success of their efforts in securing suitable settlers for Canada.

The twenty-seven return men to be supported were designated by country of operation. The British Isles were allotted fifteen, Sweden four, but France and Belgium were allotted only one each. Obviously, Hector Langevin's plea to John A. Macdonald that French and Belgian settlers ought to receive more support went unheeded.[81]

In 1906 there was a minor scandal when it became known that since 1896 the federal Liberal government had entered into a secret and private arrangement with a syndicate of steamship agents in Antwerp known as the North Atlantic Trading Company. Whereas the Conservative government had paid a commission to individual booking agents, the Liberals upon assuming power in 1896 paid the commission to a collective group of identical agents. The system did good screening and sent out only the best immigrants. Clifford Sifton was so pleased with the results that in 1899 he appointed W.T.R. Preston inspector of the agencies in Britain and Europe. To further encourage the agents of the North Atlantic Trading Company to divert settlers to Canada, the bonus for adults was to be paid for those over twelve years, rather than eighteen as had been the case. More money was also assigned for promotional literature. Between 1899 and 1906, the system brought out 71,000 immigrants at a cost of $350,000 paid to recruiters.[82]

This network of agents was to be kept secret from Parliament: "The Department does not know nor does not want to know what these agents are doing." But it also contravened emigration laws in Belgium by sending in propaganda from outside the country and by aggressive advertising in newspapers. The Canadian Pacific Railways, for example, employed Paul Watelet of Charleroi as their general agent in Belgium, and he was closely watched by Belgian officials. Canadian sentiment was that, although not strictly legal, the system netted Canada "the pick of all those who were booking from continental ports, letting the riff-raff go to the United States and to South America." When the terms of the clandestine agreement became public knowledge in July 1906, Frank Oliver, who had replaced Sifton, cancelled the agreement and opened the flood gates of immigration. The Conservative opposition and organized labour had evidence that W.T.R. Preston, Superintendent of Emigration stationed in London, James A. Smart, former deputy minister and Canadian agent of the company, and even Clifford Sifton himself had "sinister connections" with the North Atlantic Trading Company. Preston was removed from his post in London because he had worked with Louis Leopold of the Canadian Labour Bureau in London in "an enormous remunerative business" favouring the emigration of British mechanics and tradesmen. While the Canadian government appeared to have lost some of the control it had exercised over immigration from the European continent, the minister acquired more discretionary power to reject or deport immigrants.[83]

In 1911–12, Olivar Asselin was sent by the Department of the Interior to visit Belgium and France in order to make recommendations for the improvement and the extension of emigration efforts in Francophone areas. This came in response to well-founded charges that this region had not received the attention placed on the British Isles and central Europe. It occurred in the context of heated debates in Canada on imperial solidarity and bilingualism. Asselin's report made four major criticisms of the situation as he observed it. The Canadian Commissioners for Emigration in London made little effort to support effectively the exhibitions at Liège in 1905 and Brussels in 1909 and did not even join Tréau de Coeli and his staff. Secondly, none of the Anglo-Canadian steamship lines, including the CPR that has a direct line to Antwerp, sponsors lectures in Belgium, and the London office did not send Belgian farm delegates to Canada, participate in agricultural fairs or mount a circulating agricultural exhibition in Belgium. Thirdly, the high commissioner and his staff in London do not appear to have understood Belgian law and customs concerning emigration. He recommended withdrawing the Antwerp office from the control of the London office, separating Holland from Belgium, and increasing both the budget and activity of the Antwerp office. Finally, he was scandalized that the agent in Antwerp replied to French or Flemish requests for information in English only. There was a serious lack of official authorized interpreters on subsidized steamships, Canadian ports, and railway stations such as Halifax. French-language publicity was too often a grotesque literal translation from English that inspired no credibility.[84]

The publication of the uncensored report raised concerns in London because, from the point of view of "international courtesy," it contained "unfortunate reflections on conditions in France and Belgium." In fact, Belgium did not have the statutory restrictions on emigration that existed in France. The Governor-General informed External Affairs in Ottawa in a secret communication that "it is of great importance to exercise careful censorship, as regards references to foreign countries, before any report is issued by the Department."[85] While there was concern not to vex the French government, there was no immediate response to the major problem of alleged favouritism and inefficiency of the Canadian High Commission and the Commissioner of Emigration in London.

Canada had emigration agencies in Antwerp, Paris and Copenhagen before 1914, all under the direction of the chief office in London. One day before Antwerp fell to the Germans, its Canadian office closed, as did the Paris office after the first bombardment, and all records were transferred to London. The Canadian immigration office in Antwerp was not reopened in 1918. After World War I, emigrants from the European continent to Canada required a British visa on their passport. J. Obed Smith, commissioner in London, recommended that the office in Antwerp be reopened, but under London's supervision, because "there can be no dissected control on this side of the Atlantic." The Canadian government was anxious to dissociate its activities from Britain and there was some thought of making the Antwerp office the clearing house for all its continental European immigration matters.[86]

In the early 1920s, the Dominion government, the press and the business community promoted immigration, hoping to recapture the pre-war boom. The new regulations were published in Antwerp in *Le Matin*, *Métropole*, and *Handelsblad*.[87] In 1921 the Dominion government sent three immigration officers to Antwerp and Le Havre "in order that they may bring to the notice of the steamship companies any cases in which intending passengers have failed to fulfill the conditions of entry into the Dominion which has been laid down in the Canadian Immigration Regulations." This was designed to spare immigrants "the hardships entailed by rejection at the port of landing in Canada." This was direct action from Ottawa without consulting the British government or the High Commissioner in London. J. Obed Smith felt the purpose of the mission might be misunderstood as interference with Belgian sovereign rights: "Canada has no more right in Antwerp than Warsaw has in Montreal, but mutual arrangements can be made through proper channels." The Belgian Foreign Ministry was advised of the Canadian intentions.[88]

In reality, the need for renewed immigration was driven by such factors as the over-extension of the railways, the increased national debt because of war expenditures, and increased Canadian migration to the United States. Prime Minister Mackenzie King's selective immigration policy, in 1932, continued to recruit farmers, farm labourers, and domestic workers from the British Isles and "preferred countries," while placing Asiatics and eastern and southern Europeans in restricted categories. The volume of publicity decreased and only the railways seemed to take an active interest in promoting immigration. When Alex Lonay issued a polemical *Nécessité économique et sociale de l'émigration parmi les cultivateurs belges* (1926) during the post-war depression, the Ministry of Foreign Affairs issued a warning that Lonay was not acquainted with economic conditions in Canada where he suggested Belgians might profitably relocate. Several agents were suspected of misleading people. Theophile Van Lysbettens, agent for the Canadian Pacific Railway in Antwerp, had his licence taken away on orders of the governor in 1925.[89] The Canadian government had just entered into a two-year "Railways agreement" with the Canadian Pacific Railway and the Canadian National Railways (renewed in 1927) to settle farmers, agricultural workers, and domestic servants in Western Canada. The scheme encountered several problems in addition to the drought and depression that struck the region. Immigrants found it expensive to establish themselves on a farm. Some who came never intended to farm but gravitated to the towns and cities. Labourers were forced to go to urban centres because of the lack of jobs in rural areas. Unemployment was rising in the urban centres and the influx of immigrants aroused some hostility.[90]

It becomes evident that the traditional "push" and "pull" factors are not the sole elements that explain emigration and immigration. One must also consider family and regional strategies and the development of international networks. This is especially true as communication and transportation evolve toward the idealistic "global village." There was an interplay between individuals as active participants in the immigration process and impersonal historical forces.

Government policies, either to encourage emigration or to attract immigrants, alone cannot account for the movements of human population. The unpredictable results of seemingly positive governmental intervention can be illustrated from two measures. Memories of the great cholera plague associated with early Irish immigration moved the authorities to establish quarantine stations at Halifax, St. John, and Grosse Isle, Quebec, in 1869 to prevent such outbreaks. Three subsequent epidemics were interpreted as proof of the inadequacy of such action and did little to reassure the established population or prospective immigrants. Similarly, the introduction of the North-West Mounted Police and the suppression of the Métis movement, widely interpreted as the imposition of law and order, were interpreted by a few as indicative of British colonial exploitation and domination. Also, the unpublicized dumping of unfortunates, the "marginalized" and unemployed, by Britain on the Dominion reinforced a negative image.

Many factors go into the decision to emigrate, either with the intention of returning eventually or remaining away permanently. World War II was an important factor in massive Dutch emigration to Canada in the 1950s, but Belgian farmers were still interested also.[91] Governments, entrepreneurs, private corporations, etc., have motives for supporting immigration or opposing it. These are not constant in either time or place. This is well illustrated by recent developments. The point system, introduced in 1967, matched immigrants to occupational demand in order to expand the domestic market and stimulate economic growth. Eventually the "human capital" sought in Belgium, as elsewhere, included highly educated computer analysts, scientists, and engineers, as well a business entrepreneurs with investment capital. In 1991, Quebec gained control of the design, administration and delivery of settlement and integration services for immigrants from the federal government. Linguistic and cultural factors were important elements in the choice of immigrants to the province. In 1998, British Columbia and Manitoba signed similar agreements with the federal government. Alberta has an integrated program with the federal authorities. Immigration was decidedly one of several issues that became politicized in the 1990s in western Canada. There was mounting opposition from western regional politicians to continued immigration, multicultural policies, bilingualism and Aboriginal self-government. Prior to 2005 this was seen as a challenge to the elite consensus of the major political parties whose power bases were in central and eastern Canada. The Belgian experience in Canada in navigating these sometimes tempestuous waters illustrates well the complexity of the emigration/immigration process.

Migration Processes

The process of movement of peoples from one location to another has been studied historically in several different manners. First, there is the distinction between emigrants/immigrants who move with the conscious aim of establishing new family roots and sojourners who move temporarily to better their economic and social position but intend to return eventually to their native land. When Vice-Consul Robert De Vos travelled with a fact-finding mission to western Canada, he reported back to the Ministry of Foreign Affairs in Brussels in 1901 his belief that a number of immigrants were in fact sojourners who hoped to return to their native country:

> This meeting [with a farmer from the province of Luxembourg settled between Hartney and Grande Clairière in Manitoba] made an impression on me the exactitude of which was later confirmed for me: it is that our compatriot nourished the hope of leaving Canada as soon as he had some means to do so. The majority of emigrants have the same plan when they leave and still nurse it a long time after they arrive here. There is among all of them a certain repugnance, a fear of thinking that they might never see their native country again; they flatter themselves with thinking that absence from the homeland is but a transitory condition, a means of acquiring quickly the

capital which they hope to enjoy at home, in their own village. That is why, in the beginning, all their work is feverish, all their thoughts of the future as of the past being turned to their homeland. Nothing binds them to the new soil except their hope of gain.[92]

On the other hand, De Vos also noted that the regularity and cyclical nature of agricultural labour tended over time to create a certain bond between the farmer and his land. This was in some cases sufficient to convert the sojourner into a permanent settler. Established settlers did not always appreciate sojourners who were itinerant labourers, as a St. Alphonse farmer observed: "they have become wanderers and drink a lot, something this country can do without, especially here in Manitoba."[93] Clergy and emigration societies in Belgium, on the other hand, encouraged preliminary scouting as a prelude to emigration:

> In general, we cannot extol the location of Canadian farms as being suitable to the great mass of agricultural emigrants. Usually they consist of abandoned farmsteads due to soil exhaustion.... The system which we prefer to follow consists first of all in sending out a member of the family and to have him taken on as a labourer. Thus he learns to understand the country and its culture; if he does not like it, he will have earned his travel costs and will have no losses to deplore; if he persists, he will be better able to direct his family and to achieve his mission.[94]

The distinction between the two movements is sometimes blurred inasmuch as sojourners can change their minds and decide to become permanent settlers. This happened in the case of some miners from Hainaut and farm boys from Flanders who either decided to call on family to join them in western Canada or returned to recruit family and friends. Also, there were those who came with the intention of establishing permanent residence and then became discouraged or disillusioned and returned to Belgium.[95]

Scheppers College, Swan Lake, MB, 1919-32. (Author's files)
An agricultural college for Flemish boys operated by the
Brothers of Our Lady of Mercy from Mechelen, Belgium.

III

THE MANITOBA BASE

The first Belgian settlers arrived in Manitoba in the 1880s, St. Boniface becoming their initial base for settlement in the surrounding French-Canadian parishes. It became the industrial centre for many decades and remained the centre of Francophone Catholic institutions. Skilled and unskilled workers and trades people were concentrated in the eastern enclave, popularly known as Belgian Town, but it never became an ethnic ghetto. Shopkeepers, office workers and a few professionals were concentrated in the upwardly mobile sector around the cathedral and classical college. The Belgian Club, founded in 1905, was strategically located between these two urban sectors, as was the Sacred Heart Flemish parish erected later. Employment was available initially in grain processing, meat packing, in the railway yards and production of building materials. By the inter-war years, the second generation and new arrivals aspired to economic mobility through enterprises modelled on interactive business development. As Winnipeg surpassed St. Boniface, Belgians were attracted to its suburbs where they became successful dairymen, market gardeners, and after 1940, sugar beet growers and factory workers.

Those who took up agriculture, the main thrust of immigration efforts, became partners in the national development of the West as the wheat economy evolved. Families took up farms in the southern area of the province, notably around St. Alphonse, Bruxelles and Deloraine, seeking a familiar landscape as much as possible. St. Boniface remained the point of entry to the Prairies for Belgians even when Winnipeg asserted itself as the "gateway" to the West. A chain migration of Flemings used Deloraine as an interior outpost to fan out onto the second and third prairies levels.

Similarly, Walloons recruited especially by the abbé Jean Gaire moved westwards from Grande Clairière to form a short chain of Francophone rural parishes. Flemings blended into Francophone communities as easily as the Walloons, not only in St. Boniface and environs, but also in rural areas such as Ste. Rose-du-Lac and Ste. Amélie. Thus the pattern of main Belgian settlement was established – basically it was rural agricultural with some business entrepreneurship in smaller urban centres. Individuals and family units came initially and they were reinforced through chain migration. Clerical colonization projects were of minor importance in Manitoba. Internal migration resulted in dispersal over a wider area, notably the northern parklands.

Context of Initial Settlement

Settlement on the first Prairie steppe, roughly the present province of Manitoba, was stimulated by three factors. These were the building of railway lines that provided access to the vast plains; the Crow's Nest Pass Agreement of 1897 which provided access to rich mineral resources while reducing freight rates on grain destined for export and on incoming settlers' construction materials and implements; and the laissez-faire immigration policies. Federal government intervention in the settlement of Western Canada is often presented as part of a national policy, a visionary nation-building plan that is a convenient academic creation.[1] Belgians were interested in Western Canada by the time the region successfully entered the rising world wheat trade, soon ranking with the United States and Argentina in wheat exports.[2] James Trow, chair of the House of Commons immigration and colonization committee, visited Manitoba in 1877. In a series of thirteen letters, he confirmed the suitability of the North-West as a field of immigration and concluded that Manitoba was ideal for intensive agriculture.[3] The Rowell-Sirois Commission concluded decades later that because of this development after 1896, "Canadians began to believe themselves to be a great people. Their work in creating the West gave them that sense of common achievement which marks a nation."[4] After 1871, Manitoba could appoint its own agents in Europe and elsewhere "duly accredited by the General Government ". [5] Implementation of the agreement was another matter, prompting the *Manitoba Free Press* to editorialize: "Nothing more, surely, need be urged than to make a good demand upon Canada to select at least one resident of Manitoba to represent our case in Europe."[6] In fact, in August 1871, young J.A.N. Provencher was appointed by Ottawa agent for the North-West and during a three-month tour of Europe visited Belgium. His efforts were somewhat hampered by two factors: first, the lack of co-ordinated efforts by various interested government departments; second, the lack of confidence in this agent on the part of the Manitoba Francophone community.[7] Settlement was rather disappointing at first. In many years there were nearly as many cancellations of homestead entries as new entries.[8]

A second federal initiative was the provision by Order-in-Council of the Department of the Interior for bloc settlements. Among the Francophones, a few Belgians settled at Letellier, St. Pierre-Jolys, St. Malo and Ste. Anne-des-Chênes. An entrepreneur from Oudenaarde in Flanders, Louis Verhaegen, wrote to Msgr. Ireland in St. Paul, Minnesota, inquiring about the possibility of launching a bloc settlement in Manitoba. The letter was sent on to St. Bonface for a reply and action.[9] Seven years later, Métis land bought up by the Catholic Church was still available to form a Belgian bloc. By 1880 the church opposed any such settlement beyond the Red River valley parishes.[10]

The year after Trow's visit, the railway from Minnesota reached St. Boniface, the oldest Canadian settlement in the West, more important than Fort Garry [Winnipeg], and destined to become the centre of Belgian concentration and activity. The rerouting of the Canadian Pacific Railway to Winnipeg/St. Boniface instead of Selkirk, in return for a generous cash subsidy, free land for a large railway yard and buildings, and a property tax exemption set off a boom on the left bank of the river. In 1871, St. Boniface had about four times the population of Fort Garry, but by 1881 Winnipeg had a population seven times larger than St. Boniface. Nevertheless, Joseph Royal, leader of the minority Francophone legislators, attempted to maintain the traditional Red River duality in government and reassured Archbishop Taché that Belgium would send out three to four hundred thousand settlers, a fanciful view taken up in the pages of Le Manitoba.[11] Although the clergy were impressed by the industry and rapid adaptation of the few Belgians settled near St. Alphonse and Deloraine, the archbishop was becoming aware that most Belgian immigrants spoke Flemish.[12]

Winnipeg was the "gateway" geographically where the Canadian Shield had given way to fertile flat prairie land just east of the junction of the Red and Assiniboine rivers. By 1881 the CPR had reached beyond Winnipeg along the Assiniboine valley. Brandon was the western passenger terminal, but at Flat Creek [Oak Lake/Lac des Chênes] there was an important siding for outfitting incoming settlers. Abbé Gaire, a colonizing priest, identified it as his base for a triangular settlement to launch a chain of western parishes. Building material of all descriptions was stockpiled there. Two large boarding houses accommodated the railway construction crews, including a few Belgian workers. A land agency was opened at "Turtle Mountain" [Deloraine], a staging point for westward-bound Belgians.

Belgians settled in widely dispersed areas from the hub of St. Boniface, including Ile des Chênes, St. Norbert, St. Léon, Pine Falls and Ninette. The abbé G. Clouthier, a colonizing agent explained: "The whole of these places are regularly organized parishes, having schools which are kept under the immediate control of the ecclesiastical authority."[13] La Broquerie, where Jean-Baptiste Tauffenbach and Mathias Pierson settled, attracted the attention of Auguste Bodard, the colonizing agent, who entered into negotiations for a housing development for up to four hundred Belgian families. The project was probably related to the proposal of the Countess de Bruges de Gerpinne and based on the model village plan of Viscount Jules de Cuverville.[14] It was only in 1888 that the Bruneau Verhaeghe family settled in St. Boniface. Within two decades St. Boniface could claim the chief concentration of Belgians in the province.

Immigrants travelling by train from the eastern seaports were discouraged by the endless uninhabited stretches of forests and lakes between Montreal and Winnipeg, followed by the seemingly vacant prairies. But some found a familiar landscape that became a part of their identity and memory, such as those from the Ardennes who settled at Bruxelles. Others, like those at St. Alphonse or Grande Clairière created a familiar landscape with the church and its adjacent cemetery and grotto.[15] For Belgians it was important to maintain communication with a centre such as St. Boniface, to have access to wood and water, and soil suitable for mixed farming. If a familiar landscape such as Bruxelles were available, this added an emotional attachment to economic considerations.[16]

Farming in the "old country" and in the new land were both occupations designed to make nature produce marketable commodities as well as subsistence for the family. The difference was that in Belgium nature had long been domesticated and cultivated but in Manitoba it was undomesticated, wild and sometimes resistant. The immigrant farmer became a partner in the process of national development, at least economically, if not immediately in the political sense.[17]

In 1881 there appeared a strange tall building in Gretna, a grain elevator, a storage and loading facility that could save farmers the back-breaking work of hoisting nearly seven hundred sacks of wheat needed to fill a railway boxcar. Soon these vertical grain elevators appeared in all the railway towns and hamlets. In 1889–90, following cancellation of the CPR monopoly, the Pacific Northern Railway laid a line through Somerset, Swan Lake and Mariapolis, an important boost to settlement of the area where numerous Belgians were among the newcomers. The West began exporting wheat through Winnipeg and in St. Boniface flour mills went into operation. The stage was set for the implantation drama.

Early Colonization Reports

By the end of the nineteenth century, favourable reports had confirmed the suitability of the keystone province for both agricultural and working class immigrants. J.E. Têtu, immigration agent at Emerson, where immigrants entered the West arriving via the United States, reported in 1888:

> The past year, too, has witnessed a fair immigration of French and Belgian settlers, about whom I am entitled to speak as I have conducted the French correspondence for the Winnipeg Agency as well as my own at Emerson. These immigrants are of the well-to-do class, with means sufficient to purchase farms.... They are extremely self-reliant, requesting help only in one particular; of an interpreter and this but in isolated cases.[18]

In 1890, Louis Hacault, a conservative Catholic journalist from Brussels, visited the rural settlement of Bruxelles through courtesy of a free railway pass from the Canadian Pacific Railways in the interests of the St. Raphaël Society for the Protection of Emigrants. He marvelled at the warm reception by French-Canadians who had preceded them:

> The Canadians showed themselves to be perfect with respect to our compatriots. When the first contingent of Belgians arrived at Cypress River, two or three years ago, all the French Canadians were on hand to receive them. A single farmer, M.

Bernardin, lodged 45 during several weeks. That alone speaks. Canadian hospitality and generosity are beyond all praise.[19]

He met about one hundred and fifty immigrants from Luxembourg and Namur provinces and a few Flemings. All spoke optimistically of their lot; one housewife exclaimed in Flemish: "Oh, sir, we are here in heaven itself." From the highest hill in the district known as Lookout Hill, the future homestead of the Lebrun family from Marcinelle, he viewed the countryside of wooded hills and valleys and decided that he would personally take up land in the area and recruit a number of compatriots to do likewise.[20]

Hacault's enthusiasm was echoed a few years later by Georges Kaiser, an engineer who visited Western Canada in the company of Auguste Bodard, the secretary of the Société d'immigration française. In a subsequent publication, Kaiser noted that three objections to western settlement – the scarcity of wood, the lack of water, the severe climate – should not deter prospective immigrants. He underscored that the soil was fertile and natural disasters were infrequent.[21]

The consul general in Canada, Fernand Van Bruyssel, reported in detail to his embassy in Great Britain on soil conditions in Manitoba. He described it as extremely fertile, attaining a depth of several metres, the result of centuries of vegetal decomposition enhanced by the ashes of prairie fires and animal deposits. From this he concluded:

> It is, moreover, easy to cultivate; the settlers in Bruxelles and St. Alphonse assured me that one man alone can manage without extraordinary effort to cultivate, seed and harvest 50 acres of land. He only requires help for about ten days during harvesting. Add to this the fact that very well-developed agricultural machinery is in almost general use.[22]

In fact, M. De Volver, a former minister in the Belgian government, had a twenty-two-year-old son whom he wanted to send to Manitoba "to familiarize himself with the layout of large farms, cattle raising and generally all aspects of agriculture."[23]

Auguste de Pape, a pioneer in southern Manitoba, sounded a warning about sending a young member of the family to scout out possibilities abroad and the possible irremediable breaking of family and community ties.

> I find myself in a country not too convenient for young men who arrive here without parents and families, as many among them live in winter off earnings they gathered in the summer. Some go to extremes, spending the money by moving from place to place rather than becoming serious and settling down on a homestead. They have become wanderers and drink a lot, something which this country can do without, especially here in Manitoba.[24]

His opinion was published in *Les Belges au Manitoba: Lettres authentiques* alongside testimonials gathered from compatriots who had begun to clear land, plant crops and raise their families in the pioneer environment.

The immigration agent in Winnipeg reported in 1889: "there arrived during the season about two hundred Belgians, some of whom have been settled through the efforts of Rev. Father Clouthier; others, have found employment in various parts of the country."[25] On the other hand, Thomas Gelley, French interpreter for the immigration service in Winnipeg, reported that arrivals from France and Belgium were "dissatisfied men who had no agricultural tastes, but were of a roaming disposition, and who without money or the first principles of economy, came to Canada and returned home dissatisfied with our country."[26] Two years later, Gelley was commended for his efforts: "Eighty-five persons came from Belgium and have been located at St. Norbert, Deleau and St. Alphonse in Manitoba, and in Lethbridge and Calgary in Alberta."[27] Henri d'Hellencourt, a French army lieutenant who came to Manitoba in 1891 and became the editor of *L'Echo du Manitoba* in 1895, was sent by Clifford Sifton on a mission to France and Belgium, following differences that had developed between the government and its agent, Auguste Bodard. D'Hellencourt reported favourably on emigration prospects and began sending copies of *L'Echo du Manitoba* to Belgium each week.[28]

The narrow vision of the federal government, shared by the Manitoba government, appealed specifically to the aspirations of British dispossessed urban workers. Belgians had different motives for emigrating, which the Manitoba authorities failed to capitalize upon.[29] The issue resurfaced in 1907 when Armand Lavergne and Henri Bourassa attacked the Laurier government for not funding agencies in Belgium and France on the same basis as England. It reflected, they said, the personal bias of the deputy minister, James Smart, who was reported in the *Northern Express* of Liverpool on 10 February 1902 as saying that more British emigrants were required to prevent any "francisation" of Canada, an opinion often repeated in later years.[30]

On the other hand, Belgian vice-consul Robert De Vos recorded a favourable impression of early implantation: "When colonists establish themselves in groups under the guidance of an experienced person who knows English, or under the direction of a priest, as was done with success at Bruxelles and at St. Alphonse in Manitoba, it is preferable that they go farther West where it is easier to obtain good land, easy to clear and to cultivate."[31]

In his 1901 report of his western tour, he documented a number of successful farm operations: Niverville could readily accommodate another fifteen or more Belgian families; at Ile des Chênes, families who came with no capital were able in a few years to become financially independent; at Otterburne, several Flemings came with no capital, worked as farm and city labourers, accumulated sufficient cash to start their own farms, and were now securely established.

> They distinguished themselves by their behaviour, their steadiness at work, their perseverance, and their orderliness. The Immigration office classes them among the best settlers and sees with satisfaction their numbers increase. They all succeed and among the families that have prospered they cite the Bossuyt family of St. Boniface.[32]

This justified further recruitment in Belgium.

Rural Provincial Settlements

The largest rural concentration of Belgians, both Flemings and Walloons, developed rapidly in the southern area of the province. The first newcomers, François Debleekaere and five other families, Flemings who also could speak French, settled at St. Alphonse in 1882. By 1890 there were about fifty homesteads in the area registered in Belgian names. They built their first homes from poplar logs, which did not shrink when drying, quickly learned how to "make land", or use a two-bladed grub-hoe like a mattock to cut tree roots and clear away the soil. The poplar trees were cut into cordwood and hauled by oxen to the railway in Holland. Oxen were cheaper than horses, were incredibly strong, lived off the land, and when too old for such hard labour could be butchered and eaten. Many of the men, needing cash for supplies, found immediate employment on the railways.[33] The community suffered a major setback when the Northern Pacific Railway bypassed the town, giving rise to the hamlet of Mariaville, later renamed Mariapolis, five miles to the south.[34] Nevertheless, the community included a church, four schools, two sawmills, a flour mill, a couple grocery stores, a post office and a rectory. Land was selling at from $2 to $10 an acre because crop yields were already reaching thirty-six bushels to an acre.[35]

A second nucleus called Bruxelles developed north of St. Alphonse after Alphonse Bacchus took up a homestead in 1887. He opened a grocery store and obtained the franchise of the post office, a central meeting place for the community. A chain migration of Bacchus and Sauvelet relatives and neighbours ensued from the province of Luxembourg, enchanted by the panoramic views that reminded them of their homeland, its good farmland, and its abundance of wood and water. Adolescent and adult sons of thirteen families hired out to neighbouring farmers to augment family income. Little by little, family units were reconstituted. The advantage of having strong youths who could supplement family income sent a clear message to those contemplating emigrating.[36] The customary practices of unmarried children turning over earnings to the head of the household until such time as they married, coupled with the tradition for families of both the bride and groom to establish the new household fully equipped according to their means, were transplanted to the new land. The patriarchal family and the practice of pooled family resources were an asset in pioneering on the prairies.[37] The area around Bruxelles and St. Alphonse was heavily wooded. Men, especially young newcomers who had been accustomed to back-breaking work in sugar beet fields in Flanders and northern France, hired out as "grubbers" cutting bush and breaking land with a grub-hoe. They worked for board and room and a modest wage per acre cleared. They started at six o'clock in the morning, took lunch breaks at nine o'clock and four o'clock, then resumed work after the evening meal until darkness forced them to quit. In winter, they worked until the snow became too deep.[38] Joseph Hutlet was very disillusioned during his first year in Manitoba, convinced his sons had not given an accurate report of conditions, but lack of funds prevented him from returning to Halanzy. As family finances improved so did his attachment to the new homeland.[39] The Medar Glorieux family at first found that the district was "nothing but hills, stones, snakes and small lakes," thought of going farther west to Alberta or returning to Belgium, but eventually became quite satisfied with life in southern Manitoba.[40]

When Louis Hacault visited Bruxelles in 1890, he found there approximately 150 Walloons and thirty Flemings. This number was soon augmented by the arrival of more Walloon families from Luxembourg and Hainaut and Flemings from East Flanders. In 1892, he returned with his own family and a small contingent of new settlers and filed for a homestead in dense bushland. While his wife and sons assumed many of the burdens of farming, he busied himself with community and church affairs as a justice of the peace and a churchwarden.[41] August De Pape, his brother Clement and uncle John and their families hired single men, nine of whom brought their families to settle in the area, an impressive colonization success.[42] Auguste De Pape concluded that "hard work is rewarded, we can achieve a good fortune in this country by applying the same zeal and care as in Belgium."[43] He soon emerged as a community leader, serving as a churchwarden, school trustee, justice of the peace, and eventually a municipal councillor.[44] In Swan Lake, the Francis De Roo family assumed a similar leadership role soon after arriving there from Bruxelles in 1898. In Swan Lake and St. Alphonse, the Flemish group would remain predominant, spilling over into adjacent Somerset and Mariapolis.

Bruxelles remained predominantly Walloon, with a Flemish minority, and represented a wide range of occupations and talents. Louis Hacault was a journalist and man of letters who espoused conservative Catholic causes. Omer Knockaert operated a dairy farm, Julien Froidart a sawmill in the village, Ernest Deurbrouek a general store, and Joseph Hutlet was a woodworker and cabinet maker. The Hutlet clan included the Sauvelet, Mangin and Poncelet families, all from Halanzy, in the province of Luxembourg. The Poncelets operated a grocery store and lumber yard in the village. Mme Louise Nerinckx, a devout, self-effacing lady from a distinguished middle-class family, freely offered her services as *gouvernante* of the rectory for forty-five years, taught the local students their music lessons, inspired the parishioners to organize a choir and town band, and encouraged the Ursuline nuns to come to Bruxelles to open a convent school.[45] Another prominent citizen was Dr. Alphonse Van Wilghen, a graduate of the University of Louvain, who moved his medical practice to Mariapolis to be more accessible to a larger Belgian clientele in the south central region. He treated all whether they were able to pay him for his services or not.[46]

In St. Alphonse, as in Bruxelles, most were farmers but a few combined other occupations with agriculture. Alberic Schamp operated a seed business, Triphon De Pauw was a builder and accomplished beekeeper, while Francis Deschouwer was local photographer, watch repairman and also operated a sawmill on his farm. Camiel Wittenvrongel had a general store and the post office. Rural communities required this kind of self-sufficiency. There were scattered Belgian families in Notre-Dame de Lourdes, St. Léon, St. Lupicien and Holland.[47] In Swan Lake, for example, Belgians had come from southwestern Ontario, Minnesota, and even Chile, where they had initially emigrated.[48] Unlike their neighbours, the Belgians removed their children from school at age thirteen or fourteen to help on the farm. Consequently, the second generation remained on the farm, only a few going on to further education or a religious vocation. In this way, a "family farm tradition" was established with a second generation generally fluent in Flemish, French and English. A close-knit community developed as families intermarried. Eventually, Belgians became involved in business in the village itself as Pierre Jean Halleman opened a general store, Alphonse Nerynck operated a blacksmith shop, and Raymond Van Woensel started a lumber yard and hardware store. A church was built in 1913 and Brothers of Our Lady of Mercy from Malines opened Sacred Heart College in 1919, a boarding school for boys where some instruction was given in Flemish. Swan Lake had a population by 1976 that was 79 per cent Catholic of which 80 per cent of the families were of Belgian origin.

The De Vos report of 1901 provided a good summary of conditions in the early settlement period for the southern region. None of the Belgian farmers were very prosperous, but all were reasonably comfortable and satisfied. The lakes had plenty of fish and there was abundant wildlife for hunters.[49] Families corresponded with relatives in the homeland and sometimes received newspapers from overseas. The Manitoba Francophone press controlled by the clergy was accessible. In 1912, Emile Bogaert assumed the task of local reporter for the *Gazette van Detroit* that, along with the *Gazette van Moline*, circulated throughout the Flemish-speaking communities in North America, a position he held for a record forty-five years.

Settlement in southwestern Manitoba was retarded for three reasons: because of earlier warnings that "the country west of the Souris [river] is a treeless desert, in dry seasons destitute of water, and without shrub or bush thicker than a willow twig"[50]; the slow pace of the land survey; and the comparative inaccessibility until a railway reached Souris in 1886, and Hartney in 1890. Two communities served as focal points, and in some cases as halfway centres, for Belgians moving westwards from St. Boniface: Deloraine for Flemings and Grande Clairière for Walloons. The first Belgian families of Alberic Deschief, Charles Beernaert and Emile Haeven arrived in Deloraine in 1894. Two years later, five extended families arrived, followed soon thereafter by six more families from Zedelgam. Some settled in the surrounding districts west of the Turtle Mountains – Goodlands and Waskada to the south, Hartney to the north, Medora and Napinka to the west, and Boissevain to the east.[51]

Not all came as family units after this initial implantation. Single labourers married in the community and took up farming. Family histories illustrate a considerable degree of early mobility. Raymond Carels of Oostcamp, for example, homesteaded at Benson for a few years, spent two years working in lumber camps around Lethbridge, farmed at Deloraine, then worked for the Manitoba Telephone System as weed inspector and town bailiff for Deloraine. Also from Oostcamp was Jules Cuvelier who with his brother came to work on the railways in Ontario, joined a harvest excursion to Deloraine, stayed on to work as farm labourers, and finally settled on their own farms. Hector Lepoudre supplemented his income by working in Chicago during the winter months and Alfons Verbrugghe worked at the John Deere plant in Moline, Illinois, during the off-season. Likewise, Henri Kreckelburgh of Ruddervoorde came to work on a farm as a "hired man," then in a lumber camp, finally on the construction of the Hudson Bay Railway before returning to Belgium just prior to the outbreak of World War I. After the war, he and his wife returned to Canada to rejoin other families who had come from Ruddervoorde.[52] This migratory pattern was further stimulated by drought and depression. The drought in 1934 forced some to move to Foxwarren, where several other Belgians from their area had moved with cattle and horses. Others went east to the Elie, Fannystelle and Starbuck areas to cut feed and ship it back in boxcars to Medora and vicinity. A few moved to Belgian settlements in Ontario. There was also a notable change of occupation among those who came initially as farmers or farm labourers. These new occupations included operating a service station or garage, selling automobiles and selling farm implements, installing furnaces and plumbing, and working in nearby coal mines.

Deloraine also served as a halfway centre for Flemings coming from southwestern Ontario communities and St. Boniface with the intention of moving on westwards. These immigrants succeeded as individual farmers and business entrepreneurs. They also succeeded in maintaining a sense of ethic consciousness through endogamous marriages in the first generation, social interaction and in-group preference in employment. New immigrants were always assured of a warm welcome and practical assistance when they arrived from the "old country." Another dozen families arrived in Deloraine after World War I, weary of the hostilities and foreign occupation, but unsuspecting of the drought and economic trials that awaited them in southwestern Manitoba in the 1930s. They settled into agriculture, except for a mechanic who briefly continued his trade by operating a repair shop and then sold farm equipment before becoming the town's liquor agent when prohibition was lifted. All these families integrated rapidly into the larger community following the advice and support of compatriots who had preceded them.[53]

Another nucleus of immigrants, largely Walloons in this case, formed north of Hartney in the Grande Clairière and Deleau districts. This movement from Luxembourg and Hainaut provinces was initiated through the efforts of abbé Jean Gaire, a French priest who was in communication with French Canadian clerical leaders and politicians anxious to promote Francophone immigration in the West. His objective was to found a series of parishes populated by Francophone European settlers beyond the area of concentration of Francophone parishes in the Red River valley. In a letter to the archbishop in St. Boniface, he explained:

> But the western part of the province that possessed only a few Catholics lost among the Protestants of Oak Lake and Deloraine seemed to me to be absolutely empty. Between the two places there was a vast solitude. I easily obtained permission to settle there. It was thought in high places that I had illusions so they let me proceed believing that I would soon recognize

my own helplessness; but they waited in vain for my return discouraged.[54]

His project was to provide settlers upon arrival with land, farm animals, implements, seed grains, etc. This would overcome two great drawbacks to immigration – lack of capital and lack of security.[55] In the spring of 1890 he brought out eighty settlers to the "vast solitude" north of Deloraine. Recruitment of settlers was soon left to "return men" who posed as immigration agents, although they were not officially recognized as such. Edmond Fasseaux and Sebastien Deleau were quite successful in attracting forty or fifty immigrants on each expedition to Belgium and France. Fasseaux made three trips to Belgium, published articles in the press claiming he was "officially delegated by the Canadian government to inform and escort free of charge all who would like to accompany him to Manitoba."[56] In 1892, 110 Belgians came, destined mostly for Grande Clairière, but a few went to St. Alphonse, St. Léon and Lake Dauphin.[57] It was important to be near a railway line, or an anticipated line, and near to a service centre. The abbé Gaire's settlers chose homesteads near water and tall grass lands.[58] Unfortunately, Grande Clairière was by-passed by the Pipestone branch of the Canadian Pacific Railway. The consular report of 1901 remarked that besides the sandy soil, there was poor vegetation cover and only a few trees, therefore a poor choice for a new community. De Vos went on to warn against placing too much faith in clerical settlement projects because these were often inspired by narrow, even bigoted, religious objectives rather than sound economic and social judgments.[59]

Deleau, named after Sebastien Deleau who with six other families arrived from the province of Luxembourg in 1889, provided a link between the southern Belgian communities and the abbé Gaire's colonists. In 1892 the branch line of the Canadian Pacific from Souris reached the hamlet and erected a water tower at the nearby creek to service its steam locomotives. Sebastien Deleau had two sons: Désiré who went west to farm in a district later called Redvers and Gaston who raised prize Percheron and Belgian horses, beef and dairy cattle, and was elected a school trustee and a member of the Sifton municipal council.[60] Sebastien Deleau and Edouard Colleaux became "return men," in the pay of the Canadian government, whose activities were closely watched by the Belgian authorities that were alerted to fraudulent schemes and infractions of emigration regulations.[61]

Among their recruits were families who operated the general store, were the "threshermen" of the region, and were the unofficial local historians.[62] As early as 1892, Alexandre Colleaux, Joseph Nannon and Joseph Gatin pooled their resources to found a brick works that produced bricks for the construction of many fine farm homes, the local Catholic mission and the schoolhouse. Two grain elevators and a loading platform on the railway marked the economic activity of the small community. It produced fine cattle, excellent cereal crops and superb hay. The conversion of the local blacksmith shop to a garage marked a significant change that led to the decline of the village. A good highway resulted in increased car traffic to larger centres. Railway engines changed from steam to diesel and "diesel meant speed and became an express with no reason to stop in the hamlet of Deleau." This decline was also marked by a local amnesia regarding its Belgian origins.[63]

A few Belgians were interspersed in the Francophone settlements of north central Manitoba, especially around Lake Dauphin. Edmond-Marcel Didion, a successful merchant in Antwerp, became interested in Western Canada during a banquet of the chamber of commerce in Brussels. A person seated next to him, who had just returned from a trip to Western Canada in the interests of some shareholders of the Canadian Pacific Railway, depicted the region in glowing terms. In 1891, Didion pulled up stakes and headed for Ste. Rose-du-Lac. The family travelled to the end of steel and then crossed flooded swamp-land another 90 kilometres by oxcart. In scrub forest they cleared a plot and built a log cabin that served both as home and general store. The first years in this remote northern region were years of privation and loneliness, but they persevered living off the land and streams.

Compatriots soon followed. Five families arrived at Ste. Amélie, three families at Canadaville, three others at Laurier, and one at Lac Rond. At this time, the Société d'immigration française became aware of this new settlement area and directed a number of families to the region, including G. Watelet in 1897, where they became integrated in a French Canadian society. Also, Father Eugène Lecoq's recruitment efforts were rewarding, especially because of "the amount of capital brought into the country by those who have come. With hardly an exception, these colonists had sufficient money for their establishment."[64] In 1902 and 1906, in spite of opposition from some Belgian parish priests and landowners, he brought out eight Flemish families, followed by three families from Wallonia.[65] In the 1920s, the process resumed as the Klaus, Piret, Denys, Petillon, Nitelet and Pauwels families arrived from Brabant and Flanders. Ste. Rose-du-Lac soon had a certain air of prosperity, possessing several general stores, a few dealerships, lumber yard, livery barn, hotel, schools, power plant, cheese factory and creamery. Immigrants continued to trickle in until 1928.[66]

In 1931, Belgian Capuchin monks from St. Boniface accepted a missionary assignment at Toutes Aides, where nine Belgian families formed the core of the parish served by Father Willibrord, born Pierre-Henri Van Elslander, son of a St. Boniface alderman. Attempts to impose a tithe to raise necessary funds encountered stubborn resistance because in Belgium tithing was not a church commandment. In 1935, Archbishop Sinnott of Winnipeg approved the erection of a Capuchin monastery required to serve five mission stations on the northern fringe – Meadow Portage, Water Hen, Ginemar, Eddystone, and Cayer. Most of the parishioners were Indians and Métis, except at Cayer where seven Belgian families were the mainstay of the mission. The Capuchins remained in charge for forty-two years.[67]

What evidence is there that these planters and pioneers were successful in rural Manitoba? The original families not only have remained but also they have contributed enormously to the development of their communities. Secondly, there are indications of enlarged farms, of movement into service industries, and a degree of upward social mobility. Thirdly, members of the Belgian community have served on school boards, municipal boards, farm organizations, parish councils, business associations, service clubs and recreational groups. A few have won prestigious awards and others have managed stellar operations, as indicted in other sections of this study. Lucien de Burlet wrote in 1909: "It is certain that Manitoba offers important advantages to whoever wants to come to work, and to invest his money. But one must have moral strength, determination, to resign oneself to live in isolation and especially to get along with the English element in whose midst one is virtually submerged."[68]

St. Boniface Urban Hub

St. Boniface was the urban centre to which the immigrants gravitated upon arrival and where their few distinctive ethnic institutions developed. As the first rail link to the outside world, the city became noted for grain processing, meat packing and the production of construction materials when east-west transportation lines funnelled through it. By 1908, over 90,000 head of cattle passed through its stockyards in the export trade. It was this concentration of the cattle trade that led to the building of large abattoirs and meat-packing plants, with their complement of plants for the utilization of by-products. These all offered modest wages for new arrivals who required immediate employment, or who wanted time to survey the possibilities for permanent settlement. Joseph Vermander and Marcien De Leeuw observed that the clerical policy of controlling real estate transactions in order to exclude Protestants and non-practising Catholics proved harmful to the development and expansion of the city. Consul Robert De Vos also noted that by 1901 the business core had become concentrated in Winnipeg.[69] Among the first arrivals in St. Boniface in 1879 were three Bossuyt brothers – Charles, Peter, Constant – who exemplified the dual attraction of agricultural and urban life. Charles decided to launch a city enterprise while his brothers decided to take up dairying in the suburbs. By 1895, Charles had a successful stockyard and abattoir in Winnipeg. Six other families from Passchendaele and Wingene constituted the "pioneer" Belgian group.[70] In the 1890s, single men, usually farmers and labourers, began arriving at the "gateway" and if they remained in the city they found employment at Western Canada Flour Mills, in the brickyards and lumber yards. They lived at one of several boarding houses kept by compatriots. According to Joseph Vermander, very few of these immigrants before World War I were office workers.[71] On a visit back to Belgium in 1895, Charles and Constant Bossuyt convinced Edmund and Octavia Nuyttens, who were on the point of emigrating to Argentina, following what they believed to be an unjust fine for having exceeded their allowable domestic tobacco production, to accompany them back to St. Boniface. The Nuyttens started a dairy farm off Dugald Road in an area popularly known as "the Dump" which eventually was part of "Belgian Town," allegedly a centre for home-brewing of domestic beer. The Nuyttens large barn-like house became a meeting place for newcomers, as later recalled by a descendant of those pioneers:

There were always people arriving from Belgium. Room was made for them in the different farms and houses in the neighbourhood until they were able to buy or build a house of their own in East St. Boniface or Belgian Town, as it was known. The Belgians would relieve the drudgery of hard work in their first years in their adopted country with their own kind of fun and their own kind of music.[72]

When Edmund Nuytten died, his widow married a local widower, Victor Wijndels, whose son Firmin made a reputation in the Belgian community as a builder and architect. Firmin's grandson, James B. Wyndels, became the community's historian.[73]

The experience of Marcien De Leeuw and three young companions in 1906 was not unusual. The four young men had been sold cabin space on a CPR steamship by Treau de Coeli's office, but at Antwerp the agent took them to the steerage section which was filled with central and east European emigrants, jammed into the most unhygienic, foul-smelling and overcrowded conditions imaginable. They protested vociferously and paid a small bribe before they were able to occupy the cabin reserved for them. The fare from Antwerp to Quebec was $45, but the crossing could be even more costly when agents took advantage of vulnerable emigrants.[74] Marcien De Leeuw was only twenty years old when he arrived in St. Boniface, an apprentice wheelwright able to set himself up as a carpenter. Since there was no organized artisanal hierarchy, De Leeuw soon styled himself a contractor. He obtained important contracts for the erection of towers on the local city hall and fire station, the gymnasium of Provencher School where many Belgian children attended classes, and the first section of the Belgian Club on Provencher Avenue. His success continued during the inter-war years and he survived the Depression and World War II, then launched a sawmill, lumber yard, large hardware store and a prosperous home, car and fire insurance business.[75]

Others contributed at the time in less noticeable ways to the development of the urban community. Among them, for example, were Peter Van Der Veken as a house builder, Antoine Neyron in the plumbing business, and Jules Decaigny in the painting and decorating business. These entrepreneurs and some of their workmen met socially at the Belgian Club, where housing and job information was available to new arrivals, where business deals were concluded, and where economic and political strategies were discussed.[76] At the time, St. Boniface was still the leading western manufacturing centre and consequently there were employment opportunities for those who did not wish to take up a homestead in a rural area. Some pursued a migrant or seasonal worker pattern at construction during the summer months and at the Ford plant in Detroit in the winter. In addition to the meat-packing plants, stockyards, flour mills, eight brick kilns, three large grain elevators including the imposing Soubry Grain Company, several lumber yards, there were other industrial enterprises that hired immigrant workers. Louis Pauwels launched his own enterprise and the family made a name for itself in the manufacturing sector. Theodore Bockstael's family continued his business venture with success in construction management and design building.

The immigrants who arrived during the inter-war years found immediate employment in the new meat-packing plants, abattoirs and foundries. Others opened a variety of businesses, such as de Buck's travel and insurance business, De Wandel's confectionary, and the Van Belleghem brothers' purchase of the Tourist Hotel, an important rendezvous for Belgians.[77] William English organized the Belgian-Canadian Chamber of Commerce in 1932 to cement relations with Belgian firms, but the outbreak of World War II in 1939 brought these activities to a close.[78]

The Red River flood of 1950 wrought havoc in St. Boniface, particularly in the old "Belgian Town" area. However, rehabilitation projects provided renewed opportunities for small construction companies, specialists in roofing, concrete work, plumbing, heating and electrical work to establish themselves.[79] Gerard Baert arrived in 1928, and by 1933 his Baert Construction Company was on a sound footing. Flood rehabilitation projects gave the company a considerable boost so that for the ensuing twenty years it was the largest construction company in Manitoba. Bockstael Construction also enjoyed some expansion of its business as a result of the great flood. These Belgian enterprises fit the model of interactive business development. They obviously took a number of risks and were willing to accept low profits initially. Their owners aspired more to economic mobility than to social status. They did use their ethnic ties but they relied also on the French Canadian social network in St. Boniface and environs.[80]

Winnipeg also attracted some Belgians. The immigration hall through which all newcomers passed was located next to the Canadian Pacific Railway station.[81]

Belgian immigrants descending at Winnipeg, as nearly all did, would often seek out compatriots before proceeding westwards, if that were their intention.[82] The Belgian Club became an indispensable information centre after 1905. It met originally in a boarding house on Lombard Street, located next to several hotels and not very far from the Provencher Bridge across the Red River to St. Boniface. This boarding house, reminiscent of the role played by Belgian boarding houses in mining communities in Nova Scotia, remained an important ethnic focal point into the 1930s.[83] Equally attractive to immigrants was the Tourist Hotel [originally the Quebec Hotel operated by M. Van Daele] on the St. Boniface side of the Provencher Bridge. Thus, the itinerary for many an immigrant, whether single or accompanied by the family, was from the immigration hall to the boarding house or the designated hotel, and later to the Belgian Club.

Like other ethnic groups, Flemings and Walloons did not all move on to rural communities or the open prairies. By 1921, of 5,230 Belgians in Manitoba identified in the census, 1,912, or 36.6 per cent lived in the St. Boniface/Winnipeg area. A decade later the urban proportion reached 40 per cent of Belgian-origin Manitobans.[84] In Winnipeg, they were scattered throughout the city and its suburbs and were engaged in a variety of occupations. In 1887, Jerome Verhaege was employed as a locomotive engineer by the CPR, one of the few immigrants from Belgium who had some professional credentials. In 1890, Edmond Missiaen opened a bakery in the city and provided initial employment for compatriots. The itinerary of Joseph Vermander, first child of Flemish origin born in Manitoba, only fourteen years old and without a trade or experience, had to start work in a downtown overall factory to supplement his family's income. He soon found more attractive employment as an office boy in a real estate office, joined the post office department in 1909 and slowly moved up the ranks, until in 1934 he was promoted to regional post office inspector, a position which entailed extensive travel throughout Manitoba and northwestern Ontario until his retirement in 1955. His may not have been the typical career, but it augured well for his compatriots who arrived with meagre educational qualifications and occupational skills.[85]

Employment opportunities with the railways, either laying steel or making ties, attracted immigrant workers as branch lines fanned out across the prairies. In April 1928, a Belgian contractor brought two hundred workers through Winnipeg bound for The Pas. They were divided into four groups and placed on trains for Nelson, from where they were required to walk more than a hundred kilometres to the work site of the Hudson Bay Railway destined to serve the port of Churchill.[86] In addition, Winnipeg rapidly became the centre of the grain trade, including export of cereals, with an active grain exchange. At one point, the Manitoba government ventured into the elevator business but soon sold its holdings to the United Grain Growers. Local board members of this company included Remi De Roo in Swan Lake, Octave Brandt in Somerset and Emile Roeland in Mariapolis.[87] Winnipeg also became known for its garment factories turning out men's clothes, overalls, shirts, blouses etc., and offering employment to women in particular. The H.H. Stevens parliamentary committee was appointed in 1934 to investigate the spread between production costs and consumer prices in the framework of the operations of large corporations in the midst of a severe depression. It found sweatshop working conditions in Winnipeg, even at the prominent retailer, the T. Eaton Company, whose catalogues were to be found in every western Canadian household. Seamstresses, including a few Belgians, who did piece work were paid only a few pennies for dresses that sold for a several hundred percent mark-up in department stores.[88] In these conditions, there was incentive to move on to some form of self-employment such as dairying or horticulture.

Manitoba Dairy Industry

Although the Icelanders were the first to set up dairy farms in Manitoba, the Flemings soon distinguished themselves in this branch of agriculture. In 1886 there were already twenty-four cheese factories in the province, including the St. Pierre-Jolys cheese factory, opened in 1884, operated by S.M. Barre and Charles Mignault, that featured the first Danish centrifugal system installed in North America. Cheddar was the common cheese in North America but in 1892 Gruyère cheese was being produced by Belgians at St. Hubert in Assiniboia District of the North-West Territories.[89]

The Manitoba dairies exhibited some unique features compared to those in Ontario and Quebec. The Belgian dairies near Montreal, for example, were smaller, located closer to creameries and cheese factories, and enjoyed a more intensive production of milk than their western counterparts. In Manitoba, farmers who lived a distance from a large centre shipped cream by rail to the creameries and kept the skim milk for their animals, especially calves and hogs. In St. Pierre-Jolys the two cheese factories were kept well supplied by the farmers, the Belgians in particular being pleased that when they sent their whole milk to the creamery, the skim milk was returned to them to feed their animals. From

1907 onwards, special dairy trains, complete with agricultural college instructors, dairying experts and demonstration equipment, began visiting rural centres to encourage better management and production.[90]

Constant Bossuyt was one of the first Belgians to take up dairying in the region, starting a small dairy south of St. Vital with twenty cows in production, then moving to Kingston Row. He delivered milk across the Red River by barge in summer and by horse-drawn vehicle in winter to boarding houses and hotels in Winnipeg.[91] In 1892 he moved again to Fort Garry, bought the New Dairy (renamed Manitoba Dairy), then bought the Northwest Dairy and relocated in Oak Bluff, to the southwest of the city. His herd consisted of "range cattle," or interbreds, not purebreds. The Bossuyt family also had a farm in St. Pierre-Jolys, where their compatriots De Jongh and Delbecque were singled out as "practical farmers with considerable means, and can safely be classed as the most desirable class of immigrants." In St. Malo three families took up dairying and this led to the establishment of a creamery there. Louis Hacault on a fact-finding tour left a favourable report of these farms in his emigration publication.[92]

An official from the Winnipeg Health Department sang the praises of the Nuys brothers who, though both still in their twenties, unable to speak English and with no capital, had immigrated with their mother in 1889 and become established.

> They worked three years as labourers and saved $700. They bought a dairy man out and purchased his 28 cattle for $1,600, making the $700 as first payment and rented his premises for $25 a month. The first year they paid off their debt of $900 and purchased 5 acres of land of their own. The second year they built a modern house and stable on plans supplied by the Dairy Inspector. The new stable was built to hold 80 cows. All modern improvements, concrete floors, steel stanchions, individual water basins, and litter carriers were installed. Then [1895] the herd had been increased to sixty-six.[93]

After receiving this favourable report, thirty-three head of cattle had to be taken out of production following testing for tuberculosis. The Nuys brothers persevered, added tested cows to their herd, built a second dairy barn, and increased their acreage of coarse grains and potatoes.

In 1898, the French interpreter for the Department of Agriculture reported that the creamery at La Rochelle had made 50,000 pounds of butter over the summer, specifying that it "was packed in small tins of 1, 2 and 5 pounds weight for sale in the mining districts of British Columbia." This creamery was also engaged in manufacturing condensed milk and evaporated cream.[94] Consul De Vos cautioned that prospects for exporting condensed milk were limited because Europe produced vast quantities of raw milk and sugar was cheaper in Europe than in Canada, as were metal containers after visiting the condensed milk factory at St. Malo, operated by the Manitoba Dairy Company. The cheese factory at St. Pierre-Jolys produced annually 125,000 pounds of excellent cheese which found an assured market in Winnipeg and in the mining centres of British Columbia and the Yukon. Skimmed milk could be shipped in from as far distant as 350 kilometres in the railway refrigerated coaches. De Vos noted that co-operatives for butter and cheese-making had not replaced private entrepreneurs because of the small population and the restricted market. It was a situation in which Belgian entrepreneurs and producers felt comfortable.[95]

Most dairymen were doing well in the early 1900s. At Isle-des-Chênes those who had arrived virtually penniless were quickly well established. At Otterburne, Flemings worked first as day labourers and accumulated sufficient capital in a few years to engage in mixed farming, selling their milk to the creamery.[96] In his report, the Canadian immigration agent for the region was in complete agreement with the laudatory evaluation. He wrote: "Our immigration from these sources is fairly satisfactory, and the class of people coming are much to be desired.... Eighty-five people came from Belgium and have been located at St. Norbert, Deleau and St. Alphonse in Manitoba."[97] During this first wave of Belgian immigration, which came to a close with the outbreak of World War I in 1914, at least eleven Flemish dairies had begun operations in the Fort Whyte district. This rapid expansion prompted the provincial authorities to appoint a dairy inspector for what they called the "New Canadian districts." There is no indication on record whether the Belgians appreciated this presumption that they required special instruction or supervision.[98]

Who were some of these early dairymen? Boudewyn Van Wynsberghe started a dairy farm in Tuxedo in 1906 and he continued to operate it until his retirement in 1966. Jules Van Haute started a dairy farm on the eastern outskirts of St. Boniface in 1912 and continued in business until

1951. Tryphoon Anseeuw operated his dairy in Fort Whyte from 1914 to 1954. His family also operated dairies in Fort Garry and Oak Bluff. The Flanders Farm in Oak Bluff, for example, started by Hector Anseeuw, was a showpiece for the industry from the 1950s until the end of the century. These examples indicate that there was a certain stability in the industry.

There are indications that these pioneer dairymen were respected in their community. Constant Bossuyt, for example, lent money in the 1910s and 1920s simply on trust, without proper legal contracts, according to the traditional Flemish rural system of neighbourly trust. During the Depression he charged only seven cents a quart (ten cents being the normal price) and he paid his hired help twenty-five dollars a month rather than the government subsidized rate of ten dollars. His recollection was that the working-class families, who lived on very tight budgets, were the most conscientious in trying to meet their obligations.[99] In 1921, the provincial government ordered the testing of all dairy herds for tuberculosis. Unfortunately, as a result of this compulsory testing, the Bossuyts lost the majority of their herd. When the testing was found to have been inaccurate, the only compensation was that the animals that had been slaughtered were judged fit for human consumption by meat inspectors. Another challenge was change in the delivery of milk. From being loaded onto the delivery wagon from eight-gallon cans, poured into two-gallon cans from which a quart was measured out by means of a deep lid into the customer's jug or container, it was delivered in glass bottles as a more sanitary measure after 1930. In 1943, their barns burned down and some dairy cows perished in the blaze. There was inadequate insurance coverage but the rival Crescent Creamery gave generous help to the Bossuyt brothers enabling them to rebuild. Their production now went to bulk milk sales and the rebuilt farm became a showpiece for the industry. In 1971 the father and four sons were still proud to show delegations arriving from such distant places as Denmark, France, Scotland, Japan, Pakistan and Cuba an efficient and attractive dairy operation.[100] They never won awards for their milk production or breeding practices, but they developed practical advantages such as a compact barn with good feeding arrangements, above-average output per man, and good use of unpaid farm labour. Success was attributable in good measure to the business lasting longer than one lifetime and keeping the family farm intact despite some discouraging setbacks.[101]

Another success story was that of the six Van Walleghem brothers who arrived at the turn of the century. Andries Van Walleghem started the Royal Dairy in the River Heights district south of the city of Winnipeg. In 1932, this hard-working family still held to "old country ways" and they felt that twelve-year-old Walter should be contributing to the family income rather than attending school regularly. During an eight-hour day, young Walter made more than 175 door-to-door deliveries on average. In winter, milk was kept from freezing in the closed-in wagon by charcoal burners, while the driver sat outside unprotected from the elements. In 1936 a motor truck replaced the horse-drawn vehicle to deliver both raw and pasteurized milk. Belgians preferred non-pasteurized or "natural" milk but in 1950, following the disastrous Red River flood that resulted in widespread contamination of water and food supplies, health authorities made pasteurization of milk mandatory. When small dairies found compliance difficult, the Royal Dairies (as it was now called), now relocated in Elm Creek, took in the raw milk from these farms for pasteurization and delivery.[102]

There were a number of more modest Belgian dairy farms in Fort Garry, St. Norbert, Fort Whyte, Stoney Mountain, St. James, East Kildonan, and Lilyfield. The Varlez-Brunin report in 1932 remarked on the vitality of this dairy industry in the Winnipeg/St. Boniface region:

> … at Fort Garry, proximate to Winnipeg, a cluster of Belgians has won a virtual monopoly of home deliveries of milk in the urban area. They possess large barns built on the most modern lines that each house 50 to 100 cows. All whom we questioned seemed very satisfied with their lot…. They are all Flemish, many of them related and from the same village [Wingene], having encouraged each other to take up the same occupation in the belief there was room for all here.[103]

In 1959, Jean De Mytternaere came from Belgium to interview some recent immigrants. He began at Joseph Anseeuw's dairy in Fort Whyte where immigrant workers were initiated into the concepts of agro-business and he proceeded to interview families that had managed eventually to purchase their own farms. He concluded that Belgians continued to be successful when they came with some capital, were willing to adapt to new conditions, and remained frugal and hard-working.[104]

Between 1890 and 1975, Belgians operated at least forty-six dairy farms in the Winnipeg/Fort Garry/Oak Bluff area, seventeen in the St. Vital/St. Boniface region, and fourteen in North Winnipeg/East Kildonan. The small dairies were largely phased out in the 1970s as large, modern and centrally located production facilities were constructed in the urban centre. This transformation resulted from improvement in delivery services, changes in packaging and processing techniques, rising farm costs, and the other employment opportunities that presented themselves to farmers' children after World War II. Most of the Belgian suburban dairying community simply became absorbed into the urban life of Greater Winnipeg. Dairying by 2000 was scattered throughout the province. Among the dairymen recognized for exceptional milk quality were Gabriel Fifi and Derek Devos of Bruxelles, George Roels and George Michiels of Holland, J. Deblonde of Swan Lake and Bryan DeBaets of St. Alphonse.

Market Gardening

In 1900, Gustaff Vermeulen planted a large vegetable garden on Clarence Avenue in Fort Garry, the beginning of a market gardening career extending more than fifty years. Others joined him to form a series of market gardens stretching from the Pembina Highway to the east to the cement plant in Fort Whyte on the west. Initially, most gardeners sold their produce door-to-door from horse-drawn carts, an enterprise denounced by retail grocers as "peddling." Vermeulen's team and wagon were commandeered in 1915 to haul the statue of the Golden Boy from the Canadian National Railway station to the Legislative Building from the dome of which it would dominate the surroundings. Eventually, gardeners in Fort Garry, Fort Whyte and St. Vital sold their produce from stands at the front of their lots.[105]

The heavy black soil of the Red River flood plain was ideal for gardening. The federal Department of Agriculture endorsed this use of suburban land:

> Where fertile soil occurs in close proximity to a large city, or if the transportation facilities are good and costs are low, the most economical use of such land is generally the growing of

vegetables and small fruits. A small acreage is usually sufficient for the market gardener.[106]

The Red River valley escaped the brunt of the drought that struck the prairies in the 1930s. But in 1932 the worst plague of grasshoppers in decades devastated the market gardens and fodder crops of the dairy farmers in the Winnipeg region. Probably the last market garden established was the Mission Gardens in Transcona in 1940, the former farm of St. Boniface College purchased by Theophile and Augusta De Baets. It was the type of farming to which many Flemings had been accustomed in their homeland i.e. self-sufficient holdings consisting of small acreages, organic fertilization, sizeable vegetable and small fruit gardens, and coarse grain plots to feed their draught horses and a few cows. In suburban Fort Garry, St. Vital and Charlewood they relied on family labour with some seasonal help and small mechanical implements.

Prior to World War II, production was limited to the requirements of local consumption: onions, leeks, carrots, tomatoes, celery, potatoes, cauliflower and cabbages. Large quantities of vegetables were still imported because of the degree of seasonality of production and the lack of adequate storage technology. Most market gardeners had root cellars where potatoes and root vegetables could be stored for winter use, but only a limited amount was offered for sale out of season to the public. A few specialized in selling their produce on contract. Victor De Roo in Swan Lake, for example, signed a contract with the T. Eaton Company store in Winnipeg to supply the entire crop of potatoes from a twenty-acre plot.

The arrival of over one thousand Japanese Canadian evacuees in 1942, unceremoniously displaced from their homes and businesses in coastal British Columbia, marked the beginning of a decline of small market garden operations. The Manitoba Department of Agriculture encouraged market gardeners to move their operations out of expanding Winnipeg into rural areas and encouraged diversified crops such as sugar beets, sunflowers, buckwheat, soybeans, canola and flax. In 1947, a Winnipeg Gardeners' Cooperative was formed to regulate the flow of produce in order to maximize returns to individual producers. This did not meet the needs or capacities of small Belgian producers who were unspecialized with limited output. Fortunately, participation was voluntary. In 1953 a Vegetable Growers Association of Manitoba was organized to export produce but small-scale Belgian market gardeners were unable to compete with the medium producers of the association. Increasing provincial controls influenced many Belgians to withdraw from market gardening.[107] They were mostly small producers who were accustomed to selling directly from their property to the public and were not involved in commercial large-scale production. Even the medium producers became vulnerable when machinery and chemical suppliers and gigantic food processing companies began to control both input and output markets. The final stage in the demise of extensive small-scale market gardening was marked by the arrival of large corporations such as the Campbell Soup Company, Carnation Company and McCain Foods that entered into contractual agreements with agro-business farmers.

W.T. Macoun, Dominion horticulturalist, wrote in 1933 that southern Manitoba had a climate suitable for fruit growing. He cited sand cherries as being particularly drought-resistant. Of course, there were a few farmers such as A. Kool in Cromer, who specialized in wild fruits such as saskatoon, chokecherry, pembina cranberry, pin cherry and buffalo berry.[108] Theophile Gelaude in St. Vital, active in local politics and sporting events, had a particularly impressive garden featuring specialized varieties of small fruits as well as exotic flowers. His brother, Alphonse Gelaude, in rural Brunkild, cultivated a productive showcase garden and orchard that rivalled the best production of apples, pears, plums, Missouri currants and sand cherries that the Morden Experimental Farm could offer. Every Saturday and Sunday afternoon in late summer he proudly offered free tours of his property to scores of curious and admiring visitors.[109]

Sugar Beet Industry

Belgians became involved in the sugar beet industry during the Napoleonic wars when a British blockade of French ports induced Napoleon Bonaparte to subsidize the beet sugar industry in northern France. The cultivation and harvesting of this crop required a large labour force so appeals for seasonal workers were made in neighbouring Flanders. In addition to relieving the dependence on imported cane sugar, beet sugar was believed to possess remarkable medicinal properties.[110] The first refinery designed to extract sugar from beets in Canada was opened at Farnham, Quebec, in 1881. In 1901, the Ontario Agricultural College in Guelph set up test plots of sugar beets and the Berlin [Kitchener] Board of Trade sent a delegation to Caro in Michigan to recruit experienced growers, many of them Belgians. From its inception in Canada, therefore, the beet sugar industry was associated with Belgians at the level of field workers, growers and factory workers.[111] The industry was highly recommended in the *Dominion Agricultural Bulletin* for cleaning the land of noxious weeds: "The testimony of farmers in Ontario is that no other crop so effectually cleans the land, or so well fits it for barley, oats, or wheat in the following season, as a well-tilled crop of sugar beets. It will kill out, they say, the tough-lived pest, the Canadian thistle."[112]

Many market gardeners and dairymen were attracted to growing sugar beets when the Manitoba Sugar Company built a processing plant in Fort Garry in October 1940. Some local farmers had experimented with beet growing as early as 1901 and a Manitoba Sugar Company Limited was incorporated in 1925 but no plant was built. There were problems to overcome: firstly, there was a popular preference for cane sugar over beet sugar; secondly, the manufacture of beet sugar was carried on only a quarter or third of the year; thirdly, stocks of refined sugar had to be carried for considerable time if supplies were to be available for trade most of the year. Then, in November 1939, Baron Paul Kronacher, a prominent Belgian refiner with widespread investments and business connections through the Czarnikow-Rionda Company, teamed up with Baron P. Neuman de Vegvar of New York to launch the Fort Garry plant equipped with machinery from Germany and financial guarantees from Belgium.

Belgians were quite enthusiastic about the prospects of the familiar beet culture, however, from the outset the share-cropping arrangements that were imposed deprived the farmers of substantial profits. The local Catholic priest, anxious to prevent the exploitation of his parishioners, publicly criticized the evils of the share-cropping contracts. As a result of his intervention on behalf of his exploited parishioners, many of them Belgians, he was summarily transferred to the remote parish of Sioux Lookout in 1942. There were some mutterings about the connection between the church and big business but the contracts remained unchanged. There was a shortage of farm labour at the time, so the opening of the school year was postponed two weeks in order that three thousand high schools students could help harvesting grain and sugar beets.[113]

There were some serious problems by the 1950s with the business structure of the Manitoba Sugar Company. Local investors moved to prevent Baron Neuman from acquiring too much stock when Kronacker planned to expand operations into Saskatchewan after the St. Lawrence Seaway became operative in order to compete with the British Columbia refiners. In April 1954, the Beet Growers Association pointed to friction between the Belgian, American and Canadian owners:

> We believe there is considerable friction between these three interests, and the first two mentioned are doing all in their power to acquire a controlling interest in the company. We feel this would be definitely detrimental to the people of Manitoba and to the beet growers in particular.[114]

This association had little stake in the industry, however, because the growers produced under contract with the processor.

Neither the Belgian nor American investors gained a controlling interest because in 1955 the B.C. Sugar Refining Company acquired control. This came about when Neuman sold his shares to the Canadian group and Baron Kronacher was left with only four thousand of the thirty-four thousand shares. Chief Justice Rhodes Smith was appointed by the Restrictive Trade Practices Commission to investigate charges of monopoly control and collusion. The fear of competition from Ontario sugar refineries, which had for many decades hired workers directly in Belgium, especially following the opening of the St. Lawrence Seaway, induced the B.C. Sugar Refining Company to buy up all the shares, so ending the feud. This move closed off for the future "any opportunity for the public to benefit from lower prices brought about by competition."[115] Sugar beet growing continued to operate on the share-cropping arrangement but it went into decline as other cash crops on what were increasingly larger farms became more attractive.[116] Once again, Belgians were "on their own" as individuals and families in a changing capitalistic society.

Despite many gradual societal changes the urban hub remained important for the Belgian community. The new technologies, changing economic relationships, institutional evolution, and cultural heterogeneity resulted in failure of the sugar beet industry and market gardening to bring together an enduring cohesive economic ethnic bloc. Even the Flemish dairy operators eventually relinquished their dominant role. Nevertheless, these developments in no way diminished the important contribution of the group to the viability of the larger community.

Laying tracks for the Canadian Pacific Railway. (Sask. Archives R-A 6820)
The CPR encouraged immigration and hoped to attract settlers to its vast tract of arable land.

IV

WESTWARD ONTO THE PRAIRIES

From Manitoba as a springboard, and Winnipeg/St. Boniface as the point of entry to the West, settlement moved onto the second and third prairie levels. The challenges could be quite different from those encountered in Manitoba because these were mostly open treeless plains with a southern dry belt earlier identified as Palliser's Triangle, a northern extension of the Great American desert. This open region offered newcomers windswept grasslands that had once been the home of millions of bison, a semi-desert with shallow alkaline lakes, and badlands with modest buttes. Only the parkland corridor running northwestwards from the Riding Mountains to the Peace River basin offered the more familiar landscape of deciduous forest, rolling hills and scattered lakes.

Alberta and Saskatchewan emerged from the North-West Territories as autonomous provinces of Canada in 1905, marking an important stage in the economy of the region. Farming was centred on wheat-growing, a staple for which there was an open and free-trading world market. At the same time, the central Canadian industrial base, protected since 1879 by high tariffs, found a market for its goods at interesting profits in the new West. However, this also meant that duties on imported goods shut out cheaper American goods and forced western Canadians to buy high-priced domestic products. American companies circumvented this protectionism by setting up branch plants Canada, but their products were no cheaper than those of their competitors. In short, the "national policy" of the Dominion government worked counter to the interests of the immigrants.

Rural places are rooted in commodity production and their soil, climate and natural resources such as water, wood and coal are attractive to immigrants. But their social and institutional services are relatively low, their population small and the distance from major population service centres usually great. Smaller communities where Belgians settled were limited in the programs they could offer. What seemed of more immediate interest to them was the economy. The provincial government concept was that the province should be based on one dominant culture, engaged on one dominant economic activity in one dominant zone of activity. The province's destiny was focussed on wheat-production for export in the southern half of the province.[1]

When Saskatchewan, with Alberta, celebrated the twenty-second anniversary of its provincial status in 1927, it was, according to some, the "granary of the world" with the third largest population among the Canadian provinces, third largest gross domestic product, and third highest personal income. It ranked first in production of wheat, rye, oats and flax, also first in the breeding of horses. It had the largest number of telephones per capita in Canada and the number of automobile licences and of movie theatres tripled in a decade. But there were storm clouds gathering on the horizon. The long Liberal dominance of provincial politics gave way to an anti-immigrant and anti-Catholic movement, expressed explicitly in the infiltration of the Ku Klux Klan from the United States. The stock market crash of 1929 was accompanied by the beginning of nine consecutive years of climatic catastrophe, severe drought and cyclonic dust storms, grasshopper infestations, and outbreaks of equine encephalitis. The sky became dark with swirling dust and hordes of ravenous grasshoppers the hopes and aspirations of many settlers sank into deep despair.[2]

Regional Exigencies

In 1876, Belgian economist Gustave de Molinari wondered why Francophones did not seem attracted by the agricultural potential of the North West Territories.[3] There were several regional characteristics to consider. The relative inaccessibility of the region before the advent of the transcontinental railway and the construction of branch lines cannot be discounted. At first, new arrivals had to rely on freighting outfits, creaky wagons and carts, operated by "bullwackers."[4] Secondly, soldiers returning from World War I took up sparsely settled and undeveloped lands while the immigrants of the 1920s often had to settle either on marginal land or abandoned farms.⁵ Thirdly, as settlement proceeded from east to west onto the semi-arid plains, dry farming without irrigation was adopted in areas of scant precipitation. Insufficient rainfall during the growing season did not support continuous cropping, so summer fallowing and crop rotation were required.⁶ During World War I farmers were encouraged to grow wheat on a large scale as part of the war effort. But after 1918 agricultural experts encouraged crop diversification and mixed farming as a way to increase farm income and reduce soil erosion, which would become an enormous problem in the 1930s. Large grain-growing farms meant keeping many horses and large expensive threshing gangs each autumn. Technological advances such as the gasoline tractor and the combine further altered farming practices.⁷ The depression and drought added to the pattern of internal migration. It was becoming clear that settlement had been largely unplanned without much thought to what was sustainable for the rural economy. The land had been occupied either by chance – what was still available – or according to the devices of colonization agents, railway and land companies.⁸

This was the environment into which Belgians ventured. At Duck Lake, in 1901, Baron Huysmans de Deftal, agent for Crown lands, described as being helpful to "settlers of all races and beliefs who made up the population of the region," took Consul De Vos to the reserve and residential school of Okemasis and to two Belgian farmers "whose farms were developing well."⁹ This no doubt reassured him that the former Aboriginal threat had been removed and that newcomers were becoming well established. The Saskatchewan government prepared a special booklet in 1915 containing two hundred recommendations for those seeking employment as "hired men," this being a common entry point into the economy. Many newly arrived single males were unable to profit from this paternalistic advice because of a language and literacy barrier.¹⁰

The speed of immigration and railway construction resulted in a widely dispersed rural society that required an extensive and expensive system of local government, no fewer than 302 rural municipalities in Saskatchewan by 1916. These municipalities bore the burden of collecting school taxes, road building, telephone service, and some health care and welfare services. By 1930 most municipalities were faced with mounting tax arrears. Immigration had filled vacant lands but it had spawned some harsh economic realities that gave rise to a feeling that external controls, powerful interest elsewhere, were responsible, the genesis of a populist sentiment of western alienation.

Agricultural Ideology

The settlement of the region was related also to an agricultural ideology. The importance of agriculture for political and social development is a concept developed by the ancient Greeks, who espoused "an ideology in which the production of food, and above all, the actual people who own the land and do the farm work are held to be of supreme social importance."[11] Clifford Sifton, who became Minister of the Interior in 1896, was a supporter of this agrarian myth insofar as Western Canada's agricultural potential opened up opportunities for immigrants such as Belgians to advance central Canadian national objectives and assure the development of its northern democratic character. He wrote: "Agriculture is the foundation of all real and enduring progress on the part of Canada.... The possession of a preponderating rural population having the virtues and strength of character bred only among those who follow agricultural life, is the only sure guarantee of our national future."[12] Premier Walter Scott affirmed that "Saskatchewan is essentially an agricultural province, which is no misfortune. Agriculture is the basis of the business of the world. Farming is the foundation of civilization."[13]

Belgian immigrants who took up farming already espoused some basic principles of an agricultural ideology. The first objective was to buy little in the way of food for livestock or human consumption. Women assured that groceries were obtained in exchange for dairy produce, poultry and eggs. Secondly, the farmer depended on unpaid labour of family members and restricted the educational opportunities of the children. Thirdly, they believed in the virtue of the "family farm."[14] "It begins simply, with a home and a few animals, and slowly develops over the years, growing, but always with the farmers and their families owning and living on the land – independent, self-reliant and hard-working,"[15] Fourthly, although accustomed to intensive labour they were inclined to pursue some small ventures such as the farm implement business.[16]

Belgian agronomists and horticulturalists played a role in the improvement of Prairie agriculture. Four institutions provided expert advice: the Horticulture School of Vilvoorde (1836); the State Agriculture Institute, Gembloux (1860); the Forestry School, Bouillon (1864); and the

Agricultural Science section of the University of Louvain (1878). Three graduates from the Louvain agriculture faculty – Van Cauwelaert, Jeruslaem, Steurs – settled in Bruxelles in 1897, while François Rentier went to Aberdeen in 1908. Another graduate, François Smets took up large-scale farming in Saskatchewan. In 1912, Delphin Bricoux and Victor Mathurin came to Edmonton and Paul Mulie started a three-hundred-hectare farm in Whitewood.[17] President W.C. Murray of the University of Saskatchewan was impressed by this model of agricultural science in a university setting because it assured scientific research in a humane perspective, open to women as well as men. Consequently, in 1907, he insisted on a university setting, like the Louvain model, rather than the segregated college setting in Guelph, Ontario, for the Faculty of Agriculture in Saskatoon.[18]

Jean Gaire's "Chain of Parishes"

Many of the first Belgians to venture into Assiniboia District were recruited by the abbé Jean Gaire. He founded the parishes of Wolseley (1888) and Forget (1892), at the western extremity of the original triangle based at Deloraine and Grande Clairière. By 1898 his vision had been transformed into a chain of Francophone parishes stretching to the Rockies, beginning with Bellegarde, on the fourth coulee near the Gainsborough Creek just west of the extended Manitoba border. He wrote: "I saw now beyond any doubt that my first foundation would not remain isolated.... I had just found the first link in this famous chain, so great was my patriotic joy."[19]

He had gone as far west as Wolseley in 1888, where experts at the Indian Head Experimental Farm said the soil was "of an astounding fertility and admirably suited to mixed farming: cereal growing and cattle raising combined."[20]

In 1898, Alphonse Copet, Cyrille Delaite, Joseph Delaitte and Cyrille Libert set out to break land at the location the priest had designated. They were not impressed and returned to Grande Clairière for the winter declaring that the soil was too hard to plough. Gaire insisted a few rains would remedy that, therefore the following spring a larger party of Belgians and a few French set out, staked permanent claims, built huts of three-foot lengths of prairie sod for walls and boards for the roofs. Firewood was hauled from the Moose Mountain for winter. In 1894 nine families arrived[21] – from the provinces of Luxembourg and Hainaut. St. Maurice de Bellegarde would become a permanent Belgian community, although until 1900, several families retired to Grande Clairière each winter.

Even when wooden frame houses replaced the sod shacks, and horses replaced oxen, migration occurred. Alphonse Tinant stayed, his brother Auguste moved to Wauchope, and his brother Gaston moved to Vanguard in 1912. Honoré George settled permanently but his two brothers emigrated to a Belgian colony in Guatemala.[22] When the CPR extended its Souris line to Arcola it built a water tower at the Gainsborough Creek crossing but bypassed the hamlet of Bellegarde in favour of Anglophone Frys and Redvers. In spite of this, by 1905 there were 175 Francophones in the hamlet with Belgians decidedly in the majority. The parish priest reported they were imbued with "old country ideas," refused to pay the tithe to support him adequately and to send their children regularly to catechism classes. They paid little attention to "the instructions given by authorized persons." When the church burned down in 1905, the priest wanted to rebuild at Frys on the railway line, but the parishioners were attached to Gaire's site. The matter was resolved by the Anglophone Protestants in Frys who would not countenance a Catholic church. The new church remained in the hamlet, a centre of community life and identity, but business was conducted mostly in Antler.[23] In 1899 the parishioners organized their own Catholic public school district that became a convent-cum public school six years later.[24] Gaire was absent during this critical period. He had moved on to bring another group of settlers from Grande Clairière to St. Raphael de Cantal, north of Alida, in 1892. Like the two earlier links in his chain, it too was not on the railway line. Belgians were well represented among the twenty-two founding householders which within a decade counted ninety-seven Francophone parishioners.[25] However, they were a minority in "a sea of English Protestants" whose numbers increased dramatically. In 1897, Gaire developed a plan for a bloc settlement along the southern slope of the Moose Mountains where he hoped to bring a thousand settlers to form a Francophone bloc before the railway pushed through and a flood of immigrants arrived. Archbishop Langevin, anxious to promote Catholic immigration, approved the plan saying "this beautiful district belongs to us; for we will take all the places; we are there before all others."[26] Gaire conceived of another triangle of Francophone settlers with its base in Cantal and Wauchope and the apex at Forget, as compact communities isolated from external influences. Between 1897 and 1906, he made eight trips to Belgium and France to recruit settlers, but his appeals in Le Défenseur to counteract Anglophone Protestant influence in the West did not meet with much response in Belgium. Consequently, Belgians were a minority in the parishes created after Bellegarde.[27]

Wauchope was to become the springboard for Gaire's projected bloc settlement stretching beyond Moose Mountain. Five homesteads were established in anticipation of the railway, which arrived in 1901 bringing a tide of Anglophone settlers Gaire could not equal. Maurice Quennelle, who took up a homestead in 1902, opened a general store and post office and became a leading member of the Francophone community. By the 1911 census, Francophones made up 66 per cent of the population and controlled the business activity of the village that grew around the railway station, St. Regis church and convent.[28] Gaire was appointed parish priest but he expended much energy on raising funds for various colonization projects whose Belgian and French investors seemed more interested in central Canada than in western regions. The Société générale de l'oeuvre de la colonisation catholique française du Canada, which he founded in 1904 under "the high patronage of the hierarchy of Western Canada," was a small investment company whose objective was to buy up farm lands for resale to approved Catholic settlers. In 1905, he added the Société de la Ferme du Clergé français as an investment outlet for European clerics by buying up land "reserved" for approved immigrants. Although Archbishop Langevin approved of the measure, he warned that neither he nor Gaire should be seen as directors or shareholders in such a venture. In 1906 he received no further support from the Canadian government, in spite of a personal appeal to the prime minister, so his almost annual recruitment tours in Europe came to an end.[29] By 1911, funds were exhausted. Wauchope never developed into the regional service centre he had envisaged.[30]

Forget was the next link in the chain of parishes, inaugurated with the arrival of three families in 1892. A modest chain migration from Luxembourg province resulted in twenty-two homestead claims by 1896. Two years later, the Department of the Interior's report commented:

> There is also a French and Belgian settlement at Alma, on the west end of the Moose Mountains, in a flourishing condition. They have had splendid crops nearly every year, and quite a number of their friends from Bathgate, North Dakota, have come over this summer, and have taken up homesteads.... The

settlers in this district go in principally for mixed farming, and raise large quantities of stock as well as grain.[31]

A number of Belgians from Grosse Pointe, Michigan, who already possessed some capital and a working knowledge of English, settled among their compatriots at Forget. Forget became a rendez-vous for Belgians in the migratory process. In the first decade of the twentieth century, at least six families from Deloraine, and one from Deleau, came to join compatriots in the Forget district. In the same period, at least five families left for Fife Lake, two for Stoughton, and two for Coronach.[32] The 1911 census revealed that the balance had shifted in favour of the English, although the number of Francophones had doubled. The Belgian government judged that a consular agent was necessary and so appointed J. Tratsaert to that function, a position he held until February 1911. He was succeeded as vice-consul by Gaston De Jardin in October 1911, a position he held in Forget until 1915, when it was transferred to Manor until 1921.

Gaire next turned his attention to Red Deer and Rocky Mountain House as the Alberta terminus of his chain of parishes. In 1902 he established the Société de la Ferme Assiniboia-Alberta, which opened a general store in Red Deer and bought up two large estates with a view to offering small farms for sale to Francophone Catholic immigrants. The company loaned breeding stock so settlers could establish their herds upon arrival. The company was liquidated in October 1909 although it reported a profit of 8.1 per cent on its investment. A handful of Belgian families remained as a result of Gaire's initiative.[33]

Utopian Settlements

Utopianism referred in this context to the creation of ideal religious, agrarian, or social communities that a new region of settlement seemed destined to render feasible. Belgians who participated in these different projects never appear to have been involved ideologically, but rather they saw the opportunity to better themselves economically and socially by participating. In 1889, eight counts, two viscounts and a Belgian baron came to La Rolanderie, soon to be renamed St. Hubert, sixteen kilometres southwest of Whitewood, where Dr. Rudolph Meyer had begun a settlement for Swiss farmers. Meyer sold fourteen square sections to the south of the Pipestone Creek to Count de Roffignac, Baron van Brabant and Archbishop Langevin, which they later sold to the archdiocese at cost to form a Francophone Catholic bloc settlement. Work was begun on imposing stone residences, including Château Bellevue for Count Jean de Jumilhac and Château Richelieu for Count Henri de Saurras, and plans were pursued for the cultivation of sugar beets and chicory. Although the property was scarcely settled and was located sixty kilometres from the railway, the Manitoba Free Press voiced the unlimited optimism of the times:

> ... the advent of a beet sugar factory would be a great boon to farmers of the Northwest and would practically solve the question in favour of mixed farming. It would be not a little to the credit of the new Northwest if it should succeed in establishing a beet sugar factory in advance of the old province of Ontario, some of whose residents were just now making a move in that direction. Although Whitewood is scarcely a Canadian trade centre, it is claimed that the business can be made a profitable one to all concerned in it.[34]

It was an example of the marriage of utopianism and boosterism. The Territorial government intervened because of strong prohibitionist sentiments, fearing that alcoholic beverages and by-products might fall into the possession of the Aboriginal population.

The chicory project proceeded under the direction of Baron van Brabant and Count de Roffignac in a partnership known as the Bellevue French Coffee Company. The Bellevue farm was devoted entirely to growing chicory with a drying and packaging plant for the preparation of the chicory to be mixed with imported coffee. Unfortunately, the plant burned down in 1891. Although the chicory crops were good there was great difficulty in securing a suitable market.

Attention was turned next to sheep ranching and the erection of a Gruyère cheese factory under the management of M. Janet. Count Henri de Saurras organized a ranch in the Moose Mountains area for two thousand sheep imported from Europe. The cattle ranch of imported purebred stock was managed by M. De Wolffe. While the aristocrats lived in grand style organizing a brass band and church choir and holding gala balls, with occasional visits to the English gentlemen of the proximate utopian settlement of Cannington Manor, the domestic servants and farm labourers – not a few Belgians – carried on with the serious agricultural tasks. Bertram Tennyson, nephew of Alfred Lord Tennyson, wrote admiringly in *The Land of Napioa* of this "beautiful country gemmed with scarlet tiger lilies and golden marigolds" and its rolling prairie by "the long blue line of the Pipestone Valley."[35] The Baron van Brabant spent the winter of 1891–92 in Europe "attending to immigration business in connection with the colony." During the next eighteen months eighty-eight new settlers arrived at St. Hubert.[36]

The influx of new immigrants did little to change the fortunes of the venture. Baron von Brabant and his brother took over Château Richelieu and their own Richelieu French Coffee brand, flavoured with chicory of course, appeared on the market. It met with little success so the operation was turned over to Count de Beaudrap. Count Roffignac had been succeeded in the over-all management by Fernand Carnoy and the joint stock company was in deep financial difficulty, as reported in the local press:

> As far as is known at present the buildings and extensive lands of the company will lie idle, unless a customer can be found for them. The company has sunk a large sum in the enterprise, which has been quite an assistance to the district, and we are sorry their operations have not been attended with better success.[37]

Archbishop Langevin attempted to rescue the faltering project, personally visited St. Hubert in 1905, and sold it to the Missionnaires de Chavagnes from Brittany who never carried through with the immigration program.[38]

The aristocrats left, poorer if not wiser, and their utopian vision faded in the blizzards and prairie fires. But among the resilient survivors were many Belgians – the families of François Beaujot, Adolph Gatin, Elvire Raiwet, Victor Dumonceaux, Joseph Pirlot, and Justin Havelange, from Namur province. They had worked for the aristocrats and now turned their attention to their own farms. Other families came to join them, including the Moinys to work in the cheese factory; the Poncelets to take up a homestead; and the Payots to work for the parish priest in Whitewood. The agricultural expertise of the community experienced a tremendous boost with the arrival of two outstanding graduates in agriculture from the University of Louvain – François Smet in 1908 and Paul Mullie in 1911.[39]

The second utopian project was Montmartre, launched in 1893 by the Société foncière du Canada that had been founded by Pierre Forsin, Hector Fabre and some Parisian investors. The company was to supply immigrants with farm buildings, implements, domestic animals and seed grain upon arrival. When the first contingent arrived at Wolseley, the nearest rail link, there were no provisions waiting, so women and children remained in town while the men hurried south to the company property to erect temporary shelters. Théophile and Constant de Decker decided it was best to put up a sod house in the shape of a tipi and then dig a well to have access to water. Company agents appeared more anxious to construct a Grande Maison for officials than to provide for the immigrant families as winter approached. It was a miracle that most remained and survived the harsh winter that ensued.[40]

There was no crop in 1894 and a prairie fire wiped out some of what had been achieved. The de Decker brothers persuaded two other siblings, Yvon and Henri, to come to Montmartre to work as carpenters on contract for the company. Three years later, two other brothers, Camille and Désiré, immigrated and took up homesteads. By 1901 the chief landmarks of the colony, the Grande Maison and the stables, were demolished and the company reclaimed the homesteads it had granted. So the six de Decker brothers moved on, as many others had, to British Columbia. Only the butter and cheese factory that Alfred Latreille and André Gouzée from Belgium had set up in 1894 remained in operation. Gouzée had invested his capital in wheat growing and ranching but his land was reclaimed by the Dominion government in 1906, so he sold his cattle and returned to Belgium. His departure was but another indication of the failure of the Montmartre project. André Gouzée would soon return to Canada in a more important and successful role.[41]

The third venture was the aristocratic colony of Trochu. Armand Trochu, a Parisian stock broker, established a ranch not far from Three Hills in a sheltered coulee close to the Buffalo Lake trail. He recruited a number of cavalry officers in 1904 to establish ranches, as well as Count Paul de Beaudrap, who had been associated with the St. Hubert venture, and his brother Roger de Beaudrap. The most successful associate was Joseph Devilder, an ambitious and wealthy entrepreneur of Flemish origin whose father had established a banking business in Lille. Devilder invested $50,000 in the Trochu settlement, most of it in the St. Ann Ranch Trading Company which was incorporated in 1905.[42]

Devilder introduced a very rational approach to ranching in contrast to the trappings of the military and modest aristocratic lifestyle of Trochu. Several hundred feeder cattle were bought, fattened and shipped by rail to packing houses. In 1905 over one hundred fine Percheron horses were purchased, about half of which were lost in a raging prairie fire the following year. This was followed by an exceptionally severe winter which took a heavy toll among the cattle. Devilder diversified by constructing a large multi-purpose building to serve as a hotel for homesteaders passing through to take up their claims, as a dance hall and as a community centre. A blacksmith and a tinsmith were sponsored by the company to serve the community. In 1908, Devilder bought more than three hundred milch cows which were sold on a credit basis to local farmers who brought their milk and cream to the company creamery. The company kept one half of the cream cheque as payment for the cows. His only real failure was investment in oil drilling equipment which it turned out was only suitable for drilling water wells.[43]

Lommel Chain Migration

A concentration of immigrants from the Lommel/ Kerkoven region of Limburg province evolved south of historic Cannington Manor after the arrival of a branch line of the CPR in 1902 resulted in the development of the village of Manor, with the usual railway station, grain elevators, loading platform, general store and post office. A. De Trémaudan left Montmartre to set up the De Trémaudan Company in the new hamlet, selling real estate and insurance. Settlers from central Canada had begun arriving in the region south of Moose Mountain as early as 1882. The first Belgians from Lommel – Henri Clemens, Louis Engelen, and Jan Hoeben – arrived in 1912–13. Henri Clemens was joined by his brothers Jan and Jacob and Frans Michiels in April 1914. Henri returned to Belgium, where a local historian in Lommel observed: "A certain Clemens from Lommel, who canvassed the area for people willing to emigrate recruited in this way about thirty families."[44]

Manor gained a certain status in 1913 when Gaston De Jardin, who served as vice-consul in Forget, set up an implement dealership and insurance office in the village. From 1915 to 1919 he was secretary-treasurer of the village and also Belgian vice-consul from 1915 to 1921. The De Jardin family was involved in land development and investment throughout the West and they were representatives of influential Antwerp investment groups. Gaston De Jardin was instrumental in the settlement of numerous Lommel families in Manor before he moved on to join his brother in Winnipeg in the pursuit of their business interests.[45]

Veterans of World War I and war brides were just returning in 1919 when a large contingent from Lommel managed to find space on-board a vessel sailing for Canada, rather than Australia where there was also a "Belgian connection," and laid the foundation of what would be an important settlement.[46] Not all were able to settle immediately into farming, which now required some capital to make a down payment on any available farmsteads. Charel Alen worked two years in Alida to support a family of five children before returning to Manor. Drought and grasshopper plagues convinced him to move to Churchbridge where he became a successful cattle shipper. Sebastien Vanden Boer, who would later host several immigrant families, had to work two years for the CPR and three of his eldest children hired out to neighbours before the family could take up its own farm. Jef Hulsman had been Cornelius Jaenen's major competitor as a pub owner in Kerkhoven but they came to Manor together seeking a new life and prosperity.

Cornelius Jaenen and his family settled in the hamlet, and eventually took up a modest farm, unlike some who had to work for other farmers, on the railways, or in the mines. He had intended to emigrate in 1914 but the outbreak of hostilities forced him to postpone his plans. During the war he was able to accumulate some capital, especially from his pub near the Dutch border and a couple factories, where in addition to food and libations he sold unspecified "merchandise." His business was also near the Blauwe Kei–Leopoldsburg canal where shippers and line-pullers who pulled barges along with horses and manpower repaired for refreshments. A collector of village tales reported:

> Corneel Jaenen, alias den Brak, horse merchant, rented premises containing a pub with barns for the shippers' horses and a bowling alley. He also owned a farm and a considerable herd of cattle and his pub had many clients. His wife Hanne and their daughter Marie served the factory workers that came by, while Corneel played the harmonica.... The mussel festivals

that he organized were quite peppered and salted. It made his clients so thirsty that they drank like mole holes. During the womens' kermis there were tarts, farm ham, black prune pies and currant bread.[47]

Manor did not offer the same opportunities as Kerkoven. There was not even a Catholic church in the village, the nearest church being Gaire's church in Wauchope. Father A.J. Janssen from Sedley paid occasional visits to say mass with sermons in Dutch at the Manor hotel.

This chain migration continued with the arrival of five more families,[48] in March 1920 during a blinding snowstorm that left almost a metre of snow on the ground. Arnold Van Heukelom had ten children and he had to work four years on the railway and two years in a cobalt mine at Deloro, Ontario before taking a farm in Manor.[49] Jaak Van Ham had five children and Vincent Ooms had six children so their establishment was not without difficulties as well. The Flemish community was completed with the arrival of Sool Poets in 1922, and four families in 1927: Peter Tavernier, Joseph Luyten, Peter Bax, and Jaak Clemens. These all worked hard as family units, pooling the income of its members. This was an indispensable practice considering the size of some families – Louis Geysen with ten children, Joseph Luyten with twelve children, Arnold Van Heukelom with ten children, and Koob Clemens, father of the original scouts that came to the area, with ten children.[50]

Before the drought and depression of the 1930s set in, markets were stable, land was still available for mixed farming, and crop yields were good during an upturn in the economy. At least sixty cleared acres were required for a comfortable existence, which could be purchased for about $3,000, including household goods, farm equipment and a minimum of domestic animals. Catholics organized their own cemetery in Manor in 1936. Mass was said regularly in a converted bank building until a parish church was erected, symbolic of the success of the settlement.

The Limburgers were accompanied by a small number of Walloons. Fernand Gerinrose, who had come to Gaire's settlement in Grande Clairière in 1892, where he worked for the Tinant family, moved successively to Parkman, Elrose, and then Cannington Manor where he rented an imposing historic farmhouse. A daughter recalled its frontier elegance and attraction:

Our house was a stone structure with a large dance salon and almost every week during the winter a crowd of people would come and hold a dance at our place. They supplied the music and lunch and Mom [Marie-Louise Gerinroze-Tinant] provided the coffee. We had a lot of fun but I was only 10 years old so no one really noticed me.[51]

Fernand Gerinrose later moved to the village of Manor, where he was mail carrier for many years, meeting the twice daily trains that served the community.[52]

In the 1920s, Jules and Marie-Louise Minet arrived to join their daughters who also married into the Limburger community.[53] They were joined by another daughter, Victorine and husband Raymond Mottet, who first worked at the Staples ranch in Oxbow, but they did not take to agricultural life so they returned to Belgium after a few years. Jules Minet had international experience in Europe in setting up agricultural machinery, so he was kept busy repairing farm machinery by making the replacement parts in his own forge, travelling between Antler and Alida and Manor in summer months on "Louis," his dependable bicycle. Victor Renauld and Jack Pirlot from Deleau, and Philippe Revet from Bellegarde, completed the Walloon element in the Belgian community that was the mainstay of the Catholic parish. Locality of origin in Europe and family networks and intermarriage were important factors in a sense of identity and differentiation from neighbours for a couple generations.[54]

How successful was this venture onto the Saskatchewan prairies? The Lommel contingent arrived at a time of great optimism. Up to 1925 bumper wheat crops choked rural elevators and railway companies were unable to supply sufficient boxcars to transport the wheat to saltwater ports. Then there followed a series of crop failures caused by drought followed by rust. Governments launched relief and rehabilitation programs, probably assuming some responsibility for having encouraged intensive agricultural settlement of the dry belt. A Lommel commentator wrote: "In 1918 the [Canadian] soldiers and the consulates abroad depicted Canada as a land overflowing with milk and honey, the promised land, where people in twenty years could become millionaires." He concluded that "many did not find the promised standard of living and experienced a life of setbacks and accidents." He believed that many of these emigrants "with their input, their sweat and their money, would here [in Lommel] have done as well as there. But if you set your mind to it you will achieve, and some have to be far from home to prosper."[55]

Southern Horizon Country

Belgians who were accommodated at the Brandon immigration office in 1893 were not long in establishing themselves on the southern prairie beyond Gaire's parishes, as an 1894 immigration report indicated:

> The Franco-Belgians numbering some thirty families are, however, I believe, doing well. They are hard working, industrious and frugal, and being near an old settled part of the country, have profited from the example of their neighbours.[56]

Techniques of dryland farming would come with experience, although they did acquire some notions how best to proceed with cultivation, crop rotation and animal husbandry from compatriots in Bruxelles or Deloraine. Two years later, the immigration agent in Estevan reported that the region was about to receive experienced reinforcements:

> The French and Belgian settlement at Percy is in a flourishing condition; and from present prospects the immigration from the vicinity of Bathgate, in North Dakota, to that colony for the coming season will be quite large and will consist of a good industrious class of people, well acquainted with the ways of western [farm] life.[57]

An additional attraction for those coming up by the railway line from North Portal was the availability of seasonal employment in the lignite mines around Estevan and Bienfait. Since the 1880s, pioneers had dug coal with pick and shovel from the banks of a ravine at Roche Percée and hauled the precious fuel by ox team over the open prairie.

There were numerous families settled around Estevan in 1892, but they were never sufficiently concentrated to form a distinct Belgian community. Family biographies indicate they maintained social contact through the Catholic church and inter-marriage was common. Several families found employment in the town and seasonally in the coal mine. Another cluster formed in the vicinity of Weyburn and Radville. The first Belgian family arrived in Radville in 1903, followed by six more families in 1906, and another fifteen in 1910. They were mostly farmers from Flanders. Some chose not to file for a homestead but to work as labourers in Weyburn, especially at a brickyard, where a neighbourhood popularly known as "Belgium Town" emerged.[58] Belgians were familiar with eighteen different types of bricks that could be produced in a single plant and kiln from the same clay.

Four family histories illustrate the employment and migration patterns of settlers who arrived in 1910. Sylvain Goessaert, his wife and four children came to "Belgium Town" to work in home construction. He worked as a labourer putting in the town water mains, then as a hotel porter, while attending night school to learn English. He filed for a homestead in 1914 but also worked six months each year in the lignite mine at Gladmar. Joseph Wyndandts worked for the local telephone company, then in a butcher shop before taking up a homestead in the Gladmar district, as did his eldest son and some relatives. He became a community and church leader and host of Father Jacob Wilhelm of Diamond Crossing, the much-beloved pastor of the Flemish settlers.[59] Achiel Schepens worked in Weyburn at manual jobs and as a farm hand at Radville for settling near compatriots in Gladmar. Leon Uytterhagen had worked in a large sugar beet plant in East Flanders before emigrating and worked as a common labourer in Weyburn until he filed for a homestead. He was active in community affairs, serving as municipal road boss, school trustee for three decades, board member of the Wheat Pool committee and active participant in the local co-operative. These individuals gave Belgian immigrants a good reputation both with their neighbours and with immigration authorities.[60]

The Belgian community that grew up around Ceylon after 1906 came from a wide range of occupations that ranged from operating a steam laundry to hauling coal, working in the John Deere factory in Moline, or in the brickyard at Weyburn or on the Hudson Bay railway. These initial occupations indicate that there was some ethnic networking as they eventually moved into farming communities alongside compatriots.[61]

A characteristic of this early settlement was the extensive mobility of individuals and families. The movements of the Lee Van de Bon family that eventually settled in Yellow Grass illustrates this phenomenon. Van de Bon came to work during the summer for a farmer in Deloraine in 1911. During the first winter, with three other young men, he went to work in a lumber camp in Minnesota. The second winter he shovelled coal at a dockyard in Superior, Wisconsin. The third winter he went to a lumber camp in northern Saskatchewan. By 1913 he gave up on the remunerative but exacting seasonal employment and concentrated on farming activities and by 1916 he had sufficient capital to buy his own farm near Yellow Grass. In 1923 he bought a large steam engine, a threshing machine, hay racks, bunk cars, cook car, and water tanker to launch an impressive threshing outfit employing no fewer than twenty-one men each autumn. He farmed with sixteen horses, two sets of eight horses abreast, until in 1936 he sold his threshing outfit and horses and bought a tractor and combine. Successful farmers had to keep abreast of technological developments. This was the kind of progress that was much admired in the agricultural community and was crowned with a son taking over the family farm as the pioneers retired to the milder climate of British Columbia.[62]

The light brown soil belt on the western slopes of the Missouri Coteau became a major area of Francophone settlement, including some Belgians around Verwood, Willow Bunch, St. Victor, Fife Lake and Coronach. Richard De Cock, who with his siblings came to Deloraine from Brussels in 1899 and proceeded to Willow Bunch in 1901, was probably the first settler. His was a rather erratic career because he soon went to British Columbia to work as a freighter, then worked as a trapper in the north before returning to a ranch near Maple Creek. After marrying he moved back to Wood Mountain where he operated a Hereford ranch and a lignite mine. In 1927 he went off to British Columbia again, but finally settled into farming at Willow Bunch once more in 1934. He survived the depression and drought years by growing quality vegetables, a source of amazement to many. His itinerary illustrates the high mobility of some Belgian immigrants.[63]

There were a number of scattered communities in the region. Moose Jaw was the usual point of entry to this region where sympathetic agents at the Crown lands office directed immigrants to the desired destination. In 1907 the Augustin Assoignon, Désiré Denonceau and Emile Girard families from the province of Luxembourg formed the nucleus of a group of immigrants near the villages of Fife Lake and Rockglen. They were joined by a trickle of compatriots until 1914 followed by young Belgians who had joined units of the Canadian Expeditionary Force and who had obtained government loans to buy farms, stock and equipment.[64]

Farther west, abbé Marie-Albert Royer attracted Belgians to Ponteix in 1907, to Vanguard and Pambrun in 1908–09, and to Frenchville and Lac Driscoll in 1909–10. Some chose not to settle among the French Canadians therefore they filed for homesteads at Fir Mountain, Maple Creek and Robsart.[65] Some lands were settled by the abbé Royer's recruits before they were officially put on the market and the abbé Louis Pierre Gravel had to obtain squatters' rights for them. Settlement was not always a straightforward experience.[66]

The 1930s were particularly disastrous years for farmers and townspeople in southern Saskatchewan. Estevan and environs was hit first by hailstorms, then grasshopper infestations and severe drought. As many farmers migrated east and north in search of fodder for their horses and cattle, an ethnic network was again discernible because the Belgians tended to turn to compatriots in Deloraine and other southern Manitoba districts for aid.[67] Sylvain Goessaert's sons, who pioneered with their father near Weyburn, rode the rails looking for work in the forests of British Columbia and the mines of Alberta. The hard work and disappointments of those years determined seven of the eight children to abandon the prairies for British Columbia and Ontario. In Ceylon district, farmers organized haying expeditions into Manitoba in order to save their horses and cattle. Fife Lake experienced a dramatic decline in rural population. Belgians there spearheaded an exodus to Crystal Springs in northern Saskatchewan.

North Central Parklands

In 1888, only three years after the military operations associated with the North-West Rebellion, a few Belgian immigrants began to arrive at Duck Lake and Batoche.[68] François Jordens left missionary work to take up farming at Summerberry in 1906. Concentrated settlement emerged around Vonda, St. Denis and Marcotte Ranch (renamed Prud'homme in 1922). Tréau de Coeli, colonizing agent in Europe visited these settlements in 1906: "During my short sojourn, I had the pleasure of going to Edmonton and visiting the new French and Belgian colonies, along the Canadian Northern railway, at Vonda, Howell and Aberdeen where since a couple years, several Belgian families have become established and are succeeding beyond their hopes."[69]

In anticipation of the success of colonizing clergy in attracting Francophones to the Prince Albert district, the Belgian government appointed C. de la Gorgendière, clerk of the Supreme Court of Saskatchewan, its vice consul there in June 1906. A certain Baron Fallon had settled at Domrémy in 1906 and claimed to be the representative of the Belgian government. The Dominion land agent in the area, J. Dubois, complained that the baron was upsetting the school trustees, the local improvement district officials and the justice of the peace with his exaggerated claims. Belgian officials clarified his true status:

> Canada seems to be a paradise for sons of good families, failures in life, useless and troublesome. I let Mr. Dubois know that Baron Fallon was usurping the title of Vice-Consul of Belgium and that he belonged to no station whatever in a Belgian consular career.[70]

It appears that there may have been another motive, in addition to colonization, for the appointment of a vice-consul.

The Pierre Hounjet family from Liège was not untypical of the early arrivals. They were relatively poor suburban farmers who worked together in the fields. An adolescent son delivered milk during the pre-dawn hours from a cart pulled by a large dog. A pamphlet passed on by a Canadian recruiting agent aroused their desire to emigrate to better their condition. Wisely, they sent their older son François to Canada to sound out prospects in Forget, then Prud'homme. The local priest encouraged him so the family started anew at St. Denis. They were joined later by a married brother and his family, who came by way of the United States, and the Hamoline and Dutilleux families, who became active in Francophone affairs. The seven Hounjet children settled in northern Saskatchewan, made a success of farming and never regretted the decision to emigrate.[71] In 1910, twelve families from Hainaut came to Prud'homme and were all reasonably successful. Jean Hannotte served as municipal councillor for ten years, François Pirot as general merchant, Hubert Radoux as horticulturalist, and Georges Vancamphout as justice of the peace. The Baudoux family gained prominence in the community when the son, Maurice Baudoux, chose a religious life, became parish priest in Prud'homme in 1931, a zealous promoter of French Canadian causes, a chief mover in the cause for French radio in the West, and eventually was appointed Archbishop of St. Boniface.[72]

Two colonizing priests had some success in recruiting Belgians. Abbé Paul LeFloch of St. Brieux was able to attract both Walloons and Flemings to Vonda, Hoey and St. Denis.[73] Abbé Jules Pirot, a Walloon nationalist who served the Hungarian Catholic community at Esterhazy, during two trips to his native Namur region recruited eighteen Walloons for Esterhazy.[74]

Elsewhere the pattern of Belgian settlement was even more scattered and devoid of any systematic settlement strategy. The Saskatchewan Valley Land Company bought up seemingly arid land between the Qu'Appelle valley and Saskatoon at a bargain price and found no difficulty in attracting settlers, including Belgians. In Davidson, eight Belgian families were core members of the Catholic parish.[75] Near Watson, the Edward Behiels family took up homesteads north of the Quill Lakes in 1903, where they were soon joined by Peter Deschryver.[76] Achiel and Henry Tycquet pioneered south of Macrorie and four other families homesteaded south of Fertile Valley. These Belgians organized the local chapter of the Grain Growers' Association in 1918. Georges Delaporte introduced a new style of farm living, spending the winters in the village and the summers on the farm, combining village life with rural life.[77] In Elrose the Verbruggans family and the Lhoest, Grenade and Jeuris families in Mondou district were all successful farmers, retiring in most cases to Saskatoon.[78] When students of St. Walburg High School researched the beginning of their community, they came across memorable tales of rabbit hunts, building bees, card parties, masquerades and barn dances, often associated with John Van den Bergh who had come in 1906. They also noted the special affection parishioners had for Father Vandandaele who ministered for many years at Paradise Hill.[79]

In June 1907, 250,000 acres of prime farm land at Veregin, abandoned by Doukhobors who had refused to take the oath of allegiance and abandon community ownership, came onto the homestead market. Damien Van de Sempel filed for a homestead and six sons and daughters gained patents for their individual homesteads. None of their homesteads carried mortgages or any similar encumbrance throughout the three or more years it took to satisfy requirements for the patent and registration of the individual homestead.[80] Seven other Belgian families settled in the area north of Veregin and the Indian reserve. Those who left Belgium were seen by many as "deserters" nevertheless there was admiration of the rapid progress they could make, especially that a bride's family could rarely equal in dowry the amount of capital a husband from Canada possessed.[81]

Depression, Drought and Recovery

Belgians soon learned that contrarities other than strenuous labour to achieve adequate cultivation and shelter existed. The concept of free land was misleading because less than half the acreage of a township was available for homesteads. Large tracts were for sale by the government, the railway companies and the Hudson's Bay Company.[82] Secondly, the influenza epidemic in 1918 revealed the inadequacy of medical services and of governmental responses. The exodus of rural dwellers to the villages, where assistance was said to exist, resulted in a concentration of people that facilitated the spread of the contagion. Many Belgians simply turned to folk remedies such as eating garlic and boiled onions. Thirdly, the inadequacy of all governmental and institutional services in dealing with a natural disaster, economic crisis and human misery was tragically revealed during the Great Depression, marked by widespread unemployment and a drastic drop in prices for farm produce, accompanied by an unprecedented drought. Very few on the Prairies were directly affected by the stock market collapse on 29 October 1919 but the general depression it represented left none untouched.

Natural disaster accentuated the negative effects of the instability of western industrial economies. In the 1930s, drifting topsoil piled into drifts that covered fenceposts and abandoned farmsteads became common especially in the southern parts of the Prairies. Infestations of grasshoppers, in search of what little vegetation survived, and wheat rust claimed whatever had managed to survive the dry conditions. By 1931 farmers were removing the motor and steering mechanism of their cars, adding hitches and tongue to convert them into horse-drawn "Bennett buggies." Equally popular were the half versions or two-wheeled vehicles called "Anderson carts." In this way the farmers demonstrated both their adaptability and their disdain for the Conservative prime minister and provincial premier respectively. The Canadian Commonwealth Federation (CCF) and Social Credit parties attempted to organize the protest vote, but the Belgians like the French Canadians in the West tended to remain firmly loyal to the Liberal Party.

Mortgages on many farms were foreclosed, machinery was repossessed and land was abandoned. Relief supplies were sent from central and eastern Canada, but it was alleged that the authorities, mostly of British origin, in the rural municipalities and villages directed these supplies to their friends. Some farmers relocated outside the light brown soil zone. Charles Alen shipped a carload of cattle to Winnipeg from Churchbridge in 1937 which did not bring enough to pay for the freight charges. Similarly, John Jaenen in Antler shipped a carload of barley to Fort William and he received a bill for thirty-six cents as the grain was not worth as much as the freight charges. Peter Van Sprundel, in Manor near Moose Mountain which had somewhat more precipitation than most of the region, recorded the serious situation:

> Fair crops till grasshoppers flew in by the millions, cut crop green from dawn till dark but couldn't keep ahead; [grass] hoppers cleaned up all oats and barley, only a few stems left to cut with mower, Stooks too green to thresh and grasshoppers also devouring those. Plowed some fall rye under. Will only get seed back. No slough hay. Will have to locate hay in Manitoba in exchange for stock. Railroad shipping in hay free to dried out areas. Many farmers leaving for British Columbia.[83]

John Jaenen in Antler, for example, sacrificed to pay his taxes and relief supplies but the municipal officials accepted his payments and never informed him of the amnesty that had been granted. He was unable, on the other hand, to meet his mortgage payments so he abandoned his farm and moved to the Red River valley where Alphonse Gelaude, a compatriot, helped him get resettled. There was a sense of discrimination and one turned to one's ethnic group for support. As James Gray reminisced, the few jobs available went to those of British stock not the "foreigners."[84]

Nature seemed particularly pitiless as January/February 1936 was the coldest winter on record and spring came early, ushering in the hottest summer on record. At the meteorological station at Carlyle temperatures reached 43.3C. The following year was the worst year for dust storms. Belgians recalled that around Forget the creek bottoms dried out exposing large quantities of bison bones which they gathered and sold for fertilizer.

At Wauchope, trains were delayed when hordes of grasshoppers landed on the rails and were crushed into a slippery grease.

The "dirty thirties," a combination of drought and depression, was a phrase that encapsulated the economic dislocation, social turmoil, climatic change and psychological trauma of the period. It was a cruel time that broke down even some of the strongest men and dashed the hopes of countless. Guy Vanderhaeghe wrote autobiographically how his father was a victim of drought and the depression:

> That was during the thirties when we were dealt a doubly cruel hand of drought and economic depression. It was not a time or place that was kindly to my father. He had come out of the urban spread of industrial Belgium some twenty-odd years before, and it was only then, I think, that he was beginning to come to terms with a land that must have seemed forbidding after his own tiny country, so well tamed and marked by man. And then this land played him the trick of becoming more than forbidding; it became fierce, and fierce in every way.[85]

Yet, the "dirty thirties" gave rise to a romantic literature as well as a sense of community and confirmed the need for interdependence.

The role of farm women before 1940 was influenced by such factors as the lack of electricity and time-saving equipment and the care of generally large families living in poorly built houses that required a lot of upkeep and organization. These women contributed significantly to the work force during the years of drought and depression, as well as to the meagre family income by preparing and preserving food, making and mending clothing, doing farm chores, and producing and selling produce.[86] Their daughters very often had to forfeit a good education to help, and sometimes replace, their mother. When the parents were ill or handicapped, it was not unusual for girls, such as Clarice Lambert and her sister, to take over farm operations.[87] Formal schooling was replaced in many cases by a kind of apprenticeship in domesticity and home-centred industry. Hours of work depended on how long it took to finish all the multiple tasks each day. Some contributed in exceptional ways, such as Marguerite Trochu, who painted and sold postcards and Christmas cards of life in her community.[88] Eliane Silverman has described the lives of young women at this time as "a web of obedience and obligation" to family.[89] Little wonder that a quarter million people left the Prairies, defeated and disillusioned.

World War II marked a transition in image and ideology in Western Canada. Farming was no longer seen as offering certain prosperity and government responsibility for economic and social security was now firmly entrenched. Family biographies reveal that in most Belgian farm families the children moved into other occupations, especially as they were better educated than the preceding generation. By the 1970s, revenue from potash, petroleum and uranium accounted for almost 30 per cent of Saskatchewan's economy while agriculture accounted for under 40 per cent, a decline of 10 per cent in a decade.[90] A number of factors, such as expansion of the chemical industry with new herbicides, insecticides and fertilizers and the vagaries of international markets and government policies regulating wheat sales and beef production, accelerated change.[91]

The family farm, handed down from father to son usually, was considered a sign of success and evidence of continuity. After World War II sophisticated technology, specialization, international competition, credit policies and government subsidization resulted in corporate farms becoming a more successful approach. Agribusiness and diversification became the earmark of survival and success. Alphonse Jaenen and family in Fairlight, Saskatchewan, exemplified this new approach to agriculture – not only diversity of traditional and experimental crops but also diversity of enterprises that initially included an apiary and ceramics department. Through collective planning and specialized enterprises that included each of the four sons and their families, the business encompassed production of beef, poultry, and sheep and the operation of a machine shop and seed mill. A CBC program highlighted this example of diversification and consolidation in the context of rural depopulation.[92] The Jaenen corporate farm also illustrates that with Moosomin as a service centre the quality of life and the strength of social ties, long ascribed to rural and village life, have not been destroyed completely. Rural life was no longer synonymous with traditional ways of doing things.

View of the Belgian Horse Ranch, Springbank, AB, 1920s. (Glenbow NA-3350)
Belgians viewed ranching as an elitist occupation.

Dygert's Percheron and Belgian horses, Edmonton, AB, 1914. (Glenbow NC-6-4237)
Imported Belgian horses were prized for farming and urban delivery
throughout the Western provinces.

V

TO THE FOOTHILLS OF ALBERTA

The boost of activity that saw settlers move onto the third prairie level to the foothills of the Rockies began when speculators bought up lands in anticipation of where the transcontinental railway would run and where townsites were planned. The land boom began in Moose Jaw, the divisional point of the CPR, in 1882 and at Notre-Dame de la Paix Mission, the future town of Calgary where a thousand inhabitants arrived within a year. The local newspaper boasted:

> Calgary is a western town.... It is peopled by ... citizens who own religion and respect law. The rough and festive cowboy of Texas ... has no counterpart here.[1]

Belgians began arriving in Calgary and Medicine Hat in 1888, Edmonton in 1894, and Lethbridge in 1900. The federal government extended Dominion Lands legislation to the railway belt, to place these lands "upon the market at the earliest possible date," and revised regulations concerning mining, timber, and grazing.[2] Belgians were only marginally involved in ranching that developed in the southern regions of Alberta, but in the mid-north and Peace River country they would engage in mixed farming.

Immediately the question arose as to what class of immigrants should be encouraged to settle this region. Acton Burrows, a Winnipeg realtor, Archbishop Taché and Sir Charles Tupper, High Commissioner in London, deplored earlier appeals for all classes of people regardless of occupation or capital resources.[3] Bishop Grandin of St. Albert had a specific and narrower vision. He hoped to attract only Francophone Catholics, and to that end he appealed to the Société St. Raphaël in Belgium for colonists and priests who spoke French and Flemish.[4]

Boosterism, on the contrary, saw progress only in terms of unlimited European immigration and capitalistic endeavour. In 1895 the CPR began to consolidate its activities in Calgary and acquired a bloc of land withdrawn from homestead application to set up its irrigation district headquarters in Strathmore. It was here, between Baintree and Mewasin, that numerous Belgians eventually settled. In 1899, Father Delouche organized the Société d'exploitation agricole du Canada in Antwerp to attract investors to underwrite the Oblate missionaries' scheme. Lord Shaughnessy of the CPR had been approached concerning the "business undertaking" with the assurance that "Belgians are far more practical than Frenchmen." When Consul De Vos visited the area in 1901, he found Mr. Rouleau most helpful and noted that a certain M. Van Wart imported annually 30,000 square metres of timber from British Columbia to be processed at the Cushing Planing Mill.[5] However, a downturn in European financial circles resulted in the abandonment of the Delouche project in 1902.[6] By 1916, Calgary surpassed Edmonton in population, attributable in good measure to the aggressive propaganda, boosterism, of the self-styled "Denver of the north"[7] The established Anglophone population reacted in no uncertain terms to the "open door" immigration policy, as a Strathcona newspaper editorialized:

> Is this fair land to be given to the off-scourings of humanity?
> If so the government would confer a favour by telling us, so we
> can look for other quarters.[8]

Belgians were not anywhere near the bottom of the immigrant pecking order, by any means, but they shared the Catholic religion with many eastern European immigrants. Some were too closely associated in many of their settlement patterns with Francophone communities, for the liking of Anglo-Celts. This was the context of Belgian settlement on the third prairie level east of the Rockies.

Ranching and Horse-Breeding

Ranching appealed to Europeans, especially the English, with capital because it was an enterprise that promoted an ethos of the country estate, the retention of a manager-employee relationship as ranch labour was readily available, and the pursuit of a leisurely life-style. The Deputy Minister of the Interior reported in 1880:

> ... the advantages offered by the North-West for stock-raising are now receiving the attention from capitalists and experienced cattle breeders which they deserve.[9]

Ranching required large tracts because it took from twenty to fifty acres of natural range grass to feed one animal. The dry land grasses relied on shattered seed for most of their reproduction; therefore, moderate grazing was essential to permit natural re-seeding. An order-in-council in December 1881 permitted government leases of up to 100,000 acres for a term of twenty-one years at a rate of $10 per thousand acres, or one cent per acre per year. There were no "land rushes" in southern Alberta. There developed a close relationship between ranchers and the North West Mounted Police.[10]

A few Belgians took up cattle-ranching alongside English gentlemen and Canadian entrepreneurs. Adile Desmet from Meulebeke in Flanders arrived at Lethbridge in March 1893 and quickly organized a ranch at Pincher Creek. The location was chosen along a river because there were sheltering trees and swards of forage essential for winter survival.[11] The following year, the federal government prohibited all permanent diversion or exclusive use of the water of such bodies of water except by permission from the Crown.[12] In April 1904, Léon van Haverbeke and Alphonse Vanden Berge arrived from Tielt and proceeded to the Milk River district to take up ranching. The following month, six more Belgians arrived to scout out ranches, two of whom (from Meulebeke) decided to work on irrigation projects.[13] Nicolas Floener arrived at Cochrane with his extended family in July 1905, filed for a homestead and invested his entire capital in cattle. He relied on local opinion that cattle could graze out all winter. However, the exceptionally severe blizzards of 1905–06 wiped out his herd and his investment. Floener took a job in the local brickyard owned by a compatriot, Joseph Bodeur, and after many hardships decided in 1919 that the Peace River country offered better prospects. The winter of 1906–07 was no better because, as Victor Van Tighem noted in his diary: "Cattle are dying by the hundreds on the prairies."[14] The consul-general wrote pessimistically about young men who wanted to emulate English gentlemen ranchers at Wetaskiwin: "Several young Belgians from good families took up ranching at Wetaskiwin. The enterprise does not appear to have been sufficiently successful to permit them to live like 'gentlemen farmers'; on the other hand, they may not all have desired to live by manual work. Be that as it may, some abandoned the project, while others wished to continue. We do not intend to analyze the causes of these opposing determinations, which we deem to be foreign to our study of the agricultural and pastoral value of the region.[15] By 1900, the lands reserved for ranching became subject to settlement following a series of wet years which changed the perception of the dry belt and the introduction of winter wheat. Older officials who were favourable to commercial ranching lost political power after 1896.[16] Belgians were more interested in horse-ranching and horse-breeding than in cattle-ranching. The Belgian breed of draught horses, descendants of an ancient breed originating in the upper Meuse valley, were first introduced into the United States in 1866 for farm work and town dray operations. American ranchers who moved to Western Canada often brought Belgian horses with them. The Oxarat Ranch south of Maple Creek, for example, wintered seven hundred horses outside without a single loss in 1886–87. Gustave Delbeke came to the Cochrane area in 1902 from Kortrijk with several big chestnut brown Belgian horses. He made several trips to supply the demand for these work horses, and in 1907 he brought some grey-speckled Percherons as well to his Belgian Horse Ranch, south of Cochrane. The following year he filed for a homestead in Beaupré Creek Valley but he continued to train horses for area ranchers. He soon acquired a reputation showing his fine horses at agricultural fairs.[17]

In 1905, Maurice Ingeveld of Oudenarde, who had been trained in the Belgian Cavalry and the French Officers' Riding School, came to Millarville to train horses for Count Georges de Roaldes, Baron Dougat d'Empeaus and R. de Malherbe. Ingeveld filed for a homestead in 1907 and also started the Victoria Livery stables in Tilley. In 1914 he returned to Belgium but he came back permanently to Millarville in 1927.[18] Raoul Pirmez came to Calgary in 1903, bought four sections of land on the Elbow River southwest of the city to start the Belgian Horse Ranch in collaboration with Baron George Roels. In May 1910, a post office was established on his ranch, he was named postmaster, and from there mail was sorted for those west and delivered by mail carrier over dirt roads. He was also instrumental in bringing the telephone system to the area and having road access established.[19] In 1911, Pirmez, Roels and H. De Burlet formed the firm Pirmez and Company in Calgary. They became prominent members of the Ranchmen's Club, organized in May 1893 and eventually located on property belonging to Isaac Vanwart, where men of education, culture and broad world views met socially. Raoul Pirmez served as Belgian consul from 1913 to his death in 1920, with the exception of an interlude in 1916–19 when he went to England and H. De Burlet served as his interim replacement representing Belgian interests in southern Alberta. Calgary began constructing a civic identity around cowboys and ranching activities although these were marginal in its development.[20]

In October 1907 the Canadian Belgian Draught Horse Breeders Association was incorporated in response to widespread activity in the West. The plan was simple yet effective:

> Members of each club guaranteed a certain number of mares to be bred to an approved stallion, while the owner agreed to restrict the use of the stallion, at a stated service fee, to the members of the club. The federal Department of Agriculture gave financial assistance depending on the membership of the club and on the number of mares in foal.[21]

A familiar sight was the "stud horse man" travelling through the countryside, leading one of these heavy-set stallions from farm to farm. The most famous Belgian stallion in North America was 'Farceur' who sold for the phenomenal price of $47,500 in 1917. The offspring of these studs were greatly prized for work in the field and in draught horse shows. In time, they were successful in pulling contests at country fairs.

The Hector Delanoy family was probably the most active in establishing a network of these work horses. He had been convinced by a childhood friend, who had purportedly saved $20,000 in eleven years in Canada, to sell his farm and start selling draught horses in Canada. They became so familiar that during World War I the Belgian War Relief Fund used them on city streets to raise money. A son recalled:

Due to the fact that there was a big demand for heavy horses at that time, and that he and his relatives were in the horse business, in 1909 my father [in Deloraine] started to import Belgian horses from Belgium, and endowed with untiring energy crossed the ocean 13 times and on 5 crossings imported Belgian horses.[22]

The Delanoys sold horses in Nebraska and in all three western provinces. The father made his headquarters in Ste. Amelie in 1913, while his sons settled around Radville, and other relatives in Belgium kept them supplied with stallions and brood mares. They supplied the "stud circuits" of Willow Bunch, Fife Lake, Radville, and La Flèche in Saskatchewan.[23] Sales were interrupted for a decade because of the large-scale slaughter of these animals in battle and also for food during the war. The resumption of imports was marked by the arrival of five superb stallions in 1925, two of which were sold at the Regina Agricultural Fair, and the three others went on tour with a 'stud horse man.' A well-known supplier of horses was the firm of Hippolyte Steyaert & Fils in Moerbeke, which the Knight Sugar Company contacted when it needed workers for the sugar beet fields in southern Alberta. In the cities, breweries transported their barrels of beer on large wagons pulled by sturdy Belgian horses. As farmers organized local breeders' clubs, several families began to specialize in raising champion horses which they showed at local agricultural fairs, eventually at larger service centres, and ultimately at the Toronto Winter Fair. Michael De Pape and Nestor Lombaert in Bruxelles, Remi De Pape in Mariapolis, August and Charles De Pape in Holland, Jean Smeets in St. Hubert, Victor Liebaert in Mayfair, Louis Nachtelagaele in North Battleford, and Louis Dhoedt in Rivière-Qui-Barre were among the well-known breeders and exhibitors.[24]

The 1921 census indicated that there were 3,610,494 horses on the Prairies and only 38,600 farm tractors. The 1931 census showed that the number of horses had declined sharply, then during World War II horses enjoyed a brief renewed popularity. By 1944 there was a surplus of an estimated 300,000 horses in Western Canada. What happened to the large number of horses in the West? At Val Marie, in 1944, the Western Horse Marketing Co-operative was organized for the slaughter of horses and the processing of horsemeat for export. Plants were built at

Swift Current and Edmonton with the French and Japanese markets in mind. The co-operative's first contract was with the Belgian government for 10,000 tons of pickled horsemeat. Sales for canned meat for the United Nations relief programs began to decline in 1948 so attention was turned to the domestic market. Small *boucheries chevalines* appeared in many cities, including St. Boniface. Over a seven-year period, the two packing plants processed nearly a quarter million horses, a sad conclusion to a period when these noble beasts had been at the forefront of prairie farming.[25]

South Central Alberta Settlement

Leonard Van Tighem, an Oblate missionary who served multi-ethnic parishes in this southern dry belt, a successful horticulturalist and promoter of permanent irrigation through canal networks, could enter in his diary in 1905 that his efforts were being rewarded:

> Many people come to see our apple trees, loaded with apples, five trees bearing fruit; three crabs and two large sized. The Hon. Minister of Agriculture came also today, in company of Mr. MacGrath, Mayor Begin, and some other gentlemen. They were astonished when they came in the garden to see such fine fruit, apples and plums. These trees were planted in the spring of 1900.[26]

Van Tighem served mostly coalminers in the Lethbridge area, only a minority of them Belgians. His closest collaborator was William English of Bruges, manager of the local the Union Bank.[27] When Van Tighem was named to a chaplaincy in 1909, he left behind in Lethbridge a property surrounded by a fine shelter belt, a productive vegetable and flower garden, and flourishing orchard where there had been only dry bald prairie. He wrote, "I am just like a fish out of water.... I just wish to be in some small parish, with my people like in the old days of Lethbridge."[28]

Belgian investors had been attracted by the prospects of Calgary becoming the "Denver of the north." By 1901 it was already an important service and manufacturing centre, therefore. Consul E. H. Rouleau was quite proud to give Robert De Vos a tour of the important plants so that Calgary would receive a favourable mention in his impending report to the Ministry of Foreign Affairs in Brussels.[29] Rouleau was a prominent member of the small Francophone community and owner of the bloc of land known as Rouleauville, the embryonic settlement that expanded into Calgary. He had been named Belgian consul in November 1888 and served in that capacity until 1912. The influx of Belgian immigrants never surpassed a trickle.[30]

François Adam, a graduate engineer who in Jesuit college in Belgium had befriended several notable world leaders, including Ignace Jan Paderewski, came to recover his health in the North West Territories, armed with letters of reference from political and professional leaders. He contacted Prime Minister John A. Macdonald and William Van Horne of the CPR upon arrival. Consequently, he soon found himself in charge of building a section of the transcontinental line west of Calgary. In 1885, equipped with a team of horses and a wagon, Adam began a trek from Calgary which led him into the fur-trapping and fur-trading business just north of Edmonton. The following year, he began operating a trading post and a ranch at Duhamel mission, founded in 1882 by the Oblate missionaries on the Battle River. At that time, freighting by Red River cart was still a profitable business; therefore, Duhamel was an important stopping place between Fort Edmonton and Fort MacLeod. The fur trade was still of primary importance, so Adam as a wily entrepreneur ventured north of Edmonton at nine locations to purchase furs from Indians and trappers for resale. He soon came into stiff competition with the dominant Hudson's Bay Company and Révillon Frères.[31] He sold the bulk of his furs to the London company but kept back the prime pelts which he took in large consignments to London to be sold by auction. This he did for five years, the sales bringing him from $50,000 to $100,000 annually in competition with the venerable company. This also gave him the opportunity each year to visit family and friends in Belgium. On the fifth such voyage overseas he married a young woman who influenced him to invest in real estate.

The Adam ranch was transformed into a town site after François Adam learned that the CPR was planning to build a line into the area in 1905. He went to Winnipeg with a proposal to invest $100,000 in construction of a town site if the CPR promised to locate the railway station at the end of the proposed main street which would run along his property. The company agreed and Adam built twenty large commercial buildings, including the landmark Windsor Hotel, in what became Camrose. Adam realized further profits from his lumber yard because a building boom followed the arrival of the railway.

His friends in high places had enabled him to become wealthy, but his loyalty to his friends and his patriotic sentiments also caused his virtual bankruptcy. At the end of World War I, he undertook large shipments of cattle and foodstuffs to the hungry of his native Belgium and to Poland, where his old college friend Paderewski was prime minister. Political events and civil war in eastern Europe brought about the overthrow of Paderewski, the loss of Poland's best ports, and finally a Bolshevik invasion that resulted in the loss of Adam's considerable investment in aid. In 1921, Adam returned to the Peace River country and settled at Hythe. Camrose remained a permanent tribute to his enterprise but he does not appear to have encouraged his compatriots to settle there.[32]

Belgians were scattered throughout the area. In Lacombe, Eckville, and Ponoka, for example, there were a few families but they did not maintain any sustained communication with compatriots in other districts.[33] In the Castor area, several families settled and prospered. Albert Govaerts had the distinction of installing the first telephone in the community as well as having the first wind-powered electrical plant. But none captured the community's attention more than a certain Servius Coene, who filed for his homestead in 1908. On one occasion he disappeared for many weeks without warning and leaving no trace. His neighbours began to search for him, speculating that his meagre diet of bread, buttermilk and chewing tobacco must have failed to sustain him. When Louis Bierinckx thought they should auction his few personal effects for charity, Coene suddenly reappeared, explaining that in the interests of economy he had walked to Winnipeg on business, a journey that had taken a month in bitter winter weather.[34] Eccentrics and those unable to adjust to unfamiliar situations were not likely to succeed.

Only a few Belgians were involved with Dr. Tanche's utopian socialist commune established at Sylvan Lake, west of Red Deer, in 1906. This social experiment was inspired by an abortive coal miners' strike in northern France in 1905 and was based on the Fourier concept of Phalanstery, where urban dwellers learned to live together in a rural setting pursuing agricultural tasks for the common good. Tanche's colonists lived in one large building which served as living quarters for people, domestic animals and poultry. It was not a popular arrangement and the commune was dissolved within two years but some families remained in Alberta.

Pierre Féguenne, who had come to Canada in 1904, worked as a printer for the *Red Deer Advocate*, and he kept in touch with these immigrants. In 1909, he began doing some work for the University of Alberta, and in 1913 he opened his own printing business and launched *L'Union*, the only French weekly in Edmonton, in November 1917. The provincial French Canadian Association ACFA tried to buy his paper in 1928, and when he refused to sell ACFA launched *La Survivance*. Féguenne felt obliged to sell his paper in 1932 but he continued to specialize in job printing and publishing in French, German and Danish. He was recognized as one of the leading citizens in the small Belgian group within the larger Albertan Francophone community.[35]

In the Strathmore area, a few Belgians families were intermingled with the Dutch immigrants who took up CPR lands. They came at the solicitation of Father Van Aaken, a Dutch priest recruited in Montana in 1908 to promote Dutch and Flemish immigration. Upon arrival they were dismayed to find the fields unbroken and the irrigation works in a very primitive state. The colonizing priest soon disappeared. The Flemings formed a small inner group of eighty persons in the vicinity of the village and another ninety dispersed throughout the larger Dutch community. Joseph Desmet of Maulebeke, an uncle of Joseph Van Tighem, the manager of the Union Bank in Strathmore, opened his home to compatriots and mass was said there weekly by Father Camille Deman, who also served Catholics at Rockyford, Carbon, Langdon, Shepard and Chedale, so great was the shortage of bilingual priests.[36] A carpenter by trade, Desmet worked for the Canadian Pacific Land and Colonization Department building town sidewalks and bridges over irrigation channels. He eventually settled on a farm east of Strathmore.[37] None of these settlers had much capital, as family histories reveal. The Van Bavel family survived on the modest wages earned in construction of the irrigation system for the CPR. Pieter de Munta, a bachelor, lived in his root cellar in winter which was stocked with the savoy cabbage from his garden.[38] Some who lived on CPR lands, known as the Strathmore Farm, were unable to meet their annual payments and they had to beg for leniency but the Colonization Department of the railway company maintained a callous attitude toward these settlers who had in essence been misled. The Storduer family, for example, had made a down payment on their farm but they were unable to draw on their account in Belgium after the German invasion of 1914. They asked for a small refund in order to buy a team of horses but the only concession was the offer of "a team of horses from some of our culls, and a couple cows, on lien note," which would further indebt them. When the Cammaert family was unable to pay its tax bill, the CPR colonization manager paid the bill but took a chattel mortgage on all their possessions. The agent recalled that they owed a sum for seed grain they had received earlier. Consequently, Cammaert was given "some cows which he could feed his alfalfa, and turn the milk into the Strathmore Farm [and] have a portion of his cream cheques turned in against the cattle month by month."[39] The CPR Colonization Department was not very sympathetic to the problems of implantation that confronted these Belgians.

The challenges of pioneering in Alberta were vividly portrayed in a historically based novel *New Furrows* (1926). A Walloon-Flemish couple, assigned the names of Henri and Rachel Fourchette, were forced to leave their homeland because of terrible tenant farm conditions. Although most pioneering accounts failed to mention the prejudice and discrimination many immigrants experienced, the author of this novel was sensitive to Anglo-conformist pressures. On the ocean crossing they were made aware that they were destined to what was still a British colonial outpost, although "a certain amount of deference was shown them because they were Belgians and hence considered clean and thrifty, superior beings to those who came literally in hordes from Central Europe." There was an additional element in their favour: "Moreover they were going to take up land, had a little money, understood farming."[40] Once settled in the foothills of Alberta, they suffered successive crop failures from freak storms and prolonged drought. The attachment to land became obsessive and drove Henri insane. The Flemish wife held out with a martyr's determination, enduring hard work, loneliness and unimaginable dangers, the lot of many farm women at the time. The numerous children did not share the same attachment to land, nor dedication to hard work. They adopted new values and vainly dreamed of becoming wealthy. Only a daughter, Marie, saw the possibilities of success in a land and at a time when class distinctions abounded. The few established well-bred, well-educated, yet modestly wealthy, English families dominated social and political life. She concluded that through a combination of fortitude and industry with this dominant social ethos one could became a successful New Canadian.

Sugar Beet Growing

In 1902, Jesse W. Knight, a wealthy Utah mine owner, saw an opportunity to grow sugar beets under irrigation in the dry belt of the southern Alberta district of the North-west Territories. He obtained a tax exemption for twelve years as well as a sizeable government subsidy to launch the project.[41] His plan was designed also to stimulate Mormon colonization of the region but the American immigrants were not much interested in the intensive field work involved. The beets were grown from a multi-germ seed which produced several plants, consequently the rows had to be hand-thinned. Moreover, the seedlings had to be weeded sometimes as many as three times during a growing season. Finally, in the autumn, the beets were harvested by hand, the excess soil shaken off the roots, the leaves and crown cut away with hand tools. It was difficult to find workers for this back-breaking labour, so it was natural that a search should be directed to Flanders which provided experienced workers for northern France, Indiana and Michigan in the United States, and southwestern Ontario.[42]

Accordingly, James Ellison was sent to Belgium to recruit workers for the Knight Sugar Company. He was authorized to promise workers passage money and seasonal accommodation, as well as a house and a cow if they elected to settle permanently in the district. Soon there were complaints in Antwerp that the Knight Sugar Company agent gave travel vouchers to very few prospective employees, leaving others to find their own passage money.[43] Upon arrival in Alberta, many workers found that there was no adequate housing available and, in most cases, those who intended to settle permanently were never given any cows. The Belgian authorities became concerned at what they viewed as false advertising on the part of the sugar company and exploitation of field workers by the growers, identified specifically as Mormons.[44] Maximum production was reached in 1908, and thereafter there was a steady decline as it became increasingly difficult to recruit seasonal field workers. The twenty-seven Flemish families that came in 1912–13, for example, found that the company failed to honour its employment and housing engagements. Some workers had come to Raymond by way of South Bend, Indiana, where there was a sizeable Belgian community. When some families wished to return to Belgium, they were unable to do so because of lack of funds.[45] The tax exemption ran out in 1914, so Jesse Knight closed the refinery, dismantled it and moved it to the United States. The company alleged that it ceased operations because of "low beet prices, high grain prices, technical problems with beet raising, and lack of cheap labour."[46] The workers in the beet fields were left without jobs and bitter feelings toward both their employers and the Knight Sugar Company.[47]

By 1925 interest in beet growing was rekindled. The Utah-Idaho Sugar Company, a Mormon Church enterprise, opened a large modern sugar refinery in Raymond under the name Canadian Sugar Factories, The Mormon church had land settlement experience and was able to exercise a good measure of influence in southern Alberta because of its political influence and its participation in the dominant capitalist and corporate philosophies of colonizing projects in the West. Catholic workers felt insecure before such a missionary sense of social unity and the priests worried about the influence of Mormon social and sports activities on Catholic youth.[48]

The Canadian Sugar Factories held a monopoly of sugar production in the province and further entrenched its position through agreements with the beet farmers and the immigration authorities. The beet growers signed contracts committing them to deliver a certain tonnage of beets produced on a specified acreage at a price to be set by the refinery. Immigration regulations in P.C. 2668 in 1921 had been stiffened to require immigrants to be in possession of $250 upon landing. The United Farmers of Alberta, an agrarian protest movement, opposed immigration promoted by the railway and land companies, but the federal government still looked favourably on Belgians as "preferred" immigrants. The CPR collaborated in bringing out Belgian workers. The Lethbridge Northern Irrigation District was created and opened large tracts of land to cultivation through irrigation near Picture Butte and Iron Springs. An immigration agent in southern Alberta opined:

I may say that colonization of the Lethbridge Northern Irrigation district has been occupying a good deal of my time. There seems to be a sentiment with the Board of Trade Committee and the Immigration District Trustees that we would be better advised to get settlers from Central and Northern Europe than from Great Britain, or even the United States, for this project. The contention is that the Anglo-Saxon is more ready to give up and leave the land than is the European.[49]

By this time the beet industry was expanding into the Magrath district south of Lethbridge and Picture Butte north of the city.

Had working conditions improved after World War I? Field workers entered into contracts with the growers, their immediate employers, for fixed fees for each stage of field work and the stipulation that 30 per cent of the wages would be held back until completion of the harvest. Most contracts provided that growers would provide workers with suitable living accommodation. The immigrant workers almost invariably complained that the accommodation provided was in the order of a "shack," i.e., a granary, an old chicken coop, an abandoned house. This only added to the dissatisfaction caused by tedious seasonal work, low wages and isolation. In general, they were poor and ineligible for government relief and they lacked English-language skills. They were isolated and vulnerable and had little hope of satisfaction through recourse to the law. Laws existed primarily to maintain public order and to promote production rather than to guarantee worker protection.[50]

Did they fare any better than the Hungarian, Croatian and Slovak workers? Probably only to the extent that the Belgian authorities kept them informed about working conditions in Canada. When the commissioner of emigration in Antwerp learned from an agent of the Canadian Pacific Railways of a plan to recruit beet workers for southern Alberta, he informed the Minister of Foreign Affairs who in turn instructed the consul-general in Montreal to communicate with the consul in Edmonton to find out if it was preferable for workers to leave only with invitations and guarantees of work from family members or by blanket orders.[51] The CPR Superintendent of Colonization in London instructed the company agent in Antwerp, A.L. Robinson, to communicate with P.J. De Coster, Commissioner of Emigration for the Belgian government:

> In accordance with the arrangements made we are now endeavouring to arrange for one of the existing Boards in Southern Alberta to secure the co-operation of Belgian residents and organize the placement of Belgians especially in Sugar Belt work in Southern Alberta. As soon as this is made the Belgian Consul will be notified with the view of his reporting the arrangements made to his Government.[52]

But Belgian authorities were not convinced the negotiations were quite as represented. An established Alberta farmer named Camille Van Wassenhoven had started recruiting agricultural workers in Flanders. It was unclear if his efforts were related to the railway project: "I connect this affair to the present project, without at the same time having proof to support my supposition."[53]

Responses from consular officials were not altogether encouraging. Maurice Polet in Edmonton was not favourable to continued immigration to the sugar beet region of Alberta and did not think the irrigation project would prove successful. Charles Rochereau de La Sablière in Toronto warned about the proven disingenuousness of agents' promises, and A. Remes in Montreal believed bricklayers and electricians were in greater demand than farm labourers. But James Coley, who was in charge of railway colonization efforts in Calgary, encouraged Arthur De Jardin, consul in Winnipeg, to promote continued recruitment of beet workers in Flanders.[54]

How serious were the economic problems in the area in question? The experiences of the Ernest Holvoet family that arrived at Taber in 1927 may serve as an example of how to survive when only seasonal work was available. In addition to summer and fall work in the beet fields, they picked stones at fifty cents a day for the irrigation company that owned two thousand acres of the land under cultivation, and later they picked potatoes at ten cents a bag for local growers. Within a few years they bought their own farm, began to grow sugar beets and also vegetables on irrigated land for a local cannery. Holvoet was the first farmer in the district to own a beet topping machine and the first to have irrigation sprinklers instead of ditch.[55] The Holvoet success was a vindication of Father Leonard Van Tighem's dream when he exercised his ministry as a poor priest serving poor parishioners of different ethnic origins in a dwindling mining community during World War I. Van Tighem had had a vision of a productive community under irrigation in the region. When the depression struck Taber was actually beginning to enjoy more prosperity because of the expanded irrigation project.

There was a crisis in the sugar industry in the 1920s because of a world shortage and prices rose steeply. A government-appointed Board of Commerce tried briefly to fix retail prices but it had little success. Yet refineries continued to make handsome profits, until November 1920 when share-stocks of the sugar companies reached a low level as prices dropped from twenty-four cents to ten cents a pound. In 1931 the British Columbia Sugar Refineries Limited, owned by E.T. Rogers and operating Rogers Sugar Limited and Lantic Sugar Company, bought the Canadian Sugar Factories and planned to open plants in Picture Butte and Taber.[56] With consolidation came industrial strife and unrest on the sugar beet farms. Farm workers were without union protection and growers were somewhat at the mercy of the monopoly company. In 1930, the Communist Party of Canada organized the Farmers Unity League (FUL) to defend the interests of exploited farm workers. Eastern European beet workers were enthusiastic about union organization but the Flemish workers were more cautious participants. A Beet Workers' Industrial Union (BWIU) was formed and affiliated with the left-wing Farmers Unity League. The BWIU tried to form a united front of growers and hired labourers, but the Roger's company resisted all attempts to unionize farm workers and tried to sow discord between growers and field workers.[57]

The growers formed their own association to protect their interests so that there were three players in the drama that ensued – the unionized field workers, the associated growers, and the monopoly company. Confrontation erupted in 1935 when the BWIU demanded a wage of $22 per acre and better living accommodations. The Growers' Association ignored the union and offered workers on an individual basis a continuation of the $17 wage scale. The workers held out for better conditions by organizing a work stoppage. The provincial Minister of Agriculture opined that "we do not deny the right to organize on fundamental lines, but most of our growers believe the affiliation is a branch of the Communist Party." The implication was that because Communist organizers had promoted the union it was part of a Red plot to overthrow constituted authority and the free enterprise system. In fact, most beet growers came to terms with their workers offering a compromise settlement of $19 per acre.[58]

In 1936 the BWIU again demanded an improved wage of $21.50 per acre and signed up about 1,800 of the estimated 2,500 beet workers. The company held out for $20 an acre for thinning, hoeing, weeding and topping beets. E.T. Rogers out-manoeuvred the union by signing a profit-sharing agreement with the growers. Also, in 1936, a second refinery was opened at Picture Butte, north of Lethbridge. Once again there was a work stoppage and the growers decided to recruit "scab" workers. The Canadian Sugar Factories publicly threatened the union with the prospect of recruiting four hundred Belgian workers for the

Growers' Association. Frank Taylor was sent to St. Boniface to recruit field workers who had been employed by farmers who sent their sugar beets to the refinery in Grand Forks, North Dakota. These efforts resulted in about three hundred "scabs" coming to Alberta with the blessing of the provincial government, and being transported to the beet fields in buses chartered by the Growers' Association and protected by the police. The growers began evicting striking workers and their families: therefore, many of the workers went back to the fields. Fortunately, the harvest was large enough to provide paying for work by most of the original workers and the replacements. The BWIU realized that its affiliation with the Communist-oriented Farmers Unity League was a serious liability so it broke off its formal ties with the league. The Growers' Association still refused to deal with the BWIU, so the union appealed to the provincial government for recognition as a legally constituted union. The Alberta Board of Industrial Relations ruled that the beet workers were "farm labour" and therefore did not come under the statutes and regulations that were supposed to protect industrial workers.[59]

During the drought and the Depression the sugar beet industry contributed to a degree of economic stability in the Lethbridge area. Local irrigation works proved extremely valuable. The acreage under sugar beets increased from 4,845 hectares in 1930 to 8,692 hectares in 1939. A regional historian commented: "The completion of a second sugar factory in 1936 stimulated increased production; its expansion was limited only by the industry's inability to persuade housewives that beet sugar was as sweet as cane sugar. Many continued to use imported cane sugar to make preserves."[60] Belgian growers and field workers became scarce as there was a concerted effort by Mormons to buy up farmland around Lethbridge. The provincial police handled suspected organizers of farm labourers "without gloves" and regularly began arresting them on charges of vagrancy.[61]

During World War II the production of beet sugar once again became important. The BWIU reappeared as an affiliate of the Canadian Congress of Labour, and the Rogers monopoly undermined unionization by obtaining cheap Japanese labour from the internment camps of the British Columbia Security Commission. In 1950, Rogers Sugar Limited built a refinery in Taber, which remained in production until 1998. In 1956 a joint committee of the Alberta Sugar Beet Growers and the Canadian Sugar Factories recommended recruiting three hundred families for field work but immigration officials believed that number was unreasonable because of "the increase of mechanization in the sugar beet industry both in thinning and hoeing and also in harvesting."[62] G. M. Mitchell, immigration officer stationed in Brussels, was certain he could "secure agricultural families from the Flemish part of the country" but a spokesman for the Alberta Sugar Beet Growers warned:

> These people, however, are quite cautious and insist upon having a contract in hand before leaving for a new home. One of the terms insisted upon is guaranteed year-round employment for the family head for a period of one year.[63]

The sugar company and the provincial authorities thought the plan to find fifty families who would meet these conditions was sound, but they did not count on wariness that past experiences had created in the Belgian community and its network overseas. The plant in Raymond was closed in 1963, and the one in Picture Butte was finally shut down in 1978. The refinery at Taber was unable to attract Belgian field workers or factory workers. The success of the Flemish nationalist organization, Vlamingen in de Wereld, in supplying seasonal labour in southwestern Ontario beet and tobacco fields was not replicated in southern Alberta.

Northern and Peace River Country Settlements

The Athabasca district of the North West Territories was initially fur-trading country, its commercial activity dominated by the Hudson's Bay Company, and mission country as Oblate priests, among them a number of Belgians, staffed isolated mission posts. In 1821 Fort Edmonton became the dominant centre of the western fur trade. St. Albert, founded in 1861 by Father Albert Lacombe, was the chief mission centre and eventually hub of the Francophone community. In 1867 an unofficial "republic of St. Albert" was put in place by Father Lacombe and lasted a decade until the arrival of the North West Mounted Police. The St. Albert Code of by-laws was enacted by nine elected committee members who served as a kind of legislative body for an executive consisting of a *chef du pays* and two councillors. In 1870 the region became part of Canada as the North West Territories.[64]

The prospects for northern agricultural settlement were first considered in 1888. Senator John Schultz chaired a senate committee inquiring into the potential resources of the Mackenzie Basin. Schultz, who had been a leader of the Canadian Party that opposed Louis Riel and the Métis at Red River in 1869–70, was a western expansionist hostile to Catholics and Francophones. He was impressed by the agricultural possibilities of the Peace River country. The problem was that the fertile area was separated by about 400 kilometres of non-arable land from the few settlements along the North Saskatchewan River.[65]

French Canadians started a bloc settlement anchored on the old Métis settlement of St. Albert. Colonies were added at Morinville, Legal, Beaumont and Rivière-Qui-Barre. In the 1890s there were a few isolated Belgian families at these settlements as well as at Ray and Edmonton.[66] In 1897 in the Edmonton and Wetaskiwin districts there were 112 Belgians who had filed for thirty-five homesteads, had 460 acres in crops and owned 380 head of cattle. Others had settled successfully at St. Peter, Fort Saskatchewan, Stony Plain and Vegreville.[67]

In 1901, Robert De Vos visited the northern region and met many Belgian immigrants who seemed quite satisfied with pioneer conditions. He reported on several practical measures that these early arrivals had adopted. The Baert family from West Flanders had sent a son to scout out conditions in 1899, where the Verstraete and Van den Houte families were settled, before deciding to emigrate. Camile Verstraete had come to St. Albert in 1885 to raise horses, shipping several boatloads of purebreds to Belgium, thus maintaining ties with the home country.[68] Van den Houte spent the winters cutting wood to accumulate enough cash to buy a farm. Van Ackere had rented land from a colonization company but soon came to the conclusion he would do well to buy a farm outright rather than rent land. De Vos concluded:

> It should be pointed out that all the Belgians I met told me they were happy to be independent and no longer to have to work, according to their laconic expression [in Flemish]: to begin with for the lords and taxes and afterwards only for the children.[69]

Morinville he referred to as a Franco-Belgian colony because of the number of Belgians settled there but he had time only for a superficial visit so was unable to make any assessment of the state of implantation.

As was the case in other regions, chain migration as illustrated in the Behiels family history was a common experience:

> Joseph Behiels came to Canada in 1893 from Antwerp, Belgium, on a cattle boat. Mr. Louis Van Acres had hired Dad to help and care for his cattle during the two-weeks crossing. It was also necessary to bail water out of the boat at times. Upon landing in Canada they proceeded to travel to Edmonton stopping to rest at government shelters enroute. In those days the government put up shelters or rest places every thirty or forty miles for pioneers to stop to rest at. My Dad was nineteen years old, a strong young man with a vision of adventure.[70]

Young Behiels worked for Van Acres at Fort Saskatchewan until he had sufficient money in 1898 to file for a homestead near the Soetart and de Dobbelaere families not far from Morinville. By this time he had been joined by his parents and five siblings, all of whom left for Watson, Saskatchewan, in 1903 because they preferred open parklands to clearing bush. Joseph Behiels took up dairy farming and prospered, raising fourteen children in a twelve-roomed three-storey house.[71]

There was considerable mobility at the time as early pioneers sometimes decided to pull up stakes. Two notable examples were the Vandenberghes who moved to Detroit and the Laremys who took up ranching in South Dakota. In 1892, John and Edward Borle planned to take up sheep-ranching in Australia but literally missed their boat, so they came to Edmonton instead. Edward Borle farmed in the Ray district and John at Rivière-Qui-Barre. Their brother Pierre visited the area in 1895 and returned with his large family two years later, along with a nephew, Adolph Rommelaere. Perre Borle left farming and took his family to Edmonton in 1907, where he bought the Parisienne Café and built a large livery barn which proved profitable. Apparently he preferred village life because after three years he returned to Ray, bought a hotel and livery barn, built a general store and was awarded the post office. The Borles all had large families, the children usually marrying into other Belgian families so that a large network of relatives evolved. On a visit to

Belgium, Pierre Borle spoke so glowingly of life in northern Alberta that the Omer Victoor family joined them in Ray, adding to the community.[72] Small towns sometimes aspired to become cities through a combination of public and private interests. There was an ideology that depicted the cities as dangerous, immoral and selfish in contrast to "that which uplifts the community – the activities of the businessmen, the church news, the civic good accomplished by women, school gatherings ... the simple annals of the great common people who are really the foundation of this broad country of ours."[73]

The family histories of some of these "great common people" illustrate the networking and cooperation that enabled them to survive and succeed in a great lone land:

> ...Joseph Clotin came to Canada in 1906 with the understanding that if it was a good country he would let Theodore Jacobs know. Mr. Clotin and wife came to Morinville and sent back word to Belgium that there was plenty of land to rent. Mr. Jacobs and his family followed in the fall of 1907.[74]

Theodore Jacobs, his wife and four sons left their prosperous inn near Brussels convinced that a European war was brewing, so they settled on a homestead near Egg Lake. Three of the sons quickly founded a brickyard near St. Albert.[75] That same year, the Jacobs took in the six members of the Henri Verbeek family until they found lodgings and were provided with seed grain and the offer by a French Canadian neighbour to plant their first crop. The municipality offered him a job doing roadwork at $1.50 a day, a wage which helped him provide for his family. The year their mortgage fell due, a hailstorm wiped out their crops but compatriots came to their rescue.[76]

The reception at Rivière-Qui-Barre was particularly warm as all these immigrants also spoke French, the dominant language of the community. René Boddez had a family of nine children when he left Ichetyken, but they all soon felt at home when neighbours welcomed them. The presence of a Flemish-speaking priest, Father Charles Okhuysen, was a further comfort to the immigrants. Joseph Verhulst arrived in Edmonton in 1913 in a boxcar, met a compatriot who farmed near Villeneuve, and was soon settled on his own farm. He later moved to Rivière-Qui-Barre, and when the Depression struck it was several Boddez families who helped his family.

These Belgians had no formal ethnic association to give them a sense of solidarity but they maintained contact with each other and displayed a strong degree of mutual care and assistance in the face of adversity.[77]

Not all who arrived in these rural communities had been farmers in Belgium. In 1906, Gentiel Van Brabant, a brother in the Oblate order, arrived at St. Paul-des-Métis, a reserve organized by Father Albert Lacombe in 1896. In 1907, Adélard Thérien the parish priest and manager of the Métis colony, obtained the support of Frank Oliver, Minister of the Interior, to open the reserve to French Canadians. Van Brabant left the Oblates and took up a homestead.[78] Another Oblate brother who obtained a dispensation from his vows was Henri Van Tighem, who married in 1919, worked for five years at Lac la Biche on the Dunvegan or Northern Alberta Railway, then in Edmonton as a hospital worker, carpenter and real estate agent. In 1927 he took up farming at Rivière-Qui-Barre, while continuing his original trade of carpentry, building fine homes and churches.[79]

A Brussels university graduate in foreign languages, Joseph DeWetter, who arrived in 1908, worked for the Brewster Company, a ranching enterprise that supplied pack animals to surveying parties. A correspondent recalled:

> He received a degree in languages and spoke several fluently. I remember when people would bring letters to him for translation because they had forgotten how to read the language after being away from their native lands. The Government Agent and the Provincial Police often asked him to act as interpreter.[80]

In 1911 he was joined by his brother Frank DeWetter and they went over the Edson Trail to Pouce Coupé where they began farming.

In 1899, Father J.A. Lemieux obtained a tract of land from the Department of the Interior in the Peace River country. He organized the Peace River Land and Colonization Company to settle Francophones in what was conceived as a triangular bloc bounded by what became Peace River, Joussard and Spirit River, with Falher in the centre. The project was largely a failure because of the poor quality of the land, the lack of good transportation links, and the difficulty to find recruits.[81] Interest was somewhat rekindled in 1903 after Professor John Macoun, botanist son of James Macoun, undertook a survey of the Peace River country for the Geological Survey of Canada. He observed:

> While the country ... should not be settled by either the rancher or the grower of wheat until there is more satisfactory evidence that it is suited for either of these pursuits, it may be safely prophesied that after railways have been built there will be only a very small part of it that will not afford homes for hardy northern people who, never having had much, will be satisfied with little.[82]

Belgians were regarded by the immigration agents as a 'northern people' but not all were poor, as we have seen, upon arrival in Alberta. It was later observed that the region had been glaciated several times and consequently the soils were relatively thin and subject to erosion. There was usually adequate rainfall and snow cover and much less evaporation from the soil surface than on the prairie grasslands. The soil seemed sufficiently fertile to sustain mixed farming and even grain growing. The stage was set for settlement.[83]

A Société de la Colonisation de l'Alberta was created in 1912 by French Canadian community leaders in Edmonton. They opened a bureau on the city's main street but failed to establish a satisfactory network of agencies out of province to achieve their objective of recruiting in Europe as well as Quebec and New England. Grouard was to be the focus of settlement in anticipation of the arrival of the Edmonton, Dunvegan and British Columbia Railway to Lesser Slave Lake and steamer connection to the town. But the railway passed ten kilometres south of the town, which rapidly went into decline. The Dominion Lands office and many other buildings were dismantled and moved to towns on the railway line. There was suspicion the railway company wanted to build its own divisional point and deliberately bypass the Francophone centre.[84]

Between 1926 and 1930 the Francophone bloc near McLennan extended to the Falher and Donnelly districts. Among the Francophones were a number of Flemish families who introduced apiculture, which became so successful that soon there were 35,000 beehives around Falher. The Belgians were also interested in small business enterprises such as operating a garage, a general store, or an implement dealership. Mixed farming was still attractive. Jules Dechief and his son, for example, each took up a homestead at Girouxville in 1928. They had previously farmed at Lampman, Saskatchewan, but decided to move out of the dry belt. Although not officially a "return man," Dechief recruited the Joseph Deschepper family from Antwerp.[85]

By 1930 the bloc settlement period was coming to an end according to an immigration report:

> ... solid colonies of persons of the same nationality are in the minority, which means that a general mixture of nationalities of all kinds has taken place. The principle object of those coming here is to find a homestead which will prove productive and very little attention has been paid to block settlement.[86]

Belgians had come mainly as part of family and village migration or Catholic immigration projects. Throughout the 1930s there was a marked decline in homestead entries throughout the West in what has been called the "land-use shakedown." On the other hand, in the Peace River country the population increased and there was consolidation as those who remained increased their farm size.[87]

Communist leader Tim Buck arriving at Nordegg mine, 1935. (Glenbow NA-2635)
Many Belgian coal miners turned to Communist organizers to improve their working conditions.

CHAPTER VI: THE MINING FRONTIER AND PACIFIC RIM

As Belgians moved onto the third prairie level, the foothills of the Rockies, and British Columbia, they became aware of opportunities in mining, notably the collieries. In the Far West, activity began as a coastal intrusion moving inland along the Fraser riverine entrance. The Fraser gold rush attracted European attention after 1858 but coal-mining on Vancouver Island, which flourished from 1876 to 1910 attracted Walloon workers with experience in its extraction. Western Canada, perceived in certain quarters as a land of unbounded resources, was likely to possess rich mineral deposits waiting to be discovered. In 1882, the Dominion government began selling coal rights in districts believed to be likely centres of a future coal industry. This interest in coal was based on the need for anthracite coal by the railway companies for their steam locomotives and the demand for bituminous coal for domestic heating. Exploration tended "to confirm the opinion that the coal fields of the North-West may be regarded as practically inexhaustable."[1] The important mining areas that attracted Belgian workers and some investors were Turtle Mountain, Estevan, Crowsnest Pass, Lethbridge, Nordegg and Drumheller. In all these areas, as throughout North America, between 1880 and 1910, mining technology changed with the introduction of undercutting machinery and the extensive use of blasting. The degree of experience and training previously demanded of workers was less important and the supply of unskilled immigrant labour grew. In these circumstances, management tended to downgrade safety precautions.[2] In addition to the dangers associated with mining, there were the hardships of life in isolated company towns, the loneliness and alienation of foreign workers in a strange new land. The proliferation of taverns and brothels in mining communities were symtoms of a serious social dislocation. Even a respectable company such as the CPR proposed on one occasion to relocate the brothels of Cranbrook as a service to the community.[3]

The experiences in the various mining communities were intimately related to industrial unions and socialist organizations, as had been the case in Belgium. By the end of the nineteenth century, there were attempts in Western Canada to build a broad-based working-class movement by the Western Federation of Miners. But the combined power of the mining companies and the provincial and Dominion governments thwarted their efforts. The mainstream churches also tended to support management and the established order.[4] Mining was arduous work in unpleasant and unsafe conditions. Manual labour with hand tools was the chief means of production. Wages were based on contract coal tonnage. Management came mainly from Great Britain but Belgian skilled workers, especially engineers, were in great demand.[5] Seniority was virtually unknown as employees were hired and fired at will, child labour was not uncommon, mines operated erratically in response to demands for coal, and maiming and fatal accidents were all too prevalent. The immigrant workers were in a difficult position as they sometimes could not communicate with management, so were afraid of losing their jobs and therefore often deferred to their bosses. Often isolated because of their mother tongue, their traditions, their race and religion, they avoided confrontations with management as much as possible. Confrontations could lead to dismissal, to eviction from company housing, or even deportation as "criminals." That confrontations did occur was in itself a testimonial to the abysmal working conditions to which they were subjected.[6]

On Vancouver Island early settlement was more urban-oriented than rural-based. The first Belgians that arrived on Vancouver Island were missionaries from the Oregon Territory, many recruited through the American College in Louvain.[7] The Sisters of Ste. Anne, who came from Quebec, opened a girls' school, and the Oblate missionaries started a mission at Esquimalt. In 1863 St. Louis College was founded for the education of the boys in the small colony. As early as 1858, the Francophone population seemed sufficiently numerous to induce Count Paul de Garro to launch the newspaper Le *Courrier de la Nouvelle-Calédonie*. He abandoned the project after nine issues, realizing there were few subscribers and advertisers. In 1890 Belgians became involved in the development of the agricultural potential of the Okanagan valley which developed into the most prosperous fruit-growing area in Western Canada.[8]

Klondike Gold Rush

Reports of gold deposits in the Yukon reached Ottawa in 1886. A decade later, the discovery of gold at Bonanza Creek incited the Dominion government to put in place regulations that imposed "a tradition of authority, of rules and regulations established from outside" the immediate community.[9] An order-in-council of 18 January 1898 entitled any person over eighteen years of age to stake creek or bench claims after obtaining a free miner's certificate, to fish, hunt and cut timber for actual necessities of food and shelter. The Belgian community in St. Boniface became particularly interested in the Klondike and a number of men planned to proceed by way of Edmonton because it was the closest place to the Yukon by railroad. The longer "water route" down the Mackenzie was more practical than the shorter all-Canadian "overland route."[10] Edmonton became the important supply centre for groups setting off for the gold fields. Lodging and information were available at the Roman Catholic mission at St. Albert. In the summer of 1898, Adolphe, Camille and Alphonse Van Walleghem of St. Boniface and Hector Buydens of Swan Lake set off for Edmonton, proceeded to Athabasca Landing on a gumbo mud road, down the Athabasca and Slave rivers by paddle-wheel to Great Slave Lake, then down the Mackenzie river to Fort McPherson. The three Van Walleghem brothers worked for mining operators placer mining, and once they had enough money and nuggets, they descended the Yukon river to Skagway. From there they took shipping to Seattle and were back in St. Boniface in the autumn of 1900, much wiser and a little richer.[11]

Several Belgians decided that in addition to looking for gold they could profit by bringing up a herd of cattle to the Klondike. Edouard Fearon of Maple Creek drove a large herd of beef cattle over the Whitehorse Pass to Dawson City. A local historian noted: "Fresh beef was in the nature of a God-send to a mining community and they gladly paid a dollar a pound for Mr. Fearon's beef, which seemed to have dropped mysteriously from the clouds."[12] The most spectacular cattle drive was undertaken by Charles and Peter Bossuyt, accompanied by Jules Van Walleghem, Jules

Turenne and M. Lafrance. They left St. Boniface on 2 June 1898 with 150 head of cattle, four hundred sheep and fifty ponies. Charles Bossuyt had invested heavily to buy these animals for the venture, a move that greatly disappointed the abbé Willems because Bossuyt was no longer able to pay off the debt of the parish of St. Alphonse.[13] Among their many adventures was the purchase of a sawmill at Rapide-des-Cinq-Doigts so they could build barges to proceed with their cargoes. The party of twenty-two individuals arrived at destination on 23 October 1898, a trip that had taken five months. Charles Bossuyt and his daughter Marie, known locally as "Klondike Eva," ran a store but this business went bankrupt when many of the gold seekers were unable to pay the large bills they accumulated. He then became a butcher, remained in Dawson City, and appears to have gambled away much of his earnings.[14]

By the summer of 1899, the area had been virtually panned out and only a few still found the gold they sought. Still the lure of the Klondike stirred the Belgian community in St. Boniface. Florent Boone, Jules Decraene and Constant Defort decided to try their luck but they returned by the following year, quite disappointed that they had gone down too late.[15] They had also failed to consider that "supplies and all that is required [for success] are very expensive."[16] The day of the individual miner and the romance of great fortunes was short-lived and was making way for a new era of large-scale mining, dredge-working and hydraulicing. The few Belgians involved in the Klondike Gold Rush were unaware of its wider repercussions, such as alleged "gross immorality" in Dawson City,[17] the ruin of many adventurers " misled into a vast wilderness,"[18] and complaints about "the aboriginal population who were mistreated, robbed and insulted."[19]

Vancouver Island Collieries

Three factors led to the arrival of a contingent of Belgian miners from Hainaut province in 1888 to the coal mines of Vancouver Island. Firstly, there were serious economic and political crises in Belgium. The region experienced a severe economic depression after 1875 marked by industrial shutdowns, unemployment, and a rising cost of living. In 1886, when violence erupted in the Charleroi region and desperate men and women pillaged the chateaux of the mine owners, cruel repression followed, leaving the best alternative for many miners from Roux, Couillet and

Jumet to pursue an offer from the Knights of Labour to seek employment abroad in Pennsylvania, Nova Scotia, or British Columbia. François Carpent, one of the leaders of the workingmen's union accused in the "Grand Complot," went to see Paul Watelet in Thuin to arrange for emigration to Canada.[20] The second factor was the demand on Vancouver Island for experienced mine workers. Coal was first mined on the island in 1836 to supply coastal steamers. Among the miners employed by the Hudson's Bay Company was a Scotsman named Robert Dunsmuir who, upon discovering a rich seam near Nanaimo in the 1850s, established his own mine and eventually built the company town of Wellington. Initially, workers might not have found the conditions in the Dunsmuir mines as bad as those from which they came. They would later change their opinion. Thirdly, there was a favourable image projected in Belgium of conditions in the Vancouver Island mines. Baron Etienne Hulot vaunted the mineral wealth of mainland British Columbia and the coal resources of Vancouver Island. In a travel book he wrote:

> These coal deposts are the largest in the two Americas. Nanaimo, centre of the operations, situated across from New Westminster, will soon have the monopoly of coal sales on the Pacific coast.[21]

Hulot saw the advantage of monopolized control from the viewpoint of the employer, not the fear of the employees that it might encourage exploitation of the work force. Paul Watelet, immigration agent for the Bureau Central Canadien in Thuin, promised a group of workers whom he would accompany to Canada that they could expect a remuneration five or six times the amount paid in the Hainaut mines.[22] Watelet corresponded frequently with John Jessop, the federal government immigration agent in Victoria, where the official report was that the "labour market has been highly satisfactory for the greater part of the year. From midsummer to December every man able and willing to work had the opportunity to do so."[23]

Despite some negative comments and some troubling events, a flow of Belgian miners continued. Upon learning that Paul Watelet was bringing out more workers, Henri Devaux wrote from the mining town of Wellington to several Belgian newspapers warning that miners ought to beware of agents who "promise more butter than bread" because he and his sons, like several compatriots, had spent two costly weeks without work upon arrival and subsequently had worked only sporadically. Four Belgians had just returned from job hunting in the Rockies where there was little permanent work available. Those thinking of emigrating "would do better to write to a friend in America rather than inquire of an agent." They should be aware of expensive ocean passage and railway fares because the Dunsmuir collieries were "not disposed to send tickets, either free or to be refunded after arrival and getting to work." The immigration officer in Victoria regretted this intransigence because Belgians were "a desirable class of people, sober, steady, industrious and moral."[24]

In January 1899, an explosion at No. 5 pit of the Wellington mine killed seventy-seven miners, including four Belgian explosive experts. Robert Dunsmuir, as president of the provincial Executive Council, had successfully opposed in the provincial legislature amendments to the Mines Regulation Act that would have required monthly inspection. The coroner's inquest blamed careless miners for the explosion and the miners in turn blamed the Chinese workers, who were at the very bottom of the wage scale.[25] A group of 150 Belgian workers decided at this point to organize their own Republican League, not to fight for better working conditions in Canada, but to support the Parti Socialiste-Républicain in Hainaut in opposition to the cooperative movement sponsored by the Parti Ouvrier Belge. They pledged they would:

> … take a steamship and go directly to take up the struggle for
> the General Strike which will extend throughout Belgium by
> the exploited against the exploiters.[26]

A certain Joseph Geulette testified that compatriots had been forced to leave Belgium because they "were always hunted down like wild animals by Leopold II and his tax collectors."

> All these exiles because of miserable conditions swore to me that
> Belgian soil would never sully their feet before the time came
> for the Socialist Republicans to chase away the supporters of
> the tax collectors and before the coming of Universal Suffrage
> which will emancipate the People and provide us with the
> reforms necessary to resolve the great social problem.[27]

The anticlerical character of the movement was also indicated by the observation that instead of the "superstitions of a future life" direct political action in the present time was required. Nevertheless, at first, Belgian miners were not perceived by immigration officials as labour agitators and anticlerical syndicalists.

The opening of the Comox mine under Dunsmuir management would "ensure employment for all the Belgian miners" because of the favourable reports concerning "their work, care and economy in the use of explosives being one of their characteristics." The 1889 report by John Jessop in Victoria was that they were doing "reasonably well."

> The best proof that they are contented with their prospects is that on the recommendation of those already in the collieries, many of their friends and relations are constantly arriving. Coming in small parties these miners, if steady, industrious and experienced, will find no difficulty in obtaining work in the Union colliery all through the incoming year.[28]

Not many months elapsed before Belgian miners became aware that many of the adverse working conditions experienced in southern Belgium also existed in British Columbia. A lockout at Wellington in January 1889 moved workers to form a Miners' and Mine Labourers' Protective Association in February to press for conditions similar to those enjoyed by many organized American miners. Following the death of Robert Dunsmuir in April, his widow Joan Dunsmuir, as sole owner of the company, now managed by son James, took a determined stand against union activity. On 17 May 1890, six hundred Nanimo workers were joined by Wellington workers in a solidarity parade to win an eight-hour day. The work stoppage was countered by a lockout. On 30 May, eviction orders were issued, on Mrs. Dunsmuir's orders, to families that lived in company cottages. The Victoria *Colonist* painted the picture of wild-eyed "foreign revolutionaries" ready to upset the established order and supported the plan to hire strike-breakers, or "scabs," as replacement workers. By early August, fifty armed militiamen were sent in from Victoria because "a very excitable lot of men are the Belgians and there are very few constables."[29] The lockout continued fifteen months until in November 1891 the workers felt obliged to accept work on Dunsmuir's terms. Several Belgians, testifying before the British Columbia Legislative

Assembly's Select Committee on the Wellington strike, enumerated many serious grievances. Labour historian David Bercuson has contextualized the growing labour radicalism at this juncture:

> Their struggle with the boss did not begin with the morning whistle and end when the shift was over, because the entire area was company property. They lived with the company every hour of the day and night. They were grouped together to face a common enemy above ground and kept close together to face the common danger of gas, coal dust, rockfalls, below ground. They were isolated in their lives, in their work and in their too often violent deaths.[30]

When James Dunsmuir became premier in 1900, the only labour response was political action. Five local socialist organizations were consolidated in 1902 into the Socialist Party of British Columbia. The following year, it succeeded in having two members elected to the legislature from the mining districts of Vancouver Island. Disgruntled miners organized a cell of the Western Federation of Miners, an American union based in Denver, that called strikes at the Extension mine at Ladysmith and at the Union mine near Comox. Dunsmuir closed the Extension mine and evicted miners from company housing. William Lyon Mackenzie King, as editor of the *Labour Gazette*, portrayed Dunsmuir as a "selfish millionaire who has become something of a tyrannical autocrat" bent on making "serfs of a lot of free men." King was appointed secretary of the Royal Commission to Inquire into Industrial Disputes in the Province of British Columbia. The commissioners singled out Belgians as active organizers of protest marches and unionization drives.[31]

The Socialist Party members were re-elected to the legislature in 1904 and held the balance of power in the assembly, so they were able to extract amendments to the Coal Mines Regulations Act and to secure an eight-hour work day for the miners.[32] Dunsmuir remained firm in his views but the workers and their sympathizers saw themselves as "underpaid decent clean-faced miners" opposed by "villainous, bloodless owners."[33] On the other hand, the honorary Belgian consul in Victoria, T. Smith, observed blandly that the Belgians in the province "are nearly all working in the collieries of Nanaimo: they are good workers and satisfy their bosses." Most of his report consisted in comments on the extensive imports from

Belgium – cement, as used in the key bridge across the Fraser at New Westminster, iron and steel products for the railways in particular, and glass for general use. He noted that in addition to miners a few other specialized workers were immigrating, and they needed to be alerted to the fact that when coming on contract non-fulfillment of the conditions of employment on their part could result in imprisonment in Canada.[34] The report failed to describe the experience of the Belgian miners who by this time had decided to participate in the formation of a Syndicalist League of North America, whose objective was to set aside political organization in favour of "getting inside the labour movement" and employing the union to achieve a working-class "revolution."

There was plenty of strike action as the miners fought the "coal barons" in Nanaimo, Ladysmith and Extension mines from September 1912 to 19 August 1914. The United Mine Workers of America (UMWA), which had entered British Columbia in 1906 during a strike at an Ashcroft mine, backed the Vancouver Island miners and provided them with strike pay. Protest marches resulted in the provincial government sending in a thousand militiamen in the summer of 1913 "to restore order." Numerous arrests followed and Belgians became active in the organization of a Miners Liberation League to seek the release of imprisoned workers, following what they described as a "state invasion" of working-class people by violent strike-breakers hired by the capitalists. It was a re-play of the violence of the 1880s in Hainaut province in their collective memory. The outbreak of World War I and the cessation of strike pay briefly ended the confrontations.[35] On 6 February 1915, the South Wellington colliery, where numerous Belgians worked, was suddenly deluged by water from an adjacent abandoned and flooded mine, drowning nineteen men. Six days before the disaster, a mine inspector had been assured that the abandoned mine was at least two hundred metres distant when in fact it was only a metre or so distant.[36] By 1919, most of the Belgian workers had left. Only fifty-four remained in mining along with four explosive experts who were likely employed by the coal mines.[37] Strikes resumed in the 1920s and workers won the right of collective bargaining but the employers refused to collect union dues for the Mine Workers' Union of Canada, an affiliate of the Communist Party of Canada.[38]

We know little about the daily lives of these Belgian miners. Those who first came were described as "bachelor immigrants." They appear to have been employed especially as engineers in charge of blasting and as experienced workers in timbering the tunnels and hewing the coal. They were better paid than the drivers, pushers and cleaners. When families came they were housed by the company so that accommodations could become an instrument of control. Miners had to purchase their own lamps, work boots, and even explosive powder. Insurance against accidents was obtainable from the Ancient Order of Foresters but was very costly. There is no record of any women working in these coal mines, as was the case in Belgium at the time.[39] But coal miners' wives played an important role in supplementing family income through gardening and frugal management of the home. A cow, a few chickens and pigs could be raised on a five-acre lot.[40]

In Nanaimo, families saw the economic advantage of mining as an occupation in which boys would contribute to family income by working alongside a father. In 1877, education officials reported poor school attendance, truancy and lack of candidates for the high school entrance examination.

> At an early age boys are able to earn in the mines (at employment requiring neither strength nor skill) almost as much wages as are given to adults in the Atlantic region. There is thus an inducement for parents to send their boys to work as soon as they are legally entitled to do so.[41]

Ten years earlier, the situation at Wellington had been linked directly to the instability and volatility of working conditions in the community.

> Family difficulties, arising out of the unfortunate colliery strike and disputes, have seriously retarded school progress in the district during the year. The result has been a very large amount of irregularity, a low average, and little or no advancement among the pupils.[42]

In Vancouver Island mining communities there seemed little to be gained from schooling beyond basic literacy. From young adolescence, boys often worked alongside a father or neighbour. During a Legislative Inquiry in 1891, such a case was reported. Edmund Wilmer at Wellington admitted he employed an under-age son in the mine where he worked, but he denied cheating the boy of his wages. "After paying him $2.50, I was

always making $3 or $4 myself – after paying the boy company wages."
Of course, the money may simply have gone into the family income, as was
customary for both this occupational group and Belgian family practice at
the time.[43] These miners were not very occupationally or socially mobile
in the late nineteenth and early twentieth centuries.

Small Prairie Mines

The fact that rich gold lodes were discovered in northern Ontario, and
reportedly at a later date in the Duck Mountains of Manitoba and near
Edmonton, stimulated the search for the shiny yellow metal but only
poor quality, dusty lignite was found that served as a domestic fuel and
became known popularly as "Souris coal."[44] A certain Mr. Voden began
extracting coal on his homestead in the Turtle Mountains of southwestern
Manitoba in 1885 by sinking a vertical shaft twelve metres deep into
lignite seams. Settlers could obtain mining permits to extract coal on their
property in return for the payment to the government of ten cents per ton
of lignite, twenty-five cents per ton for bituminous coal, and twenty cents
per ton for anthracite.[45] The Manitoba Coal Company, formed in 1889
to develop regional mines, ceased operations after three years because
no commercial quantities were discovered. Consul De Vos reported that
Souris coal sold for $3.75 a ton in Winnipeg, while the Estevan coal sold
in Regina for $3.50 a ton. Grain elevator operators in each village usually
operated a coal shed where farmers and villagers could buy this coal.[46] In
the 1930s, there was a second wave of excitement as modest mines were
started in the Deloraine area. The Deloraine Coal Company, the Turtle
Mountain Coal Company and the Goodlands Coal Company all aroused
the hopes of the Belgian farmers in the area.

A contingent of nineteen Belgian miners, dissatisfied with their
contracts in the Maritime provinces, headed for a mine operated by
the Anthracite Coal Company west of Calgary. Consul General Van
Bruyssel stopped them in Winnipeg because the company had closed
down operations following a dispute between American and Canadian
shareholders, leaving 250 men unemployed. He obtained reduced railway
fares through the Canadian immigration authorities so the group could
continue to the Vancouver Island mines.[47] By June 1892, the Anthracite
Coal Company mine was back in operation and requested Van Bruyssel to
recruit fifty experienced miners, but he warned recruits to sign contracts

guaranteeing their return fare in case of work stoppages. Another contingent of Belgian miners from New Brunswick that arrived in Calgary refused the work offered them by the Canadian Pacific Railway Company because of the inadequate housing provided. Consul Rouleau in Calgary did what he could to resolve the dispute. Foreign Affairs in Brussels was informed of the situation:

> We had first offered them, following my approach to the Deputy Minister of the Interior in Ottawa, work in the mines of Canmore, Alberta, and they refused. They have been fed up to the present time by Mr. Rouleau [Consul in Calgary] and Mr. Pirmez, one of our ranching compatriots near Calgary.[48]

Coal-mining started around Willow Bunch, Coronach and Bengough in the 1870s, in the Estevan field, which included Bienfait and Roche Percée, in the early 1890s, and in the 1930s, strip mining was introduced at the Radville field, located between the Estevan and Willow Bunch fields. All these mines, over a hundred in number by 1940, found seasonal markets for home use. Mining companies tried to do most of their entry development work in the summer and the main extraction in the winter when some farmers sought seasonal employment. All of these areas had a sprinkling of Belgian settlers whose biographies indicate an interest in the coal deposits for their domestic purposes.[49]

Prairie mines began operation on a small scale and in a period when unions were scarcely organized. Miners worked ten-hour days in mine tunnels with barely room to stand, enduring frequent roof cave-ins because of rotting timbers, inadequate ventilation, and sometimes almost a half metre of water. The daily wage was only $1.60 with no pay for such compulsory labour as laying track, timbering, clearing roof falls and pumping water. Company housing was very sub-standard. When miners went on strike at Bienfait to win recognition for the Mine Workers' Union of Canada, they decided to demonstrate their grievances in a parade to nearby Estevan. The mayor banned the demonstration, without informing the miners, and called on the RCMP to support the local police. On 29 September 1931, remembered as "Black Thursday," the mounted police with revolvers drawn broke up the parade and a riot ensued. The melee left three strikers dead and eleven injured, and five policemen injured. Wounded miners were refused treatment at the local hospital. Public opinion in general attributed the violence to inexperienced police and unfounded official fear of a Communist coup. The Belgians were particularly cowed by the fact that Louis Revay, a compatriot, was convicted of unlawful assembly and was ordered deported to his homeland.[50] The Estevan "riot" did result in the companies involved agreeing to an eight-hour day and no unpaid labour. The miners did not win the right at this time to organize unions.

The dangers inherent in these early operations and the inadequate legislation governing them were prevalent across Western Canada. The Alberta Royal Commission on Coal Mining in 1935 asserted that since 1896 at least one thousand small mines had been opened "with little if any plant and practically no capital expenditure, often worked nothing more than a "gopher hole," usually paid poor wages, and was generally in areas without taxes and royalties."[51] The Canadian Block Coal Company, constituted in 1921 with a capital investment of a million Belgian francs for concessions obtained through an unnamed Belgian mining director residing in Calgary, left no trace in the official Belgian publication, *Annexes du Moniteur Belge*, after 1925.[52] There was little compensation for the families of victims of mine accidents. When Oscar Devolder was killed in a mine explosion at Fernie in August 1916, for example, the Belgian consul indicated he had no compensation fund and the company should be held responsible. When Arthur Vandorp was awarded inadequate compensation by the Western Collieries Limited for an accident at the Bellevue mine, the consul advised him to hire a lawyer if he believed he could obtain more.[53] A single miner who died intestate would have his property assigned to the province. When the widow of a miner killed at work asked the consulate for funds to be repatriated, there was little disposition to pay her travel expenses. It was suggested that she might be deported by Canadian authorities, at their expense, as an "undesirable" immigrant.[54]

Crowsnest Pass Collieries

The oldest coal-bearing strata in Western Canada is the Kootenay-Blairmore assemblage, the Crowsnest Pass area, straddling the British Columbia–Alberta border. The first mines belonging to the Crow's Nest Pass Coal Company were opened in Coal Creek (Fernie), Michel, Morrisey and Corbin to replace Lethbridge coal for railway locomotives.[55]

Coleman and Blairmore quickly became typical one-industry towns.[56] Belgians became involved after J.J. Fleutot and C.R. Remy, who operated Gold Fields Limited of British Columbia, bought prospective coal mines at Gold Lake, Grassy Mountain, and Frenchman's Camp (Lille). In April 1903, they founded the West Canadian Collieries Limited, backed by French and Belgian investors, absorbing the holdings of Gold Fields Limited in the new company, assuming that the enterprise would attract Francophone immigrants. The Bryson Creek and Bellevue properties were also acquired and B. Charbonnier was named superintendent of operations. Jean Menard was appointed manager. There was every indication that this would be an ideal work environment for Belgian miners and their families. A second European company, the Canadian Coal Consolidated Limited, with its headquarters in Paris, acquired the Hillcrest mine, and by 1911 there were at least four hundred Belgian and French miners in the Crow's Nest region. Their numbers declined in proportion to the number of Italians, Slovaks, and Slavs after World War I, but they remained highly respected, in spite of their socialist convictions, because they responded "patriotically" to the call to arms in 1914.[57]

The first confrontation with management took place in June 1905, when the West Canadian Collieries dismissed sixteen men who were members of the United Mines Workers of America union. A police report stated:

> It was required that the men so discharged should immediately quit and deliver up possession of the premises occupied by them and should leave the Village. I am instructed that this order was effectually carried through the instrumentality of the Royal North West Mounted Police who were called for the purpose.[58]

The police claimed they had not forced the miners to leave town but there had been "an effort to use men in uniform with all the semblance of the authority of the law, to awe those against whom proceedings have been undertaken."[59] This was a useful tactic to use against foreign workers who feared police repression and possible deportation. Even the Belgians felt insecure when dealing with authoritarian officials, although the company did function in French at the top level.[60]

The region was plagued by a number of serious mining accidents in which Belgians were victims. In 1902, an explosion at the Coal Creek Mines at Fernie claimed 102 lives, and a slide at Turtle Mountain buried part of the town of Frank and the entrance to its mine and killed seventy-six people. On 9 December 1910, an explosion tore through the West Canadian Collieries mine at Bellevue and claimed twenty-one lives and in the investigation that followed nothing was said about the non-compliance with safety standards, so the explosion was treated as an unavoidable accident.[61] The worst mining disaster followed on 19 June 1914 when 189 miners succumbed to methane gas in the Hillcrest Coal & Coke mine.

> As the bodies of the men, many of them unrecognizable, were brought to the surface, they were taken to the wash house where volunteer miners washed them, searched for their check numbers and wrapped them in white cotton sheets.[62]

A minimum compensation was offered the 130 widows and about four hundred orphans.

Family histories reveal why Belgians came to the Crowsnest Pass, how they managed to sustain their families, and how they either succeeded or failed to meet formidable challenges. The Boutry family, for example, came in order to escape seemingly intolerable conditions in the mining districts of Wallonia. Nestor Boutry and seven siblings at age seven started to pick up coal in buckets after school hours by age twelve he had to herd the family landlord's cattle for fifteen hours daily and at fifteen started to work in the coal mine. His wife came from a mining family and she too had sorted coal nuggets as a child and then learned to sew, knit and crochet like her mother, when not herding the goats, to supplement family income. A Canadian immigration agent painted an almost paradisiacal picture of life in Alberta and convinced them to emigrate. They arrived in Calgary, as their neighbours recalled, with no place to stay except the railway station:

> Food was scare, the immigrants were hungry, they were also very cold in this new climate, babies cried for lack of milk. When the Boutrys found themselves expecting another child and Rosa already very ill from the voyage and suffering from cold and hunger, Nestor Boutry took the matter to the officials

and demanded they return his wife and Nestor, Jr. to their homeland, where she could at least have food and shelter and medical care.

Immigration officials offered no assistance but fortunately Boutry found work in a mine at Morrisey, B.C., where his family joined him. They opened a boarding house for single men in Fernie which was destroyed in the fire that wiped out the business section of the town in 1904. They moved to Bellevue, where Nestor worked in the mine and his wife ran a boarding house. When fire once again destroyed their home, they moved into a farm in the country and augmented their mine wages by selling produce, poultry and vegetables at the local market. A sand and gravel pit on their property induced them to begin a business supplying construction sites. This grew into such a profitable business that Boutry gave it his entire attention.[63]

Charles and Marie Bonne came to work for the West Canadian Collieries in Blairmore in 1909. Company records indicate that the Bonnes did influence a number of families to join them, but they left the mine in 1912 to take up a homestead at Willow Valley. They eventually operated the Bellevue Transfer which proved less dangerous and more remunerative than working in the coal mines.[64] Antonio Cornil, who was not a miner, was among those influenced to emigrate. He recalled the unusual event that changed his course in life:

> I was having a game of pool with some friends when a lady came in with a letter from her husband in Canada. She was showing this letter to her brother and was preparing to join her husband the following month. Her husband told her how big and rich and nice this country was, with plenty of game and abounding with fish, and that also for $10.00 you could buy a section of land from the government, providing you were willing to make the required improvements. He had also stated miners were making from ten to twelve dollars a day. To a young guy this seemed to be a very good opportunity, and it did not take us long to decide what to do. We were going to join Mrs. Bonne and her two children on her trip to Canada. There were three of us plus her brother.[65]

Social networks could be as effective as formal recruiting agencies in attracting immigrants to western mining communities.

Not all individuals and families came directly from Belgium. A significant number had been recruited by the Imperial Coal Company for the Beersville mine in New Brunswick and by the Dominion Coal Company for its mines in Cape Breton. In 1909–10 there was a particularly bitter strike in Nova Scotia that induced the Lothier, Koentges, Lang, Maufort, Fauville and Lardinois families to seek employment in Alberta. As in Nova Scotia, miners' wives sought whenever possible to operate a boarding house for single men. This not only provided additional income for families such as the Mauforts but also created a sort of ethnic foyer where traditional food and pastimes could be enjoyed with compatriots.[66] François Spillers, who had worked in the mines in Belgium since the age of nine when his father died and he became the chief breadwinner, came to the Crowsnest Pass during a harvest excursion from Nova Scotia in 1921.[67] Frank Soulet, when interviewed about his experiences, indicated that he had come with a large party of Belgians to Nova Scotia, then had moved on to Pennsylvania for a few years, before coming to the Crownest area in 1920. He had started working underground at the age of twelve, although Belgian legislation had set fourteen as the minimum age. He had come to Alberta because he heard the pay scale was much higher and he cherished the hope of being able to retire very comfortably in his homeland. The West Canadian Collieries were perceived as a sympathetic European company with some French-speaking managers: however Soulet soon found there was a "slack time" of twenty-seven months with no benefits whatever. He became a zealous organizer for the One Big Union (OBU) in 1919 because it organized workers along industrial lines which he thought was a more effective way to advance workers' interests. Soulet had been raised Catholic but when his father was virtually excommunicated for taking up socialist activities the entire family broke with the church. He denounced clerical support of the capitalists and, in 1932, mortgaged his home to raise bail money for some of his neighbours who were imprisoned during a bitter strike. He concluded before retirement (not in Belgium as he had once dreamed) that regular work was no more assured in Canada than elsewhere in mining and that Alberta mines were probably the most dangerous anywhere.[68]

Several cases illustrate the hardship and suffering some families faced. At the Hillcrest mine, Joseph Labourier exchanged a few working days with Alphonse Heusdens, so he could meet his wife who was coming from Belgium. Heusdens was killed in one of the most disastrous mine explosions at that time. The community rallied around the widow and her son, and Labourier took young Louis Heusdens under his wing, taught him carpentry, a trade which he pursued later with success at the Kimberley mine.[69] The Oscar Capron family came to the Crownest mines in 1913 and the following year they fetched a younger son who had been left in Belgium. He arrived at the time of the Hillcrest mine disaster which had taken the life of Alphonse Heusdens and 188 others. It was an emotional introduction to a new land and the dangers inherent in mining life:

> Among those who passed for a final tour was Fernand Capron, a 12 year old boy who had just arrived from Belgium only the day before. As his father guided him between the rows of coffins with their grieving attendants, Fernand heard him say: "Son, take note of this and never go down in the mines"[70]

Young Fernand became an accomplished violinist, did his military service in Belgium in 1923, took up farming with a cousin Victor Capron in the Peace River country, then returned to Blairmore in 1940 to operate a general store, gas bar and rental cabin agency. He never forgot the Hillcrest mine disaster.[71]

Four petitions for compensation and relief that came to the attention of the provincial attorney general's office illustrate the depth of despair of some families and the bureaucratic hurdles they encountered. Juliette Vandeuren applied for compensation for herself and five children under twelve years of age, under the provisions of the Workmen's Compensation Act, after her husband Felix Vandeuren was "killed by a fall of rock from the roof of Number 4 mine" at Coleman on 31 January 1910. Five months later, the International Coal & Coke Company admitted some liability and assigned $1800 to the court, which invested half the sum "as the court directs for the benefit of the said applicant" but final payment was made only in July 1916.[72] The widow and four children of Charles Germain were awarded the usual $1,800 but the solicitor had to show "that she is of a provident nature," while a local merchant swore that she was "a person of good moral character and a fit and proper person to be entrusted with monies the Court may deem proper to place with her." A first payment came only one full year after her husband's death. It was a long seven-year struggle to obtain full payment of the compensation award.[73] The third case was that of Victorine Lobert, widow of Auguste J.-B. Lobert, who waited four months to receive an initial payment of $600 from the customary $1,800 award. She returned with her three small children to Belgium, where she had a small debt to repay, and found that her monthly payments were suspended. The Ministry of Foreign Affairs in Brussels intervened in 1920 and the consul in Edmonton wrote to the courts. The reply stated that the full amount had been paid in January 1919 but failed to provide any evidence.[74] This case was unique inasmuch as a compatriot, A. Decoux, had been charged with homicide, in spite of the fact that an inquiry had rendered "a verdict of acquittal of all responsibility" in the death of Lobert. The consul general protested the apparent unwarranted imprisonment of a Belgian national, reminiscent of an official protest six years earlier.[75] The local of the United Mine Workers of America placed the cause of the accident on "loose methods of working" and insisted the company should install safety blocks and "rectify the signalling apparatus and grading of the tracks which the jury proved utterly defective and inadequate to the general safety of the men employed in that part of the mine."[76]

The union also took up the case of Leonie Luleux of Coleman, who asked for compensation for injury and "suffocation which caused death" of her husband, a low-wage earner at the International Coal and Coke Company mine. The $1,800 award was to be paid to a local merchant in $25 monthly payments. To meet her essential needs she took in laundry, but when rheumatism struck in 1919, she was unable to work and had to borrow $105 from a compatriot to buy warm clothing. The court met her immediate need from the fund, but nothing more. The Belgian consulate refused a return fare to Belgium, where she had aged parents, because she had been born in France. In September 1920 she again asked for more money to buy winter clothing for her children: "it is hard for a woman alone with two children to live with 25 dollars a month. I do some washing but this can't provide for all we need."[77] It was not an easy period for the working class. The unions did the little they could to obtain better working conditions. Yet, the companies cannot be accused of making no provisions for their workers' families in times of tragedy.

Lethbridge Area Collieries

Lethbridge grew out of Coal Banks, where the North Western Coal and Navigation Company was organized in 1882 and miners were brought from Pennsylvania by Sir Alexander Galt to provide cheap labour.[78] Father Leonard Van Tighem, a Belgian Oblate, began coming from Fort Macleod in 1884 to say mass at Coal Bank for the "foreigners," migrant workers from the Pennsylvania mines, who were little respected by the small elite of the growing community. Léon Cabeaux, a leader of the general strike in Hainaut in 1887, found guilty by an assizes court in Mons of conspiracy in "a revolutionary plot against constituted authority" arrived in Lethbridge the following year. Not one of Van Tighem's faithful parishioners, he continued to urge his compatriots in Belgium to come join him in Lethbridge because "in Canada we Belgians, English and French form one great chain of action and when we say stop working, everything stops." This version of concerted action across ethnic lines against oppressive management illustrated his militancy: "better to be shot than languish to death," as he said. He described a virtual utopian situation in which there were allegedly few social distinctions because "priests, lawyers and magistrates are at the same level as the common people, hunting and fishing are open to all, and workers are free, hire on and leave a job as they wish." The reality was quite different from these first impressions Cabeaux gave of working conditions in Alberta collieries.[79]

Father Van Tighem's diary reveals the instability and precarious reality of life at Lethbridge in the 1890s. He observed that by 1892 miners worked only two or three days per week. On 6 March 1892, a notice was published announcing a temporary closure, which occurred on the 15th of the month. Van Tighem was certain that all the unmarried men would be discharged. "This is a very hard blow for our little town, as over three hundred miners will quit Lethbridge." However, by the end of January 1893, an extremely cold period, the miners were doing well again "as they work day and night and cannot take out coal enough to satisfy demands."[80] Later the situation was quite different again: "Our mines are closed for several days. The new Superintendent Simpson tries to cut the wages of the poor miners, but these, most justly, refuse to go to work, so the miners are on strike. Many are leaving the place...." By 5 March, work had not resumed and the company held to its decision to reduce wages by 17 per cent. About four hundred miners, mostly Slovaks, left, and on 15 March about a hundred men had no option but to return to work at the reduced wage. Van Tighem noted: "Of course, this we may call a forced action, as many have no money nor the means to leave town."[81] In 1897, the Western Federation of Miners from Montana organized the Lethbridge miners and called a protest strike against the wage cuts. Van Tighem recorded on 10 August that "many grievances must be removed before they return to their labour." Yet twenty days later he wrote that "the miners are resuming their work in the mines, no advance in wages was granted by the company." The result of this union action was that the provincial government and police put sufficient pressure on the WFM to induce them to leave Alberta.[82]

In 1903, the United Mines Workers of America began reorganizing the Lethbridge miners. By 1906, the miners were on strike once again therefore the Alberta Railway and Irrigation Company enlisted the support of the police who were unable to understand what the "foreign" workers said, much less comprehend the reason for going on strike when they were paid at least five times the wages of policemen. The police were housed and fed by the company and swore in "special constables" from among company employees. When the company tried to bring in scab workers, confrontation escalated. Louis Albert, a Belgian miner in desperate financial need, who decided to continue working, was attacked and wounded near the village of Stafford by angry strikers for being a "scab," was rescued by the RNWMP and was taken to the safety of the mine.[83] Van Tighem commented, "these are very bad times for our town," but eventually after nine months, "our strike is over, and most of the men will return to work … there is an increase of wages in favour of the miners."[84] Union workers appealed to Ottawa to intervene to prevent further violence.[85] W.L. Mackenzie King was sent in as a federal mediator and he helped draft the Industrial Disputes Investigation Act (Lemieux Act) which forbade strikes or lockouts in mines and public utilities until the dispute had been investigated by a tripartite board of arbitration representing labour, capital, and government. This compulsory cooling-off period deprived unionized workers of their most effective weapon, the surprise strike, while giving management time to recruit strike-breakers.[86]

Drumheller Valley Collieries

The first test holes for the commercial recovery of coal in the Badlands of the Drumheller valley were sunk in 1911. Eight years later, the Calgary *Eye-Opener* editorialized in 1919 that Rosedale featured an ideal hostel for single workers:

> The Rosedale Camp is one of the best equipped for the workers' comfort, with large dining hall, clean kitchens and good grub, comfortable sleeping quarters, shower baths and recreation hall, where day and night schools are held, as most of the miners during the First World War were from Europe.[87]

But the experience of the Vaast family portrayed a very different situation from this idyllic presentation. The family had come first to Glace Bay, Nova Scotia in 1918 where the father and three sons were killed in mine explosions. The widow with a surviving son and daughter came to the "western frontier" of Drumheller, where young Leo at just twelve years of age started working carrying timbers down into the Hy-Grade mine. To earn extra cash he also ran errands for the "painted ladies" in the town which was renowned for its gambling, drinking and prostitution. When he turned sixteen, he dug sewer ditches for the hospital but soon turned to working fifty-two hours a week underground. When mines started closing down during the Depression, he took up trucking. It was a hard immigrant experience – disaster, internal migration, resourcefulness, recovery.[88]

The most important immigration of miners into the area occurred after World War I. Sylvain and Louise Pans, for example, were encouraged by Canadian soldiers to emigrate, and so they came to Drumheller where there was employment in the collieries. Three years of dangerous work convinced Sylvain Pans that a job with Canadian National Railways was preferable.[89] In 1919, the One Big Union was organized in Calgary which Belgians in particular found attractive. Miners at Drumheller went on strike in May 1919 demanding recognition of the OBU as their legal bargaining agent. War veterans returning home from Europe were looking for jobs and had been passed over by the mining companies that preferred experienced foreign workers such as Belgians. Thirteen mining companies decided to hire war veterans as "protectors of mining property," plied them with liquor, armed them with crowbars, pick handles and brass knuckles, and sent them out in company cars to round up the strikers and bring them into work.[90] Violence began in the early morning hours of 9 August:

> Early Monday morning a cavalcade of cars swept along the dusty valley bottom roads to the miners' shacks strung out along the south side of the Red Deer River. The cars stopped quickly, veterans jumped from seats and running-boards and ran towards the cabins. Miners, awaked by the whoops and yells, ran for the thick brush that grew to the rear of the scattered shacks. As the attackers drew near the huts, miners threw rocks, firewood – anything handy – and stopped the charge. Both sides stood their ground as missiles and shouts filled the air. Then slowly the pursuers began to retreat to their cars. The miners followed and chased the veterans back towards the cars until gunfire began to echo through the valley. More cars were coming to reinforce the attackers. The miners quickly turned in panic and ran into the hills.[91]

By June 1921 all the mines had rejected the OBU, the scabs were released and the skilled "foreigners" were rehired. The alliance of mining companies and provincial authorities had carried the day.

But industrial peace had not been restored to the valley and its twelve thousand miners because the OBU and UMWA fought, literally with bricks, stones and clubs, to represent the mine workers. The OBU also fell into disfavour in February 1924 when the executive became more occupied with sexual scandals, including charges of bigamy, and backroom discussions of heterosexual and homosexual activities of working-class men.[92] The provincial police, when called in, patrolled with machine guns mounted on the fenders of their cars. The Canadian Block Coal Company, whose offices were in Calgary, was Belgian-financed. Its manager was a Belgian, and it had contracts with two rival unions. The majority called a strike and set up pickets night and day at all mine entrances to dissuade a minority that chose to continue working. Strikers gathered around wood fires at night and in a violent confrontation Lambert Renners hit a constable with a rock, was wounded himself by a shot fired by the police, and was arrested. The case in provincial court turned on whether picketing, or "watching and besetting," was legal. Renners lost at the provincial level so the union made it a test case by appealing to the Supreme Court of Canada. Renners lost the appeal, the court using evidence from police files to conclude that the miners had assembled on company property and "their attendance there by day and night, the fires, the shouting, their reception of the police, their threats" were proof of "not only of a nuisance, but also of unlawful assembly." Renners at least escaped deportation to Belgium.[93] Another Belgian who had a difficult role in this situation was Emile Leblanc, provincially appointed mine inspector. He had come to Crowsnest Pass in 1905, worked as a coal mine surveyor for the White Ash and Regal mines, then assumed the operation of the Bay mine at Taber in 1912, and finally during the Depression moved to Wayne to take over inspection duties in the Drumheller region.[94]

Nordegg Coal Basin

In 1906 the German Development Company and Martin Cohen Nordegg hired the banker Eugene de Wassermann to find European capital to develop an open pit coal mine at Ribbon Lake in the Kananaskis valley. Wassermann favoured a more northerly development about 170 kilometres west of Red Deer known as the Brazeau Colliery. Nordegg befriended Sir Wilfrid Laurier and Messrs Mackenzie and Mann, the railway promoters. In 1908, fifty mining engineers from Belgium, Germany, Great Britain and the United States were invited at Dominion government expense to a conference and tour of mining sites under the auspices of the Canadian Mining Institute. From this group a certain Professor Henri Potonié was invited by the German Development Company to visit claims staked at Nordegg [Brazeau Colliery] and Kananaskis.[95]

Martin Nordegg developed the rich coal-producing area, later known as the Nordegg Coal Basin, beginning in 1911. The necessary capital was raised in Europe to work the coal seams and to build a company town of over four hundred homes for more than a thousand workers on the payroll. In 1911 the Banque d'Outremer and the Banque de Commerce d'Anvers lent $4 million to the Canadian Northern Western Railway to build a 285 kilometres branch line joining the Brazeau property and the Canadian Northern Railway network at Red Deer.[96] The company town reflected a kind of caste system, or social hierarchy, as miners and managers lived in different sectors. The families of managers lived in five large elegant houses and enjoyed special privileges, including reserved front seats at the theatre. The Big Horn Trading Company, the company store, had a monopoly and employees were expected to shop there.

The operations were financed in good measure from Brussels and according to Nordegg owed much to the engineer, Ernest Gheur:

> In Toronto I opened an office in a building where Mackenzie Mann and Company and the Canadian Northern Railways were located. I started with a fairly large staff, working out the future construction and mining activity while waiting for the Belgian coal-mining engineer E. Gheur, whom I had engaged on the recommendations of the Société Générale of Brussels. When he arrived, I found that his knowledge of Belgian coalfields enabled him to adapt himself quickly to Canadian conditions in the West.[97]

Gheur had come to a Stellarton, Nova Scotiamine in 1910 with his family and when hired by Nordegg began to plan mining operations and the layout of the townsite. This occupied him from 1912 to 1917, his family having joined him at Red Deer in 1913.

Although Nordegg initially considered Gheur a "greenhorn" on matters relating to the Canadian West generally, he had absolute confidence in his expertise in laying out mining operations.[98] He even organized the construction crews laying railway track from Red Deer into eight companies of fifty men each. In a letter to his wife, when she was preparing to join him in Canada, he wrote concerning the mine:

> The extraction will take place along the flank of a ridge by way of tunnels along the two seams, without it being necessary to foresee shafts or slopes for the time being. I estimate we will be able to recover 1100 tons a day in 1914, without any great expense for setting up operations.[99]

The concession included several benches each capable of even greater production. Gheur found the deposit rich although the coal was not in his estimation of truly superior quality.

In 1917, Gheur planned another mining operation at Lac Brûlé. Unfortunately, he died from the effects of a fall in a mine before launching this project. The Nordegg mine continued to prosper. In addition to finance and engineering skill, Belgium contributed a few miners. The Alberta Royal Commission on Coal reported in 1925 that 5.5 per cent of the Brazeau miners were of Belgian or French origin.[100] In 1937, the Brazeau Collieries started making briquettes and very quickly became the largest manufacturer of briquettes in Canada. The only major mine disaster occurred on 31 October 1941, when an explosion claimed twenty-nine lives. On the whole, the Nordegg venture was a success. As far as Belgian immigrants were concerned, by the 1940s mining was no longer an attractive or viable occupation. The nature of the local economy had evolved as had the nature of immigration. An era had come to an end.

Labour Radicalism

Two different Belgian responses to labour relations reached Canada. In Quebec, a disciplined Catholic syndicalist organization prevailed as introduced by the abbé Arthur Robert (who studied at the University of Louvain and founded the school of social sciences at Laval University) and abbé Eugène Lapointe (who studied at the Catholic university in Brussels). This attempt to promote labour peace and social harmony had had some success at factories at Sérainq and Val St-Lambert. In the Maritimes and Western Canada, a left-wing socialistic collective action took root resembling the manifestations seen in the Borinage and Liège regions. Joseph Schmetz, an organizer for the Part Ouvrier Belge, left war-ravaged Belgium in 1919 with his family for Toronto, where he hoped to establish a comprehensive network of trade unions, co-operatives, fraternal societies, *mutuelles* and schools. This objective was not realized in Western Canada because Belgian workers were too small a minority within the union movement and the fragmented socialist parties to establish a comprehensive network of working-class institutions. The Belgian immigrant workers in many cases were secular, anticlerical and unrefined.[101] They also felt an affinity with the socialist movement.[102] George Vissac, manager of the West Canadian Collieries, singled out Belgians as "reds ... people with a fairly bad reputation." The UMWA at the 1917 district convention felt it necessary to adopt a motion specifically refuting the "calumny" that Belgians were largely to blame for the labour turmoil. Nevertheless, the Belgian-Italian Co-operative Society in Blairmore was branded throughout the 1920s a communist organization.[103] As supporters of workers' rights and reform observed: "it was the communists who led most struggles for jobs, for relief, against wage cuts."[104]

Religious sanction had little effect on anticlerical workers. From an "establishment" viewpoint, another way to deal with radicals, allegedly communists, was to deport them on a variety of charges. Deportation had been provided for in a statute of 1910 on grounds of moral and political unsuitability. It specified that "any person other than a Canadian citizen" (although such a category did not exist constitutionally at the time) who "shall by word or act create or attempt to create riot or public disorder" was to be "considered and classed as an undesirable immigrant."[105] So it was that Gustave Henry, who had come to the Cape Breton mines in 1912, moved to Fernie, B.C. in 1917, and ended up at Lethbridge, was ordered deported to Belgium in September 1925. The Minister of Justice issued a deportation order on the grounds that Gustave Henry had been imprisoned in Lethbridge for minor theft, and as an alien under the terms of the Immigration Act he was subject to deportation for criminal activity. His union activities were public knowledge but the order for his deportation was based on a minor criminal infraction. Upon investigation it was found that his claim that he had been a resident of Canada for more than five years excluded him from deportation on the basis claimed. The provincial attorney-general's office countermanded the federal deportation order after the Superior Court of Alberta ruled in Gustave Henry's favour.[106]

Father Neville Anderson, who was pastor at Drumheller from 1934 to 1946, left his impressions of the aftermath of the labour troubles. He wrote: "It was true that there were many among the foreign population who were careless in religious practice. The Belgians and the French (from France) were the least responsive, being generally anticlerical."[107] His views were representative not only of the Catholic clergy but also of many Anglo-Saxons. A Protestant leader proclaimed: "I believe if we were rid of these aliens we would be rid of strikes and all disturbances between capital and labour."[108] Premier John Oliver of British Columbia denounced labour agitators in 1919 in the familiar official language of the period: "Engineered by a handful of agitators there is under way throughout Canada a deliberate attempt to overthrow constitutional government and substitute therefor a dictatorship. I am convinced that the Bolshevists are behind all this turmoil."[109]

Did Belgian miners share in a common working-class culture that transcended ethnic, religious and political differences? It is evident that they did co-operate with workers of other ethnic groups, notably the Italians, Slovaks and Ukrainians, to secure better working conditions. It is also worth noting that these groups all shared a Catholic background and were often anticlerical, yet their union leaders were almost without exception Anglo-Saxon Protestants. The Walloon miners had a radical socialist European background, comfortable with political action, and so they were not averse to identifying with radical movements in Canada that promoted their interests and welfare. Unlike Finns and Ukrainians, however, they had no desire to establish locals based on language and ethnicity.[110] A. Moeller, president of the Académie Royale de Belgique, believed that "the great differences in origin, language and character of the workers" in Canada did not promote the emergence of the same class consciousness as existed in European countries. In other words, he distinguished between union solidarity, political action and class consciousness.[111]

Most Belgian observers believed that a working-class consciousness was slow to develop in Canada for a number of reasons. Firstly, industrial centres were few and scattered. Secondly, workers were divided by language, customs and country of origin. Also, agriculture was valued above mining in Western Canada. Finally, there was no effective labour party in Parliament or the provincial legislatures.[112] The Belgian socialist periodical *L'Avenir social* observed in 1902 that "the socialist movement in Canada is still in an embryonic state." Yet, in 1903, it observed with satisfaction that two Labour candidates had been elected to the British Columbia legislature.[113] On the other hand, Henri de Man visited Winnipeg in 1920 and concluded that the Winnipeg General Strike of 1919 had marked "a turning point in the Canadian labour movement" and the constitution of a working class with class power, "a characteristic manifestation of the class struggle in its simplest and most brutal form." He added that Belgians had not noted this change because they did not have access to unbiased accounts of the events of 1919, and their chief source of information was newspapers unfavourable to the strikers.[114]

Finally, it is noteworthy that Belgium provided Quebec with a model of labour relations and Catholic social action that was not transferred to Western Canada. This religiously oriented social action introduced by a few clerical intellectuals who studied in Belgium was founded on the doctrine of compassion and obligation to serve the oppressed as well as a fear of the masses, especially when they banded together to obtain redress of grievances. For French Canadian nationalists of the Henri Bourassa school, the Belgians seemed to provide an ideal program because it appeared the Catholics had wrested control of union activities from the socialists and "anarchists." Also, they had maintained a distinctive "national" character in the face of pressures from Dutch, French and German unions and had succeeded in continuing to function on a bilingual basis. On the other hand, as we have seen, it was attitudes and actions of Belgian miners and workers harbouring the left-wing ideology so manifest in the Borinage and Liège regions of Belgium that surfaced in Western Canada. The social question in Quebec was bound up with avoiding social conflicts within the ethnocultural community, whereas in the West conflicts brought ethnic groups together in pursuit of collective interests.[115]

Agricultural Settlement

In 1902, the Settlers' Association of British Columbia published a calendar advertising farms for sale.[116] The few Belgians known to have come at the time appear to have been more attracted to employment in the lumber mills and associated forestry jobs around Maillardville and Gibson's Landing. Albert Borle, for example, who immigrated in 1897, prepared log booms at Gibson's Landing for a number of years before settling into farming.[117] Although Vancouver was a good deep seaport, especially after the CPR line was extended to Granville, its commercial activity developed after the completion of the Panama Canal in 1914. Later, the activities of the Consul Léon Dupuis in using the Hudson Bay Railway, completed in 1929, made Vancouver a focal point of Belgian investment and trade.

The triangular Fraser Delta lowland rapidly attracted attention for dairy farming and market gardening. By the early 1900s, at least one hundred Flemish immigrants had settled in the area, improved by draining and dyking.[118] As early as 1891, dairying was common in the lower flood plain of the Fraser valley and southeastern Vancouver Island. The farms produced fluid milk, butter, and sometimes cheese, for the Vancouver and Victoria communities.[119] In 1913, the Fraser Valley Milk Producers Association (FVMPA) was formed as the bargaining agent and by 1920 it had become a large vertically integrated milk processing firm.[120] Some Flemish independent producers continued to supply fluid milk to the urban market. These farms around Langley and Surrey were of a modest size, normally two to three dozen Holsteins per herd, and relied heavily on home-grown hay and sillage. Little by little, the FVMPA controlled both production and manufacturing.[121] By the 1920s, large herds and barns were not uncommon, milking machines were introduced and this type of farming was becoming capital-intensive and market-oriented. In 1929, the Dairy Products Sales Act made it difficult to sell unpasteurized milk, so small producers not part of the FVMPA could not afford the cans and the sanitary equipment needed to deal with a creamery. Customers in Vancouver were sympathetic to the plight of the small producers because they preferred raw milk. By this time, few women remained engaged in dairying.[122] Some Belgian farmers survived because as the consul in Vancouver reported in 1932: " Several Belgian farmers are settled in this vicinity. Most are prosperous according to information obtained from the colonization agent of the Canadian National Railway.[123] The Dutch took over a number of dairy operations after 1945. This resulted in further mechanization, improved crop practices and feeding methods.[124] Many of the original Flemish family dairies passed into immigrant hands as sons and grandsons were more attracted to urban occupations and professions. In 1965 a research project on innovation in dairy farming in the region found that, although the Flemings were difficult to distinguish from the Dutch, the Belgian-origin dairymen tended to use more unpaid family labour and to not participate actively in adult education courses. None of the Flemish farms were large, land was used intensively, and many farmers did not adopt such innovations as heated water tanks, hay conditioners and dryers, or bulk storage for concentrate feed.[125]

In Flanders, farmers had engaged in intensive land use therefore market gardening could also be associated with a modest dairy farm. From the outset, the Flemish farmers in the Lower Fraser Valley were in competition with the established Chinese market gardeners in the growing of cabbage, asparagus, cauliflower, celery, beans and peas. Proximity to the Vancouver market and to the railway link to the Prairies were important assets because vegetables and small fruits are perishable. The advent of refrigerated railway cars and trucks made shipping to distant markets feasible. Canneries took up some of the production as well. Around Maple Ridge, the Belgians were in competition with the Japanese fruit growers specializing in strawberries, raspberries, blueberries, cranberries and loganberries.[126] As with dairying, Belgian families engaged in market gardening and small fruit farming tended, in the second and third generation, to turn to urban-centred occupations. Thus the Antonio Cloets opened the Stafford House nursing home in Vancouver and the Jozef Van Houtteghems purchased the Queen's Park convalescent home in New Westminster. Consul Léon Dupuis retired to Salt Spring Island where he tended his garden and vineyard, serving his own produce and wines to visitors who were so fortunate as to listen to his accounts of Belgian commercial enterprises in Western Canada emanating from his Vancouver office.[127]

Okanagan Valley Fruit Growing

Boosterism and patriotic sentiment were important stimuli in the development of the Okanagan Valley orchard industry.[128] An association between occupation and cultural intelligence was expressed by Lord Grey, who believed "families of refinement, culture, and distinction" colonized the best landscapes. In his words, "fruit farming in British Columbia has acquired the distinction of being a beautiful art" where "qualities of mind are necessary ... which are not so essential to success in wheat growing or ordinary mixed farming." In this view, the province would enjoy a superiority that was at once ethnic, cultural and economic.[129] Belgians were traditionally interested in fruit growing but it was capitalistic ventures that emerged from land development schemes that drew attention to the commercial potential of the central interior drybelt valley around Lake Okanagan.[130] In 1890, when the Shuswap and Okanagan Railway Company opened the valley to more intensive settlement, George Grant Murray interested eight Belgian investors in forming the Okanagan Land and Development Company Limited.[131]

In 1897, the Belgo-Canadian Fruit Lands Company was registered with a capital of $300,000 and headquarters in Antwerp. The Van de Put-Heirman Company was a major shareholder, while Raoul de Grelle became director of operations at Vernon and Fernand De Jardin was the over-all *administrateur-délégué*. More than half the shares were held by Belgian companies and slightly more than a quarter by members of the British aristocracy. The propaganda directed at investors and settlers by the Belgians was particularly optimistic. One booklet proclaimed:

> Fruit farming has acquired the distinction of being a beautiful art as well as a most profitable industry.... Fruit farming in

the Dry Belt of British Columbia is the best paying investment in the world. Those who take up fruit farming in the British Columbia Dry Belt area ... are men of the better class, people of education and refinement.[132]

The pattern of development was one of exploitation by limited liability companies, usually launched by local entrepreneurs such as the De Jardin family and financed in Europe, that bought up dry benchlands, installed modest irrigation works, subdivided the land into ten to twenty acres lots, and promoted these orchards abroad. In general, these investments were seen as worthwhile.[133]

In 1908, the Belgo-Canadian Fruit Lands Company decided to undertake the development of its land holdings itself by initiating a program of planting hundreds of fruit trees. The developers of its Vernon properties, which were devoted to sheep-raising as well as orchards, included Ludovic De Decker, Baron Pierre Verhaegen, Baron Edmond Van Eetvelde, Charles de Burlet and Maurice Cook.[134] They were also connected with the Compagnie Immobilière et Agricole du Canada (Land and Agriculture Company of Canada) that had invested some of its profits from land sales in Saskatchewan to buy up lots in Vernon and import 1800 head of sheep for ranching operations. In Kelowna the Havenith, Jacobs and Louwens families were among the pioneer fruit growers.[135] By this time, 27 per cent of the capital was subscribed by members of the Belgian nobility through the head office in Antwerp.[136]

The Belgo-Canadian Fruit Lands Company embarked on a very expensive irrigation project which included a six-mile-long main flume, to supply as much as possible of its high range land. In 1912, a subsidiary irrigation company, the Black Mountain Water Company, assumed the construction. When the first phase of the project was completed, shares were allotted to the Compagnie Immobilière et Agricole du Canada, which had been organized in 1897 by the Frédéric Jacobs Company and other Antwerp investors.[137] The majority of these shares were owned by Fernand De Jardin, Baron Edmond Van Eetvelde and Louis Van De Put. Within a year it was able to dispose of more than a thousand acres of irrigated lands.[138]

By April 1913, the Belgo-Canadian Fruit Lands Company approached the Caisse Hypothécaire Anversoise to underwrite part of its expansion plans. When the Antwerp firm hesitated, the Compagnie Immobilière et

Agricole du Canada came to its assistance. In fact, there was considerable overlap both in directors and shareholders of the two companies.[139] André Gouzée, for example, representing the Frédéric Jacobs group of Antwerp in Western Canada, was the secretary of the Alberta Company, a director of the Compagnie Immobolière et Agricole du Canada, manager of the Société Hypothécaire du Canada, president of the Société Foncière Belgo-Canadienne, and board member of the Crédit Générale du Canada from his office in Winnipeg.

The Compagnie Immobilière et Agricole du Canada [Land and Agriculture Company of Canada], backed by its Belgian investors, purchased 3,500 acres of the historic Cornelius O'Keefe ranch around Swan Lake, extending from Vernon to Okanagan Lake. A local resident was appointed manager "to attract settlers for different uses of the land." The White Valley Irrigation & Power Company was contracted to extend an existing canal to Okanagan Lake, thus irrigating seven thousand more acres of company land.[140] During World War I, the big boom seemed to collapse largely because of the failing irrigation systems. Promoters had overestimated the available water supply. Secondly, they had underestimated the water requirements of the land. Finally, they also had underestimated the capacity and desirability of their irrigation system. The provincial government intervened in 1919 with the Southern Okanagan Lands project.[141]

The Compagnie Immobilière et Agricole du Canada had organized a subsidiary known as the Belgian Orchard Syndicate in 1908. This syndicate bought two hundred acres from the parent company, planted seventeen thousand fruit trees, mostly apples, on ten-acre blocks outside the northeastern limits of the town of Vernon. A fifty-six-acre plot, for example, was ploughed and planted in trees under company management and when the owner arrived early the following spring he took over the operation of his orchard. The company would plant, irrigate, prune and spray an absentee landlord's orchard for the actual cost plus an additional 20 per cent service charge.[142] J. de la Chevasnerie, for example, negotiated in Antwerp for his property, which the Belgian Orchard Syndicate looked after for five years until he arrived to settle on his property.[143] The Belgian Orchard Syndicate operated its own packing house but when it burned down in 1930 it was decided not to rebuild. Arthur De Jardin eventually became the sole owner of the syndicate, which he operated from his L & A Ranch. It was the only project in the region that attracted a sizeable number of Belgian settlers, as a report sent to the St. Raphaël Society indicated:

> Around Vernon live some sixty Belgians, most of whom bought land from the Belgian company, the Land and Agriculture Company of Canada, which has its headquarters in Antwerp. Among these Belgians are the son of Baron Van Eetvelde de Moll, Mr. Verhaegen, former Belgian consul to the Philippines, Mr. De Decker, formerly an engineer in Egypt, and several others of the most distinguished Belgian families. All have established orchards and are very interested in the region.[144]

The Belgian Orchard Syndicate eventually owned twelve thousand acres, of which two-thirds were devoted to fruit and vegetable production. In 1932, the consul in Vancouver gave a glowing report of its success in marketing annually at least forty thousand boxes of apples. He also noted that the Belgian growers had diversified somewhat their operations:

> They harvest also a considerable quantity of pears, peaches, plums, also tomatoes and onions. In the same vein I have been informed about the presence of several Belgian growers around Enderby and Armstrong where they cultivate especially celery. They seem to succeed very well. A number of compatriots mostly farmers have settled in this part of the province.[145]

Diversification was encouraged not only because of an expanding market demand but also because of increasing costs of fruit production as packing houses, brokers, railways, jobbers and retailers all required remuneration. The Belgian Orchard Syndicate continued to manage its holdings until 1942, at which time World War II seriously interrupted its marketing strategy, so it sold its property.

Another related venture capitalized in Belgium in 1909 was the Belgo-Canadian Land Company. This company purchased 9,400 acres belonging to the Ideal Fruit Company located twelve kilometres east of Kelowna on the north side of Moose Creek. Company schemes were huge undertakings laid out by engineers such as Charles A. Stoess of the Belgo-Canadian Land Company to build large storage dams and control mechanisms to meter the flow of water from the reservoirs.[146] The construction of a dam, irrigation flumes and ditches to make six thousand acres saleable to prospective fruit growers was carried out by workers hired mostly in Italy. This venture did not have Belgian immigration as its objective, its purpose being largely speculative investment. It also had stiff competition from the Central Okanagan Land and Orchard Company, whose principal booster was J.W. Jones of Grenfell, Saskatchewan who arranged excursions for prospective buyers. After World War I, as immigration did not resume its pre-war proportions, the company sold its interests, as did the major Belgian real estate companies in Vancouver and Edmonton, enabling them to make a profit through currency exchange rates and to repatriate their funds for reinvestment at home.[147] The Vernon Orchard Company, an investment project launched and directed from Belgium as early as 1910, operated a modest tract (256 acres) east of Swan Lake until March 1930. In addition to members of the Jacobs Group based in Antwerp, the banking firm of Henri Devilder of Lille was involved. Some of the Belgians in the Vernon area may have settled on the company's tract but there is no evidence of any active recruitment of immigrants by the Vernon Orchard Company.[148]

Belgian capital and enterprising developers such as André Gouzée, Arthur De Jardin, Louis Van de Put and Raoul de Grelle, who were associated with the Antwerp-based Jacobs Group, played a major role in the initial planning and development of the Okanagan fruit-growing industry. World War I was followed by a reduction in interest and investment, as well as by the decline of the myth of western expansion. The investments capital that originated in good measure from land speculation was not accompanied by commensurate immigration. The Varlez-Brunin Report indicated two problems: a "lifestyle not adapted to the hard labour" and the prohibitive cost of transportation.[149] The Belgian families around Vernon in the northern section of the Okanagan Valley were never sufficiently numerous to form a cohesive community with its own ethnic, cultural and religious institutions.

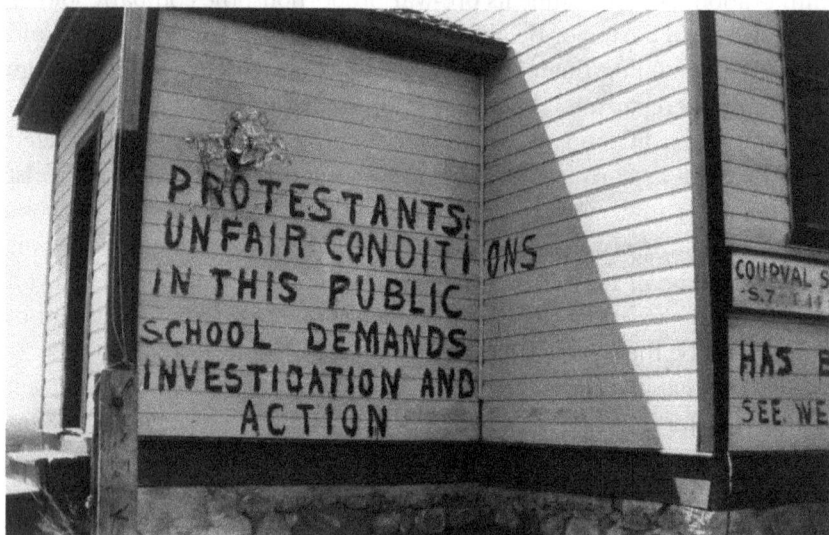

Graffiti on Courval School, 1920s. (Sask. Archives R-A 4819(4))
Belgian settlers felt threatened by Ku Klux Klan and anto-Catholic activities.

VII

LANGUAGE, RELIGION, AND
EDUCATION

Issues of language, religion and education were virtually inseparable in Belgium and remained so for most Flemings and Walloons who settled in Western Canada. Linguistic debates were commonplace in Belgium where French was the official language after independence as well as the cultural language of the upper classes, the language of secondary education and of upward social mobility. In Western Canada, English imposed itself, although there was no official language designation, but French was the first European language widely spoken in the region. By the late nineteenth century in Belgium, there was a marked increase in the Flemish-speaking population and the emergence of Flemish ethnic consciousness, culminating in the recognition of Flemish as an official language in 1898. From 1830 to 1932, Wallonia followed the *jus soli* principle so that all public education was in French, but Flanders followed the *jus personae* principle so the language of education depended on the language of the head of the family. Children of Flemish labourers in Wallonia, consequently, had no access to instruction in the mother tongue, but the Flemish elite continued to educate their children in French wherever they resided. Since 1980, Belgium is partitioned into linguistic communities with no public support of the minority language. Not without significance is the fact that the deputy prime minister, Johann Van de Lanotte, whose family had lived in Cranbrook, B.C., from 1924 to 1936, advised Canadians that Belgium, with its divisions into cultural communities and regions, was not an appropriate constitutional model for Canada to follow.[1]

Just as French Canadians identified Catholicism with their "national" identity, Flemings looked to the church to support their nationalist movement. Belgians arrived in Western Canada when the Catholic hierarchy was largely Francophone and identified with selective immigration and the ideology of agriculturalism. Immigration resulted in an increasingly multi-ethnic and multilingual society, but the dominant ethos remained British and Protestant. One consequence of the new demographic character of the region was the perception of the Catholic Church as a "French church." Walloons who settled alongside French Canadians came to share their views on language and religion, but Flemings, while remaining steadfastly identified with Catholicism, did not always appreciate its Francophone character. In Canada, educational issues often turned on Catholic/Protestant perspectives. Belgian immigrants in Western Canada rapidly became conscious of the existing conflict over religious orientation and religious instruction, as well as language of instruction, in the publicly supported schools. Flemings in particular noted that English was the language of business and government. Even after official bilingualism was instituted in the latter decades of the twentieth century, English remained the regional language of modernity and upward mobility, although bilingualism was an asset. Canada never incorporated in its constitution the absolute separation of church and state or the British model of an established church. Instead, Canadians recognized, in law or in practice, the role and contribution of organized religious groups in public institutions of education, social work, welfare and health care. It was inevitable that the Catholic Church, in particular, would become involved in linguistic issues because of this political framework and sustained immigration. The American College at Louvain [Leuven], founded in 1856, and the Séminaire Anglo-Belge in Bruges, founded in 1859, trained clergy specifically for North America. The abbé Charles Nerinckx recruited numerous candidates for Canada, among them Edouard Leo De Busschere, who served at Forget, Regina and Calgary: Achiel Marien who served in pastorates in Drumheller, Raymond, Vulcan and Lethbridge; and E. de Wilde in the mining towns of Blairmore, Coleman, Bellevue, Hillcrest, Frank and Lille.[2] Belgians, in the process of integration into Western Canada's evolving society, became active in four domains: missionary work among First Nations; outreach to

Hungarian and Ukrainian Catholics; promotion of Catholic schools; and defence of the French language. In general, the clergy were more active than the laity in these enterprises.

Amerindian Missions

Belgian missionary work in the Americas began in 1493 with the labours of two Franciscans from Ath who accompanied Christopher Columbus on his second journey to the New World.[3] Belgian Récollets and Jesuits were active evangelizers and explorers in New France and their activities took them into the far interior of the continent, including the upper Mississippi and Saskatchewan valleys. They continued to serve under British colonial rule beginning on Vancouver Island in the 1880s: Fathers G. Donckele and M. Van Nevil at the Kuper Island residential school, and M. Meuleman and E. Sobry at the Kyuquat Mission.[4] These pioneer missionaries were succeed in 1907 by the Fathers of the Company of Mary [SMM]: P. Claessens from 1907 to 1912, A. Urlings in 1912–13, and W. Lemmens in 1913.[5] These church-operated residential schools had as their objective the assimilation of Native children: therefore the Flemish missionaries taught in English. In the denominational rivalry that came to characterize these schools, the Catholics had better funding, good facilities, itinerant priests and a well-focussed school curriculum.[6] The precursors of Jesuit missionary work among the Blackfoot were Pierre-Jean De Smet and Nicolas Point, his assistant.[7] In 1845, De Smet made a three-thousand-mile journey from St. Louis into the Kootenays, where he baptized over one hundred Natives, before crossing over the Rockies to the present site of Banff. Along the Bow River he met Assiniboines suffering from famine and disease. He reported: "I rendered all the services in my power to the invalids, baptized six children and an old man who expired two days after; he was interred with all the ceremonies and prayers of the Church."[8] He went on to Fort Jasper where he baptized forty-four persons and blessed seven marriages of Iroquois who were engaged in the fur trade in the interests of Montreal merchants.[9]

The Oblates of Mary Immaculate (OMI), who arrived in 1845, had the largest contingent of Belgian missionaries in the West. Most held ultramontane views but became more liberal as they came to appreciate many qualities in the life-style and belief system of the First Peoples. Bishop Grandin of St. Albert obtained permission from the Archbishop of

Mechelen [Malines] to preach in his seminaries and colleges and was able to recruit fifteen men. He confided: "I want Belgian missionaries ... they have the advantage that they can speak Flemish and that is why they easily learn English and German."[10] Among his recruits were Brother Henri Scheers, who came to Lac la Biche in 1874 and continued to labour in the Native missions in the North-West Territories until 1904, and Leonard Van Tighem, who served the Blackfoot and a multilingual community at Lethbridge. Brother Victor Van Tighem of the Van Dale congregation of the Oblates left Antwerp in February 1886 to join Leonard in the North-West Territories. In serving the Piegan mission he noted that the settlers set a very bad example of civilized behaviour. As for Hayter Reed's supposedly "new improved system of farming" for promoting Native self-sufficiency, while avoiding competition in the exchange economy, Van Tighem concluded that government officials had little understanding of how to promote industry, had little sympathy for the poverty of his charges, and were more interested in protecting farmers and ranchers from any possible competition.[11]

More than thirty Oblates served in Western Canadian missions before 1940. Their careers as teachers, community builders and counsellors were outstanding and they merit a separate publication. Roger Vandersteene, for example, had an illustrious and controversial career serving the Cree of northern Alberta until 1976. He said, "A Fleming understands better than anybody that the language of a people is its main artery." The Cree called him Ka Nihta Nehiyawet, which translates as "the one who really speaks Cree." His understanding of and admiration for Cree symbolism and spirituality led him to create a syncretic Cree liturgy, an innovation that won the respect of his parishioners but disturbed his conservative superiors. The hierarchy did not countenance much departure from traditional forms so his efforts were frustrated although Cree tunes and drumming were accepted. He was installed a Cree elder and medicine man. Shortly before his death, he gave his medicine pipe to an old friend, Harold Cardinal, who had left the Catholic Church. His case illustrates in some measure the linguistic tensions that existed within the Oblate order. Most of the Prairie missionaries were Flemish while most of those in the northern region of the North West Territories were Walloon. Vandersteene worked in a region dominated by Francophones. Moreover, his Flemish nationalist activities were public knowledge, including participation in a pro-Nazi movement for the creation of a separate Flemish state.[12]

Outreach to Hungarians and "Ruthenians"

Belgian missionaries and parish priests served a wide range of ethnocultural communities, most notably the Hungarians and the Ukrainians, known at the time as "Ruthenians." The French Oblate, Albert Pascal, even before he was named bishop of Prince Albert in 1907, advised Prime Minister Laurier that the government should recruit immigrants of diverse ethnic backgrounds and should also provide advisors, teachers and doctors with appropriate language skills. Pascal had broken with French Canadian objectives, had learned several Native languages, and taught in English. It was a multicultural approach long before its time in which some Belgians shared.[13]

The abbé Jules Pirot, a Walloon nationalist, served the Hungarians at Kaposvar (1904–15) and Esterhazy (1919–54) in their mother tongue while writing poetry in his Walloon dialect. He believed that all groups valued their mother tongue and this should receive some official recognition: "How often in a country where English predominates I saw Hungarians, Slavs, Germans, French run to me beaming because I spoke their language."[14] The Fathers of Scheut dismissed him with the comment, "he lacks a missionary calling," and the Benedictines at Bruges deemed him to be "a revolutionary and not what might be called an interesting person."[15] He spent two years in a parish in Namur ministering to the working-class poor where he imbibed the ideals of the Christian socialists. Somewhat ironically, this priest of humble origins and liberal views accepted to labour among the colonists of the Count of Esterhazy under a conservative prelate, Mgr Langevin, who needed a priest who could speak German and would learn Hungarian. The early assessment that he had no gift for evangelizing could not have been more erroneous because from Kaposvar he established ten missions nearby and six farther to the west where settlement was just beginning. He was also an unofficial colonizing agent, eventually recruiting his own family and eleven other Walloon families.[16] The Vanderhaege family, whose grandson Guy distinguished himself subsequently in the literary field, was part of the Belgian community in the Hungarian bloc settlement. Pirot's early ministry at Kaposvar was troubled by school controversies, but in the inter-war years he travelled hundreds of miles by buggy in summer and cutter in winter from Esterhazy to visit the scattered Hungarian settlements in Lipton, Cupar and Markinch. Pirot was fondly remembered as an avid gardener, a good hunter, and a kindly and simple man of learning who could be most stubborn. He never lost his love of nature, writing to his friends in Belgium about the marvels of prairie flowers, colourful songbirds, delicious wild fruits, wide horizons, beautiful sunsets and dazzling northern lights.[17]

Belgian Redemptorists reached out to other ethnic groups soon after their arrival in the West. When the Redemptorist provincial toured the West in 1892, he saw the lack of adequate services among the various ethnic communities and he was convinced that the future belonged to those who spoke English. Initially, he sent Father Willem Godts to minister to the Germans and Flemings around Regina and Edmonton, an astoundingly immense field.[18] Archbishop Langevin invited the Redemptorists to accept a charge at Brandon in 1898, with Willem Godts as superior and Edouard Verlooy as assistant, from where they could serve four missions among the Ukrainians.[19] The following year, Achille Delaere of Lendelede in West Flanders, arrived in Brandon to minister to Ukrainians and Poles at Huns Valley, Shoal Lake, Glenella and Rossburn. He noted that the Ukrainians had their own liturgy in Old Slavonic, rites common to the Eastern churches, a married secular clergy, yet were in full communion with Rome since 1596. In 1894, Propaganda Fide decreed that only celibate Ukrainian priests would be permitted to serve in North America, thus effectively cutting off recruitment in Eastern Europe.[20] The Belgian missionaries were alerted to three dangers in their ministry: i) resistance to any effort to Latinize them; ii) the temptation to attend Russian Orthodox churches that shared the same rites and customs; iii) proselytizing by Presbyterian-trained clergy of the Independent Greek Church.

Delaere was challenged by a schismatic movement led by Stefan Ustivolski, exiled from Tsarist Russia, who passed himself off as a metropolitan bishop of the Orient.[21] Delaere confirmed that he "has ordained about hundred men who are simple workmen who can barely read or write and who travel among the people to deceive them. Ordination costs fifty dollars."[22] The schismatic "Seraphim popes," or preachers, warned the people about surrendering church property to the "French" episcopal corporation. In Saltcoats the schismatic priest was none other than Ivan Kamarnizki, agent for the Dominion Lands office in Yorkton.[23] Delaere's second challenger was John Bodrug, a former Catholic cantor who had been ordained by Seraphim, who gathered some of the better-educated schismatics into an Independent Greek Church in 1904 under the direction of the Presbyterian Church and Manitoba College. This group was able to organize for its own purposes many of the Ukrainians who resisted the Latin version of Catholicism.[24]

In 1904, the Belgians established a monastery in Yorkton, and Delaere soon was joined by Evariste Vrijdaegs, and later by Louis Adam, Ludwig Boske, Henryk Boels, Charles Techeur, and Noel-Marie De Camp. The more than eight hundred families to whom they were to minister in twenty-three churches were not very enthusiastic at first because the Redemptorists were celibate monastics who followed the Latin rite and spoke little Ukrainian.[25] Two years later, Delaere received an indult from Rome permitting him to inculturate to the Ruthenian rite for a five-year period. He would follow the Julian calendar, say mass in Slavonic, administer communion in both kinds, administer confirmation immediately after baptism, wear the traditional Eastern Church vestments, but on no condition might he marry. His Walloon colleagues, Louis Adam and Charles Techeur, were not comfortable working in a Flemish establishment. Louis Adam left the congregation to become a diocesan priest serving the Ukrainians and Charles Techeur returned to Belgium and was replaced by Louis Van den Bossche.

When the Consultor General of the Redemptorists, Francis Ter Haar, visited Yorkton in August 1914, thirty Belgian priests were now serving in Canada, five of them in Yorkton following the Ruthenian rite – Delaere, Decamps, Boels, Van den Bossche, and Brother Idesbald Monstrey – to support eight Ukrainian secular priests.[26] A monastery was founded at Komarno, in the Interlake region of Manitoba, in November 1916 by Delaere and Van den Bossche to serve thirty-nine mission stations. Decamps and Boels opened a minor seminary in Ituna and were joined by Louis Regaerts and Petrus Ivens. The end of World War I enabled seven more Belgian Redemptorists to join their coreligionists in the course of the next few years: Richards Costenoble, Albien Van Biesen, Jozef Gherkiere, Frans Van den Bossche, Jaak Janssens, Hubert Gelin, and Albert Delforge.[27] Yorkton remained the central house with Komarno and Ituna as smaller units of the Vice Province under Camille Van de Steene in Brussels.

A sermon preached by Van den Bossche at Hafford in 1918, during the visit of the recently appointed Bishop Nykyta Budka of the Ruthenian rite, declared that any person who sent a child to a public school or a Ukrainian *bursa* [residence for students] was in danger of hellfire. This led to a public disturbance and a humiliating court case charging Budka and Van den Bossche with sedition. At a meeting of the Ukrainian intelligentsia in Saskatoon in 1918, the Ukrainian Greek Catholic Brotherhood was organized in order to "remove from our church celibacy, which is demoralizing our clergy and people ... to send the French-Belgian missionaries to preach the Roman faith among their own people or among the heathen."[28]

In 1923, Delaere began publishing a modest journal, *Holos Spasitelya* [Redeemer's Voice], to challenge the propaganda of Cyril Genik in *The Canadian Farmer*. Delaere was faced with two additional problems. Firstly, he found that many of the young seminarians recruited were poorly qualified academically and ill behaved, so many either quit or were dismissed. Six Flemish priests were so discouraged that they returned to Belgium. Secondly, the monastery and mission were transferred to the Toronto province of the Redemptorists, where the prevailing ideology was assimilation and anglicization. Delaere left for Belgium in the summer of 1930, after a colleague confided in a letter in Flemish: "The sun comes out after the rain, the spring comes after winter, even in Canada. But just between us, the worst is that the English will always remain English."[29] This was further underscored when a Conservative anti-immigration mayor was elected in Yorkton and the Ku Klux Klan celebrated the victory by burning a cross in the centre of the town. In 1935, Albert Delforge, a remaining Belgian, was shot by a disgruntled parishioner. It seemed time for the Belgians to close this chapter of their missionary efforts. Many Ukrainians were grateful that the Belgian missionaries had provided the nucleus from which a Ruthenian ecclesiastical province developed.[30]

Relations with Protestants

Belgians did not emigrate from a country noted for its religious diversity. The Catholic Church was in fact a national institution with which three-quarters of the population in the provinces of emigration identified closely. Members of the United Protestant Church in Belgium, did not emigrate to Canada, although from the seventeenth to the nineteenth century there was a trickle of Walloon Protestants to the United States. There was an active Jewish community in the cities which is known to have maintained some contact with Canadian Jews, notably in Montreal. Free-thinkers and agnostics were more common in the mining and industrial zones of Wallonia. In spite of this lack of significant religious diversity,

Belgian Catholics in Western Canada generally got along well with their Protestant and unchurched neighbours. Common occupational, economic and social concerns played a more prominent role than religious differences. In wartime and during the Depression, interdenominational social and charitable activities were common. Individual priests such as Leonard Van Tighem, Jules Pirot, Chrysostom of Kalmthout and Hubert Heynen reached out to the entire community regardless of religious affiliation. This toleration may have had its roots in the movement for Belgian independence when religious liberals and conservatives, along with freethinkers, united against the oppressive Dutch Calvinist influence.

In Western Canada, people and clergy lived and worked in a predominantly tolerant secular milieu while in their church life traditional customs remained. Although the Quebec-origin clergy insisted upon wearing clerical garb in public, for example, the Belgian-trained clergy opposed it in a largely Protestant milieu to avoid being ridiculed as "men in skirts" and "men in petticoats."[31] Colonizing projects launched by business interests considered it normal to exclude Catholic clergy probably because the latter had organized their own recruitment campaigns.[32] Protestant clergy and church boards carried out surveys of immigrant communities to determine their alleged adaptability to the moral and civic standards they associated with "Christian citizenship." Belgians were categorized as requiring specific programs of assimilation in spite of being ranked by the government among the "preferred" immigrants.[33] In Lethbridge, for example, Father Leonard Van Tighem refused to join the Presbyterian minister's vociferous public denunciation of alcohol abuse, gambling and prostitution, but he proceeded instead to work quietly to remedy the social environment that promoted vice in mining communities.[34] The Protestants were not long in seeking revenge; they prepared a petition to have the Catholic school cut off from public funding. In December 1895, the mayor, who was also a local lumber merchant, ordered the Catholic Church closed during an outbreak of measles in town. Van Tighem refused to comply, noting in his diary: "The finest piece of bigotry ever enacted yet in our town."[35] At this time, the Orange Lodge and several denominational organizations pressured the Dominion government to abolish immigration agents, especially missionary colonizers.

Serious opposition came from the Ku Klux Klan in the late 1920s and early 1930s in Saskatchewan in particular. The KKK campaigned openly on behalf of the Conservative Party for the prohibition of religious garb and symbols in school and the elimination of French from the curriculum. Directly affecting Belgian settlers was the KKK demand that all Catholics born outside Canada should be deported. Klan activities targeted Catholic schools and churches and even touched the Capuchin mission in Manitoba, as Father Chrysostom recorded in his diary: "During the night a huge cross was erected behind our grounds. By whom and for what purpose? People think that it is a warning from the Ku Klux Klan that they will put everything to the torch! May God protect us."[36]

In southern Alberta, Belgians faced a more subtle pressure on their religious, family and community life. Coalminers and beet workers in particular felt pressure from the Mormons' aggressive evangelization through highly organized social, sports, recreational and cultural activities that attracted the youth. Van Tighem and other clergy saw the danger of young people being lured into these social and recreational activities that encouraged fraternization and possibly inter-marriage. Although Van Tighem had made several converts to Catholicism, he was distressed when a couple young women left his congregation to marry Protestants: "May God forgive these unfortunate girls ... and may not the tears of their aged parents cry for vengeance to Heaven."[37] Mixed marriages were a problem that Mgr Langevin had underscored as early as in 1899: "It is really devastating for me to record the large number of these nefarious marriages which make us lose a lot of Catholics."[38] Of course, Msgr Jules Bois in Bellegarde could report that through such marriages he had gained several converts for his parish.

There was also the presence of a few Belgian Protestants and freethinkers who challenged the image of a homogeneous Catholic community. In 1914 a Belgian evangelist, E. Petrequin, probably associated with the Eglise Missionaire Belge in Pennsylvania, came to the Crowsnest region to preach "A New Christianity, Social and Anti-Clerical."[39] There were many lodges in the coal-mining town and most miners belonged to them, ignoring church sanctions, because of the insurance and social amenities they offered. Pastor J. E. Duclos, minister of Erskine Presbyterian Church in Edmonton, began a bilingual mission in Bonnyville in 1909, purchased a small farm near the village and opened a modest hospital and school. By 1916 a small congregation, that included some Belgians, emerged at this Duclosville. He then held successful missions in Cold Lake and at St. Paul-des-Métis. In Edmonton he opened a night school for adults and a boarding house for students of French Canadian and Walloon origin.[40]

How large was the defection? Belgians in Canada never converted as a community as had happened in Wisconsin under Joseph René Vilatte of the Old Catholic Church.[41] The 1931 census listed religious affiliation of Belgians as 24,673 Catholics and 2,912 Protestants, or more than 10 per cent higher than the ratio of Catholics to Protestants in Belgium.

Although the clergy viewed Belgians as independent thinkers and somewhat given to contention, Flemings appeared more pious and more conservative than Walloons. At the popular level, were these evaluations well-founded? Firstly, Western Canada was different from Flanders and Wallonia. "Americanism," or the movement to accommodate to liberal concepts of democracy, popular rule and the virtual separation of church and state posed a challenge to the clergy because it introduced greater personal liberty in church affairs. Secondly, church organization and support were different. The vesting of property rights in the episcopal corporation instead of in the local parish council strengthened central control. The role of local churchwardens was limited compared to the powers of Protestant trustees. Thirdly, societal change was so rapid and pervasive that popular opinion and practices outstripped convention and teaching. A generation gap could pose profound challenges to community leaders. The Catholic Church had evolved by 1940 from a mélange of immigrant churches to a national multi-ethnic institution. Francophones were no longer a dominant element in the West, although still an important component. New generations succeeded the immigrant parishioners, priests and professors, and Belgians, like others, began to question clerical celibacy, the circumscribed role of women in the church, and unquestioning obedience to the hierarchy in social and personal matters. Fourthly, the charitable attitudes and actions of Protestant leaders and benefactors acted as a goad to Catholics from time to time. Diversity at the community level resulted in increasingly tolerant views of "others" on the part of neighbours. It would take a century, nevertheless, for official pronouncements by church leaders to move from labelling of "heretics" to "separated brethren."

Belgian Parishes

Canon law provided only for territorial or geographical parishes, not ethnic-based congregations. What had no canonical provision had to be organized on a practical basis, as was done in Winnipeg for the Poles and

Germans. In 1913, Archbishop Langevin informed the Vatican that there were three rural Flemish parishes in Manitoba: St. Alphonse, Bruxelles, and Swan Lake. He also reported that there were two Flemish priests for six hundred parishioners in St. Boniface and Ste. Amélie.[42] Two problems arose in parishes where Belgians were numerous: firstly, Francophone priests who insisted on delivering their sermons and announcements in French to Flemish parishioners; secondly, priests who spoke Flemish and used English in parishes with a significant number of Francophones. In an encyclical to the Canadian hierarchy in 1916, Pope Benedict XV addressed the problem of such divisions: "we urge all priests engaged in the sacred ministry to become thoroughly conversant in the knowledge and use of the two languages, and discarding all motives of rivalry, to adopt one or the other according to the requirements of the faithful." This was official bilingualism before its time with no recognition of other ethnolinguistic needs and demands.[43]

The parishes in south central Manitoba grew out of mission stations of St. Leon parish, Theobald Bitsch serving as both priest and immigration agent. In 1883, a log building used as both church and school was erected at St. Alphonse with abbé Télesphore Campeau, who began to learn Flemish, as its first resident priest.[44] The abbé Gustave Willems immigrated to Brussels in 1892 and ministered in both Flemish and French. In 1897, abbé Hubert Heynen, a Dutch priest from Limburg, was transferred from Deloraine and its missions as far west as Forget and Estevan, to Bruxelles, where he served until his golden jubilee in 1946. He ministered in both languages and brought out Catholic settlers from both Belgium and Holland.[45] In 1913 a church was built in Swan Lake with Dom Boniface Diedericks as first resident priest.

There was a Walloon concentration west of Bruxelles, at Grande Clairière, Deleau and Bellegarde, part of Jean Gaire's utopian dream. The Belgians at Manor attended mass in Wauchope until 1925. In 1929, a vacant bank building served the parish until a church was built in 1950. In 1974, St. Joseph's parish, Manor, was downgraded to a mission, with the priest resident in neighbouring Carlyle, and was deconsecrated in April 2006. The descendants of the original Belgian families had moved on.[46] In southern Alberta, near Strathmore, a number of Flemings joined the settlement of Dutch Catholics of abbé Van Aaken, popularly known as Aakenstad. Leonard Van Tighem took up residence in Strathmore in 1909 as priest at the Sacred Heart parish with its core of Flemish adherents.

They organized charities in support of the Don Bosco Home in Calgary, missions in India and Peru and a special relief society to bring assistance to victims of the Depression. Here also, by the outbreak of World War II, the Belgians were lost in a multicultural community.

The largest concentration of Belgians in the West was in St. Boniface and adjacent St. Vital and Fort Garry. All Belgians, both Flemings and Walloons, originally attended mass at the cathedral. Archbishop Beliveau designated a chapel at the rear of the cathedral where a succession of priests – De Munter, Van Den Bossche, and Everard Kwakman – said mass every Sunday and gave catechism classes in Flemish in the afternoon. Some Flemish community leaders asked for a "national church" in 1911 but the proposal failed to obtain widespread support among the parishioners. The chairman of a planning committee reported: "having regard to the disposition of the large majority of Flemings: I thought it wise to abandon the project of a Flemish church."[47] It was an attitude that would continue to plague the project of a Flemish ethnic parish. The underlying problem was that the majority did not want to assume the huge debt load such a project would entail. In Belgium there was generous state support of the church, the absence of which in Canada immigrants did not always understand. They even resented the compulsory payment of tithes.

Eventually, in October 1917, the Flemish parishioners indicated their desire to proceed with the plan, leaving the Walloons to continue worshipping at the cathedral with other Francophones. Msgr Beliveau presided over the canonical erection of the parish: "We recognize and erect as a Catholic parish for the service of the faithful of the Flemish language of the parish of St. Boniface ... under the invocation of the Sacred Heart, the same territory as that of the parish of St. Boniface."[48] On Plinquet Street in the "Belgian Town" sector, a house served as a rectory with the church on the same lot. Technically, it was a linguistic parish within the cathedral parish, although the parishioners regarded it as the "national parish," saying that "Belgian means a Fleming and speaking Belgian means speaking Flemish."[49] It took on a more Flemish character in 1928 when the Capuchins assumed charge of the parish and built a monastery under the leadership of Father Chrysostom.

The Flemish community did not support the Capuchins to the extent required. Catechism classes in Flemish were stopped in 1935, parents preferring English instruction for their children. In 1955, even sermons in Flemish were no longer offered because of the lack of interest. This erosion of the use of the Flemish language may be attributed to the lack of sustained immigration to reinforce the original community, and to assimilation into mainstream society of the third generation through the school system, community pressure and the influence of the media. Flemings found English relatively easy to learn and virtually obligatory for the conduct of business.[50] Attendance and financial support declined over the years until Archbishop Baudoux, a Belgian who had great pride in the community, found it necessary to hold a consultative assembly regarding the future of the parish. There was little interest in maintaining a costly Flemish institution: therefore the committee, on which R. Bockstael represented the community, recommended closing the church and winding down parish affairs. In later years, a few parishioners and some Capuchins regretted the decision and tended to blame the archdiocese.

The Capuchins expanded their activities with a second monastery at Toutes-Aides under the rule of the mother house in St. Boniface. In addition to serving the parish that had a number of Belgian families, as did nearby Ste. Rose-du-Lac, the Capuchins undertook missions to Native peoples of the region. They received a young Native novice, Brother Arsene Spence, who was to be sent to the Detroit house, but the Americans would not accept a Canadian Indian because "past experience shows Canadians cannot conform to our life and surroundings and cause a lot of trouble."[51] When informed he could not attain to the priesthood, he left. His superior surmised: "Maybe our life seems to be monotonous. One young brother alone with older priests, who would converse mostly in Flemish even in recreation. But the instability of this Indian boy and his longing for freedom are not to be excluded from his final decision."[52] The cultural divide was as great between the First Nations and the Capuchins as with other religious orders. In 1972, Cardinal Archbishop Flahiff of Winnipeg asked the Capuchins to turn over their parish and several western missions to the Oblates.

In Greater Winnipeg there were numerous scattered Belgian families that worshipped in English at Holy Cross parish in Norwood, at St. Maurice in Fort Garry, and St. Ignatius in south Winnipeg. The rapid integration of Flemings into mainstream society resulted, in part, from this involvement in multi-ethnic parishes. Even an ethnic parish such as "Sacred Heart of the Belgians" in St. Boniface succumbed to local apathy and urban and occupational integrationist pressures.

Belgians in the Hierarchy

The Western Canadian hierarchy, in the late nineteenth and early twentieth centuries, distinguished itself as being conservative and pious rather than scholarly and open to new social and demographic changes. A breath of fresh ideas came from priests and bishops who had frequented the American College of the University of Louvain, founded in 1857 on the initiative of Peter Paul Lefevre, Belgian administrator of the diocese of Detroit. Among its outstanding graduates were two future Pacific coast bishops of the archdiocese of Oregon, which extended originally from California to Alaska and included Vancouver Island: Jean-Baptiste Brondel of Bruges and Charles-Jean Seghers of Ghent.[53] In 1903, the diocese of Victoria was detached from the American church although many Catholics did not like the thought of becoming part of a French-Canadian-dominated church.

In September 1862, Charles-Jean Seghers left Louvain to take up missionary work among Native "no stockings" and settler "short stockings" on Vancouver Island. One of his first acts was to visit the flourishing mission of August Joseph Brabant at Hesquiat on the west coast of the island.[54] Seghers, who spoke English, French, German, Flemish and several Native dialects, and read nine languages, quickly sensed a British air of superiority to everything foreign and Catholic.[55] Seghers was consecrated bishop of Victoria in June 1873, named coadjutor at Oregon City in 1878, then archbishop in 1880. In 1886 he resigned to return to Vancouver Island and then devoted himself to missionary work in the Yukon, where he was murdered.[56] Seghers was a scholar who declared that "a bishop without books is like a soldier without arms." He left a special collection of more than four thousand books, now at the University of Victoria.[57] Jean-Baptiste Brondel came to the Oregon territory in the 1860s and in 1879 succeeded Segher as Bishop of Victoria. His episcopacy was brief because he was transferred to Helena, Montana, where there were also Belgians.[58] His auxiliaries and compatriots, Louis Lootens and Joseph Nicolaye, were passed over as his successors because the Holy See recognized that the Anglophone constituency did not want any more French and Belgian clergy and bishops.[59]

In contrast to the Pacific coastal region where Belgian bishops were immigrants, on the Prairies three Canadian-educated prelates distinguished themselves and their community. Maurice Baudoux was born at La Louvière in Belgium and came to Prud'homme, Saskatchewan, at the age of nine. He was ordained in 1929 and served in his home parish of Prud'homme until his appointment as bishop of St. Paul in 1948, and then archbishop of St. Boniface in 1952. As a Walloon who grew up in a predominantly French Canadian and French parish, he engaged in the traditional Francophone struggle for language, educational and cultural rights. In St. Boniface his constant defence of minority rights and promotion of inter-cultural harmony won him the distinction of being the first Western Canadian prelate to receive an honorary degree from a Protestant institution, United College in Winnipeg.[60] Archbishop Baudoux's successor was also a Belgian, born in southern Manitoba. Antoine Hacault, grandson of pioneer Louis Hacault and Leontine Tilmont of Bruxelles, was ordained in 1951, named auxiliary bishop in 1964, and then coadjutor with succession rights to Archbishop Baudoux in 1972. Like his grandfather, he was conservative in his views and habits.

From Swan Lake, Rémi De Roo, son of Raymond De Roo and Josephine De Pape, second generation Flemish Canadian farmers, was raised by the Ursuline nuns in Bruxelles after his mother's untimely death. He was ordained in 1950, served as parish priest at Holy Cross in Norwood, a multi-ethnic parish, and rose to episcopal rank in 1962. As Bishop of Victoria he was active in the peace movement and human rights issues. He became particularly outspoken on economic issues and was perceived as the most liberal and outgoing member of the episcopacy. He was named to the Pontifical Commission for Culture and was a major contributor on social affairs and economic policy for the Canadian Conference of Catholic Bishops. Although he was temporarily disgraced for an alleged mismanagement of diocesan funds, he was vindicated subsequently and his important contribution to Catholic social thought was honoured. The intellectual trajectory of the two Manitoba-born bishops is illuminating: Hacault was a descendant of a controversial outspoken Walloon journalist and became a conservative administrator, while De Roo was a descendant of a conservative farmer and became an outspoken liberal reformer. That the Holy See named Hacault to St. Boniface and De Roo to Victoria was not haphazard.

In the Second Vatican Council, Baudoux assembled a group of young consultants who later became bishops: Remi De Roo at Victoria, Antoine Hacault at St. Boniface, and Noel Delaquis at Gravelbourg. This group made a special contribution as Baudoux addressed the Council seven times and his team submitted twenty-three written texts. Among the innovative ideas they presented were the use of the vernacular in the mass and breviary, the updating of pastoral care, and the importance of Biblical studies. They were strongly supported by Cardinal Soenens of Brussels and Cardinal Liénart of Lille.[61]

Religion in Education

Belgians were involved in two historic struggles known as the "Manitoba School Question" and the "Territorial School Question." Public education was originally under the control of the several colonial administrations that came together to form the Dominion of Canada in 1867, with territorial additions thereafter. The division of powers under a federal system of government left public schooling in the jurisdictional domain of the provinces. In Manitoba and the North-West Territories there was originally a dual confessional system of public schools, Protestant and Catholic, each in control of its own curriculum, teacher training, inspection system, and languages of instruction. The Pacific coastal colonies of Vancouver Island and British Columbia had a common non-sectarian system with instruction in English. When the provinces of Alberta and Saskatchewan were created in 1905, they adopted a separate school system, based on the Ontario model. This system set up common non-sectarian schools and permitted within each school district the organization of a separate Catholic or Protestant school if numbers warranted. All schools followed a common curriculum and teacher-training program in this system. Belgian immigrants came into a situation that was in transition and open to acrimonious conflicts. The Public Schools Act, 1890, abolished the Catholic public school system in Manitoba, creating a single public system out of the Protestants school sector. Although the act seemed unconstitutional, the federal government avoided disallowing it, preferring to let the courts decide if there were appeals.[62] These actions were undertaken because the libertarian rhetoric of the Protestants held that only public schools promoted unity and freedom.[63] At that moment, an ultra-conservative Catholic journalist from *Le Courrier de Bruxelles*, Louis Hacault, was touring the West with a Belgian delegation. He had carried on a vociferous campaign in the Belgian press against "godless schools," Free Masons and agnostics. He quickly turned to denouncing the same "enemies of virtue" in Manitoba, but his loud protests made little impact on government officials. Catholic officials were somewhat embarrassed by the vituperation of his allegations: "Although it seemed the theories were pushed somewhat to the extreme, he advanced nothing without some proof, and if it was difficult to accept some of his ideas, it would have been very embarrassing to attempt to refute them."[64] The schools in the parishes continued to operate much as before without the official Catholic designation. In the St. Boniface region, where the majority of the new arrivals were concentrated, the schools operated largely in French under the supervision of T.A. Bernier, former provincial Superintendent of Catholic Schools. Bernier was a friend of the archbishop, a correspondent of the Société Saint-Raphaël, and an immigration agent working on the Belgian file.

In order to maintain instruction in French and religion, *écoles libres*, or "free schools," were organized in some localities supported by voluntary donations and funds raised by the clergy from the wider Catholic community. Msgr Langevin had encountered the term "free schools" in Belgium signifying self-supporting institutions distinct from those benefiting from state support. In St. Alphonse, abbé Campeau had the school continue with the voluntary labour of students and financial sacrifice of the parents. The students undertook to gather wood for fuel, haul water, shovel snow, till the school garden and clean the classroom. In Bruxelles, abbé Willems transformed the public Ecole Ste. Marie into a "free school" in 1895 and personally taught the curriculum set out by the province. Dr. Alphonse Verwilghen sacrificed time from his medical practice to teach English to pupils and adults who wanted to learn the dominant language of the wider community.[65] The Lorne municipal council, which included Belgian members, gave an annual grant to these schools. Flemings united with Walloons in demanding a Catholic education, although a few were in favour of the non-sectarian system. The archbishop opined "we count on changing their minds."[66] Gradually, some rural Catholic schools frequented by Belgian children accepted the public non-sectarian system and inspection.

Appeals were made to the consul general to organize support in Belgium for the beleaguered Catholic schools. Jules de Bernard de Fauconsol noted "what discreet reserve I am obliged to observe in this Canadian political question." It would be impolitic to advertise in Belgian newspapers for contributions to a Manitoba Schools Fund. On the other hand, he observed, "the most practical method, in my opinion, would be to send the abbé Willems to recruit emigrants in Belgium and perhaps bring back money." He offered to contact the Minister of the Interior "to obtain for him a free return ticket, and the position of an immigration agent."[67] Following the accession to power of the Liberals under Wilfrid Laurier in 1896, negotiations were initiated with the Manitoba government, resulting in a compromise known as the Laurier-Greenway Agreement, 1897. It introduced a system of bilingual public schools alongside the common schools.

In the North-West Territories the erosion of the dual confessional system was incremental and aroused less public outcry than in Manitoba. In 1901, a Department of Education was created and all schools were subject to this central administration. Although the legislative trend was clear, application in specific cases could be somewhat different. In Lethbridge, in 1889, Father Leonard Van Tighem opened a school and brought the Faithful Companions of Jesus to operate the boarding institution. The local newspaper deplored the move, advocating a single public school to assimilate the immigrants' children because "many of them bring hatred of Government, hatred of liberty, and hatred of humanity."[68] The social leaders in the community belittled Van Tighem's work among the "foreign element" and proceeded to attempt to block his efforts to obtain Territorial funding for his school. He responded: "there are now [1893] over eighty children attending of which a dozen are Protestants. Thus has the so-called separate school become more public than the public school."[69]

The Walloons in Bellegarde believed they would encounter fewer difficulties in organizing a Catholic public school because they formed a religiously homogeneous community, unlike Lethbridge.[70] In September 1899, they organized Bellegarde Catholic Public School No. 50 but encountered difficulties in recruiting and retaining suitable teachers. They persisted in their efforts and were successful in retaining their Catholic instruction through both the school crisis and the municipal restructuration crisis that followed. The crisis in the North-West Territories was resolved differently than in Manitoba. Both jurisdictions had originally followed the Quebec model of a dual confessional system. Manitoba eventually moved to the Maritime model of a single non-sectarian public system while the Territories, upon attaining provincial status in 1905 for Saskatchewan and Alberta, adopted the Ontario model that permitted a separate Catholic system alongside the common schools.

Belgians found themselves supporting different school system depending upon the provincial jurisdiction in which they lived.

Language and Education

The Canadian West was originally a jurisdiction known as the Mer de l'Ouest, with headquarters at Fort Kaministquia [Thunder Bay, Ontario], frequented by Montreal-based fur traders and itinerant Catholic missionaries. Its Métis population adopted French as its European language. After the British conquest, the region became the territory of a royal charter company, the Hudson's Bay Company, that permitted the Earl of Selkirk to found a small Red River colony at the junction of the Red and Assiniboine rivers, where the Catholic mission of St. Boniface developed. Following the sale of the territory to the Canadian government in 1869, Louis Riel's provisional government maintained the established bilingual character of the settlement, and this passed over "in practice," but not law, into the constitution of the province of Manitoba, 1870.

Religious rights and linguistic rights were confused because Catholics often used their schools to offer instruction in French. European immigration resulted in demands for recognition of languages other than English and French as mediums of instruction, on the one hand, and measures to assimilate the "new subjects" through an integrationist Anglo-conformist curriculum and school system, on the other hand. In Bellegarde, for example, the inspector's report in 1903 was very critical. It said: "The teaching is mainly in French and the pupils are not gaining much ability to use English." The solution proposed was clear. "They are not likely to improve in the use of English unless English is used and the pupils are required to use it.... There seems to be no necessity for the constant use of French."[71] During the first provincial election in Saskatchewan in 1905, the archbishop reminded parishioners in a letter read from pulpits that the Conservative Territorial government had increasingly restricted French and Catholic instruction from 1885 to 1901. The publication of the pastoral letter was widely viewed as clerical interference in secular affairs. Bellegarde voters supported the Liberal candidate, a clear indication that these Walloons followed the example of their French Canadian neighbours.[72] The Liberal government that came to power in 1896 in Ottawa was seen as open to increased immigration and a resolution of the Manitoba School Question. The Laurier-Greenway Agreement provided for a system of bilingual schools, shifting the emphasis away from religion to language. Clause 258 of the revised Manitoba Public Schools Act, 1897, provided that "when 10 of the pupils of any school speak the French language, or any language other than English, as their native language, the teaching of such pupils shall be conducted in French, or such other language, and English upon the bilingual system."[73] The English-French bilingual schools would serve the Walloons as well as a number of Flemings who also spoke French. Rome was convinced that the clergy should adopt a more conciliatory approach.[74] On the other hand, Roman authorities supported the efforts of Hacault and others to work secretly for restoration of the Catholic schools.[75]

Following the implementation of the terms of the Laurier-Greenway Agreement in 1897, former Catholic public schools and "free schools" transformed themselves into English-French bilingual schools. Flemish parents in St. Boniface living along the banks of the Seine River petitioned their school board for an English-Flemish bilingual school, but the board was unable to supply qualified teachers. The request was never taken up subsequently. In the St. Alphonse, Somerset and Swan Lake area, seventeen one-room rural English-French bilingual schools were organized.[76] Louis Hacault led a press campaign on the premise that it was impossible to separate French instruction from a Catholic curriculum and environment in both Canadian and Belgian publications.[77] Abbé Jean Gaire also took up the fight to raise money for schools through articles in a bulletin called initially *Les Annales du denier du Manitoba*, in *Le Défenseur du Canada catholique et français*, and in *La question des écoles ... appel à la France et la Belgique*. Although the Francophone communities retained much of their cultural identity under the bilingual school system, the church was less assured about other ethnocultural groups such as the Flemings.

With the outbreak of World War I there were numerous expressions of fear the country was becoming "balkanized," through inadequate instruction in English language and literature and inappropriate civic attitudes. John W. Dafoe in the *Manitoba Free Press* expressed this sentiment: "There is a real danger that Canada may become a multilingual country, inhabited by different peoples, speaking different tongues, and cherishing divergent national ideals."[78] In this charged atmosphere, the newly elected Liberal government of T.C. Norris in 1915 considered abolishing the bilingual system and introducing compulsory school attendance. Charles Newcombe, Superintendent of Schools, conducted an investigation of the schools. The tenor of his report did not support the charges made by the *Manitoba Free Press* and the *Winnipeg Tribune*. Newcombe found some "administrative difficulties," such as a tendency in the English-French schools to use French as the medium of instruction throughout the day for the primary grades, but he made no recommendation for abolition of the bilingual system. There was also the problem that only one bilingual school existed in some multilingual settlements, so that one or two Belgian families had access only to an English-Ruthenian bilingual school. In Bruxelles and Grande Clairière the teachers lacked frequent contact with native speakers of English. There were 126 English-French rural and village schools with 234 teachers and 7 393 pupils. In St. Boniface Provencher School, with ninety-eight Belgian pupils, and St. Joseph's Academy, with sixty-five Belgian pupils, pupils were taught by religious orders and were performing efficiently: "at a relatively early age, acquiring ease and fluency in the use of English." In Ste-Rose-du-Lac village school, the students had a better understanding of English than the teacher and had reached a "fairly good" standard. At Ecole Ste-Marie in Bruxelles, although both teachers were English-speaking, junior pupils were unable to converse in English. However, in all schools, virtually all children were fluently bilingual by Grade 8, contrary to assertions appearing in the press and voiced publicly and in the legislature by opponents of the system.[79]

Newcombe's findings were also supported by inspectoral reports of the period for southern Manitoba. In 1915, rural school districts near St. Alphonse, Somerset, Swan Lake, St. Leon and Holland were added to the inspectoral duties of an Anglophone, Dr. D.S. Woods, whose comments on "twenty districts, comprising 30 departments serving children of French and Belgian extraction" were revealing. He wrote:

> The convent schools are outstanding examples of attractive surroundings, comfort and neatness. I was particularly pleased in the latter type of school with the sense of respect, courtesy and good manners of the children. In English composition and conversation good progress has been made in St. Alphonse, Bruxelles, Somerset, the senior room of Lourdes. And the junior room at St. Leon, and also in the following rural schools – Cleophas, Faure, Montcalm and Pike Lake.[80]

Nevertheless, the Norris government proceeded to repeal the bilingual clause. The *Manitoba Free Press* did not believe in "abolishing the French language from the schools" because the French were entitled to "special treatment" as a founding partner. The *Winnipeg Telegram*, on the other hand, found no convincing argument for abolition and believed the Liberals were influenced by "extreme influences" within the party.[81] The government alleged that Robert Fletcher, Deputy Minister of Education from 1903 to 1939, had found the bilingual system in "near collapse." Fletcher later denied such a view:

> By 1916 the schools were producing young people with a fair knowledge of English. There was a marked improvement in this respect in the secondary schools in French communities, and the leaders among the French set themselves the task of seeing that their young people destined for the teaching profession measured up to the required standards.[82]

Immediate implementation of the full scope of the legislation did not occur. Belgians everywhere continued to support bilingual schooling. The Belgian Club sent a letter of support to opposition members of the legislature. In 1917, the inspector in Deloraine reported on the last bilingual classes: "Flossie school, in a Belgian settlement in the Turtle Mountains, continues to do excellent work. Here the pupils speak with scarcely a trace of accent." The convent school in Bruxelles continued to operate under public school jurisdiction and drew the commendation: "It would not be fair at this point to overlook the success that has been made by the staff of Bruxelles village school, where in three years time the pupils from the lowest to the highest grades have learned to speak English very well." In all the Belgian rural school districts, the inspector in 1918 found that "considerable effort had been made to better physical conditions" and teachers were upgrading their qualifications.[83]

In both Saskatchewan and Alberta, communities tried to staff their schools with teachers of their own ethnolinguistic group. This usually satisfied Walloons settled in Francophone communities. The practice was tolerated because it was assumed by some educators that English could be taught best to non-English speakers through the medium of the mother tongue. This assumption was challenged by Norman F. Black in *English for the Non-English* (Regina, 1913), who asserted that success would be achieved only through the exclusive use of English in the classroom, school premises and community activities. This idea was taken up by school inspectors, as demonstrated in one report: "Teach the children to speak, to read and to write English – this is our first and great educational commandment. Our second commandment is like unto the first – through the common medium of English within our schools build up a national character." French Canadians combined language and religion; English Canadians combined language and nationalism.[84]

Belgian Relief Fund, Regina, SK. (Sask. Archives R-B 9525)
Throughout Western Canada people generously supported the Relief Fund for
German-occupied Belgium, 1914-18.

VIII

ECONOMIC, POLITICAL AND MILITARY ACTIVITY

In the economic domain Belgians were promoters and pioneers but in the political domain they were participants for the most part. Belgium played a major role in economic and industrial development and diversification in Western Canada through investment in capital and technology and the creation of jobs for thousands of Canadians beyond the wheat economy. Investment played an important role in nation-building in the region as Belgians became involved in land speculation, construction, resource exploitation, mining operations, commercial agriculture, and research. Their role in dairying, market gardening, fruit-growing and sugar-beet culture have been examined in earlier chapters. In manufacturing, the transformation of raw materials into other goods, they operated or worked in flour mills, sugar refineries, brickworks, lumber mills and cheese factories. Oil and gas discoveries in Alberta and the beginning of uranium and potash mining in Saskatchewan broadened the economic base and invited investment. These developments stimulated the service sector, trucking, marketing and manufacturing. Agriculture was no longer the main underpinning of the local economy and began to develop into agro-business.

The growing pains of a new economy spawned regional political parties that Belgians were reluctant to support. The drought and depression of the inter-war years underscored not only the weaknesses of the capitalist system but also the vulnerability of immigrant agriculturalists. Thus they were willing to consider government intervention in the economy and some central planning of production and distribution. It was easier to accept the health care and social services of a welfare state that eventually evolved than controls in agricultural production and marketing. Two world wars resulted in an image of a "brave little Belgium," war relief campaigns, and close military ties.

Belgians in Western Canada participated modestly in political activity and organization out of their own class and occupational interests. Miners and beet workers were accustomed to union activities, the former in particular having a strong political legacy. All Belgians were somewhat acquainted with monarchy, parliamentary institutions, political parties and elections before coming to Canada. Office-holding was not a priority for newcomers but most were involved in neighbourhood organizing and community activity. They did not participate visibly in the political elite. However, they played an important, but less conspicuous, role at the local and regional levels. A few were elected to the federal parliament and provincial legislatures, where careers are usually brief and their decision-making powers are greatly curtailed by party solidarity and the caucus.

Commercial and Industrial Investment

Commercial interest in Canada predated Confederation. In August 1848 Arthur Hart of Montreal wrote to the Belgian ambassador in London offering to serve as consul in Canada. The Chamber of Commerce in Antwerp contacted the Ministry of Foreign Affairs in Brussels suggesting that it would be useful to have a consular official either in Montreal or Quebec "to enlighten Belgian traders about the unknown resources" of Canada with a view to both import and export trade. Two years later, Jesse Joseph, a frequent visitor to Belgium with European business contacts and involvement in immigration projects, was named honorary consul in Montreal.[1] There was a problem, however, in establishing direct commercial ties because article XV of the Anglo-Belgian Treaty of 1862 subjected the British North American colonies to British control of commercial and diplomatic affairs. After Confederation, Sir Alexander Galt opined that no further treaties should restrict Canadian commerce without the consent of the colonial authorities.[2] Still, good commercial exchanges were not forthcoming, partly because Britain expressed considerable concern about Belgian exploitation of the Congo up to 1914.[3] Nevertheless, the Métallurgie of Tubize built a public building in Ottawa for the Dominion government in 1886 and the following year the S.A. Internationale de Construction entered into a number of public works contracts with the government of Quebec. The Grand Trunk Railway bought its steel rails from Cockerill of Liège. These activities marked the beginning of Belgian investment.

Antwerp and Brussels investment firms became interested in Canada largely through the efforts of Ferdinand Van Bruyssel (Consul-General, 1885–94), who enjoyed the favour of the Prince of Chimay, Minister of Foreign Affairs, who consorted with the economic elite of the day. Members of the Belgian royal family, cabinet ministers, the nobility and notables involved in the exploitation of the Congo and investments in Egypt were among those speculating on the profits to be reaped in Canada. In February 1888, a Comptoir Belgo-Canadien, presided jointly by P.S. Stevenson of the Grand Trunk Railway and Clarence de Sola, was organized in Montreal to attract Belgian capital and to facilitate the importation of Belgian glass, cement and rails.[4] This initial initiative was marred somewhat by the personal involvement of Van Bruyssel in secret business deals, using government funds for personal gain and lobbying inconsistent with his diplomatic status.[5] In 1891, Van Bruyssel informed Premier Greenway of Manitoba that three engineers from the Belgian State Corps of Mining Engineers associated with the University of Liège were prepared to undertake a two-year survey "to call attention of capitalists and metallurgists in Belgium ... to investments ... mining property and establishing metallurgical industries in Canada."[6] In addition, the *Recueil Financier* in 1893 drew attention to the Canadian Pacific Railway and the agricultural promise of Western Canada.[7] A network of honorary consuls involved in business was set in place: Victoria 1892; Vancouver 1897; Winnipeg 1901; Prince Albert 1906; Regina 1908; Edmonton 1908; Forget 1903; and Manor 1915. Consul Robert de Vos advised offering "advances on crops, mortgages, loans for buying building material, livestock or horses, savings and other banking services, even arrange agricultural real estate and possessions, create agricultural industries or contribute to their creation."[8] It was known in Europe that "high officials of the Department of the Interior" favoured speculator friends by manipulating the submissions so that "certain important people, partisans of those in power, had every opportunity to make off with the best lands at the lowest price."[9]

Belgium, as a country of heavy industrialization, developed a model based on linking heavy industry and the banking system that motivated financiers and industrialists to seek foreign markets.[10] Three periods of investment activity can be discerned, originating in Brussels and Antwerp respectively. In the period prior to World War I, the Brussels groups concentrated on the eastern provinces, while Antwerp entrepreneurs turned their attention to the West, after Ferdinand de Jardin's visit in 1906. The Banque d'Outre-Mer, the Banque de Bruxelles, Paribas, in conjunction with the Emile Francqui group that included Ernest and Edmond Solvay, Jules and Jean Jadot, formed the Société Minière du Canada in 1910. Its objective was to expand activities in Western Canada, including the construction of a railway link in Alberta to the Brazeau mines and investment in two silver mines in British Columbia.[11] In 1912, the Société La Canadienne [Belprise] was formed by Baron Maurice Fallon, John de Marnix, Charles de Burlet, Mme Capelle-Henry, Maurice de Laminne and Baron Pierre Verhaegen for construction projects in Calgary.

The Antwerp investors belonged to the Frédéric Jacobs group, which included Jean Berchmann, André Gouzée, Xavier Bareel, and Frédéric Jacobs, and formed the Alberta S.A. Belge du Nord-Ouest Canadien in 1905 which bought 70,000 hectares of land along the projected Canadian Northern Railway line between Battleford and Edmonton.[12] Also involved in this venture were Ludovic De Dekker, Emile de Bontridler, Albert Peeters and Albert de Bary. The influential director of its business affairs was André Gouzée, who had come initially to the Montmartre area to engage in cattle-raising. He became intimately involved with another of the Jacobs group enterprises, the Belgo-Canadian Fruitlands Company organized in 1908 in the Okanagan valley. Land speculating could be risky, and this prompted the Belgian consul in Calgary to warn about "wild catting," the sale of worthless lands at exorbitant prices.[13] In 1906, the Frédéric Jacobs group set up the Land and Agriculture Company of Canada [Compagnie Immobilière et Agricole du Canada] with offices in Winnipeg, where Ferdinand de Jardin was in charge. The company bought up 65,000 hectares of prime farmland along the Grand Trunk Pacific and Canadian Pacific Railways, and another seven thousand hectares in the Vernon area of British Columbia. Shareholders included Baron Edmond Van Eetvelde, Louis Van de Put, and André Gouzée "a member of the local board of directors."[14] Closely related to this investment company was the General Financial Corporation of Canada which dealt in loans, mortgages, investments, securities, stocks and bonds. Once again the interlocking directorate was noted: "Mr André Gouzée is one of the managing directors and in charge of the company's affairs in Canada. The head office of the company is in Antwerp, and the Canadian head quarters are at Winnipeg."[15]

In 1907, the Société Hypothécaire du Canada [Mortgage Company of Canada] with 10 million francs capital from the Société Générale, Banque Commerciale d'Anvers and Banque J. LeGrelle, and private funds from Baron Delbeke, Baron Van Eetvelde, Robert De Decker, Ernest Goethals and the Jacobs brothers among others, entered the Western Canadian market. Once again the extent of this investment drew attention: "The company controls large sums of European capital, which is invested in first-class mortgages on properties accepted as safe risks only after the very closest inspection."[16] In 1911, the Antwerp investors of the de Bary group launched the Belgian Estate Company of Canada [Société Foncière Belgo-Canadienne] with a capital of 12.5 million francs to undertake housing developments in Winnipeg and Edmonton. Its activities continued until May 1976. Crédit Général du Canada, capitalized by Oscar Vandermalen, Paul Lambert-Mandron, Thomas Moreau de Bellaing, Remacle Bonjeon, Jules de Borchgrave, Fernand Dauwe and Florent Lambert, invested in Winnipeg and Vancouver. This also represented investment from the Walloon cities of Namur and Liège.

Of more than passing interest was the corporate linkages as Ferdinand de Jardin and E. de Grelle of the Land and Agriculture Company of Canada, and André Gouzée of the Mortgage Company of Canada figured prominently among the directors of the Crédit Général du Canada and the Belgian Estate Company, both chartered in 1911. Ferdinand de Jardin was appointed chief administrator by the Jacobs group of all these companies, along with Louis Van de Put. Xavier Bareel was involved in the Jacobs Group and he was connected also with the Banque Belgo-Luxembourgeoise and its manifold investments. Baron van Eetvelde, renowned secretary of state for the Congo Free State under Leopold II, chaired the over-arching board of directors. The Lille bank of Henry Devilder, which was involved in the Trochu settlement in Alberta, was also a shareholder.

Several smaller projects merit attention. In 1910, the Banque Josse Allard of Brussels obtained a 15 per cent share in the Nordegg and

Brazeau Collieries. In 1914 Raoul Pirmez[17] and George Roels, with a couple friends in Calgary, inspired by a rumour started by a Scottish geologist that the properties along the Elbow River were sitting on a sea of oil, formed Petrol Limited. The capital was to be raised in Belgium but the outbreak of war and the German invasion of Belgium put an end to the project.[18] In 1913, fifteen small entrepreneurs in Brussels banded together to launch the Belgo-Canadian Co-operative Society, which bought up 250 lots of land in the Moose Jaw area for resale.[19] It proceeded to sell, at "exorbitant prices," some lots in subdivisions of Moose Jaw called Fairmont and Glenora.[20] The company was dissolved by 1919 and purchasers were left with undeveloped and unserviced lots of farmland five kilometres beyond the city limits that were then offered for sale for payment of arrears of taxes. The acting consul in Calgary observed: "this company was directed by a band of rogues and the whole affair was a massive swindle."[21]

The non-payment of taxes on property during World War I created a problem for some Belgians. Baron Maurice Fallon, for example, owned properties in Prince Albert and Vancouver for which he was unable to pay taxes because he spent the war years confined to his estate in Namur, except for two brief periods in jail in Germany. Belgian authorities interceded to stop the sale of these properties for tax arrears on the ground that it was unreasonable to deal unjustly with a citizen of an allied nation under German occupation who was anxious to pay the arrears to retain his possessory rights.[22] The consul in Calgary explained, to the newly appointed Consul in Vancouver, the injustice that Baron Fallon faced in the projected sale of valuable Point Grey properties purchased in 1911: "Belgians have invested a very considerable amount of money in Canada before the war in real estate, loans, etc. and the conditions in which they have found their investments after the war is anything but encouraging. The exchange is so high against Belgium and the payment of these taxes will cost Baron Fallon 100% more than it would have cost him before the war."[23]

During a second period of activity from 1919 to 1939, only four of the early Belgian companies flourished – the Land and Agriculture Company, the Mortgage Company of Canada, the Belgian Estate Company of Canada, and the General Credit of Canada, all part of the umbrella Jacobs group based in Antwerp.[24] In these inter-war years, much of the early optimism about the future prosperity of Western Canada evaporated. Belgians were primarily concerned with reconstructing their own economy which had been shattered by war. Nevertheless, the Antwerp-based investors launched two new trading companies – the Belgo-Canadian Trading Company in 1919, and the Canadian Pacific Ocean Services Agency in 1921. The Canadian Block Coal Company, financed by Brussels bankers and chartered with Belgian managers at Taber to exploit concessions in Alberta, appears to have ceased operations by 1925.[25] When a certain Gaston Pootmans proposed to set up a sales outlet for Belgian products in Regina in 1922, the consul advised him to consider Winnipeg instead of Regina because the small city did not serve a sufficient Belgian clientele for such a venture.[26]

Investment and trade were expected to rebound significantly with the granting of "most favoured nation" status to Belgium by the Commercial Treaty of 1924. In this context, Captain Léon Dupuis in Vancouver campaigned with some success for increased imports of glass, structural steel, etc. via the Hudson Bay route to Western Canada. He had arrived in Vancouver in 1920 as the Official Delegate of Belgian Industries on a mission to establish commercial and industrial exchanges. As founder of L.J. Dupuis & Company Limited he was also the agent for the Union Commerciale Belge de Metallurgie S.A., exporter of structural steel. In 1928, a Chambre de Commerce Belgo-Canadienne, supported by the Banque Bunge and the Banque d'Anvers, was organized in Brussels, and, in November of the same year, Dupuis invited members of the Vancouver business and commercial elite to form a parallel organization. On 22 February 1929, the first meeting of the Canadian-Belgian Chamber of Commerce was held at Hotel Vancouver with its objective "to encourage trade between Canada and Belgium."[27] Leon J. Ladner MP was elected president from among the twenty-two charter members from such important organizations as the Canadian Manufacturing Association, the CPR, the CNR, the Royal Bank of Canada, the Bank of Montreal, the Canada Grain Exporting Company, Pacific Coast Terminals and the H. R. MacMillan Export Company. The charter specified among its objectives: "to investigate questions pertaining to their commercial and industrial relations, to collect and distribute statistics and information relating to the object of the Chamber... to encourage and facilitate the transactions of business."[28] *Lloyd Anversois* published a notice in 1931 stating that "in manufactured goods the West buys abroad more than the East, proportionately speaking, and it seems that it is there that the future of

Belgian trade in Canada lies." Consul Van Rickstal was sent west from the eastern provinces as director of the Office Commercial de l'Etat and wrote a series of pertinent articles in the *Bulletin Commercial*.[29] Baron Louis Empain drew the attention of the Solvay group to the western provinces.[30]

A third period of investment began after World War II, chronologically beyond the general bounds of this study yet indispensable for an understanding of the extent of Belgian participation in the economy of the West. Belgian companies made a rapid recovery after 1945 because of the Galopin doctrine: to avoid the pillaging of Belgian factories during the German occupation by continuing to produce. Belgian companies such as Petrofina, Canadian Hydrocarbons, and Sogémines/Genstar installed themselves in Canada in order to gain access to the American market. Foreign investors were attracted because of a number of favourable conditions: a stable democratic government favourable to capitalists, exceptional urban growth. untapped mineral and other resources awaiting exploitation, an expanding consumer market, and the discovery of large reserves of oil and gas. Belgian investments abroad were characterized by multi-industrial interests of multinational dimensions in metallurgy and mining, energy, transportation and construction.[31]

The real estate market became so attractive in the 1960s and 1970s that Belgians organized two other companies in Canada – the Union Financière, engaged in consulting activities for the creation and management of capital, and the Mutualité Anversoise. The Belgo-Canadian Real Estate Company continued to be active at this time. Henry Vandernoot of Ghent, chairman of Franki Canada Limited, which specialized in foundation and piling construction, expanded his activities as chairman of Caisson Drilling Services with headquarters in Edmonton.[32]

Multinational corporations organized holding companies to provide managerial and financial services to other companies, the majority of whose equity or shares it owned. Sogémines Development Corporation, for example, expanded from construction, through Inland Cement throughout the Prairies and through BACM construction in Winnipeg, to the oil and gas boom through corporations such as Canadian Petrofina, Canadian Hydrocarbons and Genestar Limited.[33] They relied on supplies from their own subsidiaries such as Iroquois Glass, Eastern Electric Casting, Rothesay Paper and Brockville Chemicals. They proceeded to buy Ocean Cement, then Seaspan International, the largest marine transportation company, and also drydock operations in Vancouver. By 1976 they also controlled Abbey Glen Property Corporation, the sixth largest publicly owned real estate development company in Canada.[34]

In 1953, a group of Antwerp businessmen with the Banque Lambert group and Sogémines set up Canadian Petrofina, a subsidiary of Petrofina S.A., for gas and oil exploration in Alberta and a refinery in Montreal.[35] After the OPEC energy crisis, Petrofina invested in Syncrude and the oil sands project. With the introduction of the National Energy Policy and the creation of a national company called Petro-Canada, Canadian Petrofina was bought out for $1.7 billion in 1981. According to a Belgian economist this was a bonanza for the shareholders: "In other words, the government paid 120 dollars a share for stock that had been selling on the market shortly before for 60 dollars even taking inflation into account."[36] In 1968 Sogémines changed its name to Genestar Limited to reflect a broad-based conglomerate in a large number and variety of industries of a general nature. It expanded into the port of Vancouver, took control of Canada Permanent Mortgage Corporation and of Canadian Trusco in 1985. The giant glass multinational Glaverbel by the end of the 1970s controlled the lion's share of all distribution of glass in Western Canada.[37]

Canadian Hydrocarbons Limited and Great Northern Gas Utilities were part of Baron Edouard Empain's energy empire, the chief supplier of natural gas and propane in Western Canada. Soon Canadian Hydrocarbons was producing and distributing diesel fuel, electricity, and oil derivatives such as asphalt throughout Canada. Through its subsidiaries, Baron Edouard Empain took personal charge of the Empain-Schneider Corporation and acquired an important interest in Canadian Homestead Oils Limited. The OPEC crisis enabled it to prosper, its shares rising by 87 per cent in value in a single year. By 1976 it owned all the shares in Homestead Oils but government restrictions on foreign-owned companies forced it to sell its assets to Intercity Gas Company just when it was beginning exploration in the Beaufort Sea.[38]

From 1960 to the early 1970s, Belgium ranked third largest foreign investor in Canada, after the United Kingdom and the United States, and thirty years later it was still ninth. This reflected important economic shifts in Belgium and Canada. Belgians had correctly gauged the fact that in Canada industrial capital moved westwards after 1970 with Calgary and Vancouver emerging as corporate command centres, a shift that reflected the massive concentration of capital in oil and gas, forestry and mining sectors in Alberta and British Columbia.[39] Investors bought into the myth of development, an exploitative attitude toward nature, unaware of a possible environmental crisis overtaking the region.[40]

The success of Belgian investment continues with expansion to every sector of modern technology. Pauwels has made Winnipeg its Canadian headquarters. Agfa-Gevaert, Bekaert, Interbrew, Solvay, Imasco, Umicore, Mestdagh, Puratos and Symfo are not household names, yet they played a significant role in the marketplace. Interbrew, formed when Flemish brewers of Stella Artois merged with Walloon-based brewer Piedboeuf, merged with the Brazilian company AmBev to form InBev and acquired John Labatt Limited in July 1995 to become the leading global brewer. The financial ties with Belgium remain strong to the present as Paul Desmarais Sr. of Power Corporation of Canada, for example, is a business partner of Albert Frère of Groupe Bruxelles Lambert, a Brussels holding company. Together they have merged Suez and Gaz de France to create the world's third largest energy company.

Four Canadian Investment Awards went to Belgian firms in May 2003: to Union Minière of the Umicore Group for research with the University of Alberta and innovative production at Leduc and Fort Saskatchewan; to Solvay S.A. for its advanced work in pharmaceuticals and plastics; to Katven Natil N.V. in Edmonton for its logistical services to the petroleum industry; and to Arinso International in Vancouver for comprehensive business consultation services. In 2005, Belron became the major glass operation by acquiring Autostock, which included Speedy, Apple, Lebeau and Novus. GSK acquired ID Biochemicals. The following year, the Belgo-Luxemberg Arcela-Mittal integrated with Dofasco to become the world's largest steel company.

Regional Political Action

In Western Canada, the labour movement did not benefit from Gustave Francq's numerous initiatives in Quebec on behalf of the working class. His views were clearly expressed in *Le Monde Ouvrier/The Labor World*, which had no fewer than eight thousand subscribers. In the street railway troubles in Winnipeg in 1907, and again in the Winnipeg General Strike of 1919, the Flemish community of St. Boniface/Winnipeg saw the general strike as a left-wing plot to overthrow legitimate authority.[41] The Walloons, recruited mostly by colonizing priests and settled in rural communities, were generally conservative and practising Catholics, unlike their compatriots engaged in mining. Even the Depression failed to arouse much support for the protest movements apart from mining in the Estevan and Drumheller districts and beet culture in southern Alberta. The few Belgian women that worked in the Winnipeg garment industry sweat shops to supplement or provide family income in the 1930s were not militant protesters but as newcomers they were anxious to retain what employment they could get. Similarly, in the work camps, organized across Canada by the federal Conservative government to meet the unemployment crisis, Belgians were among the number who decided to protest peacefully.[42] This was in sharp contrast to the Walloon coal miners who played a prominent role in both Alberta and Vancouver Island.

Belgians were reluctant to support prohibition because the coercion advocated by evangelical Protestants was often intemperate, xenophobic, a violation of individual rights and frequently anti-Catholic.[43] During World War I there was an effort to link prohibition with patriotism. The local paper in Cypress River, where a number of Belgians were settled, observed just before voting day that "anyone who will vote in favour of liquor might as well enlist under the Kaiser as far as patriotism goes."[44] Moreover, the "beer parlours" that were created in "wet" towns and villages throughout Western Canada through provincial legislation violated Belgian social customs by removing consumption of beer from the family setting and parochial functions. Belgians, like most European immigrants, remained quite perplexed by the liquor legislation and did what they could to circumvent it.[45] As one observer commented, the problem with beer parlours was that only drinking was allowed and so there was neither food nor women as "waiters emptied barrels of beer into bored customers."[46] Prohibition ran into more opposition when widespread bootlegging undermined respect for the law. In 1920 the Manitoba Moderation League was formed, strongly supported by the Belgian Club, and three years later the brewers and hotel-keepers formed a Beer and Wine League to promote responsible use of alcohol.[47] A liberalization of government restrictions ensued as cultural norms changed after World War II. Still, Belgians did not find quite the same congenial atmosphere of their "old country *estaminets*" even when their traditional brews like Stella Artois and Leffe appeared in bars and restaurants.

When Belgians arrived as newcomers in the West, they felt somewhat marginalized and alienated from the politics of the region, especially as these were very much a perpetuation of the issues of eastern Canada. Thus, there was a time lag, typically into the second and third generation, from newcomer arrival to integration and full political participation. Only in St. Boniface was there significant political participation which may be explained by the presence of a civic community with common interests. In most rural communities the established host society, composed largely of Ontario and British Isles settlers, monopolized political activity. Many Belgians distrusted the emerging CCF party not only because of its alleged socialistic philosophy but also because of its Anglo-Protestant leadership and its fusion of the social gospel with politics. Tommy C. Douglas, its leader now remembered as the "father of medicare," embraced the eugenics movement and one of his advisors had been a Ku Klux Klan organizer. From 1933 to 1942, the Church viewed the CCF as a socialist movement opposed to the principles and tenets of Christianity. The few Belgians who achieved political office did not exhibit any behaviour or pursue policies that favoured their ethnic group but acted as representatives of the community. In general, the Belgians voted Liberal until the 1920s, and in Saskatchewan until the 1940s. Electoral success was attributable to its effective political machine that included even the highway and road inspectors, as well as the provincial liquor store operators.[48] The Conservatives, whose organs such as the *Winnipeg Tribune* and the *Calgary Herald* opposed immigration from non-British sources, were perceived as linking Canadian identity to British ideals and values, including Protestantism. A popular treatise on immigration expressed surprise that immigrants from Belgium "come in the lower half of the table" of percentage of persons naturalized.[49]

Belgians generally stood aloof of right-wing political and social movements such as the merger of the United Farmers of Alberta and the Non-Partisan League in 1919, with its concept of "group government," later expressed under the Social Credit and then the Reform Party labels. When by 1933 many saw the Depression as a product of systemic failure, rather than personal defeat, and they turned to fringe political parties – the CCF and Social Credit – Belgians remained more intent on toppling the Conservatives. Not until 1943 did the bishops concede that "the faithful are free to support any political party upholding the basic Christian traditions of Canada, and favouring needed reforms in the social and economic order."[50] Belgians in Bellegarde continued to vote Liberal, while Antler and Redvers, its neighbouring communities, voted for the CCF party. Belgians voted as they did, probably not because they followed the directions of their traditionalist parish priest, but more likely because they were not involved in the urban labour movement, were repelled by the Protestant social gospel, and were unable to perceive the CCF as a viable response to their agrarian problems. Nor was the new party's attempt to appeal to the women entirely successful.[51] The feminist movement came to realize that political activity tended perhaps to draw attention to gender similarities that their rhetoric had discounted.

Social Credit in Alberta, and as it spread into neighbouring provinces, did not appeal to Belgians because its strong religious character, rooted in pre-millennial fundamentalist Protestantism, had little relevance to them. The emphasis on sovereignty of the people did not accord well with their concepts of collective rights and traditional hierarchical authority structures. The monetary and financial philosophy of the movement was barely understood by the farmer, small businessmen and blue-collar workers. On the other hand, Belgians did become involved in one regional political revolt. They shared the political and economic complaints of their neighbours in the Peace River Valley regarding the Alberta provincial and federal governments. A quarrel between the federal and provincial governments over a proposed winter road from Grimshaw to Yellowknife resulted in a popular secessionist movement in 1938 to create a new province out of the Peace River region, the Yukon and the Northwest Territories. It was a resurrection of a similar but less popular demand in 1917–18 for the creation of a similar province.[52]

More recently, there is less reason to believe that Belgians remain attached to a traditional old-line political party. They share a feeling of western alienation like their neighbours and believe the federal system in the past benefited the eastern region of the country more than their own. Now they feel part of the prosperous and dynamic elements of society – those who have acquired wealth and success in oil, ranching, farming, and construction, who believe in themselves, their region, and the potential of the West.

Not many Belgians aspired to or attained high political office. Jules Pynoo, a popular alderman from St. Boniface, ran in the federal election of 1949 as a Labour-Progressive candidate but his left-wing affiliation resulted in a crushing defeat. Marcel Lambert, whose mother was Belgian, served as a member of parliament from 1957 to 1984, became Minister of Veterans' Affairs in the Diefenbaker cabinet and Speaker of the House of Commons in 1962–63.[53] From St. Boniface, Robert Bockstael sat in the House as a Liberal from May 1979 to October 1984 and served as a parliamentary secretary to various ministers from 1980 to 1984. He had the support of the church and the business community as well as his ethnic community. Walter Van de Walle sat as a Progressive-Conservative member of parliament for Pembina constituency in 1986, and he was re-elected for St. Albert in 1988.

At the provincial level, only Joseph Van Belleghem was successful as a Liberal, in November 1949, because he had the "necessary connections" in St. Boniface. He had served on city council for many years and had won the support of the French Canadian population and his own Flemish group through leadership in a wide range of community organizations. He felt restricted in caucus and was convinced that Premier Douglas Campbell was a Francophobe, so in the election of 1953 he decided to run as an Independent Liberal Progressive. He was defeated, the archbishop having given his blessing to a grand nephew of Louis Riel as a more suitable representative of the community.[54] In Saskatchewan, John Cuelenaere, mayor of Prince Albert, was elected to the provincial legislature for Shelbrook constituency in 1964 and was appointed Minister of Natural Resources, a portfolio he held until 1966. In Alberta, Arthur Soetaert of St. Albert broke the family tradition of voting Conservative and sat as a Liberal member of the legislature from 1955 to 1959.

The Belgian clergy was not averse to publicly promoting community issues. Abbé Maurice Baudoux of Prud'homme joined a delegation of Saskatchewan Wheat Pool representatives in 1942 to petition the Mackenzie King cabinet to consider the plight of western farmers. Within a couple of years, he became the driving force in Radio-Ouest Française because the CBC station at Watrous gave little attention to French programming. By 1948, Baudoux had succeeded in winning a broadcasting permit and was named to the episcopacy. Bishop Remi De Roo was also an activist, founding member of the World Conference of Religions for Peace, chairman of the Human Rights Commission of British Columbia, an outspoken critic of capitalism and champion of Latin American liberation theology. Archbishop Antoine Hacault, during his brief episcopacy, was a forceful promoter of ecumenism, holding dialogues with Anglicans and Lutherans, while also working with the Canadian Council of Churches.

At the municipal level, the non-partisan Belgian Club in St. Boniface was where political issues were discussed and plans were laid to select

Belgian candidates for various offices. Nicolas Pirroton, a Liégeois, was elected alderman in 1929 for the ward including "Belgian Town," where Victor Wyndels owned considerable property and thirty-two extended Belgian families resided. He chaired the local Belgian Relief Fund in 1914–18, served as president of the Belgian Club from 1926 to 1935, was bandmaster of the city band, and founded the Belgian Benefit Society. When Pirroton died suddenly in November 1943 he lay in state at city hall. It was then that Joseph Van Belleghem decided to take up political life more actively in order to perpetuate a Belgian presence. Van Belleghem served as an alderman from 1931 to 1938, and from 1943 until 1950, when he was elected to the provincial legislature. He was mayor of St. Boniface from 1954 to 1960, during which time he championed the historic role of St. Boniface and fiercely opposed amalgamation with Winnipeg, the "unicity" movement which would deprive St. Boniface of much of its historic identity. He served again as mayor from 1963 to 1955, when he was appointed Belgian consul for Manitoba. He was an outstanding native son, educated locally, spoke five languages and served his community honourably. St. Boniface at this time had four chief officers who were Belgians: Mgr Maurice Baudoux as archbishop; Joseph Van Belleghem as mayor; Joseph Bockstael as city engineer; and George de Cruyenaere as chairman of the school board.[55]

Throughout Western Canada the common career pattern was to become involved in community affairs before seeking political office. Jules Pynoo, for example, immigrated in 1929, built up Pynoo Construction Company, was a distinguished member of the St. Sebastien Archery Club and, beginning in 1950, served on city council for eighteen years. Although he was not a practising Catholic, he was widely respected by the electorate for his social activism. Similarly, Arthur Soetart served as mayor of Morinville for sixteen years and then as a Liberal member of the provincial legislature from 1955 to 1959. He also worked as farm manager, was director and treasurer of the Alexander Band Farm Trust and was greatly appreciated by the First Nations band.[56] Gordon Van Tighem was elected mayor of Yellowknife NWT after serving for twenty-four years in marketing management for the Bank of Montreal, the last eight years in the North West Territories. One of ten children in a family of modest means, he worked as a replacement for absentee workers at minimum wage in a Firestone tire plant during the summer months to finance his university studies. He rose to tire inspector in the plant and went into banking upon graduation. Reminiscing, he wrote: "I realized if I wanted something I had to work hard to get it. No one gets something for nothing."[57] It was the work ethic that won Belgians the praise of early immigration officials. He was founding director of the Stanton Hospital Foundation and the Side Door Youth Centre. In 2006 he was elected chairman of the Northern Forum of the Federation of Canadian Municipalities. A sibling, John Van Tighem, served as superintendent of the Calgary Catholic School for thirteen years. John Cuelenaere was elected to city council in Prince Albert in 1942 and was named chairman of the finance committee. He became a staunch supporter of Marion Gilroy's program to set up regional libraries throughout Saskatchewan. He campaigned against the popular concept of the time that such libraries would entail onerous levies used to indoctrinate young people in socialist philosophy. In 1948, he was elected mayor, an office he held until 1955, and the following year he was responsible in good measure for the creation of the North Central Saskatchewan Regional Library, a system subsequently widely adopted. He served a final term as mayor in 1961–62 and left a third of his estate to the Prince Albert Public Library.[58]

In rural towns and villages many Belgians served their communities well and their contribution has passed largely unheralded. Ross Dujardin in Deloraine, for example, member of town council from 1962 to 1966, mayor from 1966 to 1975, made his mark first in local business, Catholic benevolent organizations, the hospital board, and the Elks Lodge, to become known affectionately in town as "Ross the Boss."[59] August DePape, a self-educated man who read and wrote both official languages and his native Flemish, served as an immigration interpreter, insurance agent, municipal councillor for ten years, school trustee for twenty years, justice of the peace and first president of a local grain marketing board. Likewise, Maurice Delichte served as a school trustee for twenty-three years and as a director of the Manitoba Milk Marketing Producers' Board. Remi DePape served as secretary of the Somerset school board and was a member of the Swan Lake hospital board before being elected mayor of the village of Somerset in 1962.

Family Businesses

The early emphasis on wheat-growing led to urban growth as well because it required grain-handling facilities, agricultural equipment dealerships, railway stations, loading facilities, grocery stores, banks, and insurance offices. The counterpart of the traditional family farm was the family business. The rural community was dependent on the village community and the village community survived because of the surrounding farm families. Villages, serving as local service centres, were strung out about fourteen kilometres apart along the railway lines, the indispensable transportation links, and only later were they connected by highways.[60]

Three village institutions in particular attracted Belgian planters: the "general store," the implement sales business, and the local hotel. The village grocery store constituted a meeting place as well as a supplier of a wide range of goods: "meats and smoked fish, hardware, machines and tools, canned goods, hats, dishes, crockery, paper goods, tobacco, toiletries, groceries, and whatever else. Sometimes also the local post office."[61] These stores carried a large inventory and the mark-up on goods varied between 30 per cent and 35 per cent. They dealt with Winnipeg, sometimes Vancouver, suppliers and usually granted credit, the bills payable after fall harvesting. Among the successful family "general stores" were John Van de Sempel's in Veregin, serving the Doukhobor community, and Nicolas Rondelet's in Girouxville, serving a French-Canadian clientele.[62] The evolution of this prairie institution was documented by Emile Bosmans of Antwerp who came to Bittern Lake NWT in 1889. In 1902 he built a trading post and stopping place for incoming settlers taking up homesteads, expanded the following year into a general store and post office. Eventually he ran a feed mill and cheese factory, then began selling farm machinery. Finally, he donated land for the construction of a railway station and sold part of his property for the townsite of Roundhill.[63]

The local hotel was in some ways a social centre replacing the Flemish and Walloon café or estaminet. However, the Canadian version lacked the conviviality of the open-air shaded tables and the variety of beers and food, restricted as it was both in venue and service by provincial statutes. The Tourist Hotel in St. Boniface, operated initially by M. Van Daele and later the Van Belleghems, was the first stop for many arriving from Belgium. Flemings seemed particularly attracted to operating village hotels. Omer Huybrecht at St. Lazare, Maurice Vandermeulen at Oak Lake, Alphonse Jaenen at Manor, among many others, chose this occupation which entailed work for the entire family as this institution not only offered overnight rooms, but also provided a dining room, a beer parlour, and sometimes a pool hall or dance hall. In the beer parlour many deals were closed, local gossip was exchanged, and politics and religion were discussed. The hotel provided indispensable lodging and food for travelling salesmen and the occasional work gang.

Military Connections

Unlike Canada, Belgium grew out of revolution with the result that military ideals and virtues remained prominent, conscription was normal and expenditures on defensive works, weapons and training were voted regularly by parliament. Her standing army was never large because Article VII of the Twenty-Four Articles (1839) recognized Belgium as an "independent and perpetually neutral state" under the collective guaranty of the Great Powers. The violation of these articles, the "mere scrap of paper," by German armies advancing on France on 4 August 1914 aroused strong feelings in Canada.[64] On October 15, King Albert I ordered his small army to retreat behind the Yser River line, where the Belgians held on to five hundred square kilometres, including forty villages, of native soil the Germans never conquered. With military headquarters at La Panne, and the government in exile in London, Albert I passed into history as the courageous "soldier king." An enduring stereotype of Belgium and Belgians was established.[65] A few Belgian Canadians escaped to neutral Holland. Maurice Ingeveld who had enlisted in Calgary, for example, rejoined his former regiment in Antwerp and escaped with some compatriots to Holland, where he was interned. He managed to escape to England and then rejoined Belgian forces in France. Michel Burgelman, who worked on a ranch near Burmis, also fled to Holland after the fall of Antwerp, managed to make his way to England, and from there back to rejoin his family at Frank in June 1915. It appears that he would have been considered a deserter if he did not rejoin the army.[66]

There was an immediate response in Canada to Belgium's plight. On August 6, only two days after the German violation of Belgian neutrality, Maurice Kimpe, the consul in Edmonton, took action. He inserted the following announcement in French in *Le Progrès Albertain*: "General mobilization of the Belgian army having been decreed, military personnel residing in Canada are required to present themselves immediately, by the quickest and shortest route, directly to the depots and forts where their arms and equipment are stored."[67] On December 10, this call to arms was repeated in both French and Flemish, after two Francophone contingents had left Edmonton for the war zone. Miners in the Crowsnest Pass area and workers at the Trochu ranches had also returned to serve the homeland. Louis Houbregs in Blairmore left a wife and six children under twelve years of age. Edouard d'Arippe of the Big Hill Ranch, near High River, had to arrange with the Bank of Commerce to conduct the sales of his stock while he was at the front. Others, such as Jacob Clemens in Carlyle, joined the Canadian Expeditionary Force as an effective way to come to the aid of Belgium while assuring a good reception eventually for the family in Canada.[68] Jean Melkenbeke, for example, was identified in this manner: "He is a Belgian subject and has not been naturalised Canadian. He, therefore, has the choice between being sent by me [Consul] to the Belgian army or volunteering with the Canadian forces."[69] Nevertheless, Canadian naturalization was not officially recognized in Belgium as granting exemption from military service[70] In August 1915, there was a third call for "every member of the French and Belgian colony in Edmonton and suburbs, who has not yet been called to the front and who desires to join, can be enrolled on Saturday next."[71] By this time, the Canadian "colonial" troops had distinguished themselves and established their reputation at the second battle of Ypres, when on 24 April 1915 the full brunt of a chlorine gas attack, a violation of the Hague Convention (1897) on chemical warfare, failed to break their ranks.

The question of call-up of Belgian reservists and the classes mobilized while residing in Western Canada raised a number of practical questions. Firstly, many did not respond to appeals published in local newspapers across the country because they did not subscribe to or read these English and French newspapers. Nor did they pay attention to notices posted in local post offices. Those reservists who did respond voluntarily wanted certificates confirming that they had volunteered in Canada in order that they be discharged in Canada at the termination of hostilities.[72] Raymond van de Sype, for example, who farmed at Ceylon, Saskatchewan, had gone to work in a coalmine at Blairmore, Alberta, in the winter of 1916–17 when he received his military call. The consul in Calgary considered that he was a resident of Blairmore and so he faced the challenge of selling his livestock and renting his farm in Saskatchewan.[73]

Those who failed to respond to the call to arms were treated as deserters and were subject to court martial. There remained the problem whether they had in fact received official notification, place of residence not always known by the authorities, especially if they had never registered at the nearest consulate upon arrival in Canada. Joseph Private of Blairmore, who had volunteered for the Belgian army, returned to Alberta after thirty months of active duty in France and required a four months extension of his leave because of travel difficulties. The acting consul in Calgary warned: "You must not count on an amnesty because there will never be any for deserters and you will never be able to return to Belgium.... That would be regretable after thirty months of good service, but the law is the same for everybody." He added, "Moreover, he sees around him young Belgian men who refuse to leave and who escape not only Belgian conscription but also Canadian conscription."[74] Canadian employers did not want to be accused of harbouring "deserters." Pat Burns, a prominent business leader in Calgary and strong supporter of the Belgian cause, made a point of checking with the consulate on the status of his employees. L. Stockett, director of collieries for the CPR, told Consul de Burlet in 1917 that, "miners should not be called up because the mines are short of men especially here in the West." He added: "it is absolutely necessary that the coal mines can be worked regularly so that the functioning of the railroads, the zinc, copper and iron foundries, and consequently the munitions factories, not be hindered." The message was passed on to higher authorities.[75] Belgians employed in the Canadian civil service who had been granted leave to do their military service "shall be entitled to receive regular salary during such period of service," by order of the Privy Council.[76]

A few Belgian subjects who had served in the Canadian Expeditionary Force, upon discharge and return to Canada, requested financial assistance for repatriation from Belgium. The Department of Militia and Defence paid the railway fares from Montreal for six Belgian reservists to their Western Canadian residences – three to Winnipeg and one each to Weyburn, Vanguard and Ponteix. The reservist from Ponteix was Léon Courmont, a farmer whose land had provided no income during his absence, who had served three years at the front, was seriously wounded and crippled for life and had spent a year in hospital in Brussels. He had been granted a three months' convalescence leave to settle his affairs in Saskatchewan. The abbé Napoleon Poirier, a personal friend, parish priest at Bellegarde and colonization agent, petitioned for a reduction of Courmont's transportation fares to return to Belgium to continue his medical treatment. All the Department of Militia and Defence would authorize was "transportation on repayment from Ponteix, Sask., to

Montreal, and third class passage to England, at government rate." In other words, minimum assistance even for honoured allies.[77] Also, there were petitions to the Belgian consulates for assistance. These requests were directed to the Canadian Patriotic Fund, a charitable institution designed specifically to assist the wives and children of soldiers in the Belgian army or the Canadian Expeditionary Force who were the sole support of the family.

King Albert appointed a royal commission to gather information on alleged atrocities, such as the use of poison gas on troops, the bombardment of civilian targets, ambulances and medical facilities, and some alleged torture and killing of civilians. In England, the Lord Bryce Commission report, a propaganda instrument designed to arouse humanitarian and patriotic sentiments, concluded there had been "mass rapes, the splitting of babies on bayonets, the cutting off of children's hands and women's breasts, hostage murders, Germans excreting on private possessions." Eventually, diligent reporters challenged the accuracy of these serious allegations.[78] The alleged "atrocities" referred quite often to the killing of civilians as they tried to flee to France. Fact and fiction were intermingled in unlikely statements, in reminiscences decades later, such as "we saw people being burned in ovens and other people being buried alive."[79] Jules Minet, on the other hand, maintained that as hundreds clogged the roads into northern France some people were killed in battles between German and French troops, artillery strikes, etc. The only "atrocities" he recalled were those against civilians who took up arms against German troops. A young man in the village of Spy, for example, climbed into the church spire to fire on advancing Germans and was captured and dragged behind a horse through the village streets as a warning to civilians to respect the rules of war.[80] Much was made of alleged atrocities in the village of Tamines. Professor Peter Buitenhuis investigated the "atrocities myth" and concluded that the Bryce Report was "largely a tissue of invention, unsubstantiated observations by unnamed witnesses, and second-hand eyewitness reports, depending far more on imagination than on any other factor." Furthermore, "there was no attempt at scholarly investigation and evaluation of the evidence. Most significant of all, the documents and testimony of the witnesses disappeared from British records at the end of the war," making it impossible to check the evidence.[81]

The Belgian Mission, commissioned to publicize the plight of Belgian civilians, entered Canada by train from Boston to Saint John and Montreal, where it was received with enthusiasm by a crowd of an estimated 25,000 at Windsor Station. The Chambre de Commerce Belge in Montreal had made all the arrangements for the publicity throughout Canada "to bring to light as much as possible the great role the small Belgian population played in this formidable conflict … to arouse more intense sympathy for the noble sovereign." The Belgian Mission was headed by Henri Carton de Wiart, Belgian Minister of Justice (1911–18), an influential aristocrat whose brother Edmond was the secretary of King Albert and a director of the Société Générale de Belgique.[82] The most important role of the mission was fund-raising and the message in the English-language Montreal press was transmitted across the country. Gustave Francq, prominent Belgian Canadian labour leader in Quebec, hosted the Montreal headquarters of a relief committee that was organized and he printed the trilingual *Pro Belgica*, the authorized mouthpiece of the Belgian Relief Fund, from 1915 to 1919 on his presses.[83]

Emile Francqui, managing director of the Banque d'Outre-Mer, and Herbert Hoover in the United States organized the National Relief and Food Committee, but the Canadian agency was the Belgian Relief Fund. Within a few months, Saskatchewan people had contributed nine railway cars of food. In St. Boniface, the Relief Fund, quite appropriately, was administered by Nicholas Pirotton through the Club Belge.[84] J.H. Woods, editor of the Calgary *Daily Herald*, was honorary secretary-treasurer of the Belgian Relief Fund for southern Alberta. He was ably seconded by his secretary, Della James, an indefatigable fund-raiser, Maude Riley who rallied the support of the social elite of Calgary, Pat Burns of the business community, and Baron de t'Serclaes of the Belgian community. A scholarly driving force behind the Belgian Relief Fund was Dr. S. Mack Eastman, prominent history professor at Vancouver and Calgary, who gave a series of lectures across Alberta in support of the fund. He said: "These lectures have been well attended and have resulted in a considerable accession to the Belgian Relief Fund, besides which I am sure that they have given much information concerning Belgium to a number of Alberta communities." It was an important exercise in fund-raising and public education.[85] The Imperial Order Daughters of the Empire sponsored a series of lectures accompanied by lantern slides by Professor Eastman in seven Alberta towns as well as a concert of Belgian instrumental and vocal music in Calgary.[86] The only misfortune was that on 6 December 1917 a Norwegian ship sailing out of Halifax harbour with relief supplies for

Belgium collided with a French munitions ship causing a gigantic explosion that claimed 1 600 victims and destroyed much of the city. In 1919 the Belgian Relief Fund was succeeded by Relief Work for the Victims of War in Belgium, an organization mandated to "receive and collect money, food and other articles in Canada or elsewhere," directed by Robert John Dale, insurance broker and future Belgian consul in Winnipeg, and Gustave Francq, printer and labour organizer.[87] The organization remained active for a number of years and was replaced in 1937 by a federally chartered Belgium-Canada Association with an exchange mandate that included the facilitation of industrial and agricultural development and the promotion of cultural and scientific projects.[88]

Mgr Hebbelynck, delegated by the University of Louvain to go to Canada, solicited aid "in money and in books to rebuild the university library and the commercial school affiliated with the university" which had been damaged in the course of hostilities.[89] Among private donors, none was more successful than François Adam of Camrose, who sent shipments of beef and pork to the hungry population of Poland and Belgium.[90] The consuls in New York and Calgary were quite unaware of Adam's illustrious career or his important national and international contacts.[91]

Another unusual offer of help came from an association of ranchers in Medicine Hat that owned more than twenty thousand horses. They offered to send five thousand horses of the type suitable for farm work to Belgium to replace the horses lost during the war years. It was an indication of the interest and sympathy aroused in Western Canada for the plight of Belgian civilians.[92]

Belgium was firmly implanted in the Canadian consciousness. Belgians, in turn, remember solemnly Canada's contribution to the liberation of their country, especially battles at Ypres and Mons. At Passchendaele every evening, regardless of adverse weather or other activities in the city, some citizens of Ypres, now including children of a third generation, gather at a war memorial to remember the 15,654 Canadian casualties, a perpetual and extraordinary act of remembrance without parallel anywhere. Also remembered is the fact that, following the armistice on 11 November 1918, the corps of the Royal Canadian Engineers began to reconstruct the bridges, clear the canals for navigation, and rebuild the railway lines of Belgium.

Canadians played a less conspicuous role in Belgium in the Second World War in 1939–45. The Department of External Affairs agreed that Belgian nationals conscripted by Belgian authorities would not be admitted to the Canadian armed forces "merely as a means of escaping obligations to serve in the Belgian Army," nor would Canada enlist Belgian nationals "until their cases have been referred to the Belgian authorities."[93] Nevertheless, Lt. Maurice Henri Pirenne and twelve compatriots who had pursued graduate studies in the United States and were stationed with the Belgian Military Training Unit in Cornwall, Ontario, were expected to serve either in the Belgian forces or in the Royal Air Force.[94] In May 1943 the Air Liaison Mission in Ottawa approved the enlisting of a restricted number of Belgian nationals as part of the British quota at Canadian facilities, to be trained in Canada at the expense of the Canadian government.[95] In 1944 the Canadian government made no apparent effort to locate ninety-one Belgians in Western Canada listed as "deserters" because they had not responded to mobilization orders.[96]

The First Canadian Army undertook the task in 1944 of opening the Channel ports for the supplying of the invasion forces. The Twelfth Manitoba Dragoons liberated Ostend on 6 September and Bruges on 12 September. The last pockets of German resistance in Flanders collapsed at Walchteren on 9 November. By the beginning of December, thousands of tonnes of stores landed at Antwerp, which became the principal Allied supply port in northeastern Europe. Two events flowed from victory. Firstly, Belgian Canadians, like Max Emke, for example, who had been trapped in Belgium by the blitzkrieg and had been interned, were liberated.[97] Secondly, Belgian brides of Canadian soldiers, 649 in number, were rapidly given passage to Canada. Naturally, the approach of final victory was suitably observed at home:

> Winnipeg and vicinity Belgians celebrated Sunday morning for the partial liberation of Belgium. They met at the Belgian Club on Provencher Avenue, and with flags waving and band playing, proceeded to the Belgian Sacred Heart Church on Plinquet Avenue, where a Te Deum mass was sung by Father Peter…. Father Peter gave an address in the three languages. After Mass, the celebrants returned to the cenotaph on Provencher Avenue where a prayer was said and the Last Post sounded.[98]

Belgium had entered the Canadian imagination as a "preferred country" whose emigrants were deemed frugal, industrious and innovative contributors to the Canadian socio-economic fabric. They never lost their status although the demands of Canadian society evolved over the decades with the development of a more diversified economy and multicultural society. Two world wars had further strengthened the bonds between the two countries.

Martha and Mary Maufort, 1900. (Glenbow NA-3903-42)
Daughters of August and Aline Maufort, settlers at Blairmore and Coleman.

ETHNICITY AND CULTURE

Two types of nationalism emerged in nineteenth-century Europe: territorial-political nationalism and romantic-ethnic nationalism. In the case of Belgium, in the mid-twentieth century ethnolinguistic nationalism gradually replaced the mid-nineteenth century territorial nationalism of the new kingdom. This transition within the framework of the territorial nationalism was beginning to manifest itself in the second period of emigration to Canada, that is to say in the inter-war years of 1919–39. Upon arrival in Western Canada, Belgians discovered that the dominant Anglo-conformist ideology was based on assimilationist territorial nationalism. Yet in the context of large-scale immigration the demographic development was polyethnic. A majority in 1900 envisaged the nation as fundamentally British and English-speaking but the existence of a sizeable Francophone minority with strong historical roots contested this uniformist ideology. Unless Belgians could integrate rapidly into the mainstream cultures they could find themselves underprivileged.

In addition to the gradual emergence of a multicultural Canadian identity there was a sense of regional community. Regionalism was based on resource exploitation and development of the hinterland, initially in the interests of the central provinces of the Dominion, so that with the passage of time a sense of western alienation developed. All the ethnic components of the regional population, including Belgians, found a new regional identity, partly through participation in local community activities that transcended their ethnocultural diversity. In this experience of adaptation to a new environment, of transformation and integration into an evolving social, political and economic milieu, the immigrants brought their own cultural practices and values. These cultures consisted of their whole way of life, material, intellectual, and spiritual. In this way, their cultures were not only a product of the past but became creators of their future in the land of adoption. This did not mean uninterrupted cultural progress because a merging of new and old involved both affirmative and negative properties. Tradition tempered the idea of progress so that it is more accurate to think in terms of change, not continuous progress. What emerged in the Belgian experience are altered values, norms, and social relationships with concurrent continuity of aspects of traditional life and thought. Certain distinctive characteristics, habits and attitudes of "Belgianness," whether Flemish or Walloon, survived.

Ethnic Institutions

Belgian communities in Western Canada lacked institutional completeness, as defined by Raymond Breton, i.e., the structure of organizations to provide most of the services required by the group. Firstly, they did not constitute a homogeneous community but sometimes identified themselves as Flemings or Walloons. Secondly, they found in mainstream society many of the services and amenities they desired. Within Francophone settlements and parishes, Walloons found a congenial environment that precluded any need for particular Walloon institutions. They utilized and supported the educational, socio-political and cultural institutions of Francophone minorities throughout the Western provinces and territories. Flemings, whether settled in Anglophone or Francophone districts, on the other hand, on occasion made ethnic distinctions. Two Flemish institutions emerged to meet this cultural need – Sacred Heart parish and the Capuchin monastery in St. Boniface and the Scheppers Institute or College in Swan Lake. In 1905, both Flemings and Walloons desired a social centre in St. Boniface. Le Club Belge reflected both the linguistic situation in Belgium and the ethnic nature of Belgian immigration in Canada. It was frequented and supported largely by Flemings, but French was the language of its early records and proceedings. The Belgian communities in Manitoba were sufficiently concentrated in St. Boniface by 1900 to feel a need for a centre to give themselves a better sense of community and the possibility of offering practical assistance to newcomers. Le Club Belge, its official name since its incorporation in 1905 under the Manitoba Joint Stock Companies Act, was founded by Louis de Nobele and his father-in-law Theophile Elewaert to assist incoming immigrants. This Belgian club had as its objectives:

> To provide and maintain a social intercourse between the members of the Company; to consider and discuss all questions affecting the interests of the Belgian residents in Manitoba, to procure delivery of lectures on any subject of interest to the Company; to form and maintain a library; to render voluntary aid or otherwise to any member of the Company or to any Belgian residing in Manitoba; to purchase, hire or otherwise acquire for the purposes of the Company any real or personal property, that is, land, buildings, furniture, books, household effects, musical instruments, apparatus, appliances, conveniences and accommodation.[1]

The first club room for the forty-five charter members was in a large Belgian boarding house at (84) Lombard Street (originally Post Office Street because at the eastern extremity was the wharf on the Red River at which the steamboats from Minnesota tied up) at the hub of commercial activity. The charter members represented an interesting cross-section of the Belgian population, including twenty-two labourers, three farmers (one a widow), four florists, two carpenters, two bakers, two masons, a butcher, and a restaurant owner. In 1906, there was need of more spacious quarters close to the small concentration of Belgians settled in St. Boniface, first near the Dubuc Block then at the east end of Provencher Avenue, where construction of a single storey clubhouse was begun by Wynant and De Leeuw. In 1911, Theophile Bockstael was awarded a contract for the addition of a second storey, followed in 1914 by another addition on the east side of the clubhouse. This completed the building program, with a post office located at the rear of the building. There were about two thousand members, Flemings and Walloons, who were enrolled upon arrival in Manitoba for a $2 fee, one half going to membership according free entry to all events and the other half a share in the company. There were also associated members, mostly French Canadian businessmen interested in socializing and familiarizing themselves with the Belgians, their talents, needs and aspirations. From the beginning, observance of Independence Day on 21 July was accompanied by a dinner, free refreshments and a band concert. In 1915 the club adopted the policy of reading all reports in both French and Flemish. The majority of the members were Flemings and a few may have had some difficulty understanding official statements in French. Although the club remained non-political, in 1916 the executive strongly supported those politicians who spoke out against the abolition of the bilingual school system. Again, in 1938, a formal protest was sent to the Canadian National Railways because of lay-offs at their Transcona marshalling yards which affected many Belgian workers.[2]

World War I gave the club prominence as a centre for Belgian military affairs and headquarters for the Belgian Relief Fund. But membership dropped significantly because of prohibition legislation in 1916 that curtailed business to the point that by 1917 Le Club Belge was virtually bankrupt, telephone service was cut off, annual taxes were unpaid, and some employees were laid off. In 1918, a Congress of all Belgians in Western Canada was held with twenty delegates in attendance to promote business enterprises and to promote club membership but conditions did not improve. A Belgian Veterans Association was formed in 1920 but it could not provide much financial aid. In March 1921, the club was closed and did not resume its activities until 1925 with the imposition of annual fees on the members. Four years later, the Belgian Veterans Association and its Ladies Auxiliary affiliated with the Royal Canadian Legion, assuring the veterans a measure of financial security. Women were admitted during the war years if they were escorted by a member. In November 1926, a Ladies Auxiliary was formed to provide clothing to destitute families and to visit the sick and elderly. They put on an annual banquet at the clubhouse for senior citizens, distributed Christmas and Easter parcels to the aged and shut-ins, and organized a "Christmas Tree" or concert for the children. Significantly, St. Nicholas did not come on the eve of December 6 like in Belgium, but the customs of the host society were adopted in order not to confuse the children who at school, at church and in the wider community were exposed to the gift-giving and Santa Claus on December 25.

The end of prohibition in 1928 enabled the club to recover from its indebtedness and to survive the Depression rather well as activities expanded. The proclivity for beer drinking led to "regular suspensions of members for gambling, drunkenness, brawling, obscene language and unbecoming behaviour." A ladies committee attempted to "further the moral and material aspirations of the Club," as did the Flemish parish priest in 1938. In 1955, the club issued a number of regulations with the same objective, and the following year decided to pay the local police to patrol its parties and dances. The Belgian community did not attract the attention of the law enforcement agencies for violent crimes, only for overly exuberant club activities and house parties.

On the more positive side of the ledger, club services expanded greatly. It had to deal with some social problems because the urban governments failed to intervene effectively, the business community was preoccupied with economic returns and investment, and the elite in St. Boniface and Winnipeg were often self-made men who resented any limits on their laissez-faire habits. There was an incentive, therefore, for the Belgian community to pursue its own social program. In February 1928, the Belgian Mutual Benefit Society of Manitoba was organized with membership open to "any Belgian by birth (male or female) and the children of such Belgian and the lawful wife or husband of such Belgian" on the payment of a fee ranging from $3 to $6 on an age basis and a nominal assessment on the death of a member. It was a distress fund as well as a death benefit. Membership soon reached just under five hundred by 1960. Over a period of forty-five years, benefits were provided for 271 members. In 1939, the club expanded its activities to a branch clubhouse in Ste-Rose-du-Lac and Father Damas of the Flemish parish succeeded in organizing the Belgian Sacred Heart Credit Union Society with the support of area dairy farmers and a few more prosperous parishioners at Holy Cross parish in Norwood. In 1951, the Club Belge invested some of its funds in this credit union and assumed much of its direction under the name of the Belgian Credit Union. By this time, the Club Belge had 2,600 shareholders and five hundred associate members. In February 1939, women were accepted finally as regular members and shareholders, a source of financial gain because over a number of years the club was able to offer about $15,000 in scholarships to children of members to enable them to continue in post-secondary studies. This indicated the progressive steps from early generations that had little interest in educational pursuits, to a generation in which sons generally followed the father's trade or occupation, to a generation interested in higher education.

The language question never became a public issue. In 1928, the by-laws were printed in English only, although all notices to meetings were issued in Flemish, French and English. The Varlez-Brunin report (1929) on Belgian communities contained a revealing comment on linguistic balance:

A Mr. Perroton, master cabinetmaker from Liege, expressed the wish that the library [of the Club Belge] should be made up of seven-tenths books in Flemish and three-tenths books in French and English, the latter being easier to purchase in Winnipeg. The members of the Belgian club who take very scrupulous care to prevent the language question to arise among them, have asked me to support this request to you.[3]

By 1943 all club business was conducted in English, while at social functions three languages were still heard. By 1969, at the ephemeral Council of Belgians in Ottawa the discussions were in English "with Flemish and French translations available on request." The Belgian Club had originally provided a bonding network for Belgians but it later provided a bridging network to other groups for mutual benefit.[4]

Belgian Sacred Heart parish was erected on Plinquet Street in response to Flemish requests for services in their own language apart from the masses, confessions and catechism classes offered in uninspiring facilities at the St. Boniface cathedral. The Sacred Heart parish boundaries were coterminous with those of the cathedral parish so did not include the Flemings of Norwood, St. Vital, Transcona and Fort Garry.[5] In 1928, Capuchin monks established a monastery in the vicinity and assured regular services in Flemish until the parishioners, especially the Canadian-born, indicated a preference for English services. Through a daughter house, the Capuchins provided multilingual services in Ste. Amélie and Ste. Rose-du-Lac for a couple decades, until the Archbishop of Winnipeg transferred all missionary work to the Oblate order. They also provided services in Flemish in Dugald, where a number of Belgian families who found employment in the CNR yards in Transcona resided.

The role of Scheppers Institute (Sacred Heart College), located in Swan Lake, in serving the Flemish community is not well known. It represented an important attempt to provide a practical education to rural youth in a traditional Flemish setting. In 1919, Sister Angêle, a Ursuline on a home visit to Thildonck in search of support for a school for senior boys to complement the convent for girls in Bruxelles, met a Brother Amadeus of the Brothers of Our Lady of Mercy who were involved in educational work overseas.[6] Although Rome preferred they would direct their efforts to the Congo, the Brothers were attracted to the prospect of working in Flemish in Manitoba. In August 1919, two brothers sent to scout out the situation and report on the climate and customs bought a half-section farm (325 ha) from George Couch, a pioneer who had farmed there near the village of Swan Lake since 1887.[7] Four brothers soon joined them at the farm and they all spent the winter cutting wood as farm machinery, lumber, cement, door and window frames, and bricks arrived at the village destined for the Institute. They bought nine work horses, milch cows, pigs and chickens, and when spring came they planted the fields in wheat, barley and oats. Their objective, in line with the philosophy of the Canadian Agricultural Instruction Act of 1913, was to inculcate values and build character through a "spiritualizing of agriculture."[8] There was some debate about the size of the building to be erected, but it was resolved to build an imposing Belgian-style two-storey brick-faced edifice with large high-ceiling rooms on a raised basement that proved to be inadequately insulated and too costly to heat in winter.[9] Firmin Wyndels contracted to build the college for $70,000 but raised the price to $80,000 as modifications were added. The brothers eventually spent over $120,000 on the project which included two reception rooms, two refectories, a pantry and kitchen, a music room and two classrooms on the main floor; a chapel, two infirmaries, two dormitories, a concert hall and a lavatory on the second floor; a manual training room, recreation room, provisions room, boiler room, laboratory, etc. in the basement. Unfortunately, the day the main building was completed the farm buildings, with the furniture, personal belongings of the staff, and school equipment, burnt down.

Classes began in October 1920 with forty residents and fifteen day students from the village. Archbishop Beliveau insisted that the teaching be in French and English, but the staff felt unable immediately to satisfy this requirement so some students returned to their former schools. When the Superior of the brotherhood visited the school in 1921, he opined that the Institute was financially unstable and religious exercises were inadequate. The director resigned and left the brotherhood, and he settled in nearby Mariapolis. The new director transformed the school into an agricultural institute to the satisfaction of the Archbishop, who was of the opinion that the Manitoba Agricultural College in Fort Garry was an Anglophone Protestant institution, 85 per cent of whose graduates did not actually farm. He observed: "Our students are all sons of dirt farmers who will have to help their parents on the family farm. Educate them in theory and practice. Thus you will instill in them a love of the soil, and our countryside will remain Catholic."[10] By 1921, there were sixty boarders at the institute, good relations had been established with the local Belgian communities, four novices were received, and the farm buildings were moved close to the institute. Students were anxious to have their studies meet provincial standards and grant them credits therefore the brothers eliminated courses in agriculture and the use of French as a medium of instruction. When a priest-inspector visited the school and reported these changes to the Archbishop, strained relations ensued.[11] In August 1926, two more brothers arrived from Belgium to initiate a commercial course and a science course similar to those in the program of studies of the Jesuits at St. Boniface College. A bountiful crop on the farm enabled the brothers to buy new textbooks and equipment for the chemistry and physics laboratories. When St. Boniface College burned down, many of their students in commerce wanted to attend Scheppers Institute but Msgr Beliveau instructed the clergy not to permit such a transfer. By 1927 the Superior in Huberdeau, Quebec assessed the deteriorating economic situation at Swan Lake and concluded that the farm and its equipment should be rented out to a local Belgian farmer. The number of students declined sharply and maintenance costs mounted sharply. In October 1932 an order arrived to liquidate the assets and to have the institute equipment and furniture accompany the brothers to the orphanage at Huberdeau. The empty building was left in the care of the parish priest and a certain M. Goethals, who purchased the farm land. The local Belgians gathered to thank the Brothers of Mercy for their devoted service to their youth and community, but it was evident that the Institute had outlived its purpose and that the depression made any continuation of such a project impractical. The buildings remained vacant for years as negotiations with the federal government to open a training facility failed to mature. Only the faint outlines of foundation stones remain on the outskirts of the village of Swan Lake as a memorial to an experiment in Flemish education.

Ethnic Behaviour

The Flemish community retained several markers of folk culture, while the Walloons found it easy to adapt to French-Canadian folkways.[12] Pigeon racing and bicycle racing were equally popular among Flemings and Walloons but also very popular among the British-origin population with the result that pigeon racing became a trans-national competitive sport and bicycle racing took on a community character in which the entire city of Winnipeg became involved. Pigeon racing was formally introduced in 1917, when Theophil Nuyttens, Camille Van Drissche and Charles Van Cauwenberghe organized the St. Boniface Racing Pigeon Club, associated with the Club Belge in 1921, to compete with a Winnipeg club organized by English breeders. The pigeons that were popular were a cross-breed between the smerle and tumbler breeds of the Low Countries and the English carrier pigeon. The Belgian system of allotting a prize for every ten pigeons in the races held every weekend from mid-May to mid-September was adopted. There was a special 400 kilometres Young Bird race and an 800 kilometres Old Bird race in late July. The longest west-east race recorded was from Banff to Winnipeg in 1924, and the longest south-north race was from Oklahoma to Winnipeg in 1935. As many as three hundred pigeons were entered in a race. Finalists often went on to compete at an international race in Detroit.[13] Omer Van Walleghem, who specialized in long-distance racing pigeons, imported his stock from West Flanders. Adolph Van Walleghem made enough prize money in 1930 to pay his fare and his wife's fare for a trip to Belgium.[14] Constituent clubs were organized in Winnipeg and Norwood which eventually amalgamated in 1976, when interest was still keen but participants were fewer. In 1949, André Gobert, who played hockey for the Detroit Red Wings, was stricken with polio and he decided to return to an earlier interest in pigeon racing which he shared with his father Remi Gobert. He was hired by Cornell University in Ithaca, New York, to manage its pigeon loft and participate in a research project on the homing instincts of pigeons.[15]

The Flemish settlers in southern Manitoba do not appear to have had the same interest in pigeon racing as their urban compatriots. On the other hand, Walloons in the Crowsnest Pass region showed some interest in this traditional sport. In the late 1930s, Antoine Cornil organized a Homing Pigeon Flying Club in Coleman. The birds were imported from England and a number of interested persons set to work building the appropriate lofts. Cornil left an interesting description of the special timing device required to record the flight time:

> Each of us had to have special clocks to ascertain the arrival time of our birds from the race. This clock is almost eight inches in diameter and near the top is a little hole about ½ inch by 1 inch where you place the little tin box in which you place

the ring taken from the leg of your bird which is registered in your name. This is clicked in the apparatus and it registers on your clock the time in hours, minutes and seconds. From the time you clock in, nobody can open it during the race except the secretary at the end of the race. If anyone tampers with it he is disqualified.[16]

Immigrants from France introduced bicycle racing to Western Canada. Belgians quickly took up the sport and A. De Cruyenaere, J. Cortvrient and Camille De Buck organized the St. Boniface Cycling Club in 1916, which by 1933 had no fewer than fifty active members. Races were held throughout the 1930s in a dirt track velodrome on Wilkes Avenue in Tuxedo. Beginning in 1932, there were a number of highly competitive races in which a number of ethnic groups participated. The local papers published photographs of these races and posted the names of winners, especially for the races from the city to Winnipeg Beach.[17] Theophil Dubois was the winner for successive years, setting a record equal to the best European racers. By 1940, Viv Nuytten had emerged as the equally successful champion. The longest race in which Belgians participated in significant numbers was from Winnipeg to Kenora. They had a particular velodrome race in which the last rider of each lap was eliminated until only two final riders remained to contest the prize, a handsome sum of money. In 1934, five members of the St. Boniface Club went to Detroit to compete in the American North-Western Amateur championship. Dubois won in every race he entered. Thousands of people from all over the continent lined the streets of Windsor and Detroit during the six-day competition for significant cash prizes. Races ranged from novices to seniors and women. Astride feather-light frames of steel tubing, cyclists reached speeds of 65 kilometres an hour. Back in Manitoba, the old Tuxedo velodrome was no longer considered adequate, so a new velodrome was officially opened on Des Meurons Avenue in St. Boniface on 6 July 1935, accompanied by all the appropriate municipal fanfare. The Belgian Club now made the Letellier-St. Boniface race its annual event and this was interrupted only by the advent of World War II. Cyril Raes, internationally renowned racer in the Tour de France, settled in Deloraine in 1927, where he quickly organized a local racing club.[18]

The Flemish communities retained a number of folk games, "traditional, local, active games of a recreational character requiring specific physical skills, strategy or chance, or a combination of these three elements." Researchers have wondered if Flemings had an anachronistic perception of their homeland as a unitary nation in which their rural ancestors had little or no cultural identity or socio-economic prestige? What is evident is that among Belgians, the folk games are almost exclusively Flemish.[19] Pole archery is the most prominent of these sports and has its roots in mediaeval popinjay shooting. The Manitoba version of pole shooting requires a thirty-metre pole pinned by two posts so that a tree of five branches can be lowered when necessary to have a full rack of thirty-nine birds on the perches (thirty-four one-point small birds, two two-point *kalle* birds, two three-point side birds, and one four-point high bird) attached. The archers shoot at the perch that is slightly angled toward them from a distance of twenty metres using blunt arrows. Bows with sights and mechanized bows are not permitted. The game appears to have been introduced in St Vital in the 1920s at the farm home of Theophile Gelaude. The St. Sebastien Archery Club was formally constituted in 1926 and had a companion club in Ste. Amélie that met at the farm of Ernest Beyt from 1925 to 1945, when activities were moved to the farm of George Verhaegen under the presidency of Albert Pauwels. In March 1929, the Manitoba Pole Archery Association was formed, bringing in several English archery groups, to standardize the rules for the game. In 1929, the Robin Hood Club was added with a branch in Ste. Rose-du-Lac, presided by Pierre Brabant. The Ste. Rose and Ste. Amélie clubs amalgamated in 1934, under the presidency of Jules Catyn, with over fifty enrolled members, including a few in St. Louis. World War II saw a lull in activities, and although the annual tournaments were revived in 1946, the sport never regained the popularity it had experienced in the inter-war years. By 1974, four archery clubs were associated with the Belgian Club – the Manitoba Pole Archery Association, the Robin Hood Pole Archery Club, the St. Sebastien Archery Club, and the Seven Dwarfs Archery Club.

Belgian bowling, or *rolle bolle*, did not attract the same public attention as pigeon racing or bicycle racing nevertheless it remained quite popular in scattered Flemish communities. The men's game resembles curling. In fact, Omer Van Walleghem, an expert lawn bowler, won twenty curling championships, including the Silver Bowl in the Manitoba Curling Bonspiel in 1964. Unlike curling, the losing competitor keeps on leading until he has a winning bowl, and then his opponent leads. It is played on a *trage*, a dirt alley about eleven metres long and four metres wide, slanted slightly to the middle. The object of the game is to roll a flat, oval, cheese-shaped hard bowl as close as possible to the feather peg at the far end of the alley. The women's game is played on a six-metre-long flat alley with a metal hoop at each end in which each player rolls a five-pin bowl.[20] P.J. Hallemans of Swan Lake introduced the game to southern Manitoba communities. Soon there were clubs in Holland, Cypress River, Glenboro, Baldur, Mariapolis, St. Alphonse, Bruxelles, Somerset and Deloraine.[21] There were even some in non-Flemish communities and in North Dakota.[22] When the Deloraine Community Centre was opened in 1973, it was equipped for the usual games but also for Belgian bowling and a new game called "Dobbelaere 9-pin bowling" in honour of René Dobbelaere, who arrived in 1930 and served as president for many years of the Deloraine Belgian Bowling Club.[23]

In rural Manitoba, Flemings from East Flanders played *bak schiaten*, box shooting, a game not unlike toss the bean bag. The object is to pitch a round metal slug through a small opening in a square board, along a three-metre wooden board. It is a game for two players, each having two slugs to shoot. The Flemish dart game requires a special board with five concentric coloured circles of 25, 20, 15, 10, and 5 points respectively and a bull's-eye in the middle that counts for 50 points. Each player has four darts and they play ten rounds in singles in turn. In 1948, an annual international tournament was started in Detroit to which the Belgian Club in St. Boniface sent entries each year.

Card playing was a common pastime at family and neighbourhood gatherings. Belgian Whist was popular, but the most ethnically specific game was *bien*, which required a special deck of cards from which all cards from two to six had been removed. The game is played by two sets of partners, each of whom is given sixteen match points to commence and then the object of the game is to get rid of these points in order to win. In the pioneer era, there were also a few pipe-smoking contests. The contestants used imported long-stemmed clay pipes and fine-cut cigarette tobacco. The object was to keep the pipe continuously alight for as long as possible. The alleged North American record was 106 minutes of continuous smoking.

Initially, upon arrival in the west, Belgians participated within their own community to sustain collectively a part of their traditional recreation. This would appear to be a normal ethnic maintenance strategy.[24] It is more likely that the continuation, or introduction, of such recreational activities as pigeon racing and bicycle racing were "subcultural recreational norms," not particularly related to social class differences or to under-participation in mainstream leisure. Nor were these activities restricted to members of the Belgian community. This complementary approach postulates that if members of an ethnic group find the host culture lacking certain activities, or not sharing them generously, they organize their own association to fill the gap. This would seem a better explanation of the situation in St. Boniface and Ste. Rose-du-Lac.[25] Alongside these recreational pursuits, individuals in the group also participated in community leisure – baseball, hockey, and curling thus there was never a deep sense of marginality expressed because of the lack of accessibility or opportunity to participate in the recreational activities of the wider community. In rural areas, activities centred on the school and/or village were always comprehensive. Finally, one may ask if André Gobert as a professional hockey player, or Omer Van Walleghem as a champion curler with a city club, had compromised his ethnic identity. The question appears no more valid than asking an English person who won the St. Sebastien archery tournament, or a German who won at *rolle bolle*, if he had compromised his ethnic identity.[26]

Ethnic identity also expresses itself through traditional dishes and preparations in the home and at family and community gatherings. What are these traditional foods? Belgian pastries, spice cakes, chocolate and waffles readily come to mind. Flemish farmers and labourers ate ham or bacon and eggs, cheese, strong coffee and thick cereal bread for breakfast. Their Walloon compatriots were satisfied with fresh-baked bread dunked in a large *jatte* of strong coffee. The other meals might feature rabbit with prunes, or *vlaamse stoverij*, stewed meat in a sauce fortified with dark beer. A thick chicken soup was sometimes augmented by the addition of *trippe*, a kind of choice lean pork sausage. The favourite vegetables were red cabbage cooked with apples, and *jut*, a preparation of cooked cabbage and mashed potatoes seasoned with cream and salt. Another favourite was *cassette*, a home-made cottage cheese pressed into balls, put into crocks to cure, and then eaten spread on bread like butter, seasoned with salt and pepper, or else with sugar and cinnamon. Desserts ranged from crème caramel, rice pudding, applesauce, or thick fruit pies to a variety of sweet waffles. In Western Canada, Belgians were able to find most of the ingredients for their traditional dishes.

Apart from the food prepared and consumed in the home, the connection with ethnic identity is largely spacialized, i.e. located at particular events such as the *kermess*, buildings such as a church hall or club, enclaves such as a "Belgian Town."[27] Most Belgian immigrants were classed among the "common people," characterized by the Flemish stereotype of hefty drinkers and hearty eaters in convivial groups. This social behaviour was not always understood by the more rigorous Anglo-Celtic host society. Belgian families could be the objects of police investigations for the brewing of domestic beer (which was generally legal if not offered for sale), and a few were believed to engage in illicit distilling. The social setting of communal drinking was quite different in Western Canada from the camaraderie of the local café or bistro in Belgium.[28]

In Belgium, each town had its annual festival, usually following the harvest thanksgiving mass, known as the *kermess*. It was not unlike a country fair with its sports competitions, food shows, street dancing and parades. In general, there was abundant food and drink, folk music, and singing as people visited relatives, neighbours and acquaintances expecting generous hospitality. Evelyn Simoens Baltessen organized the Kermess Week activities of the Belgian Club for many years. The Flemish communities in southern Manitoba did organize a few *kermess* but the custom did not became entrenched because the fall fair and the community fowl supper intervened.

Carnivals marked the advent of the Lenten season, and sometimes a mid-Lenten break as well. These celebrations were marked by colourful parades of mythological beings such as the plumed giant Gilles of Binche and Ros Beiaard, the huge horse of Dendermonde, marching bands, and general merriment. Religious processions such as the Precious Blood in Bruges and the Penance Procession at Veurne drew large crowds of pilgrims and the less devout. In Western Canada, the carnival saw itself reduced to a family celebration and the religious processions, controlled by the clergy, eliminated the secular celebrations. The Procession of Our Lady of Flanders was restricted to Ontario. The Corpus Christi procession wound its way through the streets of St. Boniface each year, led by the La Verendrye brass band, but it was more a French Canadian event than a Belgian one. In Canada there were none of the more secular parades such as the Procession of Cats in Ypres. Another common Belgian custom was the maypole celebration, quite distinct from the English maypole dance, to celebrate a person elected or appointed to an important office. The community gathered to congratulate the office-holder, expecting some refreshments, usually in the form of making available a keg of special beer. Belgians quickly learned not to attract attention, especially of the police, or to upset wider community standards.

The activities surrounding the feast of *Sint-Nikolaas* on 5 December originated in the Dutch/Flemish region of the Low Countries and spread into the Walloon areas and northern France. In Belgium, St. Nicholas in his red episcopal robes and mitre, riding his faithful white horse Amerigo, brings presents to the good children who have left their shoes by the stove or fireplace with carrots and sugar cubes for Amerigo. He rides high in the sky, accompanied by black helpers in Moorish dress, the *Zwarte Pieten*, or Black Peters. At one time, a lump of coal might be left instead of presents to indicate St. Nicholas's displeasure with the behaviour of certain children. In the Francophone region, St. Nicholas is accompanied by *Père Fouettard*, the flogger who carries a bundle of sticks to punish naughty and disobedient children. These customs were observed in Canada during the early years of settlement, but they rapidly gave way to the customs of the host society. Globalization has reversed the flow of customs from North America to Europe with the popularization of the Christmas tree, Santa's reindeer including Rudolph, the giving of presents on 25 December, etc. becoming part of the Belgian celebrations.

Cultural Activities

Belgians reached out very rapidly to the wider community after their own successful implantation. The Belgian-Canadian Association of British Columbia, for example, had as its dual objective "encouraging social contacts between Belgians and organizing cultural activities" with appeal to the general public, although not to the same extent as in Quebec, where they provided leadership in higher education, music, theatre, art and sculpture.[29] Nationally, Nicholas Goldschmidt, whose father was Belgian, directed the CBC opera and the Centennial choir and organized the musical celebrations of Canada's centennial in 1967. César Borré, a Walloon who conducted the Royal Flemish Orchestra, taught choral singing and Gregorian chant throughout Canada. Watson Kirkonnell commented that although Belgians engaged mostly in agriculture in Western Canada, "they have shown unusual talent in drama and music and have been prominent in Le Cercle Molière and La Société Lyrique de

Gounod, at St. Boniface."[30] The Cercle Molière, Canada's oldest theatre company, founded in 1925 with Belgian-born André Castelein de la Londe as its artistic director, quickly won national recognition. Arthur Boutal succeeded him from 1928 to 1940, at which time Pauline Le Goff Boutal became artistic director, as well as continuing as actor, set designer and costume designer. The Cercle Molière continued to provide the best of French theatre to appreciative audiences and eventually had its own concert hall in the Centre Culturel Franco-Manitobain in St. Boniface.

In Flanders most rural villages had amateur drama groups, a tradition exported by the Onder Ons drama club which tried to keep language and music flourishing. In December 1916, the Belgian Club in St. Boniface accepted a locally organized Onder Ons group, which presented plays in Flemish in St. Boniface and a few rural communities. In the 1930s, Vlanderen's Kerels, a group from Chatham, Ontario, visited Manitoba communities to raise enthusiasm for the preservation of Flemish culture. After World War II, the association Flemings in the World, led by Arthur Verthé, took up the cause. It organized a few chapters in the west, working through the Belgian Club and some local Belgian-Canadian business associations. Apart from keeping alive a sense of ethnic identity, it did not succeed in Manitoba in rekindling the same interest in Flemish culture and language as it did in southwestern Ontario.

The Belgian Club in St. Boniface had its own concert band, and in the 1970s it sponsored the Belgian Folkdancers of Winnipeg which performed at various civic functions. Brass bands, the *fanfare*, existed in virtually every village in Belgium in the early twentieth century. A brass band was organized in Holland, Manitoba in 1894 and in St. Alphonse in 1897. In May 1899, the Société de Musique de Bruxelles was formed by Gustave Hutlet, Jean Agarand, Benjamin Haegerman, Emile Hutlet, and Alphonse Bacchus. In June of the same year, a second band appeared, a parish band known as the Fanfare Paroissiale, also known as l'Union de Bruxelles, which became the leading band and over the years included members of the founding families of the parish – the Hutelet, Hacault, Schumacker, Poncelet, Nicloux, Sauvelet, François and Fifi clans. It provided music for special events throughout the province. The St. Boniface *fanfare*, known as the La Verendrye Band, was organized in 1912 by Joseph Vermander, bandmaster from 1921 to 1943. It played at civic celebrations, community events and religious processions, invariably including in its repertoire a special Belgian processional march.[31] The tradition continued as Gustave

Hutelet organized a brass band in Swan Lake and Adolph François did likewise in Holland in 1949.

Every parish had its choir, and there was usually a soloist expected to perform at Easter and Christmas services. Joseph Hutelet started the first choir in St. Alphonse in 1892 which sang in Latin, French and Flemish. Music was an essential part of community gatherings. Nicolas Rondelet and three members of the Capron family, for example, were the community musicians in the Falher and Girouxville area of northern Alberta. Victor Capron taught music and his wife was an accomplished pianist, Fernand Capron played the violin, and his cousin Victor Capron played the clarinet, saxophone and trumpet.[32]

Across the West, there were Belgians who had higher aspirations than the "song and dance" associated with folkloric multicultural events. In 1971, a number of university professors decided to form the Canadian Association for the Advancement of Netherlandic Studies (CAANS) for the promotion of Flemish and Dutch culture, language, and literature, as well as cultural exchanges of young people. Pianist Jenny LeRouge Le Saunier came to Red Deer in 1907 and taught there until 1922, when at the request of Sir Ernest MacMillan she moved to Edmonton to pursue a brilliant musical career until 1971. Frank J. Simons came to Winnipeg in 1921, taught the harp and was a valued member of the Winnipeg Symphony Orchestra. Both Le Saunier and Simons publicized the compositions of their fellow Belgo-Canadians César Borré, Jules Hone and Frantz Jehin-Prume. In St. Boniface, the Société Lyrique de Gounod gave well-attended concerts and provided training in choral singing. In sculpture, Marcel Braitstein and Auguste Hammerechts' artistic realizations in Quebec set a standard for young Belgians elsewhere. Brent Gelaude of Vancouver, known for his wooden images and busts of Inuit people, stands in the tradition of Pierre Hagvaert, who worked on the Quebec pavilion at Expo 67. Throughout rural areas there are artists and small galleries that remain known only locally such as the Van Walleghem art studio in Winnipeg, the Patti Hacault studio in Holland, the Leopold Simoens studio in Bruxelles. Stephanie Deleau is widely respected as stylist arbiter in the fashion world. In 1911, Henri Hoet of Antwerp, a skilled cabinet-maker, arrived in Cardston, Alberta, and within a couple years was hired to craft the intricate woodwork and honeycomb ceiling of the Mormon temple, then on the interior of the Prince of Wales Hotel in Waterton. He built a spectacular mansion, Cobblestone Manor, around an original log-house, featuring the finest craftsmanship in its cabinets, furniture, panelling and decorative lighting. The many windows on each side of the house, the exterior of which was covered with stones gathered at a nearby creek, were double-glazed and coated with an ammonia mixture to create the first thermal windows. Cobblestone Manor survives as a restaurant and is preserved as a provincial historic site.[33]

Before radio, television and the internet became common sources of information, people relied on oral communication and print for news and opinions. Three journalists played a role in informing Belgians in Western Canada: Louis Hacault took up the cause of Catholic schools in Manitoba; abbé Jean Gaire, in his efforts to attract immigrants and raise money for his settlements, published *Le Défenseur du Canada*.[34] Pierre Van Paassen, correspondent for a number of foreign newspapers while working for the Toronto *Globe* and *Daily Star*, lectured extensively across Western Canada from 1931 to 1938 on international affairs.[35] Most ethnic groups in Western Canada launched their own newspapers and printing establishments. Flemings depended on Flemish newspapers published in the United States such as the *DePere Standard* and the *De Volksstem*. In 1907, the *Gazette van Moline* began publication with Camille Cools as its Detroit correspondent, specializing in news from immigrants from East Flanders and those settled in Manitoba. On 3 August 1914, the Cools-Vinckier Printing Company published the first issue of the *Gazette van Detroit*, a weekly selling for one dollar for a one-year subscription. It began to surpass the Moline paper in readership, especially after Emile Bogaert submitted weekly reports, first from Bruxelles, Manitoba, then from Winnipeg over a forty-five-year period. In 1940, it assumed the subscription list of the *Gazette van Moline* and reached a peak of eight thousand subscribers. After World War II, the readership declined sharply until what appeared to be the last issue was sent out on 2 August 1974. It soon reappeared in Dutch and English format, backed by West Flanders industrial magnate René De Serrano, became a bi-monthly of reduced size in 1989 and survives operated by three elderly widows, assisted by two correspondents in East and West Flanders, from the basement of Father Taillieu's retirement home for Belgian-Americans.[36]

Walloons had access to the French Canadian press as well as papers sent from Belgium and France. Nevertheless, they felt a need to issue their own news bulletins. *L'Avenir de l'Ouest* managed a few issues only in St. Boniface, and none appear to be extant. From May to December 1888, a monthly *Le Courrier du Nord-Ouest* appeared but it seems to have attracted insufficient readers to continue publication. The weekly, *Le Soleil de l'Ouest*, founded in 1911, was taken over by Louis Baloche who owned a small printing shop in Norwood. It was financed largely by his Belgian wife, Mme Collomb, took on a socialist tone, which made it unpopular with the French Canadian clergy, and after the small Collomb fortune was exhausted the paper folded in March 1916. During World War I, two experiments in a trilingual paper – French, Flemish, English – also ended in failure. *Le Démocrate* managed five issues in 1914. *Le Fanal* survived from August 1916 to November 1918. A certain G. Lévesque had vowed to keep tabs on local St. Boniface politicians, whom he called the Clique de l'Hôtel-de-Ville. He explained the purpose of his newssheet:

> What we want is rigorous accounting in the administration of our city's finances. We want to and need to raise the financial position of our city because its future depends on it. What we want to do is show the public of St. Boniface what has been done in the past by our municipal administration and so permit our readers to judge, by giving them the facts and figures.[37]

La Petite Feuille, a French-only paper launched in August 1912, managed thirty-three issues but it too finally faltered in April 1914. There was another attempt in 1916 with *La Libre Parole*, which seems to have survived to 1919, but again there are few copies extant. This proliferation of local papers emanating from the Walloon community indicates a certain dissatisfaction with the religiously oriented French papers published in the West. There was also a specialized paper, *Le Rancher*, printed in St. Boniface whose circulation and fate remain equally elusive.

Pierre Féguenne launched *L'Union* in November 1917, which served the Francophone community in Alberta until 1932. The Association Canadienne-française de l'Alberta tried on numerous occasions to buy *L'Union*, but Féguenne continued to believe the community required an independent news outlet not subservient to a religious and educational lobby. For many years his wife was the only female Linotype operator in Canada.[38] In recent times, the nationalist organization in Antwerp, Vlamingen in de Wereld [Flemings in the World], issues an electronic newsletter for the Flemish community. Likewise, for the Walloons, the Union Francophone des Belges à l'Etranger, with headquarters in Mons, issues a bi-monthly paper, *Le Journal des Belges à l'Etranger.* Neither of these ethnic bulletins has a wide circulation in Western Canada.

Until recently, the Belgians in the West have not had their own historians. Yvette and George Brandt in Swan Lake amassed an impressive collection of documents and photographs, some of which was featured in the jubilee history *Memories of Lorne* (1981) and the Bruges exhibition guide by Marc Journée, *Go West* (2006). In the summer of 1975, a Belgian History Committee consisting of eight persons, spearheaded by James B. Wyndels and Professor Keith Wilson, began soliciting information for a history of Belgian settlement in Manitoba. The result was *The Belgians in Manitoba* (Winnipeg, 1976). Several family reminiscences followed, such as *Hutlet Heritage, 1680–1972* (Swan Lake, 1977), *Belgian Canadian Builders: De Pape–De Roo Families* (1993), and *Our Van Walleghem Roots* (2001). The only comprehensive survey remains the article "Belgians" in Paul Robert Magosci, ed., *Encyclopedia of Canada's Peoples* (1999). The settlement and contribution of Belgians in Western Canada figured prominently in the International Colloquium on the Belgian Presence in Canada held at the University of Ottawa in October 1999.

Apart from official reports, missionary journals and travellers' tales, the Belgian community has received little literary attention. In 1907, Georges Schoeffer, using the pseudonym Forestier, published a novel depicting the disillusionment of settlers in the northern parklands. Pioneer life in this novel was depicted as utter misery at Ste. Rose-du-Lac.[39] The abbé Jules Pirot as pastor in Hungarian parishes in Saskatchewan wrote many poems and short stories in his Walloon dialect describing the natural beauty of the prairies. In three dramatic works he reflected on some of the problems of his pastorate. *Les Fils de la Sociale*, a moralistic play in three acts, highlighted the dangerous influence of atheism and bad company. *Les Martyrs*, a drama in three acts, celebrated the early Christian martyrs as a dedication to the struggles of Mgr Langevin. *Les Ouvriers trompés*, a one-act play, warned against syndicalist propaganda. Two novels touched on regional history: *Avant les Neiges* (1926) described pioneer life in a multicultural West; *Elle vit* (1949), somewhat autobiographical, was about a Hungarian immigrant family and the role of a priest in guiding and comforting them in their trials. It was a sympathetic, not realistic, depiction of life on the western prairies in the pioneer age. He confided to a friend: "Here, religion is simple and sincere; respect of persons is totally unknown."[40]

Far less sympathetic in certain respects were two novels by Hélène de Harven, daughter of an Antwerp businessman, who spent two years in the West, from 1890 to 1892. In both *L'Exilé, Histoire du Nouveau Monde* (Tournai, 1938) and *Waïada: Dans le crépuscule des Peaux-Rouges* (Bruxelles, 1949) she decried the destruction of traditional Native life-style and the disappearance of the bison herds resulting from European settlement and the advent of the railway. More representative of a well-integrated Belgian writer, Guy Vanderhaege, whose grandfather settled in Pirot's Hungarian parish, has moved beyond the pioneer age in his novels. Only in *Man Descending* do we see the utter demoralization of his father as the Depression robbed him of his self-esteem and hope. In 1920, Berthe Gusbin, accompanied by her sister Marthe and husband, left Brussels to join their older brother Edmond Gusbin in The Pas. She married a French journalist and set up a studio in The Pas, wrote poetry and taught violin. In *Au Nord du 53e* she recorded the adventures and exploits of a number of remarkable northerners but recorded few of her own observations and sentiments.[41] Less fortunate, Patricia Anne Van Tighem, in an autobiographical work, *The Bear's Embrace*, recounts a harrowing encounter with a grizzly bear and her courageous struggle with post-traumatic stress to which she finally succumbed.[42] In a sense, this closed the circle of images of Western Canada that began with European warnings about the severe climate, wild tribesmen and ferocious animals of the region. It was a region of the mind as well as a geographical region.

Integration, as opposed to the concept of assimilation, is a process of immigrant settlement that to date awaits a strong theoretical definition. It stands in contrast to the dehumanizing implications of assimilation, according to which immigrants must shed their inherited culture to adopt a new lifestyle and mentality. The American sociological model of the "melting pot" assumed there was a host society into which only the new immigrants were expected to "melt." Assimilationist rhetoric in Western Canada, under the form of Anglo-conformity, was prevalent before World War II, but it gave way to pluralistic views as the British element in society became less dominant and proportionately reduced in the total population of the region. Integration involves a sense of social justice and a desire to participate in civic affairs. In this process a new identity emerges, involving a sense of being Canadian, of incorporation into mainstream society, while retaining certain distinctive characteristics, habits and attitudes of "Belgianness," whether Flemish or Walloon.

Behind the issue of integration is the process known as socialization, or the way in which individuals learn to behave in a certain society and develop a sense of self in a new social environment. According to theorists, the chief agents of socialization are the family, the mentors, and the age peers. Belgian families were particularly effective, in the first two generations of life in Canada, a period when the family was also an economic unit, in implanting values of personal responsibility, conformity, and group solidarity. In rural agricultural communities, with a concentration of Flemish or Walloon families, internalization of this cultural transmission followed with facility. Children and adolescents in this environment shared these values with their equals, their age group. Their mentors were their teachers and members of the clergy who reinforced their traditional values.

In the more complex social environment of the towns and cities, parental influence gradually weakened because of reciprocal socialization, or the influence of competing agencies, which tended to modify some traditional views. The peer group is quite diverse in an urban setting and the mentors come from a variety of recreational, athletic, cultural, social and professional groups. There are also indirect nonpersonal sources of communication such as radio and movies, and eventually television, videos and computer networks that influence the thinking and behaviour of all persons, young and old, rural and urban. There are no available statistics to indicate whether Belgians were more or less susceptible to formal socialization than other ethnic or national groups.

School, leisure and recreation activities socialize and homogenize diverse cultures, or at least afford youth the opportunity to learn about other cultural practices and develop friendships across ethnocultural backgrounds. Adults through widened contacts through farmers' and business organizations experience a similar cross-fertilization of ideas and values. The result of these social relationships is integration and social inclusion. For Belgians, of course, schooling, sports and entertainment in Canada resembled in many respects the cultural norms of the home country. Traditionally, family loyalty, interdependence and emphasis on obligations were cherished values, yet it was easy to accept the emphasis on individual achievement and personal growth that characterized the host society in Canada. Parents wanted their children to succeed occupationally and financially, but in the first generation they did not have high educational expectations for their children. This reflected their own general socio-economic status. The school systems, public and separate, were inclusive or open to almost all children of given ages and provided a general comprehensive education that included some civic indoctrination. Catholic-oriented schools provided more insulation from competing values and mores to several ethnic communities than did the common public schools. Until World War II, the public schools had a secularized Protestant ethos not unlike the civil religion of American public schools. This ideology was based on the assumptions that British institutions were divinely blessed with high ethical standards and they had a moral mission in the world, especially towards immigrant communities that were sometimes categorized as "lesser breeds." This ideology was clearly expounded in provincial curricula and in J.T.M. Anderson's *The Education of the New Canadian.* The objectives were clearly assimilationist in an Anglo-conformist sense but there is reason to believe that the results appeared more integrationist than assimilationist.[43]

The recent development affecting integration is rural restructuration, marked first by the creation of larger administrative units and followed by a decline in rural population. This began with the disappearance of rural one-room schools and the building of larger village schools that also offered secondary level courses. Homogeneous settlement patterns were disrupted as a result. Larger school units with large centralized schools succeeded the consolidated schools and further encouraged a mixing of young people from a variety of ethnocultural backgrounds. Declining Belgian rural activity, as in dairying, market gardening and sugar beet cultivation, is part of persistently declining rural population in the West. The primary cause of the disappearance of many village communities and shrinking farm population is increasing agricultural productivity that implies less need for rural labour. On the other hand, the disappearance of many villages has been accompanied by the growth of strategically located service centres that in turn indicates a continuing interdependence between rural and urban populations. This population shift is visible in the prairie landscape as the wooden grain elevators that stood as sentinels in every village have been demolished and replaced by a few concrete silos at widely dispersed locations. The new service centres offer new trades, business and professional opportunities for the sons and daughters of third and fourth generation agriculturalists. This relocation accompanied the abandonment of subsistence farming in favour of agro-business by the more enterprising farm families. For the historian and demographer this mutation implies accelerated integration and increased challenges to self-identity for ethnocultural groups.

It would be misleading to assume that there was an unopposed one-directional flow of events in favour of adopting majoritarian views and practices. The clergy in the early settlement period, for example, was anxious to set and maintain boundaries to protect shared norms, values and behaviour. Community leaders on occasion joined in opposing public dances, mixed marriages, inter-denominational services, and divisional and regional sports leagues. As we have seen, there was concern on the part of the clergy and parents in southern Alberta because the Mormons exerted undue pressure on Catholic youth to join in their cultural and recreational activities which had an avowed assimilationist motivation. This boundary maintenance never developed into a counter-culture, as was the case with the Hutterites. Belgians, however, were sometimes included among individuals and groups behaving outside the boundaries of acceptable behaviour set by conservative Protestant leaders, prohibitionists and suffragettes. These informal agents of social control did not provoke Belgians to the point of public confrontation and principled challenges. Belgians remained true to their own social norms, within the confines of Canadian law, while resisting or ignoring what was perceived as outrageous proscription. Far from being deviant, this in-group behaviour helped to maintain a sense of identity.

The existence of a cluster of Belgians in the east end of St. Boniface did not result in the formation of a ghetto and in negative economic consequences, as some ethnic studies postulate. Instead, the immigrants integrated well because they were located near to attractive employment and they were able to learn the second official language to their benefit. Belgian Towns in Glace Bay, St. Boniface and Weyburn belied any relationship between segregation and poverty. Indeed, their existence was an indication of gainful employment and networking. Furthermore, this clustering, whether in urban St. Boniface or rural southern Manitoba communities, provided a sense of social and cultural comfort.[44]

The first generation of immigrants who settled in rural communities were too preoccupied with meeting their material needs to be concerned about problems of integration. Arthur Vermeire in southern Manitoba remembered his youth, not in terms of community events, but in terms of strenuous farm labour:

We had a six-foot binder pulled by three horses and I drove
the binder when I was eleven years old, and did the stooking
also. I never went further than grade eight, even though I went
to school till I was almost seventeen, but only in the winter
time. In the summer time twelve-year old boys were expected
to stay home to help with the work. We always ran barefoot in
summer.[45]

Francis De Roo had similar memories, but he added a detail that
underscored the degree of co-operation across ethnolinguistic lines that
pioneering encouraged. When the father and the sons were busy cutting
green poplar wood for sale in the village, the roof of their shanty house
caught fire from an overheated stovepipe. A seven-year-old lad quickly
enlisted the help of a couple neighbours – an Englishman and a Frenchman.
The three men worked as a team: one in the well getting water, another
mixing it with snow, and the third tearing sod off the roof to pour in the
watery mixture. They communicated by signs only because De Roo spoke
only Flemish, Le Bain only French, and Couch only English.[46]

The Walloon communities often felt the weight of the rigourist theology
of the French Canadian hierarchy and clergy. They were not always in
agreement with the ban on mixed marriages and public dances, nor the
ruling that if a father sent his children to a non-Catholic school, he would
be penalized by "no sacraments for him and no first communion for his
children."[47] These directives were effective in bringing about compliance
only among very devout Catholics. Even a school inspector like P. Rochon
dared ignore an episcopal order to have teaching appointments subject to
clerical approval. A liberal-minded prelate like Bishop Mathieu in Regina
was very reluctant to join in the crusade against public dances and balls
where Catholics would socialize with non-Catholics because he was very
aware of the sentiments of the European-origin population in his diocese.[48]

The Walloons who integrated into the French-Canadian community
participated fully in Francophone educational, cultural, and religious
organizations on the prairies. Abbé Maurice Baudoux, as already
mentioned, was not only an influential supporter of their initiatives but
also an innovator in the movement for their full participation in the public
media.[49] In Willow Bunch, for example, the St. Jean-Baptiste Society
sponsored other associations such as an educational committee organized
in 1913 and an independent model parliament for adults and youth to

develop their oratorical skills. A musical committee was formed and soon had a twenty-six-voice male choir under the direction of Dr. Godin, accompanied by a twenty-piece band. It was fine for the clergy to sponsor events through an association like the St. Jean-Baptiste Society but there was resistance to any attempt to control all activities. In Gravelbourg, some of the laity resented clerical control and organized an Association Catholique de la Jeunesse Canadienne to initiate fortnightly young peoples' discussion groups. Beginning in 1921, it introduced drama, musical concerts, operettas and lectures. Conflict developed between the local cultural elite, consisting of the clergy, staff of Collège Mathieu and the Gravel family, on the one hand, and a large community group who espoused only popular cultural activities, on the other hand. The Walloons were divided in their loyalties. In British Columbia, where the Francophone community was relatively small, its Belgian component was quite active in organizations such as the Société française de Bienfaisance et Secours mutuel de Victoria. Joseph Haegart, for example, was a principal organizer of the Alliance Française in Victoria in 1907. The social milieu was very favourable for the development of these initiatives because the British elite of Vancouver Island was quite Francophile. This was reflected in the number who spoke French and the prominent role given to French instruction at Royal Roads College. This favourable climate continued to the World War II period, when Belgians became active in Le Club Canadien français and supported the local paper, *L'Echo de la Colombie*, in the 1960s. Their participation was recognized when Arthur Chéramy was elected first general president of the Fédération canadienne-française de la Colombie.

In the coal-mining districts of the Crowsnest Pass, the Walloons displayed some distinctive traits and behaviour. Unlike the Italians, they had no formal organizations, socializing instead by visiting and house parties around a keg of beer. In fact, they did not even frequent the saloons as did other ethnic groups. Mistaken quite often for French, they remained quite different although they shared their socialist views and even anti-clericalism. They were better educated than most of their Central European co-workers and they had smaller families than other Catholic groups.[30] In Bellegarde, a Walloon Catholic farming parish, the social pattern was not too different. A long-time teacher in the parish observed:

The coffee drinkers, the *cafteurs*, and the drinkers who swallow their alcohol in one gulp, gather together. Among the Belgians, they like to "spread the table," that is to say to entertain, and of course they talk in patois, the language of the old Walloon hamlet in the old country.

Hospitality, in popular culture, had wider implications. Yvette Le Gal continues to explain:

As there are no hotels, it is the rule that one welcomes those who pass by. If the inhabitants of a house are absent, the passer-by may go in, light a fire and eat. But he must put out the fire, cut and bring in wood before leaving. For this reason no one must lock the door of his house. None however fears for his safety.[51]

The concept of separate gender spheres requires closer analysis when applied to Belgian rural families, if only because men had an appreciable domestic existence just as women had. Most fathers clearly took great interest in the development of their children and felt responsible for providing them with the opportunity to fill a useful occupation upon reaching adulthood. This was in addition to a pride in being able to provide the basic necessities, and some small comforts, for the family. This was an aspect of paternal responsibility that was severely challenged during the Depression of the inter-war years. Men also experienced the need to support their wives who were primary nurturers and educators by governing family affairs and inculcating in the children the need to learn and to obey. As children grew into adolescence and became more independent, in part because of the democratic ethos of public education, fathers sometimes felt their authority challenged. Although the patriarchal position of men in society tended to support paternal authority in the home, the traditional Flemish and Walloon stratified family structure was questioned. Men, more than women, functioned in both the public and private sphere and therefore were more exposed to a larger community where the tight-knit extended family and paternal authority were less common and less valued.

Women's work took on added importance in village and farming communities during the Depression and during work stoppages and strikes in mining communities. On the farm, women provided income from the eggs, butter, cream and meat they sold, or for which they obtained credit, at the general store. In difficult economic times, a woman's workload increased as gardening, preserving, knitting, sewing and mending clothes from scraps and flour and sugar sacks became essential.[52] Possession of a traditional craft such a lace-making did not provide much income or recognition in Western Canada. Rachel Mannens in Bruxelles, Manitoba and Mariette Buydens in Hudson Bay Junction, Saskatchewan found their skill fulfilled their personal artistic and aesthetic sense but the lace-making tradition was not passed on to become a permanent aspect of Flemish-Canadian culture.[53] For women generally, relief came in winter with a round of card and house parties, a few concerts, radio programs, and the party line telephone. Men met at the livery barn, general store, barber shop, post office and railway station to discuss mutual problems. None of this was particularly ethnic in nature although it replicated to a degree the conviviality of the Walloon and Flemish village.

CONCLUSION

This study is based in good measure on the archives of the Ministry of Foreign Affairs in Brussels and family biographies in local and district jubilee histories. The experiences of Belgian promoters, planters, and pioneers in Western Canada indicates that both ethnic behaviour and national culture affected their implantation as an immigrant group and eventually conditioned their integration into the evolving mainstream society of the region. They came as investors and participants in a developing economy and settled as planters on the vast stretches of open prairie and verdant river valleys, veritable pioneers in the creation of a new West. They promoted four agricultural pursuits – dairying, market gardening, sugar-beet culture, fruit-growing – with distinction in Manitoba, Alberta, and British Columbia. Aside from a few radical union leaders who sought refuge in North America, these immigrants were not the destitute, dispossessed, or persecuted. The majority were agriculturalists, labourers and miners in search of better economic conditions. They were recruited by land speculators, immigration agents, steamship companies, railway companies, employment agencies, "return men," and colonizing clergy. It was common, during the first wave of immigration before 1914, for sojourners to remain as pioneers.

Belgians were protected by their home government in matters of recruitment procedures and emigration provisions and in the fulfillment of contractual obligations on the part of steamship lines, colonization companies and Canadian employers. Fact-finding missions from Belgium followed up on conditions of settlement and corroborated consular reports. Irregularities and fraud in emigration/immigration were of great concern to Belgian authorities. Canada never launched a massive campaign to attract Belgians as it did in the British Isles. Nevertheless, Belgium was thought to be in the "preferred" category in Canadian immigration legislation and regulation.

In spite of an assimilationist Anglo-conformist ideology in Western Canada throughout the period to 1940, Belgians were able to accommodate readily to a social milieu whose base over time became less that of a common descent, common ancestral traditions, or common religion. Politically, Flemings and Walloons had come from a duo-ethnic nation that idealistically upheld equality under political union and that believed the solution of problems rested with the attitude of the majority, but also with a consideration of the aspirations of the weaker partner. Flemings identified especially with the heterogeneous Anglophone community in the West, while most Walloons identified with the Francophone minority.

Both Belgian immigrant communities brought to the new environment their own cultural practices and values, some of which were "national," others predominantly ethnic Flemish or Walloon, and others occupational or class. Thus, there appeared to be a common work ethic, sense of social justice, and desire to participate in civic affairs. On the other hand, there were political and religious differences between agriculturalists, miners and investors. Integration into the complex mainstream, itself in continuous progression, was facilitated by the fact Belgians lacked institutional completeness, the structure of organizations to provide most of the services they required. Also, there was no great social distance, or marked cultural differences, between them and the predominant Anglophone and Francophone communities. Although they did retain some sense of historic identity and a level of popular culture within their own group, they did not politicize these group concerns and differences. The Belgian experience, therefore, falls into a category of partialized or fragmented ethnicity because some aspects of an individual's life remained within the confines of ancestral expectations while other segments followed the mainstream culture. Some Flemings appear to be taking on an affective ethnicity in response to rising manifestations of Flemish nationalism in Belgium. This explains the self-identification as "Flemish" in recent multiple-origin census returns, although at the same time English is indicated as the home language. On the other hand, many Walloons have retained their mother tongue and they usually identify themselves as Francophone Canadians of Belgian origin.

Although Canadian immigration officials perceived Belgians as belonging to the "preferred" class, or readily assimilable, and able to contribute immediately to the regional economy, these immigrants did retain a sense of their own identity. This sentiment of ancestral identity was rooted in a number of factors. Locality of origin in Belgium, such as Halanzy, Wingene, or Lommel, was transmitted through chain migration to new communities in Western Canada. Family networks and community intermarriage were important factors in maintaining a sense of belongingness. The Catholic church was usually an influential social centre and communication with the homeland aided in sustaining a degree of differentiation from the multiethnic neighbourhood. Although there were no official Belgian bloc settlements, there were concentrations of planters in rural communities and urban enclaves that were reinforced by continuing immigration and religious patronage. In the first two generations, the experience of pioneers and planters was situational, with some significant differences between predominantly Flemish and Walloon concentrations of population. Walloons almost invariably became integrated into the Francophone community, whereas Flemings, except in the first generation in St. Boniface, adopted many Anglophone host society views and customs. Still, in St. Alphonse and Swan Lake a Flemish flavour persisted and Bellegarde retained an unmistakably Walloon quality.

In the various communities where Belgians settled, they were in contact with a host society, or mainstream, that was itself situational and evolving over time. They came to a southern Manitoba that was markedly Anglophone western Ontarian, a Saskatchewan that was quite multicultural and polyglot, a southern Alberta that was predominantly American, and British Columbia that was characteristically British. They acculturated to a variety of sub-host cultures, in other words, that in turn were modified by a continuing stream of diverse immigrants. Belgians, unlike some immigrant groups, promoted the monarchical, liberal democratic, Christian and bilingual character of society. They presented no formal claims for distinctive political, economic or socio-cultural institutions. On the contrary, the paucity of their ethnic parishes, schools and associations was a factor in the rapid integration of the bi-ethnic community. The only institutions of consequence were the Club Belge, the Belgian Sacred Heart parish in St. Boniface, and Scheppers Institute in Swan Lake.

Family histories provide evidence of the role of family, mentors and age peers in the process of socialization. In the first two generations in Canada the family, especially a farm family, implanted values of personal responsibility, conformity, and group solidarity and a work ethic. Children and adolescents shared these values with their age group, while the teachers and the clergy as mentors reinforced their traditional values. In the more complex social environment of towns and cities, parental influence was somewhat weakened, the peer group was more diverse, and mentors came from a variety of recreational, social and professional groups. By the third generation, non-personal influences, such as radio, movies, television and the automobile, influenced the thinking of all persons, young and old, rural and urban. School, leisure and recreational activities developed friendships across ethnocultural backgrounds. Adults through widening contacts in farm and business organizations, labour unions and professional associations experienced a cross-fertilization of ideas and values. Marriages that were contracted originally within the Belgian community, in the second generation included the wider Catholic community, and thereafter the entire community, indicating that Belgians were susceptible to formal socialization. Social relationships resulted in integration and social inclusion, justifying the "preferred" immigration status. Both Flemings and Walloons valued individual achievement and personal growth and, in the initial stages of implantation, they wanted to succeed occupationally and financially. Nevertheless, in general, Flemish farmers and Walloon coalminers did not have high educational expectations for their children. The school systems provided a comprehensive education to all and Catholic-oriented schools provided insulation from competing values and mores. There were occasions when boundary maintenance was required, such as during Mormon social pressure on youth in southern Alberta, pressure to join new political parties, and from informal agents of social control such as religious leaders, prohibitionists and suffragettes. Walloon communities sometimes resisted the rigourist theology of the hierarchy and clergy concerning marriage, schooling, recreation and tithing. The Flemish family tradition of pooling the income of all its members survived for several decades.

Rural restructuration, marked first by the creation of larger administrative units, then the disappearance of railway branch lines, grain elevators and smaller villages, disrupted homogeneous settlement patterns. New service centres offered new trades and business and professional opportunities for the sons and daughters of the third and fourth generation Belgian-Canadians. Employment in the early collieries was replaced by opportunities in the petroleum and potash industries. These mutations implied accelerated integration and increased challenges to self-identity.

The story of Belgian life in Western Canada illustrates the major eras and developments of the region. From the image of an untamed wilderness to the granary of the world, Belgians participated in the wheat economy. They excelled in the cultivation of sugar beets, vegetables and small fruits, the operation of dairy farms, and the raising of fine horses. They mined coal from the Souris valley to Vancouver Island, organized unions and battled the bosses, even when they were compatriots. They endured the challenges of war, drought and depression. The financiers of Antwerp and Brussels invested heavily in land, resource exploitation, construction and industrial development, while farmers, labourers, small business men, housewives and miners toiled, raised their families, and participated in the affairs of their local communities. Missionaries, priests, nuns, teachers, and professional people helped to sustain the popular image of Belgians as industrious, frugal and successful. Others distinguished themselves in the arts, music and literature. Two world wars, in which Canadian troops alongside Belgians fought valiantly, confirmed the moral fibre of the Belgian people and further endeared them to the Canadian public. These are the observations that emerge from the generational record of family histories. The archival record confirms that while Belgian authorities were wise to interest themselves in the fate of their emigrants, they were gratified that they integrated well as pioneers in Western Canada, promoted industry and commerce, and generally succeeded as model planters.

APPENDIX

Table 1. Distribution of Belgian Origin Population in Western Canada, 1901–91.

	Manitoba	Saskatchewan	Alberta	British Columbia	Total
1901	940 (56.6%)	NWT 310 (18.7%)		410 (24.7%)	1,660
1911	2,430 (39.6%)	1,538 (24.8%)	1,269 (20.5%)	938 (15.1%)	6,198
1921	5,320 (41.9%)	3,477 (27.4%)	2,590 (20.4%)	1,334 (10.4%)	12,711
1931	6,323 (41.9%)	4,458 (29.5%)	2,726 (18%)	1,597 (10.6%)	15,104
1941	6,715 (42.5%)	4,250 (26.9%)	2,919 (18.5%)	1,930 (12.2%)	15,814
1951	7,733 (43.7%)	4,079 (23.1%)	3,006 (17%)	2,867 (16.2%)	17,685
1961	9,698 (38.4%)	5,464 (21.6%)	5,152 (20.4%)	4,948 (19.6%)	25,262
1971*	9,055 (41.7%)	3,555 (16.4%)	4,265 (19.6%)	4,840 (22.3%)	21,715
1981*	6,500 (37.2%)	2,830 (16.2%)	4,305 (24.6%)	3,830 (21.9%)	17,465
1991**	14,715 (33.7%)	6,515 (14%)	11,045 (25.3%)	11,420 (25.3%)	43,695

Source: Statistics Canada, Catalogue 92-913 to 92-727.

*Census takers tended to ignore ethnic origin; therefore, figures tend to be low.
**Multiple origins for both "Belgians" and "Flemish" as separate categories.

Table 2. Province of Origin of Belgian Emigrants Destined for Canada, 1912–40.

West Flanders	30.6%
East Flanders	21.6%
Brabant	14.9%
Luik/Liège	10.6%
Antwerp	9.8%
Hainaut	7.8%
Luxembourg	3.1%
Namur	1.1%
Limburg	0.5%

Source: *Statistisch Jaarboek*, 1940; cited by Marc Journée, pp. 62–66.

Table 3. Belgian Origin Population in Canada.

Census	Belgian Origin	Born in Belgium
1901	2,984	2,280
1911	9,664	7,975
1921	20,234	13,276
1931	27,585	17,033
1941	29,711	14,773
1951	35,148	17,251
1961	61,382	28,253

Source: M.C. Urquart and K.A.H. Buckley, *Historical Statistics of Canada* (Toronto, 1965), Series A83, A182.

Table 4. Periods of Belgian Immigration to Canada.

Period	Immigrants	Description
1900–14	15,891	First wave of immigration
1914–18	402	World War I
1919–28	13,263	Second wave of immigration
1929–39	1,966	Depression
1939–45	76	World War II
1946–50	3,809	Reconstruction period
1951–60	15,200	Third wave of immigration

Source: *Report of the Royal Commission on Biculturalism and Bilingualism* (Ottawa, 1970), vol. IV, Table A-1.

NOTES

CHAPTER I: THE VIEW FROM BELGIUM

1   Jean Stengers, *Emigration et immigration en Belgique au XIXe et au XXe siècles* (Bruxelles: Académie Royal des Sciences d'Outre-Mer, 1978), 23, 29.

2   *Annales parlementaires, Chambre, 1855–56*, 7 April 1856, 1043; *Annales parlementaires, Sénat, 1888–89*, 13 February 1889, 111.

3   Jean Volders, "La fièvre d'émigration," *Le Peuple*, 8 January 1889. To facilitate reading of the text, we have translated all citations and newspaper dates into English.

4   Jules Leclercq, *Un été en Amérique. De l'Atlantique aux montagnes rocheuses* (Paris: Plon, 1877), 84–85.

5   Henri de Man, "Lettre du Canada. Les progrès du mouvement ouvrier," *Le Peuple*, 22 April 1920.

6   AMAE, dossier 2946, Letter from Governor of Luxembourg, 31 December 1887. The Archives du Ministère des Affaires Etrangères in Brussels has been a major source of information for this project.

7   Gustaaf Vekeman, "Lettre d'un émigrant," *Le pionnier de Sherbrooke*, 19 July 1883.

8   Octave Laurent, "De Chicago à Québec," *Bulletin de la société royale belge de géographie* 18 (1894): 273–74, cited in Serge Jaumain, "Le Canada des récits de voyage et brochures de propagande diffusés en Belgique (1867–1914)," in

Serge Jaumain, ed., *Les immigrants préférés: Les belges* (Ottawa: Presses de l'Université d'Ottawa, 1999), 79.

9   Georges Kaiser, *Au Canada* (Bruxelles: A. Lesigne, 1887), 223; Eugène Goblet d'Alviella, "Souvenirs d'une excursion au Canada," *Revue de Belgique* 29 (1881): 49, 119; Octave Laurent, 'De Chicago à Québec,' *Bulletin de la société royale belge de géographie* 18 (1894): 287, 294; Léon Brabant, "L'émigration vers le Canada," *Le Peuple*, 29 April 1911.

10 AMAE, dossier 4093, Rapport sur la Nouvelle Confédération du Canada, 19 March 1868.

11 Baron Etienne Hulot, *De l'Atlantique au Pacifique. A travers le Canada et le nord des Etats-Unis* (Paris: Librairie Plon, 1888), 264.

12 Kaiser, *Au Canada*, 243, 266.

13 *Recueil consulaire, 1908*, Ketels, "Rapport générale," 140.

14 Louis Strauss, *Le Canada au point de vue économique* (Paris: Librairie internationale, 1867), 21.

15 Hulot, *De l'Atlantique au Pacifique*, 267–69.

16 A. J. W. *Les aventures de Coquelicot au Canada* (Bruxelles: Librairie Veuve Willems-Van den Borre, 1911),120.

17 *Le bien public*, "Canada: L'or dans le Nord Ouest," 24 July 1897; "Canada. Au Klondyke," 18 November 1900; "Canada. Un compot au Klondyke," 24 November 1901.

18 Tréau de Coeli, *Le Canada occidental* (Paris, 1910), Letter of Emile Girard, Forget, 20 February 1910, translated and cited in Richard Lapointe and Lucille Tessier, *The Francophones of Saskatchewan. A History* (Regina: Société historique de la Saskatchewan, 1986), 74.

19 O. De Meulenaere, *Un 'trip' aux Etats-Unis et au Canada* (Bruxelles: A.G. Beulens frères, 1911), 75.

20 E. Ducpetiaux, "Budgets économiques des classes ouvrières en Belgique," *Bulletin de la Commission centrale de statistique* 6 (1885): 261–440.

21 Christian Douchant and James R. Richtik, "Belgian Migration to Manitoba to 1930," eds. H. John Selwood and John C. Lehr *Reflections from the Prairies: Geographical Essays* (Winnipeg: Department of Geography, University of Winnipeg, n.d.), 27–28.

22 AMAE, dossier 2808, Report of Robert De Vos to Minister, 21 March 1901, 7–8.

23 G. Lennox, *Guide universel de l'émigrant* (Bruxelles: Librairie universelle Rozez, 1885); *Guide universel de l'émigrant. Fédération canadienne: La Colombie brittanique* (Bruxelles: Librairie universelle Rozez, 1886).

24 Brother Berchmans [Victor Van Tighem] to Leonard Van Tighem, 25 March 1884, eds. Mary Eggermont-Molenaar and Paul Callens, *Missionaries among Miners, Migrants and Blackfoot* (Calgary: University of Calgary Press, 2007), 27.

25 Gommar De Pauw, *The Educational Rights of the Church and Elementary Schools in Belgium* (Doctor of Canon Law dissertation, Catholic University of America, 1953), 76–77.

26 Dirk Mussehoot, *Wij Gaan Naar Amerika. Vlaamse Landverhuizers naar de Nieuwe Wereld, 1850–1930* (Tielt::Lannoo, 2002), *passim*. This is the standard work on 'push factors' for Flemish emigration.

27 Jean Stengers, *Emigration et immigration en Belgique au XIXe et au XXe siècles* (Bruxelles: Académie Royale des Sciences d'Outre-Mer, 1978), 29, 59;

V. Aelbrecht, "L'immigration ouvrière belge à Tourlaing durant le Second Empire," *Revue Belge d'histoire contemporaine* 21, nos. 3-4 (1990): 351-381.

28 AMAE, dossier 4093, Report of Consul in Quebec, 21 March 1885.

29 AMAE, dossier 2940, viii, 21 March 1891; ibid., dossier 2669, bis II, I, Law of 14 December 1876, Regulation of 2 December 1905.

30 Jozef Van Mullem, *Belgian Emigration to Canada* (Brussels: Ministry of Small Enterprises, Trades and Agriculture, 1999), 21.

31 Ginette Kurgan-Van Hentenryk, "Belgian Emigration to the United States and Other Overseas Countries at the Beginning of the Twentieth Century," eds. Ginette Kurgan and Emy Spelkens *Two Studies on Emigration through Antwerp to the New World* (Bruxelles: Center for American Studies, 1976), 21–22, 28.

32 See, for example, the issue *Belgique-Canada* 2, no. 5 (1919): 10.

33 AMAE, dossier 2669 bis, I-B.

34 C. P. Kindleberger, *Europe's Postwar Growth* (Cambridge: Harvard University Press, 1967), chap. 4; L. Bockstaele and A. Olivier, *Canada. Vestigingsmogdijkheden van landbouwers* (Bruges: Provinciaal Comite voor Landbouw, 1955); Cornelius J. Jaenen, *The Belgians in Canada* (Ottawa: Canadian Historical Association, 1991), 16–19.

35 AMAE, dossier 2669 bis, VI, Memorandum on emigration. The author identified the AMAE sources and André Vermeirre compiled the emigration information from the archival material.

36 *Journal de Bruxelles.* 25 June 1886. Translation.

37 "La crise ouvrière et l'émigration," *L'Opinion,* 4 August 1886.

38 Ministère des Affaires Etrangères, *Le service de renseignements concernant l'émigration* (Bruxelles, 1888), 7.

39 AMAE, dossier 2947, Governor of Luxembourg to Minister of Foreign Affairs, 20 February 1891.

40 Luc Devolder, "Of Stations Passed," *The Low Countries* (Bruges: Die Keure, 2004), 34–35.

41 Van Mullum, *Belgian Emigration to Canada*, 13.

42 Ministère des Affaires Etrangères, *Loi et règlement sur le transport des émigrants* (Bruxelles: Moniteur Belge, 1876), 27.

43 AMAE, dossier 2669 bis, VI, Circular of 27 December 1884.

44 AMAE, dossier 2954, III, VI, VII, VIII, IX.

45 AMAE, dossier 2669 bis, IV, file 320.

46 AMAE, dossier 2669 bis, VIII, Regulation of 25 February 1924; ibid., dossier 2669 bis, IB, Commissioner to Françoise Deroover, Director, MAE, 10 January 1929.

47 *Le service de renseignements concernant l'émigration.*

48 AMAE, dossier 2669, Report of 26 March 1897; ibid., dossier 2958, Count Walbott van Bassenheim to Minister, 15 April 1897.

49 "Les travailleurs de l'Ouest," *Le Canada*, 23 October 1907, cited in J. E. Vignes, *La vérité sur le Canada* (Paris: Union International d'Editions, 1909), 203.

50 AMAE, dossier 2669 bis, II, liasse 4, dossiers of Michel Biet, Jacques Rosenfeld.

51 AMAE, dossier 2958; LAC, MG 10, G-I, f. 138, Clarence de Sola to Minister of Foreign Affairs, 28 March 1905.

52 Ibid., files of Adolphe Bayot, Emile Van Iseghem, Emile Van den Neste.

53 Ibid., files of Charles Beernaert, A. J. De Brucques, Pierre Lehoucq.

54 Ibid., file of Aimé Gyselbrecht & Frères with CPR telegram of 27 March 1923.

55 Ibid., files of Albert Stevens, Adolphe Marchand, A. Demarée, Hector Laeven, Albert Beun.

56 AMAE, CCC, Letterbook 4, H. De Burlet to Claude Robinet, Maple Creek, 28 March 1919, 381–82.

57 AMAE, dossier 2669 bis, IV, file 320, Teaching Club, 18 July 1926 to 25 May 1927.

58 Ibid., file 320, Report of L. E. Van de Velde, 10 March 1927. Byt Willem Laetsman, one of the accused, was later convicted in Holland.

59 AMAE, dossier 2669 bis, IV, file 320, Butterfly Publicity Company; *Journal de Charleroi*, 11 December 1923; Commissioner of Emigration to Minister, 22 November 1933.

60 AMAE, dossier 2669 bis, II, liasse 4, file 320, Minute of 12 August 1927 to Mr. de Coster, Commissioner for Emigration. There are also letters to the Minister of Foreign Affairs and the Consul in Detroit.

61 The objectives of the society were as follows: "L'Oeuvre, without taking part either for or against emigration, considers it to be an established fact; it counsels the emigrant on the countries that best suit him and the means of transport; iprotects him at Antwerp, in the ports of call and disembarkation through the instrumentality of men of confidence; finally, it maintains contact with the public through its bulletin." AMAE, dossier 2669 bis, II, Extract of report of Antwerp committee, 1890–91, 3–4.

62 AASB, Fonds Taché, Walbott de Bassenheim to Hippolyte Lory, s.j., December 1888.

63 AASB, Fonds Taché, Bernier to Msgr Taché, 25 January 1889.

64 AASB, Fonds Langevin, LB 3, Langevin to Walbott de Bassenheim, 9 June 1896; Archives of Archdiocese of Edmonton (hereafter AAE), Fonds Grandin, LB 3, Grandin to Walbott de Bassenheim, 22 August 1892; *Oeuvres de l'Archange Raphaël pour la protection des émigrants. Comités d'Anvers. Rapport pour les exercices 1890–1891* (Anvers: Typographie Bellemans Frères, 1891); AMAE, dossier 2669 bis, III, Memo on charitable societies.

65 Jean Stengers, *Emigration et immigration*, 57–58.

66 *Manuel des émigrants* (Bruges: Planche Frères, 1892).

67 AMAE, dossier 2958, I, Van Bruysel to Minister 3 April 1893.

68 Julian Devos, "L'émigration belge au Canada" (typescript, 1969), 68–69.

69 Jennifer Vrielinck, "De Vlaamse en Nederlandse migrantenpers in Canada: een historische doorlichting," in Leen d'Haenens, *Het land de Ahorn. Visies of Canada* (Gand: Academia Press, 1995), 159–81.

70 J. Willequet, "Un facteur d'expansion commerciale: Le système consulaire sous Léopold I," *Bulletin de l'Académie royale des sciences d'outre-mer* (1964): 805–36.

71 AMAE, Pers. 793 I Robert Carter & Company to S. Wandeweyer. Belgian Ambassador in Great Britain, 15 April 1850.

72 *Recueil consulaire* (Bruxelles, 1857), 31.

73 His first initiative was to establish direct steamship connections between Antwerp and Canadian ports, each country to provide a yearly subsidy of $30,000, but the Belgian parliament refused to co-operate fearing the repercussions of its farmers to the importation of Canadian cereals.

74 AASB, Fonds Taché, Bodard to Taché, 10 October 1887; Georges Kaiser, *Au Canada* (Bruxelles, 1897), 202, 204–5; LAC, Agriculture Papers, vol. 590, file 66685, Watelet to Lowe, 27 August 1888.

75 AMAE, dossier 2940, Wilmert to Minister, 24 November 1887; ibid. Van Bruyssel to Minister, 12 June 1888; AMAE, dossier 2940, VIII.

76 AASB, Fonds Taché, Walbott de Bassenheim to Lory, 25 December 1888; Bernier to Taché, 25 January 1889; Pelletier to Taché, 20 November 1889. The immigration agent in Montreal complained in 1892 that "a Belgian society under pretext of charity or philanthropy sent this year to Canada some settlers without means or morality,"

released convicts. Canada, *Sessional Papers* (Ottawa, 1892), No. 2, Report of A. Bodard, p. 36.

77 E. J. Auclair, *Le curé Labelle: Sa vie et son oeuvre* (Montréal, n.d.), 153–64. LAC, RG 17, Hacault to Lowe, 7 August 1890; Hacault to Minister, 2 August 1890. Louis Hacault, *Les colonies belges et françaises au Manitoba* (Bruxelles, 1892), 3.

78 *Recueil consulaire* (Bruxelles, 1897), Report of 28 May 1897.

79 AMAE, dossier 2958, Letter of J. Wégimont, 11 January 1899.

80 AASB, Fonds Langevin, Delouche to Langevin, 28 June 1898.

81 AMAE, dossier 2958, Consul general to Minister, 3 November 1900. Appended a letter of R. de Vos, vice-consul.

82 Canada, *Sessional Papers*, No. 25 (1901), Report of Léon Roy, 20 August 1900, p. 127.

83 Canada, *Sessional Papers*, No. 25 (1901), Report of Tréau de Coeli, 25 August 1901; AMAE, dossier 2808, dossier 1360/14, liasse VI, Entreprises diverses, Memorandum of 9 March 1901.

84 AMAE, dossier 2828, Report of Robert De Vos to Minister, 21 March 1901, pp. 123–24.

85 AMAE, dossier 2808, Memorandum of Consul General, 21 June 1901 attached to the Report of A. E. De Vos, 21 March 1901.

86 AMAE, dossier 2958, J. Berckmans et al. to Minister, 14 February 1905, 30 March 1905.

87 AMAE, dossier 2958, Minister to J. Berckmans, 14 April 1905; *Recueil financier* (Bruxelles, 1921), vol.II, p. 1355. The Antwerp investment firm of Frederik Jacobs et Fils had a controlling interest in four companies established in Canada: Cie Immobilière et Agricole du Canada (1906), Société Hypothécaire du Canada (1907), Crédit Général du Canada (1911), Société Foncière Belgo-Canadienne (1911).

88 AMAE, dossier 2669 bis, I-B. Director General to Minister, n.d. [1929]. The

sixteen page report is in the same dossier.

89 AMAE, dossier 2669 bis, I-B, Report of Louis Varlez and Lucien Brunin, 1929.

90 AMAE, dossier 2669 bis, I-B, Consul general to Minister, 16 November 1932.

91 AMAE, CCC, Letterbook 3, H. De Burlet to Dr. Van Raemdonck, Linching, China, 17 April 1917, p. 182.

92 Ibid., Letterbook 4, H. De Burlet to Charles Meuffels, Liège, 24 April 1919, p. 411.

CHAPTER II: THE PROMISE AND CHALLENGE OF THE WEST

1 C.L. Higham and Robert Thacker, eds., *One West, Two Myths. A Comparative Reader* (Calgary: University of Calgary Press, 2004), 6–8.

2 Alan G. Green, *Immigration and the Postwar Canadian Economy* (Toronto: University of Toronto Press, 1976), 9.

3 Gustaaf Vekeman, *Voyage au Canada* (Namur, 1885), 23.

4 LAC RG 20, Ai, vol. 1098, file 1520, Cablegram Mackenzie Bowell to Sir Charles Tupper, High Commissioner, 27 July 1894.

5 AMAE, dossier 2951, I. 4.

6 AMAE, dossier 2669 bis, I-B, Report of Louis Varlez and Lucien Brunin [1929], p. 2.

7 An early revision of the myth of the West as a land of unlimited promise was Adam Shortt, "Some Observations on the Great North-West," *Queen's Quarterly* 11 (1896): 183–87.

8 *Manitoba Free Press*, 19 April 1873.

9 House of Commons, *Debates*, 21 February 1905.

10 Charles Croonenbergh, S.J. *Trois ans dans l'Amérique septentrionale, 1885, 1886, 1887* (Paris: Delhomme et Briquet, 1892), 150; Chevalier de Hesse Wartegg, "Métis et Indiens dans le Nord Ouest du Canada," *Revue Générale* 2 (1885): 855.

11 J.E. Vignes, *La vérité sur le Canada* (Paris: Union Internationale d'Editions, 1909), 61–75.

12 Léon Brabant, "L'émigration vers le Canada," *Le Peuple*, 5, 12, 19 April; 5, 11 May; 29 June; 6 July 1911.

13 André Vermeirre, "Projets d'implantation belge au Canada" (manuscipt, n.d.), pp. 52. This was part of a project with Cornelius J. Jaenen sponsored by the Secretary of State for the Generations Series of ethnic histories.

14 *House of Commons, Debates*, 1890, vol. 24, appendix 5, 12 March 1890; ibid., vol. 25, appendix 5, pp. 121–23; ibid., 1892, vol. 26, appendix 2, p. 148; ibid., 1903, vol. 38, appendix 2, p. 39.

15 James Gray, *Red Lights on the Prairies* (Saskatoon: Western Producer Prairie Books, 1986), 2.

16 LAC, RG 76, box 16, file 179, Letter of 18 October 1892.

17 Alan F.J. Artibise, *Winnipeg. A Social History of Urban Growth, 1874–1914* (Montreal: McGill-Queen's University Press, 1975), 184.

18 AMAE, dossier 2958, file on Joseph Van Hove, 5 June 1900.

19 AMAE, dossier 2958, Minister to Consul General, 8 July 1904; Charmanne to Minister, 13 September 1904; NAC, MG 10, G1, File F-138, Petition of Van Hove, 10 May 1904, on Palace Hotel stationery. Agent McCreary in Winnipeg commented that the petitioner was probably seeking a permanent appointment.

20 Klaus Peter Stick, "Canada's Century," *Prairie Forum* 1, no. 1 (1976): 26–27; Paul F. Sharp, *The Agrarian Revolt in Western Canada* (St. Paul: University of Minnesota Press, 1948), 14–15.

21 W. A. Waiser, "A Willing Scapegoat. John Macoun and the Route of the CPR," *Prairie Forum* 10, no. 1 (1985): 65–82. Brian W. Blouet and Mervin P.Lawson, eds., *Images of the Plains: the Role of Human Nature in Settlement*

(Lincoln: University of Nebraska Press, 1975), 75–97, 155–58.

22 Lewis G. Thomas, *The Canadian West to 1905. A Canadian Sourcebook* (Toronto: Oxford University Press, 1975), 1–3.

23 *Manitoba Free Press*, 22 July 1876, p. 2.

24 Bernard Penisson, "L'Emigration française au Canada (1882–1929)," in *L'Emigration française: Etude de cas* (Paris: Publications de la Sorbonne, 1985), 55–56.

25 John H. Archer, *Saskatchewan: A History* (Saskatoon: Western Producer Prairie Books, 1980), 105; Gerald Friesen, *The Canadian Prairies: A History* (Toronto: University of Toronto Press, 1984), 248.

26 Norman Macdonald, *Canada, Immigration and Colonization, 1841–1903* (Toronto: Macmillan, 1966), 122.

27 Friesen, *The Canadian Prairies*, 249.

28 House of Commons, *Debates*, 1910, 22 March 1910, 5850.

29 LAC, MG 26, G, Laurier Papers, Fabre to Laurier, 12 June 1901, fol. 56840-43.

30 Cited in Olivar Asselin, *L'émigration belge et française au Canada* (Ottawa: C. H. Parmelee, 1913), 5–6; Ramsay Cook, ed., *The Dafoe-Sifton Correspondence, 1919–1927* (Altona, MB: D.W. Friesen, 1966), Sifton to Dafoe, 18 November 1920, 42.

31 *Receuil consulaire*, 1908, Report of F. Van Bruyssel, 1 March 1908, p. 10.

32 Lorna McLean, "To Become Part of Us. Ethnicity, Race, Literacy and the Canadian Immigration Act of 1919," *Canadian Ethnic Studies* 36, no. 2 (2004): 19.

33 H. F. Angus, "Canadian Immigration: The Laws and its Administration," *American Journal of International Law* 29, no. 1 (1934): 84–85.

34 D.C. Corbett, *Canada's Immigration Policy: A Critique* (Toronto: 1957), 3; George A. Rawlyk, "Canada's Immigration Policy, 1945–1962," *Dalhousie Review* 42, no. 3 (1962): 289; Peter S. Li, "Canadian Immigration Policy and Assimilation Theories," in J. A. Fry, ed., *Economy,*

Class, and Social Reality (Toronto: Butterworths, 1979), 411–22.

35 Ronald Wardaugh, *Language and Nationhood: The Canadian Experience* (Vancouver: New Star Books, 1983), 137–40.

36 Freda Hawkins, *Canada and Immigration: Public Policy and Public Concern* (Montreal: McGill-Queen's University Press, 1988), 156–62; Jacques Brossard, *L'immigration: Les droits et pouvoirs du Canada et du Québec* (Montréal: 1967), *passim*.

37 AMAE, dossier 2669 bis, II, Extract of the report of the Antwerp committee, 1890–91, p. 6. The Redemptorist clergy in Flanders opposed emigration, alleging that overseas Flemings would lose their faith and their culture.

38 [Marguerite Thomson], *Belgian Canadian Builders: De Pape-De Roo Families, 1893–1993* (private printing, 1993), 77–78.

39 Olivar Asselin, *Emigration from Belgium and France. Report on an enquiry made during the winter 1911–12* (Ottawa, 1913), 6.

40 The Minister of Foreign Affairs warned the consul general in Montreal that his government viewed Ontario requests for workers with great suspicion because "generally it facilitates illegal entry into the United States of the self-styled recruits." AMAE, 2669 bis, I-B, Hymans to Remes, 29 November 1927.

41 Robert Painchaud, "The Catholic Church and the Movement of Francophones to the Canadian Prairies, 1870–1915," (PhD thesis, University of Ottawa, 1976), *passim*.

42 AAE, Fonds Legal, abbé Philippe Casgrain to Mgr. Legal, 24 April 1912; AAR, "Colonization and Immigration," T. Stedman to Mgr. Mathieu, 25 April 1912.

43 Macdonald, *Canada, Immigration and Colonisation*, 38.

44 *Canada, Sessional Papers*, 1872, doc. 4, p. x; ibid., 1883, vol. 16, no. 12, John Lowe to Joseph Marmette, p. 93b.

45 LAC, RG 25, A1, vol. 15, John Carling to Sir Charles Tupper, 10 August 1888.

46 LAC, RG 7, G14, vol. 88(1), E. Vidal to
    Marquis of Lorne, 12 February 1879.

47 *Canada, Sessional Papers*, No. 7 (1892),
    Immigrant workers in the North-
    West, 1891, pp. 182–83; LAC, RG 17,
    No. 80347, La Rivière to Carling, 22
    September 1891; No. 81660, LaRivière
    to Carling, 22 December 1891; LAC,
    RG 76, vol. I, Lowe to Burgess, 28 April
    1892.

48 LAC, RG 18, A1, vol. 67, file 461-92;
    LAC, RG 6, A1, vol. 80, file 2833, L.A.
    Catellier to F. Van Bruyssel, 11 October
    1892.

49 J. Herreboudt, *Le Canada au point de vue
    de l'immigration* (Bruges: Herrenboudt &
    Claeys, 1890), 14. Tréau de Coeli was
    originally from Antwerp, having left
    for personal reasons, AMAE, dossier
    2858, I, cited in Serge Jaumain, "Survol
    historique de l'immigration belge au
    Canada," in *Les Immigrants préférés: Les
    belges* (Ottawa: University of Ottawa
    Press, 1999), 39.

50 Société historique de Saint-Boniface
    [hereafter SHSB], Langevin Papers,
    L12424, Tréau de Coeli to Langevin, 3
    September 1898.

51 LAC, RG 76, vol. 295, file 271343, part
    1, Tréau de Coeli to W.T.R. Preston, 1
    January 1904.

52 Serge Jaumain, "Les Belges au Canada,
    Des immigrants très courtisés," in
    Anne Morelli, ed., *Les émigrants belges*
    (Bruxelles: EVO, 1998), 121.

53 Abbé Pascal-Joseph Verbist, *Les
    Belges Au Canada* (Turnhout: Antoine
    Van Genechten 1872); *De Belgen in
    Canada* (Turnhout: Antoine Van
    Genechten, 1872). The best studies of
    the propaganda publications are Serge
    Jaumain, "Le Canada des récits de
    voyages et brochures de propagande
    diffusés en Belgique (1867–1914)," in
    Serge Jaumain, ed., *Les immigrants préférés:
    Les belges* (Ottawa: Presses de l'Université
    d'Ottawa, 1999), 75–100; Vera Van
    Coillie, "Propaganda en voorlichting
    met bettreking tot de Belgisdche
    overzeese emigratie, 1880–1914"

(licentiate thesis, University of Ghent,
    1980).

54 LAC, RG 25, R1, vol. 6, J. Lowe to Sir
    A. Galt, 30 December 1882.

55 Gustaaf Vekeman, *Le Canada, ou notes
    d'un colon* (Sherbrooke, 1884), 28.

56 LAC, RG 25, A1, vol. 11, J. Lowe to G.
    Vekeman, 14 February 1885.

57 LAC, RG 25, A1, vol. 14, G. Vekeman
    to Sir Charles Tupper, 10 October 1887.

58 LAC, RG 25, A1, vol. 15, H.B. Small to
    Sir Charles Tupper, 5 August 1890.

59 G. Lennox, *Guide universel de l'émigrant.
    Amérique anglaise. La province du Manitoba
    dans les derniers documents officiels*
    (Bruxelles: Librairie Universelle Rozez,
    1885); G. Lennox, *Guide universel de
    l'émigrant. Amérique anglaise. Fédération
    canadienne. La Colombie britannique*
    (Bruxelles: Librairie Universelle Rozez,
    1886).

60 LAC, RG 25, A1, vol. 14, J. Lowe to J.G.
    Colmer, 11 October 1886.

61 Stanislaus Drapeau, *Canada, le guide
    officiel du colon français, belge, suisse, etc.*
    (Ottawa, 1887), 27.

62 Alfred Bernier, *Le Manitoba, champ
    d'immigration* (Ottawa, 1887).

63 Louis Hacault, *Les colonies belges et
    françaises du Manitoba. Notes du voyage au
    Canada en 1890. Avec des extraits des rapports
    des fermiers délégués de Grande-Bretagne*
    (Bruxelles: Vromant, 1892).

64 J. H. Ellis, *The Ministry of Agriculture
    in Manitoba, 1870–1970* (Winnipeg,
    1970), 72–79, 92–93, 112–13, 116–17.
    Agricultural workers were the object
    of this propaganda. In keeping with
    the cultural bias of the first federal
    Immigration Act, recruiting was
    directed to "preferred countries," among
    them Belgium.

65 Gustaaf Willems, ed., *Les belges au
    Manitoba: Lettres authentiques* (Ottawa,
    1894), 8–11, 18, 25.

66 AMAE, dossier 2958, I, Tréau de Coeli
    to Minister, 6 April 1899.

67 *Géographie du Canada et atlas de l'ouest canadien* (Ottawa: Ministère de l'Intérieur, 1905, 1910).

68 *Le Canada occidental*, February 1911.

69 *Etablissez-vous au Canada sur les terres du Canadien Pacifique. Renseignements relatifs aux fermes toutes montées et aux pr'ts aux colons* (Bruxelles: CPR, 1913), p. 10, 4; *Manitoba et le Canadien Nord-Ouest. Renseignements pour les Colons* (n.p., n.d.), 3.

70 AMAE, dossier 2955, Musée commercial de Bruxelles; J. Herreboudt, *De l'avenir de nos relations commerciales avec le Canada* (Bruxelles, 1892), 16.

71 LAC, RG 25, A1, vol. 11, J. Lowe to Sir Charles Tupper, 4 April 1885; Vol. 12, Cablegram of 8 September 1888.

72 LAC, RG 25, A1, vol. 14, Richard Berns to Sir Charles Tupper, 7 November 1886.

73 LAC, RG 25, A1, vol. 14, J. Lowe to Sir Charles Tupper, 26 December 1886.

74 LAC. RG 25, A1, vol. 12, Telegram to Sir Charles Tupper, 8 July 1885; ibid., vol. 14, Berns to Tupper, 9 November 1886

75 Canada, *Sessional Papers*, No. 25 (1906), Report of Tréau de Coeli, agent in Belgium, 2 July 1905, p. 62.

76 *Le livre d'or de l'exposition universelle et internationale de Bruxelles en 1910* (Bruxelles, 1910), 624, cited in Serge Jaumain, "Les Belges au Canada: Des immigrants très courtisés," in Anne Morelli, ed., *Les émigrants belges* (Bruxelles: EVO, 1998), 121–22; House of Commons, *Debates*, Speech of Hon. M. Lemieux, 14 March 1911.

77 Macdonald, *Canada. Immigration and Colonization*, 110–11.

78 LAC, RG 25, A2, vol. 119, file I, 13/8, W.D. Scott to J. Bruce Walker, 1 March 1907; [Liberal Party of Canada], *L'immigration française au Canada* (Ottawa, 1908), 18.

79 AMAE, Pers. 1193, I, dossier B, No. 1091, 13 June 1891.

80 *La Belgique*, 21 January 1891.

81 Canada, *Sessional Papers*, No. 13, Report of the Department of the Interior, 1894, p. 5; LAC, RG 17, Hector Langevin to J. A. Macdonald, 24 August 1890.

82 D. J. Hall, *Clifford Sifton* (Vancouver: University of British Columbia Press, 1981), vol. I, 261; "Clifford Sifton: Immigration and Settlement Policy, 1896–1905," in Howard Palmer, ed., *The Settlement of the West* (Calgary: University of Calgary Press, 1977), 68, 71–72.

83 House of Commons, *Debates*, 1901, vol. 36, appendix 1, pp. 362–65; ibid., 1903, vol. 38, appendix 2; LAC, Laurier Papers, vol. 350, file 93603-5, Sifton to Laurier, 11 January 1906; House of Commons, *Journals*, Appendix II, Select Standing Committee on Agriculture and Colonization, 1906, pp. 231, 232, 282, 323, 335, 349.

84 Olivar Asselin, *Emigration from France and Belgium to Canada, Report. On an enquiry made during the winter 1911–12 by Mr. Olivar Asselin, at the request of the Department of the Interior* (Ottawa: King's Printer, 1913), 10–12, 28.

85 LAC, RG 25, G1, vol. 1136, file 1278, Governor-General's Secretary to External Affairs, 7 January 1914.

86 LAC, RG 25, A2, vol. 183, file 17/57, J. Obed Smith to High Commissioner, 6 October 1921.

87 LAC, RG 6/7, G1, vol. 390, file 132.

88 LAC, RG 25, A2, vol. 183, file 17/57, E. Phipps to H. Jaspar, MAE, 11 August 1921.

89 AMAE, dossier 2669 bis, IB, Director General's letter, 1926; ibid., dossier 2669 bis, II, liasse 4, 28 December 1925.

90 M. F. Smeltzer, "Saskatchewan Opinions on Immigration from 1925 to 1939" (Master's thesis, University of Saskatchewan, 1950), *passim*.

91 L. Bockstaele and A. Olivier, *Canada. Vestigingmogelijkheden voor landbouwers* (Bruges: Provincael Comite voor Landbouw, 1955); Patrick Bailly, *Etude sur la politique migratoire du Canada. L'exemple belge* (Bruxelles: Université Libre de Bruxelles, 1998).

92 AMAE, dossier 2808, Report of Robert De Vos to Minister of Foreign Affairs, 21 March 1901, p. 65.

93 Evelyn Simoens Baltessen, "An Investigation in how progress and educational directives affect the integrity of a minority group" (Winnipeg: unpublished paper, n.d.), p. 1A.

94 AMAE, dossier 2940, Count Walbott de Bassenheim to Minister, 25 May 1893.

95 The author has examples of both occurrences in his own extended family. A couple sojourners in Saskatchewan eventually decided to settle permanently and encouraged a contingent from Limburg, including my paternal relatives, to join them. On the other hand, an aunt and uncle who had come to join my maternal relatives from Namur returned after several years to Brussels.

CHAPTER III: THE MANITOBA BASE

1 Kenneth Norrie and Douglas Owram, *A History of the Canadian Economy* (Toronto: Harcourt Brace Jovanovich Canada, 1991), 301.

2 C. Knick Harley, "Transportation, the World Wheat Trade, and the Kuznets Cycle, 1850–1913," *Explorations in Economic History*, 17, no. 3 (1980): 218–50.

3 James Trow, *A Trip to Manitoba* (Quebec, 1875), 75, 86–87.

4 Royal Commission on Dominion-Provincial Relations, *Report* (Ottawa: King's Printer, 1940), Book I, 79.

5 PAM, MG 12, A1, No. 455, E. Murdock to Archibald, 30 August 1871; nos. 471, 477, 486, G. Powell to Archibald, 10 September, 21 September, 22 September 1871.

6 *Manitoba Free Press*, 19 April 1873.

7 Robert Painchaud, "The Catholic Church and the Movement of Francophones to the Canadian Prairies,

1870–1915," (PhD thesis, University of Ottawa, 1976), 299, 358–59.

8 K.H. Norrie, "The Rate of Settlement of the Canadian Prairies, 1870–1911," *Journal of Economic History* 2 (1975): 410.

9 AASB, Fonds Taché, Louis Verhaegen to Msgr Ireland, 27 April 1882; Taché to Dewdney, 21 January 1882; Dewdney to Taché 21 February 1889.

10 PAA, Fonds Oblat, B II, Taché to Lacombe, 6 April 1880, 612–14.

11 AASB, Fonds Taché, Royal to Taché, 14 March 1882.

12 AASB, Fonds Taché, de Bassenheim to Lory, 25 December 1888.

13 Canada, *Sessional Papers*, No. 5, 1889, Report of Rev. G. Clouthier, 29 December 1888.

14 AASB, Fonds Taché, Abbé A. Pelletier to Taché, 20 November 1889; ibid., Jules de Cuverville to Taché, 17 March 1893; *Paris-Canada*, 9 September 1886.

15 Robert Sack, *Homo Geographica; A Framework for Action, Awareness, and Moral Concern* (Baltimore: Johns Hopkins University Press, 1997), 135.

16 J. P. Wiesinger, "Modelling the Agricultural Settlement Process of Southern Manitoba from 1872 to 1891. Some Implications of Settlement Theory," *Prairie Forum* 10, no. 1 (1985): 84–102.

17 On the concept of "development" see H.W. Arndt, "Economic Development: A Semantic History," *Economic Development and Social Change* 29 (April 1981) :461.

18 Canada, *Sessional Papers, 1889*, no. 5, Annual report of Emerson Immigration Agent, 31 December 1888, 114.

19 Louis Hacault, *Les colonies belges et françaises du Manitoba* (Bruxelles, 1892), 26.

20 Hacault, *Les colonies belges*, 22, 43; Yvette Brandt, comp. *Memories of Lorne, 1880–1980* (Altona; Friesen Printers, 1981), 145–46; Personal communication from Dr. Richard Lebrun, who served as rector of St,

Paul's College, Winnipeg. E. Lebrun
and his sixteen-year-old son Eugène
left Marcinelle in April 1891, worked
for a local family in Bruxelles, filed for
a homestead, bought two oxen and a
sleigh to haul the wood they cut during
the winter, and they were soon joined
by two other sons. *Les belges au Manitoba*
(Ottawa, 1894), E. Lebrun to Minister,
10 December 1893, 10–11.

21 Georges Kaiser, *Au Canada* (Bruxelles,
1897), 202.

22 *Receuil consulaire, 1897* (Bruxelles, 1897),
Report of 28 May 1897; Canada,
Sessional Papers, 13 (1897) Part I, p. 15; 13
(1898), Part IV, 189.

23 AASB, Langevin Letterbook, L11934-7,
Institut St. Louis to Mgr Langevin, 31
May 1898.

24 Evelyn Simoens Baltessen, "An
investigation into how progress and
educational directives affect the integrity
of a minority group" (unpublished
paper in Canadian Studies, University
of Manitoba, n.d.),1A. PAM, P5564,
f.1, August De Pape Journal, 1893,
unfortunately relates only the journey to
Winnipeg.

25 Canada, *Sessional Papers*, No. 6, 1889,
Report of W.C.B. Graham, 1889.

26 Canada, *Sessional Papers*, No. 13, 1900,
Report of Thomas Gelley, 1 January
1900.

27 Canada, *Sessional Papers*, No. 25 (1902),
118–19.

28 LAC, MG 26, G, Laurier Papers, file
88134, d'Hellencourt to Rodolphe
Boudreau, 19 July 1904.

29 "Experience and Opinions of Settlers,"
Manitoba Official Handbook (Liverpool,
1892), 40–44.

30 Canada, *Debates, House of Commons*, 9
April 1907, 6151; Robert Painchaud,
"French-Canadian Historiography and
Franco-Catholic Settlement in Western
Canada, 1870–1914," *Canadian Historical
Review* 59, no 4 (1978): 448–49.

31 *Recueil consulaire*, report of Consul
General, 1 October 1896.

32 AMAE, dossier 2808, De Vos report,
1901, 44–46.

33 Marcel Haegeman, "The Belgians of
South-Central Manitoba," (typescript,
1994), 1–2.

34 PAM, MG 9, A56, Marie-Anna-A. Roy,
"La Montagne Pembina au Temps des
Colons," 32, 55–56; Louis Hacault,
Les colonies belges et françaises au Manitoba
(Bruxelles, 1892), 48.

35 PAM, MG 9, A56, Marie-Anna-A. Roy,
"La Montagne Pembina au Temps des
Colons," 32, 52–55, 57; Hacault, *Les
colonies belges*, 48.

36 Hacault, *Les colonies belges*, 11, 18.

37 Brandt, *Memories of Lorne*, 208–10.

38 Haegeman. "The Belgians of South-
Central Manitoba," 3.

39 Brandt, *Hutlet Heritage*, p. 109; Hacault,
Les colonies belges, 43.

40 *Holland, Manitoba, 1877–1967* (Altona :
Friesen Printers,1967),197.

41 Roy, "La Montagne Pembina," 30–32,
79–81; Manitoba Museum of Man and
Nature (hereafter MMMN), tape 573,
"Autour de Nos Clochers – Bruxelles";
SHSB, Carton "Belges," E. Fontaine,
"Histoire de la Paroisse de Bruxelles," 8.

42 Ibid., 13.

43 [Marguerite Thomson, comp.], *Belgian
Canadian Builders. De Pape-De Roo Families.
Celebrating a Century in Canada* (private
printing, 1993), 2.

44 PAM, A5564, f.1, Auguste De Pape
Journal, 1893.

45 SHSB, Carton "Belges," E. Fontaine,
"Histoire de la paroisse de Bruxelles," 8.

46 Brandt, *Memories of Lorne*, p. 212; Roy,
"La Montagne Pembina," 32, 81.

47 Joseph Delmelle, "Les Brabançons
de la Montagne Pembina," *Le folklore
Brabançon*, no,214 (1977) :136.

48 George H. Hambley, *Historical Records
and Accounts of the Early Pioneers of the
District of Swan Lake, Manitoba from its
Early Settlement, 1873–1950* (Altona:
Friesen Printers,1952), 68–71.

49 AMAE, dossier 2802, Report of De Vos 1901, 52–53; *Receuil consulaire, 1901*, 441–43; Canada, *Sessional Papers*, 13 (1897), part I, 15; 13 (1898), part IV, 189.

50 H. Y. Hind, *Narrative of the Canadian Red River Expedition of 1857, and of the Assiniboine and Saskatchewan Exploring Expedition of 1858* (London, 1860), IV, 299.

51 Annette Saint-Pierre, *Almanach français du Manitoba* (St. Boniface: CEFCO, 1984), 28; Lake Alma Over 50 Club, *Settlers of the Hills* (Altona: D.W. Friesen,1970),77–78.

52 These family histories are recorded in *A History of the Riverside Municipality, 1879–1967* (Dunrea; n.p., 1967), 82–83; *Deloraine Scans a Century, 1880–1980* (Altona: D.W. Friesen, 1980), 42,44, 375, 430, 432, 537, 539, 581, 647, 660, 663, 693, 732.

53 *Deloraine Scans a Century, 1880–1980* (Altona: D.W. Friesen, 1980), 430, 725, 732.

54 AAW, Grande Clairiere, Gaire to Langevin, 8 October 1896.

55 AASB, Fonds Taché, Gaire to Taché, 7 September 1886.

56 *La Belgique*, 21 January 1891.

57 *Le Manitoba*, 6 April 1892, 10 January 1893.

58 J. P. Wilsinger, "Modelling the Agricultural Settlement Process of Southern Manitoba, 1872 to 1891. Some Implications for Settlement Theory," *Prairie Forum* 10, 1 (1985): 84–102.

59 AMAE, dossier 2808, De Vos Report, 1901, 64.

60 SHSB, Robson, "The Story of Deleau", 4.

61 *Hartney and District, 1882–1957* (Deloraine: Deloraine Times,1957), 20–21.

62 *Hartney and District*, p. 22; Canada, *Sessional Papers*, 25 (1902), Part II,119.

63 SHSB, Robson "The Story of Deleau," 4.

64 Canada, *Sessional Papers*, No. 13 (1896), 122.

65 AASB, Fonds Langevin, Lecoq to Langevin, 22 February 1902.

66 A. Théoret, *Sainte-Rose-du-Lac* (Winnipeg: n.p., 1948), 126–37.

67 Marie-Anna-A. Roy, *Les Capucins de Toutes-Aides et leurs dignes confères* (Montréal: Editions franciscaines, 1977): 17–36, 77–93, 121–22; MHSO, Bel. 2001, Archives of the Belgian Capuchins, Nos. 26, 27, 28, 30, 31, 32, 39A.

68 Lucien de Burlet, *Au Canada. De Paris à Vancouver* (Paris: Librairie Ambertm 1909),. 240.

69 MMMN, tape 5, Joseph Vermander, 1971; tape 108, Marcien De Leeuw, 1971; AMAE, dossier 2808, Robert de Vos, "Canada: La coloinisation agricole dans l'ouest, 1901."

70 SHSB, Carton "Belges," Clippings, Obituaries. Nathalie Van Brabant, daughter of Peter Van Brabant, was the first Belgian to enter the order of the Grey Nuns in St. Boniface.

71 MMMN, tape 5, Joseph Vermander, 1971.

72 Raymond Loudfoot, "The Nuyttens of Belgian Town" *Manitoba Pageant* 19, no. 3 (1974) :16.

73 Keith Wilson and James B. Wyndels, *The Belgians in Manitoba* (Winnipeg: Peguis, 1976); James B. Wyndels, *Joseph Van Belleghem, Une biographie* (Trois Rivières: Editions du Bien Public, 2002).

74 MMMN, tape 108, Marcien De Leeuw, 1971.

75 MMMN, tape 108, Marcien De Leeuw, 1971.

76 SHSB, Carton "Belges," clippings.

77 MMMN, tape 28, Camille de Buck, 1971; James B. Wyndels, *Joseph G. Van Belleghem: A Biography* (Ottawa: J. Merriam Print, 2004), 4.

78 MMMN, tape 75, William English, 1971.

79 The author served in the St. Boniface office the Red River Flood Rehabilitation Board as a bilingual clerk processing claims during July/August

1950 and was able to assess the extent of the damage caused as well as the reconstruction opportunities for small entrepreneurs.

80 R. Waldinger, "Immigrant enterprise. A critique and reformulation," *Theory and Society* 15 (1986) 249–85; A. Langlois and E. Razin, "Self-employment among ethnic minorities in Canadian metropolitan areas," *Canadian Journal of Regional Science* 12 (1989): 335–54.

81 Alan F. Artibise, "An Urban Economy: Patterns of Economic Change in Winnipeg, 1879–1971," *Prairie Forum* 1, no. 2 (1976): 163–88.

82 Rosa A. Minet, *Journal* (npublished travel journal, 1925), n.p. In addition to addresses obtained before leaving Belgium, travellers made useful contacts during the transatlantic crossing. These indicate there was communication between Belgians in southern Ontario and Manitoba.

83 The author recalls that as a young boy, accompanying his parents to Winnipeg with a carload of cattle destined for the St. Boniface stockyards, it was at the boarding house on Lombard Street that they lodged.

84 Paul Voisey, "The Urbanization of the Canadian Prairies, 1871–1916," *Histoire sociale/Social History* 8 (May 1975): 77–101.

85 MMMN, tape 5, Joseph Vermander, 1971. He is the author of "The Use of the Bow by our Indians," *Transactions of the Manitoba Historical Society*, Series III, no. 22 (1965–66).

86 Keith Wilson and James B. Wyndels, *The Belgians in Manitoba* (Winnipeg: Peguis, 1976), 73.

87 Yvette Brandt, comp., *Memories of Lorne, 1880–1980* (Altona, 1981), 273.

88 Alvin Finkel and Margaret Conrad, *History of the Canadian Peoples* (Toronto: Copp Clark, 1998), II, 249.

89 *Moosomin Courier*, 13 October 1892, 1; *Whitwood Herald*, 19 May 1952, 21. For more information see Gordon P. Church, *An Unfailing Faith. A History of the Saskatchewan Dairy Industry* (Regina: Canadian Plains Research Center, 1985) passim.

90 Manitoba Dairy Association, *Fifty Years of Dairying in Manitoba* (Winnipeg, 1935),17, 18, 21; Veronica McCormick, *A Hundred Years in the Dairy Industry* (Ottawa, 1968), 110; Paul Phillips, *Manitobe Dairy Study* (Winnipeg, 1984), 161.

91 MMMN, tape 77, C.A. Bossuyt, 1971.

92 Canada, *Sessional Papers* (1889), 48; ibid. (1891), 102, 103; C.H.P. Killick, *Manitoba Dairying. A Century of Progress* (Winnipeg, 1971),101–5; Louis Hacault, *Les colonies belges et françaises du Manitoba* (Bruxelles, 1892), 19.

93 P.B. Justin, "Golden Opportunities for Manitoba Dairymen," *The Dominion* 12 (1895): 16.

94 Canada, *Sessional Papers* (1898), no. 13, 190.

95 AMAE, dossier 2808, report of Robert De Vos, 1901, 47–48, 88.

96 *Recueil consulaire* (Bruxelles, 1901), Report of 21 March 1901, 436–38; C.H.P. Killick, *Manitoba Dairying: A Century of Progress* (Winnipeg, 1971), 102–4.

97 Canada, *Sessional Papers* (1902), No. 25, 118–19.

98 MMMN, tape 77, C.A. Bossuyt, 1971; MMMN, tape 65, W.G. Van Walleghem, 1971; Manitoba Dairy Association, *Fifty Years of Dairying in Manitoba* (Winnipeg, 1935), 30.

99 MMMN, tape 77, C.A. Bossuyt, 1971.

100 MMMN, tape 77, C.A. Bossuyt, 1971; A.A. Innes, *The Dairy Industry in Canada* (Toronto: Ryerson Press, 1937), 128.

101 H.L. Patterson, *The Dairy Farm Business* (Ottawa, typescript, 1945), 6–12, 17.

102 Killick, *op. cit.*, 102–4; MMMN, tape 65 W. G. Van Wlleghem, 1971.

103 AMAE, 2669 bis, I-B, "Canada" Report of Louis Varlez & Lucien Brunin, 1932, 11–12.

104 LAC, RG 30, vol. 5915, file 194, Jean De Mytternaere interviews.

105 Avis Mysyk, *Manitoba Commercial Market Gardening, 1945–1997: Class, Race and Ethnic Relations* (Regina: Canadian Plains Research Center, 2000), 1–5.

106 R.W. Murchie, *Agricultural Progress on the Prairie Frontier* (Toronto: Macmillan, 1936), 48.

107 James W. F. Ross, *A Static Model of Economic Efficiency in Vegetable Production in Manitoba: An Application of Line Programming* (MSc thesis, University of Manitoba, 1969), 2–3.

108 George Chapman, *Fruit growing in Manitoba, Saskatchewan, Alberta* (Winnipeg: Country Guide, 1933), 3, 17.

109 Personal reminiscences of the author whose family was a neighbour of the Gelaudes, 1941–43. The Andries family in the Turtle Mountain district was particularly successful in developing specialized varieties of berries.

110 Frank Mann, "The History of the Sugar Industry in Wallaceburg" (typescript, 1977), 2.

111 Ella M. Cressman, "The Sugar Beet Industry," *Waterloo Historical Society Papers*, vol. 60 (1972): 91–93; Mann, 3–4; *Wallaceburg News.* 17 April 1902; AMAE, Report of Consul General, 26 June 1902.

112 Cited in J. Castell Hopkins, *The Canadian Annual Review of Public Affairs, 1909* (Toronto: Canadian Annual Review Publishing Company, 1909), 206.

113 *Winnipeg Tribune*, 12 August 1942, 13.

114 Heather Robertson, *Sugar Farmers of Manitoba* (Altona: D.W. Friesen 1968), 105.

115 Restrictive trade Practices Commission, *Report concerning the Sugar Industry in Western Canada and proposed merger of Sugar Companies* (Ottawa: Department of Trade and Industry, 1957), 182.

116 Ibid., 90, 117–19.

CHAPTER IV: WESTWARD ONTO THE PRAIRIES

1 Bill Waiser, "Our Shared Destiny?", in Gregory P. Marchildon, *The Heavy Hand of History: Interpreting Saskatchewan's Past* (Regina: Canadian Plains Research Center, 2005), 7–29.

2 Randy Boswell, *Province with a Heart. Celebrating a Hundred Years in Saskatchewan* (Toronto: CanWest Books, 2005), 66–68.

3 Donatien Frémont, *Les français dans l'ouest canadien* (Saint-Boniface: Editions du Blé, 2002), 9.

4 John Hawkes, ed., *The Story of Saskatchewan and its People* (Regina: S.J. Clarke, 1924), II, 681.

5 *The Prairie Provinces in their Relation to the National Economy of Canada* (Ottawa: Dominion Bureau of Statistics, 1934), 30–32.

6 M.W.M. Hargreaves, *Dry Farming in the Northern Great Plains, 1900–1925* (Cambridge: Harvard University Press, 1957), 3.

7 J. H. Thompson, "The Adoption of the Gasoline Tractor in Western Canada," *Canadian Papers in Rural History* 2 (1980): 9–40; B. Bruce Shepard, "Tractors and Combines," *Prairie Forum* 11, no. 2 (1986): 253–72.

8 T.W. Schultz, "the Increasing Economic Value of Human Time," *American Journal of Agricultural Economics* 54, no. 4 (1972): 843–50.

9 AMAE, dossier 2808, Robert De Vos, "Canada. La colonisation agricole dans l'ouest," 1901, pp. 79–80.

10 Saskatchewan, Department of Agriculture, *Practical Pointers for Hired Hands* (Regina: King's Printer, 1915).

11 Victor Hanson, *The Other Greeks* (New York: Free Press, 1995), 7.

12 Canada, *Sessional Papers*, 1911, No. 52, Commission on Conservation, p. 25.

13 Cited in Gordon L. Barnhart, *Saskatchewan Premiers of the Twentieth Century* (Regina: Canadian Plains Research Center, 2004), 18.

14   Kenneth M. Sylvester, "Rural Land in the 1901 Census, Inequality, Gender and Property," *Historical Methods* 33, no. 4 (2000): 243–46; Kenneth Michael Sylvester, "All things Being Equal: Land Ownership and Ethnicity in Rural Canada, 1901," *Histoire Sociale/Social History* 35, no. 67 (2001): 46–47.

15   Derek Poitras and Hartley Furtan, "Unravelling the Mystique of the Family Farm on the Canadian Prairies," Saskatchewan Institute of Public Policy, *Policy Dialogue* 14 (Winter 2007): 22.

16   E.B. Mitchell, *In Western Canada before the War A Study of Communities* (London: John Murray, 1915), 153–62.

17   *Revue Agronomique de Louvain* (1907), 192; (1908), 383; (1909), 236; (1912), 336; (1913), 288, cited in Marc Journée's thesis, "De lokroep van een nieuwe frontier, Belgische emigratie en expansie in Canada, 1880–1940" (licence, Katholieke Universiteir Leuven, 1981), 59.

18   Grant MacEwan, *Between the Red and the Rockies* (Saskatoon: Western Producer Prairie Books, 1979), 192–93.

19   Abbé Jean Gaire, *Dix années de missions au Grand Nord-Ouest canadien* (Lille: Imprimerie de l'Orphelinat de Don Bosco, 1898), 118.

20   Ibid., 202.

21   The Sylvestre, Stringer, Carbotte, Revet, George, Tinant, Legros, Pierrard, Stevenot families.

22   Antler and District History Committee, *Footprints in the Sands of Time* (Altona: Friesen, 1983), 531–44; *The Optimist* (Redvers), 24 March 1982.

23   AAR, Parish of St. Maurice de Bellegarde (1897–1949), 12 September 1901, 6 September 1902, 3 October 1902, 11 October 1905; *Esquisse historique de la Paroisse de St, Maurice, Bellegarde, Sask.* (Bellegarde, 1948), pp. 7–11; SHS, dossier R80-27-0, file Father Gervais.

24   AAR, Parish of St. Maurice de Bellegarde, 22 April 1903, 9 June 1903, 11 October 1905, 5 November 1905.

25   AS, Pamphlet file: "Bellegarde"; Pierre Morissette, "The French settlements of Cantal, Bellegarde, Sainte-Antoine, Wauchope and Forget" (typescript, n.d.), 11–12.

26   AASB, Fonds Langevin, Letterbook 6, Langevin to Gaire, 5 April 1898.

27   AAE, Fonds Legal, Gaire to Legal, 3 May 1905; Canada, *Sessional Papers*, 25 (1902), Part II, p. 119.

28   AAR, File "Wauchope," Gaire to Langevin, 21 August 1903; Canada, Census of 1911.

29   LAC, MG 26 G, Laurier Papers, Gaire to Laurier, 13 March 1906.

30   Wauchope disappeared from the census in 1971, having been officially "disorganized" the previous year. The convent was moved to Bellegarde, the church building remained without a priest or services, the grain elevators and railway station were demolished, and by 1978 the four remaining houses were ordered demolished by the municipal council because they constituted a public danger. All that remained, apart from a very few rural descendants of the pioneers, was an historic cairn on Highway 13 and the well-tended grave of abbé Gaire in the churchyard.

31   Canada, *Sessional Papers*, No. 13 (1898), part I, p. 13; part IV, p. 189.

32   SHS, dossier R80-176, p. 4; *Deloraine Scans a Century, 1880–1980* (Altona: Friesen, 1980), p. 423.

33   *Le défenseur du Canada*, No. 1, p. 4; No. 3, p. 17; No.4, pp. 5–7; No. 5, p. 18; No. 15, pp. 26–33; No. 25, pp. 6–13.

34   *Manitoba Free Press*, 11 November 1890.

35   Bertram Tennyson, *The Land of Napioa and Other Essays in Prose and Verse* (n.p., 1896).

36   "The Romance of the French Counts at Whitewood, Assiniboia," in John Hawkes, *The Story of Saskatchewan and Its People* (Regina: S.J. Clarke1924), II, 937–46; A.W. Rasporich, "Utopian Ideals and Community Settlement in Western Canada, 1880–1914," in Henry Klassen, ed., *The Canadian West*

(Calgary: Comprint Publishing, 1977), 37–62.

37   *Whitwood Herald*, 12 April 1894; Betty McCormack, *Memories of St. Hubert* (Whitewood, 1940), pp. 5–7; John A. Archer, *Saskatchewan: A History* (Saskatoon, 1980), 124; Alex MacDonald, *Cloud-Capped Towers. The Utopian Theme in Saskatchewan History and Culture* (Regina: Canadian Plains Research Center, 2007), 67–69.

38   AASB, Fonds Langevin, Letterbook 5, Langevin to Baron de Boisseau, 25 April 1903; ibid., Letterbook 7, Langevin to Fort, 31 March 1904; ibid., Letterbook 8, Langevin to Fort, 11 August 1906.

39   Betty McCormack, *Memories of St. Hubert* (Whitewood, 1940), 57–59, 110–16, 123–24, 166–70, 175–76.

40   Désiré De Trémaudan, "Chronologie de Montmartre, Saskatchewan," typescript, n.d., pp. 8, 10,20, 25, 29, 31; *Le Colonisateur Canadien*, 15 October 1893; LAC, MG 26, Laurier Papers, Cory to Laurier, 25 September 1907.

41   Bernard Wilhelm, "Montmartre, Un Village en Saskatchewan," *Vie française* 27, nos. 4–5 (1973): 121; AS, A. B695, Arthur J. Boyce Papers, D.T. de Trémaudan to Boyer, 23 June 1943; ibid., Boyer to Scriver, 24 Januray 1954.

42   Donatien Frémont, *Les français dans l'ouest canadien* (St-Boniface, 1980), 131; A.W. Rasporich, "Utopian Ideals and Community Settlements in Western Canada, 1880–1914," in Henry Klassen, ed., *The Canadian West* (Calgary, 1997), 51–52.

43   Sheilagh S. Jameson, "The Story of Trochu," *Alberta Historical Review* 9, no. 4 (1961): 1–6.

44   R. Kortleven, *Kerkoven, daar gaat niks boven* (Lommel, 1979), vol. I, p. 142. Jacon Clemens was still in Canada when war broke out and Belgium was occupied by the Germans. He enlisted in the 28th Battalion, Canadian Expeditionary Force, and was a victim of a mustad gas attack from which he never fully recovered. He married Irma Minet from Namur province after the war and they settled in Cantal. He had been a factory worker in Belgium, not a farmer, and the land the Soldiers Sttlement Board allocated to him was unsuited to intensive farming.

45   G. H. Dickin, "History of Manor" (typescript, 1985), n.p.

46   The first arrivals in September 1919 included the Charel Alen, Cornelius Jaenen, Antoon Vreys, Jef Hulsmans, and Ferdinand Van Broekhoven families. In October, another group consisting of the Sebastien Danden Boer, Koob Clemens, and Louis Geysen families joined them.

47   G. Michiels, *Dorpsverhalen: van mensen en dingen uit het dorpsverleden* (Lommel, 1983), 43–44.

48   Arnold Van Heukelom, Jaak Van Ham, Vincent Ooms, Jan Reynders, Charel Nuyts.

49   P. Luykx, *Genealogie Van Heukelom* (Lommel, 1972), pp. 203–7.

50   Adriaan Vanden Boer, "Naar Canada willen wij varen. Lommelse uitwijking naar de Nieuwe Wereld (1913–1927)" *Te Lomelle op die Campine* 15, nos. 1–2 (1989): 1–60.

51   Manor and District Historical Society, *Memories are Forever* (Altona: D.W. Friesen 1982), recollection of Germaine [Jimmie] Forsyth, née Gérinrose, 215.

52   Gerinrose daughters married into the Limburger community: Emily to Frank Ooms, Regina to Alphonse Jaenen.

53   Irma to Jacob Clemens, Rosa to John Jaenen and Helene to Mathew Jaenen.

54   Manor and District Historical Society, *Memories are Forever* (Altona, MB: D.W. Friesen 1982), 60, 135–36,141, 195, 215–21, 267, 288, 325, 337, 386–92; interviews with Mathew Jaenen and Irma Clemens, Manor, 15 July 1981; Carlyle and District Historical society, *Prairie Trails to Blacktop* (Altona: D.W. Friesen, 1982), *passim*. St. Joseph's parish, Manor, closed in 2005 following the virtual disappearance of the business sector of the village and the

out-migration of most of the Belgians' descendants.

55 R. Korteleven, *Kerkoven, daar gaat niks boven* (Lommel, 1979), 143.

56 Canada, *Sessional Papers*, No. 13 (1894), part III, 1 November 1895, p. 134.

57 Canada, *Sessional Papers*, No. 15 (1896), 3 November 1896.

58 Radville Book Committee, *Our First 50* (Weyburn, 1960), 12–14, 128; AS, Pamphlet File, Local Histories, "Ralph, from Oxcart to Oilwells."

59 Alice Henderson, comp. *Homesteading in Surprise Valley* (Gladmar, 1970), 63–65, 106–7.

60 Ibid., 52, 58–59.

61 History Committee of the R.M. of the Gap, *The Building of a Great Land* (Altona; Friesen,1980), 425, 463, 469, 485, 495–96, 515, 517, 565.

62 Yellow Grass Heritage Committee, *Yellow Grass: Our Prairie Community* (Altona: Friesen.1981), 573–75.

63 Wood Mountain Centennial Committee, *They Came to Wood Mountain* (Wood Mountain, 1967), 70–73.

64 Fife Lake History Book Committee, *Gathering of Memories* (Fife Lake, 1981), *passim.*

65 AEG, dossier Ponteix, Gravel to Langevin, 8 March 1909; AMAE, dossier 2669 bis, I-B, "Canada", Consul at Calgary to Minister, 10 June 1919; Georges Hébert, *Les débuts de Gravelbourg* (Gravelbourg, 1965), 159.

66 *They Came to Wood Mountain*, 211–21; Robsart Jubilee Committee, *Robsart Pioneers Review the Years* (Robsart, 1955), 81–82.

67 *Deloraine Scans a Century, 1880–1980* (Altona: Friesen,1980), 729.

68 AS, Saskatchewan, Department of Agriculture, Land Branch files, pp. 1–12; 17–19; 41–43.

69 Liberal Party of Canada, *L'immigration française au Canada* (Ottawa, 1908), Tréau de Coeli report, 31 March 1907, translated from French.

70 LAC, MG 10, G-1, Microfilm F-138, Dubois to Ketels, 21 March 1907; AMAE, dossier 2958, Ketels to de Favreau, 28 March 1907.

71 SHS, dossier R80-11, "La famille Hounjet: Histoire générale"; SHS, dossier R80-12, "Mémoires de Henri Hounjet"; AS, Pamphlet file, Local History, Gilles Leroy, "Prud'homme."

72 Interviews with Mgr. Maurice Baudoux, 6 July 1981; 31 August 1983.

73 LAC, MG 26 G, Laurier Papers, LeFloch to Laurier, 11 July 1908; LAC, RG 76, No. 47 1120, W. P. Scott to H. Péranm, 24 August 1906.

74 Lucien Léonard, *Un littérateur wallon du Canada* (Namur, s.d.), *passim.*

75 Davidson and District Historical Society, *Halfway Happenings* (Davidson, 1980), 49; John Hawkes, *The Story of Saskatchewan* (Regina, 1928), I:808.

76 Ben Putnam et al., *Fifty Years of Progress: Chiefly the Story of the Pioneers of the Watson District from 1900–1950* (Muenster: St. Peter's Press, 1950), 69, 73. Interview with Michael Behiels, 14 January 2005.

77 W.A. Cohoon, *Jubilee Reminiscences* (Macrorie, 1957), 32, 84, 108–9.

78 Sanctuary Community Club, *A Tribute to the Bygone Communities of Saltburn, East Gap, South Dean, Sanctuary and Hamlet* (Elrose: Elrose Review, 1970), 21, 24.

79 Students of St. Walburg High School, *The St. Walburg Story* (St. Walburg, 1955), 26, 36.

80 John Hewett, "Canada Beckons" (typescript, n.d.), pp. 11–12, 14. Their experience was remarkable because 57 per cent of homesteads in Saskatchewan were never "proven," that is patented following successful completion of the required cultivation and building.

81 Ibid., pp. 18, 21.

82 W.R. Motherwell, *Methods of Soil Cultivation Underlying Successful Grain Growing in the Province of Saskatchewan* (Regina: King's Printer, 1910), Bulletin No. 21, p. 11; Chester Martin, *Dominion Lands Policy* (Toronto, 1938), 409.

83   Manor and District Historical Society, *Memories are Forever* (Altona:D.W. Friesen, 1982), 392.

84   Personal recollections of the author who lived in a drought-stricken area until 1940; James H. Gray, *The Winter Years: The Depression on the Prairies* (Toronto: Macmillan, 1966), 126–27.

85   Guy Vanderhaeghe, "What I Learned from Caesar," *Man Descending* (Toronto: Macmillan, 1982), 70.

86   Sara Brooks Sundberg, "Farm Women on the Canadian Prairie Frontier: The Helpmate Image," in Veronica Strong-Boag and A. Fellman, eds., *Rethinking Canada: The Promise of Women's History* (Toronto: Copp Clark Pitman, 1986), 95–106.

87   PAA, P73.585. File Clarice Lambert Demers.

88   Lafond Historical Committee, *Dreams Become Realities: A History of Lafond and Surrounding Area* (Lafond, 1981), 125.

89   Eliane Silverman, "In Their Own Words: Mothers and Daughters on the Alberta Frontier, 1890–1920," *Frontiers*, 10. 2 (1977): 38; "Explanation of Migration,"*Annual Review of Sociology*, 404.

90   Brenton M. Barr, "Reorganization of the Economy since 1945," in P.J. Smith, ed., *The Prairie Provinces* (Toronto, 1972), 65–82.

91   John Stahl, "Prairie Agriculture: A Prognosis," in David Gagan, *Prairie Perspectives* (Toronto: Holt, Rinehart & Winston, 1970), 68–70.

92   *Farm Light & Power*, 15, no. 8 (1973): 1, 6; personal communications with Elva and Alphonse Jaenen.

CHAPTER V: TO THE FOOTHILLS OF ALBERTA

1   *Calgary Herald*, 12 November 1884; Jack Peach, "Looking Backward: Mission District was the French Quarter of Calgary," *Calgary Herald*, 9 August 1980. Canada, *Sessional Papers*, 5 (1889), pp. 59–60; 13 (1895), part III, p. 157; 25 (1902), part II, p. 119.

2   Kirk L. Lambrecht, *The Administration of Dominion Lands, 1870–1930* (Regina: Canadian Plains Research Center, 1991), 45.

3   Acton Burrows, *North Western Canada: Its Climate, Soil and Productions* (Winnipeg, 1880), 76.

4   AASB, Fonds Taché, Taché to Viscount Jules de Cuverville, 4 April 1893; Canada, *Sessional Papers*, No. 13 (1896), Report of Sir Charles Tupper, 1895, p. 6: AAE, Fonds Grandin, Letterbook 3, Grandin to Count Walbott de Bassenheim, 22 August 1892. The Catholic church carried on its independent recruitment, not wanting liberal, independent-minded, socialist, syndicalist Belgians, LAC, RG 17, Deputy Minister Correspondence, Cloutier to John Lowe, 29 February 1892.

5   AMAE, dossier 2803, De Vos report [1901], p. 87.

6   AASB, Fonds Langevin, Delouche to Langevin, 28 June 1898; 12 August 1898; 14 September 1898; Langenin to Shaughnesy, 9 January 1899; Provincial Council at St. Albert, 7–9 April 1902.

7   Among the grossly inflated claims see *The Manufacturing, Jobbing and Commercial Center of the Canadian West* (Calgary: City of Calgary, 1911); *The Land of Plenty* (Calgary: Board of Trade, 1907); *Commercial Metropolis of Western Canada* (Calgary: Hundred Thousand Club, 1907).

8   *Alberta Plaindealer*, 18 May 1898.

9   Canada, *Annual Report of the Department of the Interior* (Ottawa, 1880), p. viii.

10 Patrick A. Dunae, *Gentlemen Emigrants. From the British Public Schools to the Canadian Frontier* (Vancouver: Douglas & McIntyre, 1981), 88–89.

11 Elliott West, "Against the Grain: State-Making, Cultures, and Geography in the American West," in Carol Higham and Robert Thacker, *One West, Two*

Myths (Calgary: University of Calgary Press, 2004), 14.

12 *North-West Irrigation Act*, S.C. 1894, c. 30.

13 Eggermont-Molenaar and Callens, *Missionaries among Miners*, 87, 158, 390.

14 Cochrane and Area Historical Society, *Big Hill Country. Cochrane and Area* (Altona, MB: D. W. Friesen, 1977), 636, 641. Belgian authorities listed three Belgian enterprises in Alberta in 1905: the Adam ranch in Duhamel, the Pirmez ranch near Calgary and the Bodeur brickworks in Cochrane. See AMAE, dossier 2808, dossier 1360/14, liasse VI.

15 E. Van Bruyssel, *Le Canada* (Bruxelles, 1898), 411.

16 David H. Breen, *The Canadian Prairie West and the Ranching Frontier, 1874–1924* (Toronto: University of Toronto Press, 1983), 74–76, 11–113, 127–29.

17 Cochrane and Area Historical Society, *Big Hill Country. Cochrane and Area* (Altona,MB: D.W. Friesen, 1977), 296–97.

18 Glenbow Archives [GAI], M2682, NA227, Maurice Ingeveld Fonds.

19 Foothills Historical Society, *Chaps and Chinooks: A History West of Calgary* (Calgary: Northwest Printing, 1976), I, p. 136; II, pp. 189, 398.

20 *Calgary Herald*, 12 October 1920; GAI, M3112, M6192, M7425, BK Ranchmen's.

21 Keith Wilson and James B. Wyndels, *The Belgians in Manitoba* (Winnipeg, 1976), pp. 75–76. In Quebec the government bought the horses for distribution throughout the province to similar associations on the understanding that the animals were to be kept for breeding and were to remain in the province for at least three years. Quebec, *Journal de l'Assemblée Législative, 1910*, Interpellation en Chambre, 13 mai 1910.

22 SHS, dossier R80-55 "Famille Delanoy."

23 History Committee of the R.M. of the Gap, *Building of a Great Land* (Altona,,MB: D.W. Friesen, 1980), 571–72; *The Yesteryears* (Radville: Radville Laurier Historical Society, 1983),

442–44; *Le Patriote de l'Ouest*, 16 May 1912.

24 Remi De Roo, "The History of the De Pape and De Roo Families," (Typescipt, n.d.): 30–48; *Memories of St. Hubert* (Whitewood, 1980), p. 204; *Holland, Manitoba, 1877–1967* (Altona,MB: D.W. Friesen, 1967), 131–34, 167–68.

25 G. E. Britnell and V.C. Fowke, *Canadian Agriculture in War and Peace, 1935–50* (Stanford: Stanford University Press, 1962), 277–78.

26 Deschatelets Archives, HEF 3282. L57C3, Codex historicus of Leonard Van Tighem, 25 July 1905.

27 In 1914 William English married Stella Burns, sister of Pat Burns, millionaire meat packer. He later pursued his career in Winnipeg. He had a brother, Joseph, who was a famous Flemish artist.

28 Deschatelets Archives, HEF 3282. L57C3, Codex historicus, 23 June 1909.

29 AMAE, dossier 2808, De Vos report, pp. 86–87.

30 Canada, *Sessional Papers*, No. 25 (1903), pp. 97, 119.

31 *Camrose Canadian*, 15 July 1980; Marcel Saxé, *Two Centuries of Fur Trading, 1723–1923. Romance of the Revillon Family* (Paris: Draeger Frères, 1923), 75, 81–83.

32 *Camrose Canadian*, 19 March 1947; 23 January 1957; 15 July 1980; *Edmonton Journal*, 18 May 1961. François Adam died at the Lacombe Home, Midnapore, at the age of 103.

33 *Ponoka Panorama*, pp. 359–60; Eckville District Historical Society, *Homesteads and Happiness* (Eckville, n.p., 1979), 195.

34 Jessie J. Campbell, ed., *Chatter Chips from Beaver Dam Coulee* (Lacombe, 1974), 180, 236–37.

35 *Edmonton Journal*, 25 October 1974; Copy of letter from Gordon J. Grierson, Publisher, *The Red Deer Advocate*, to Eloi DeGrace, Provincial Archives of Alberta, 19 April 1979.

36 Rev. Camille Deman set up a refugee colony, for Belgians who had fled to

England, in the Peace River country during World War I.

37 *Strathmore. The Village that Moved* (Red Deer: Adviser Graphics, 1986), pp. 277, 318.

38 Ibid., pp. 317, 469, 551.

39 Glenbow Archives, CPR Papers, file 64, Manager to Dr. Rutherford, 7 October 1914; 3 November 1914; 3 November 1914, second letter.

40 Flos Jewell Willaims, *New Furrows. The Story of a Belgian Immigrant Girl's Life in the Alberta Foothills* (Ottawa: Graphic Publishers, 1926), p. 15.

41 Heather Robertson, *Sugar Farmers of Manitoba* (Altona, MB: D.W. Friesen, 1968), 20.

42 Roberston, *Sugar Farmers of Manitoba*, 127–50.

43 British Columbia Sugar Museum (Vancouver), Knight Sugar Company Papers, Peter De Blieck to J. Ellison, 11 March 1913, 12 March 1913; Ellison to De Blieck, 26 February 1913.

44 Glenbow Archives, Knight Sugar Company Papers, Ellison to Hallstead, 22 February 1908; Ellison to Friedl, 28 January 1913; *Raymond Roundup, 1902– 1967* (Lethbridge, 19667), 353, 530, 666.

45 Interview of Celine Audenart by Howard Palmer, typescript, August 1980. Howard Palmer and Tamara Palmer, eds., *Peoples of Alberta: Portraits of Cultural Diversity* (Saskatoon: Western Producer Prairie Books, 1985), p. 16.

46 Howard Palmer and Tamara Palmer, *Alberta: A New History* (Edmonton: Hurtig, 1990), 200.

47 Glenbow Archives, Knight Sugar Company Papers, Collection files 3–4-1-, 3-4-2, 3-4-3, 1-12-1.

48 L.A. Rosenval, "The Transfer of Mormon Culture to Alberta," in L.A. Rosenval and S.M. Evans, eds., *Essays on the Historical Geography of the Canadian West: Regional Perspectives on the Settlement Process* (Calgary: University of Calgary, Department of Geography, 1987), 122–44, 137–38.

49 LAC, MG 26, Mackenzie King Papers, J1, vol. 84, file 71592, Buchanan to Magrath, 14 December 1923.

50 John Bank, "Farm Workers: Victims Outside the Law," *Labour Gazette*, 75, no. 6 (1975): 368–74.

51 AMAE, dossier 2669 bis, I-B, "Canada," Loney to Minister, 17 November 1927; Hymans to consul-general Remes, 29 November 1927; Minister to Remes, Order 587.

52 AMAE, dossier 2669 bis, I-B, file 1151. De May to Rawlinson, n.d. [1926].

53 AMAE, dossier 2669 bis, I-B, "Canada," Lonay to Minister, 17 November 1927.

54 AMAE, dossier 2669 bis, I-B, "Canada," Polet to Remes, 15 February 1928; Remes to Minister, 15 March 1928; Rochereau de La Sablière to Remes, 26 March 1928; Coley to De Jardin, 20 April 1928.

55 Taber History Committee, *From Tank 77 to Taber Today* (Altona,MB: D. W. Friesen, 1977), 189–90.

56 Restrictive Trade Practices Commission, *Report concerning the Sugar Industry in Western Canada and the proposed merger of Sugar Companies* (Ottawa: Department of Justice, 1957), *passim*.

57 Ivan Avakumovic, "The Communist Party in Canada and the Prairie Farmer: the Interwar Years," in David Bercuson, ed. *Western Perspectives* (Toronto, 1974), 78–87.

58 John H. Thompson and Allen Seager, "Workers, Growers and Monopolists," *Labour/Le Travailleur* 3 (1978): 160–61.

59 J.H. Thompson and A. Seager, "Workers, Growers and Monopolists. The Labour Problem in the Alberta Sugar Industry," *Labour/Le Travail* 3 (1978): 168–73.

60 Hugh A. Dempsey, ed., *Lethbridge: A Centennial History* (Lethbridge: Historical Society of Alberta, 1985), 121.

61 Cecilia Danyk, "Showing these slaves their class position: Barriers to organizing Prairie farm workers," in David Jones and Ian MacPherson, eds.,

Building Beyond the Homestead (Calgary: University of Calgary Press, 1988), pp. 163–78.

62   LAC, RG 27, vol. 290, file 1-26-56-1, James Lynn to Department of Immigration, 4 September 1956.

63   LAC, RG 27, vol. 290, file 1-26-56-1, W. B. Grunewald to C.E.S. Smith, 30 August 1956; W.W. Dawson to C.E.S. Smith, 11 September 1956.

64   "The amazing case of the republic of St. Albert," in *Alberta in the 20th Century* (Edmonton: United Western Communications, 1991), I, p. 282.

65   Canada, *Report of the Select Committee of the Senate* (Ottawa, 1888), pp. 13, 107.

66   Walter P. Fitzgerald, *The Wheels of Time* (Rivière-Qui-Barre, 1978), pp. 125–26, 168.

67   Canada, *Sessional Papers*. No. 13 (1899), pp. 14–15.

68   St. Albert Historical Society, *The Black Robe's Vision: A History of St. Albert and District* (St. Albert, n.p.,1985), pp. 267–68.

69   AMAE, dossier 2808, De Vos Report [1901], pp. 100–101.

70   Maurice Behiels and Laura Behiels, "The Behiels Heritage," (typescript,1985), p. 2.

71   Ibid., pp. 3–4.

72   Fitzpatrick, *Wheels of Time*, 122–19, 168, 351; *The Black Robe's Vision*, 454. The Van Hecke family thought that the region was too far north for farming therefore he declined to take a homestead, according to an interview with Brother Arthur Van Hecke by Eloi DeGrâce, 27 April 1981.

73   *Peace River Record*, 27 March 1924; Ronald Rees, "Reconsidering Antiurban Sentiment," *Landscape* 28 (1985): 26–29.

74   Fitzpatrick, *Wheels of Time*, p. 226.

75   *The Black Robe's Vision*, p. 399.

76   Ibid., pp. 348–49.

77   Ibid., pp. 110,122, 350–51.

78   *St. Paul Journal*, 17 February 1981.

79   *The Black Robe's Vision*, p. 130; *Wheels of Time*,. 347–48.

80   Lillian York, ed., *Lure of the South Peace* (Fort St. John, 1981), pp. 25–26.

81   David Leonard, "The Great Peace River Land Scandal," *Alberta History* 39 (1991): 9–16; Gilles Boileau, "Les Canadiens Français de Rivière-la-Paix" (typescript, Société Canadienne d'Etablissement Rural, 1960), p. 30.

82   Cited in Gordon E. Bower, ed., *Peace River Chronicles* (Vancouver: Prescott Publishing, 1963), 213.

83   E.C. Stacey, *Peace Country Heritage* (Saskatoon: Western Producer Book Service, 1974), 74–77.

84   *Grouard News*, 9 August 1913, 19 September 1914, 10 & 24 April 1915; Richard Brown, "A Town Bypassed: Grouard Alberta," *The Archivist* (May–June 1990): 10–12.

85   Wayne Jackson, "Ethnicity and Areal Organization among French Canadians in the Peace River District, Alberta," (MA thesis, University of Alberta, 1970), pp. 22–34; PAA, 3,86.587/399, Canada Colonization Association, Annual Report, 17 March 1941; Lucie St-André, ed., *Histoire de Girouxville* (Calgary: D.W. Friesen, 1977), 58–59.

86   PAA, file 86,587/706, CPR, Department of Immigration and Colonization, Annual Report, 1930.

87   James Gray, *Men against the Desert* (Saskatoon: Western Producer Prairie Books, 1967), 186.

CHAPTER VI: THE MINING FRONTIER AND PACIFIC RIM

1   Geological and Natural History Society of Canada, *Report of Progress for 1880–81–82* (Montreal: Dawson Brothers, 1883), p. 14; G. C. Hoffman, "Coals and Lignites of the North-West Territory," in Geological Survey of Canada, *Report of Progress, 1882–83–84* (Montreal: Dawson Printers, 1885).

2   United States, *Abstracts of the Immigration Commission* [Senator Dillingham Commission] (Washington, 1911), p. 646.

3   Glenbow Institute Archives, CPR Records, file 2339, V. Hyde Baker to J. S. Dennis, 8 October 1909.

4   Paul Phillips, *No Power Greater: A Century of Labour in British Columbia* (Vancouver, 1967), 27–41; Charles McMillan, "Trade Unions in District 18, 1900–1925: A Case Study," (MBA thesis, University of Alberta, 1969), pp. 38–41.

5   T. H. Patching, ed., *Coal in Canada* (Montreal: Canadian Institute of Mining and Metallurgy, 1985), 134.

6   Irving Abella and David Millar, eds., *The Canadian Worker in the Twentieth Century* (Toronto, 1975), 4–5.

7   *Guide to the Province of British Columbia for 1977–78* (Victoria ,BC: T.N. Hibbem, 1877), 268, lists Bishop Seghers of Victoria, J. Jondau at Esquimalt, Lemmens at Nanaimo, and Auguste Brabant and Joseph Niolije at Hesquiat.

8   W.E. Ireland, "The Historical Evolution of the Present Settlement Pattern," *British Columbia Natural Resources Conference. Transactions No. 9* (Victoria,BC: 1956), 197–200, at p. 199.

9   Glenbow Archives, M 8374, Emile Leblanc Fonds.

10 Harold Fryer, "The Klondike Trail," *Alberta: The Pioneer Years* (Langley, BC: Stagecoach, 1977), 141–46; James MacGregor, *A History of Alberta* (Edmonton, 1972), 155.

11 *Our Van Walleghem Roots* (Altona, MB: D.W. Friesen, 2001), 19–22.

12 John Hawkes, *The Story of Saskatchewan and its People* (Regina: S.D. Clarke, 1924), II, p. 927.

13 AASB, Langevin Letterbook, L11719-11, G. Willems to Langevin, 4 April 1898.

14 MMMN, tape 77, C.A. Bossuyt, 1971; J.G. MacGregor, *The Klondike Gold Rush through Edmonton, 1897–1898* (Toronto: McClelland & Stewart, 1970).

15 Camille De Buck, *Le Club Belge: Fifty Years of History* (Winnipeg, 1955), 6–7.

16 J. Castell Hopkins, ed., *The Canadian Annual Review of Public Affairs, 1904* (Toronto: Canadian Annual Review Publishing, 1904), report of Mr. Justice Britton, 1 August 1904, p. 547.

17 J. Castell Hopkins, ed., *The Canadian Annual Review of Public Affairs, 1908* (Toronto: Canadian Annual Review Publishing, 1908), 544–45.

18 Msgr Emile Grouard, *Souvenirs de mes soixante ans d'Apostolat dans l'Athabaska-Mackenzie* (Winnipeg: La Liberté, s.d.), 364.

19 PAA, Anglican Papers, A281/149, box A-32. Holmes to Young, 28 May 1899; Diane Newell, "The Importance of Information and Misinformation in the Making of the Klondike Gold Rush," *Journal of Canadian Studies* 21 (1986–87): 95–111.

20 Jean Puissant, "Quelques témoignages sur l'émigration hennuyère,1884–1889," *Académie Royale des Sciences d'Outre-Mer, Bulletin de Séances* 3 (1973): 457–58.

21 Baron Etienne Hulot, *De l'Atlantique au Pacifique* (Paris: Librairie Plon, 1888), 312.

22 *La Liberté* (Wasmes), 5 February 1888; *La République Belge* (Bruxelles), 2 December 1888.

23 Canada, *Sessional Papers*, No. 6 (1890), Annual Report of the Victoria, B.C. immigration agent, 31 December 1889.

24 *La République Belge*, 14 April 1889; Canada, *Sessional Papers*, No. 4 (1888), p. 82.

25 Terry Reksten, *The Dunsmuir Saga* (Vancouver: Douglas & McIntyre, 1991), 85–87.

26 Puissant, *op. cit.*, p. 458.

27 *La République Belge*, 2 December 1888; Puissant, *op. cit.*, p. 458.

28 Canada, *Sessional Papers*, No. 6 (1890), Annual Report, 31 December 1889.

29 Recksten, *op. cit.*, p. 117.

30 David J. Bercuson, *Fools and Wise Men* (Toronto: McGraw-Hill Ryerson, 1978), 254.

31 Reckston, *op. cit.*, p. 177.

32 Martin Robin, *Radical Politics and Canadian Labour, 1880–1930* (Kingston: Industrial Relations Centre, Queen's University, 1968), 43.

33 C.F.J. Galloway, *The Call of the West* (London: T. Fisher Unwin, 1916), 89–92.

34 *Receuil consulaire* (1904), Report of T. Smith, Victoria, 6 January 1904.

35 P. G. Silverman, "Aid to the Civil Power: The Nanaimo Coal Miners Strike, 1912–1914," *Canadian Defence Quarterly* 4 (1974): 16–52; Lynn Bowen, *Boss Whistle: The Coal Miners of Vancouver Island Remember* (Lantzville, BC: n.p., 1982), 131–98. Cf. also *Three Dollar Dreams* (Lantzville, Blichan Books, 1987).

36 British Columbia, *Annual Report for the Minister of Mines for the Year ending 31 December 1915* (Victoria, 1915), pp. 328–34.

37 Bureau of Mines, British Columbia, *Special Report on Coal Mine Explosions* (Victoria, 1918), pp. 529–30; British Columbia, *Sessional Papers* (1919), vol. I, Sec. H, Report of the Department of Labour for 1918, pp. 1–35.

38 John Manley, "Communism and the Canadian Working Class during the Great Depression: The Workers Unity League, 1930–1936" (PhD thesis, Dalhousie University, 1984), *passim*.

39 Patricia Hilden, "The Rhetoric and Iconography of Reform : Women Coal Miners in Belgium, 1840–1914," *Historical Journal* 34, no. 2 (1991): 411–36.

40 Carol Giesen, *Coal Miners' Wives: Portraits of Endurance* (Lexington: University Press of Kentucky, 1995), *passim*.

41 British Columbia, *Department of Education, Annual Report* (Victoria, 1887), Report of Inspector for Wellington, p. 222.

42 British Columbia, *Department of Education, Annual Report* (Victoria, 1877), p. 19.

43 British Columbia, *Journals of the Legislative Assembly, 1891* (Victoria, 1891), Report of the Select Committee, p. cccxx. A general overview of regional labour issues is Paul Phillips, *No Power Greater: A Century of Labour in British Columbia* (Vancouver: British Columbia Federation of Labour, 1967).

44 Herman Ganzevoort, *A Dutch Homesteader on the Prairies: Letters of Willem de Gelder, 1910–13* (Toronto: University of Toronto Press, 1973), 35, 98.

45 AMAE, dossier 2808, Robert De Vos report [1901], p, 130.

46 Ibid., p. 62.

47 LAC, MG 10, G1, No. 2958, Van Bruyssel to Foreign Affairs, 23 July 1888; Josef Van Mullem, *Belgian Emigration to Canada* (Brussels, 1999), p. 35.

48 AMAE, dossier 2808, Charmanne to Baron de Fabereau, 2 June 1904.

49 P.L. Broughton et al., "Lignite Coal Reserves of Southern Saskatchewan," in G.R. Parslow, *Fuels: A Geological Appraisal* (Regina: Saskatchewan Geological Society, 1974), 81–94.

50 LAC, RG 26, vol. 16, Deportation of Communist agitators, 1931–1937, cited in Irving Abella, *On Strike* (Toronto: Oxford University Press,1974), 57.

51 Alberta, *The Report of the Royal Commission Respecting the Coal Industry in the Province of Alberta* (Edmonton, 1936), p. 81.

52 G. Kurgan-van Hentenryk and J. Lauryssens, *Un siècle d'investissements belges au Canada* (Bruxelles, 1986), 43, 54.

53 AMAE, CCC, Letterbook 5, H. de Burlet to Arthur Vandorp, 26 February 1920, p. 351.

54 Ibid., George Roels to Consul General, 10 September 1919, p. 135.

55 A.A. den Otter, "Bondage of Steam in the CPR West," in Hugh Dempsey, ed., *The CPR West: The Iron Road, the Making of a Nation* (Vancouver: Douglas & MacIntyre, 1984), 200, 202.

56 PAA, Department of Municipal Affairs Papers, 74–174, box 76, file 1040; ibid., box 77, file 1048.

57 Personal communication from Allen Seager, Burnaby, 19 June 1989.

58 LAC, RCMP Records, Section A-1, v. 300, no. 517, L.P. Eckstein to W.A. Galliher, MP, 9 June 1905.

59 Ibid., F. White, Comptroller, to W.A. Galliher, MP, 29 June 1905.

60 Taped interview of Frank Soulet, Blairmore, by Howard Palmer, August 1980, in possession of author.

61 David J. Bercuson, "Tragedy at Bellevue: Anatomy of a Mine Disaster," *Labour/Le Travailleur 3* (19780: 221–31.

62 Crownest Pass Historical Society, *Crowsnest and Its People* (Calgary: D.W. Friesen 1950), 222.

63 Ibid., 435–36.

64 Ibid., 426.

65 Ibid., 475–76.

66 Ibid., 526, 632, 660, 691.

67 Ibid., 853.

68 Ibid., 851; taped interview with Frank Soulet, Blairmore, by Howard Palmer, August 1980.

69 Ibid., 592.

70 Frank W. Anderson, *Canada's Worst Mine Disaster* (Calgary: Frontier Publishing, 1969), 37.

71 Lucie St. André, ed., *Histoire de Girouxville* (Calgary: D. W. Friesen, 1977), 50–51.

72 PAA, Attorney Generel's files, Acc. 82.235, file no. 4.

73 PAA, Attorney General's files, Acc. 82.235, file no. 5.

74 PAA, Attorney General's files, Acc. 82.235, file no. 12.

75 LAC, RG 13, A2, vol. 62, file 1102, R. de Wouters d'Oblinterz to A. Aylesworth, 28 July 1910; LAC, RG6, A1, vl. 115, file 2284, Memorandum of Joseph Pope, Under-Secretary of State, 22 Octrober 1904.

76 LAC, RG 13, A2, vol. 162, file 1102, T.J. Harris & Maurice Barrell to W.L. Mackenzie King, Minister of Labour, 1 August 1910.

77 PAA, Attorney General's files, Acc. 82.235, file no. 93.

78 A. A. den Otter, "Sir Alexander T. Galt and the Northwest. A case study in entrepreneurialism on the frontier" (PhD thesis, University of Alberta, 1975), p. 230; Patching, *Coal in Canada*, 152.

79 *La République belge*, 9 September 1888, cited in Jean Puissant, "Quelques témoignages hennuyère 1884–1889," Académie Royale des Sciences d'Outre-Mer, *Bulletin de Séances* 3 (1973): 455, 460.

80 Mary Eggermont-Molenaar and Paul Callens, eds., *Missionaries among Miners, Migrants and Blackfoot. The Van Tighem Brothers Diaries. Alberta. 1875–1917* (Calgary: University of Calgary Press, 2007), 71–85.

81 Ibid., 96–109.

82 Ibid., 120; A.A. den Otter, *Civilizing the West: The Galts and the Development of Western Canada* (Edmonton: University of Alberta Press, 1982), 290–92.

83 LAC, RG 18, RCMP Papers, AI, vol. 316, file 238-06, Wilson to Commissioner, 4, 6, 8 April 1906; "Crime Report, Re. Strike at Lethbridge. Assault on Louis Albert," n.d.; Willam M. Baker, "The Miners and the Mounties: The Royal North-West Mounted Police and the 1906 Lethdridge Strike," in W.M. Baker, ed., *The Mounted Police and Prairie Society, 1873–1919* (Regina: Canadian Plains Research Center, 1998), 137–71.

84 Eggermont-Molenaar and Callens, *Missionaries among Miners*, 167–68; James J. MacGregor, *A History of Alberta* (Edmonton, 1972), 185.

85 Canada, House of Commons, *Debates 1906*, 26 March 1906, pp. 573–74 LAC, RG 18, RCMP Papers, AI, vol. 316, file 238-06, Sherman to Verville, 31 March 1906; Lake Streisel, "The Miners Strike Out. The Lethbridge Coal Miners Strike of 1906," *Alberta History* 52, no. 4 (2004): 2–6.

86 The Lemieux Act was found unconstitutional in 1925 when applied to industries outside federal jurisdiction.

87   Harold Fryer, *Ghost Towns of Alberta* (Langley, BC: Stagecoach, 1976), 90.

88   Drumheller Valley Historical Association, *The Hills of Home: Drumheller Valley* (Altona,MB: D.W. Friesen, 1973), 505–7.

89   Ibid., 321–23.

90   Anne B. Woywitka, "The Drumheller Strike of 1919," in Irving Abella and David Millar, eds., *The Canadian Worker in the Twentieth Century* (Toronto: Oxford University Press, 1978), 218–26.

91   David J. Bercuson, *Fools and Wise Men. The Rise and Fall of the One Big Union* (Toronto: McGraw –Hill Ryerson, 1978), 199.

92   Steven Maynard, "Rough Work and Rugged Men: The Social Construction of Masculinity in Working-Class History," *Labour/Le Travail* 23 (1989): 159–69.

93   Bora Laskin, ed., *A Selection of Cases and Materials on Labour Law* (Toronto, 1947), pp. 137–42.

94   Glenbow Archives, M 8374, Emile Leblanc Fonds.

95   Canada, *Sessional Papers* VII (1909), No. 26, pp. 16–18.

96   Ginette Kurgan-Van Hentenryk and J. Laureyssens, *Un siècle d'investissements belges au Canada* (Bruxelles, 1986), 23–24.

97   T.D. Regehr, ed., *The Possibilities of Canada are Truly Great: Memoirs 1906–1924 by Martin Nordegg* (Toronto: Macmillan, 1971), 171–72.

98   Gratien Allaire, "Ernest Gheur et Nordegg, Alberta," *Le Franco*, 1 August 1986, p. 4.

99   Bernard Gheur, *Retour à Calgary* (Paris: Ace Editeur, 1985), 115.

100   *Report of the Alberta Coal Commission, 1925* (Edmonton, 1926), p. 181.

101   Gary Gerstle, "The Franco-Belgians," in *Working-class Americanism* (New York: Cambridge University Press, 1989), 70–71, 83–85.

102   *La République Belge*, 1 July 1888; Canada, *Sessional Papers*, No. 4 (1888), p. 69; Cornelius J.Jaenen, "Le contexte

socio-économique de l'immigration belge au Canada," *La question sociale en Belgique et au Canada* (Bruxelles, 1989), 157–58.

103   Personal communication from Professor Allen Seager, Burnaby, 19 June 1984.

104   Ben Swankey, "Reflection of an Alberta Communist: The Hungry Thirties," *Alberta History* 27, no. 4 (1979): 4.

105   LAC, RG 76, file 653, 1910 Act (Bill 102), 22 March 1910.

106   PAA, Supreme Court of Alberta, Appellate Division, *Rex. v. Gustave Henry*.

107   Cited in M.B. Vinini Byrne, *Fron the Buffalo to the Cross: A History of the Roman Catholic Diocese of Calgary* (Calgary: Calgary Archives and Historical Publishers, 1973), 354, 361.

108   Rev. Captain Wellington Bridgman, *Breaking Prairie Sod* (Toronto: Musson, 1920), 196.

109   Address by Premier Oliver at New Westminster, 10 June 1919, cited in J. Castell Hopkins, *The Canadian Annual Review of Public Affairs, 1919* (Toronto: Canadian Annual Review Publishing Company, 1920), 789.

110   Donald Avery, *Dangerous Foreigners. European Immigrant Workers and Labour Radicalism in Canada, 1896–1932* (Toronto, 1979), 39–74; A. Ross McCormack, *Reformers, Rebels and Revolutionaries: The Western Canadian Radical Movement, 1899–1919* (Toronto, 1977), 65–75; Martin Robin, *Radical Politics and Canadian Labour, 1880–1930* (Kingston, 1968), 104–15.

111   Dr. A. Moeller, "Le Canada," *Revue générale 2* (1911): 124.

112   "Le mouvement syndical au Canada," *Le mouvement syndical belge*, 14 February 1920, 20 November 1920, 15 January 1921, 22 July 1922, 4 August 1923, 16 June 1924.

113   *L'avenir social*, 1902, p. 675; 1903, pp. 497–98.

114   Henri de Man, *Cavalier seul: 45 années de socialisme européen* (Genève: Editions du Cheval ailé, 1948), p. 113; "Winnipeg," *Le Peuple*, 7 May, 6 July, 11 July 1920.

115 Yvan Lamonde, "La trame des relations entre la Belgique et le Québec (1830–1949): la primauté de la question sociale," in Ginette Kurgan-van Hentenryk, ed., *La question sociale en Belgique et au Canada: XIXe–XXe siècles* (Bruxelles: Editions de l'Université de Bruxelles, 1988), 173–83.

116 Alfred H. Siemens, ed., *Lower Fraser Valley: Evolution of a Cultural Landscape* (Vancouver: Tantalus Research, 1968), 108.

117 Walter P. Fitzgerald, *The Wheels of Time* (Rivière-Qui-Barre, 1978), 128.

118 Marc Journée, "De lokroep van een nieuwe frontier: Belgische emigratie en expansie en Kanada, 1880–1949" (Licence, Katholieke Universiteit Leuven, 1981), pp. 49–50.

119 H. R. Dare, *Dairy Farming in British Columbia* (Victoria, BC: Kings Printer, 1928), *passim*.

120 Siemens, *Lower Fraser Valley*, 108.

121 R.H. Campbell, "Dairy Farm Organization in the Lower Fraser Valley of British Columbia," *Economic Annalist* 27 (1957): 29–34.

122 Marjorie Griffin, "The Decline of Women in Canadian Dairying," *Histoire sociale/Social History* 27, no. 34 (1984): 307–34.

123 AMAE, dossier 2669 bis, I-B. "Canada" file CLL 814/43, Possibilities of immigration in British Columbia [1932].

124 E.M. Gunn, "The Dutch and dairying," in Siemens, *op. cit.*, pp. 117–38.

125 Coolie Verner and Peter M. Gubbek, *The Adoption or Rejection of Innovations by Dairy Farm Operators in the Lower Fraser Valley* (Ottawa: Agricultural Economics Research Council of Canada, 1967), 4–24.

126 R.W. Murchie, "The Sociological Aspects of the Agricultural Problem," *Canadian Political Science Association. Proceedings* 3 (1930): 145–52.

127 Personal interview with Captain Léon Dupuis, Ganges, 13 October 1983.

128 British Columbia Archives and Records Service (BCARS), Add. Mss. 1584, A-1008, Pooley Family Papers; Paul Koroscil, "Boosterism and the Settlement Process in the Okanagan Valley, British Columbia, 1890–1914," *Canadian Papers in Rural History* 5 (1986): 73–105.

129 Jason Patrick Bennett, "Apple of the Empire: Landscape and Imperial Identity in Turn-of-the Century British Columbia," *Journal of the Canadian Historical Association* 9, New Series (1998): 72, 78.

130 M. Anne Kerr et al., *Okanagan Fruitlands: Land-Use Change Dynamics and the Impact of Federal Programs* (Ottawa: Lands Directorate, Environment Canada, 1985), 112.

131 D.S. Shackelton, "Lord and Lady Aberdeen: Their Okanagan Ranches," *Beaver* (Autumn, 1981): 12–15; D.G. Patterson, "European Financial Capital in British Columbia: An Essay in the Role of Regional Entrepreneurs," *B.C. Studies* 1 (Spring, 1974): 40–41.

132 J.S. Redmayne, *Fruit Farming in the Dry Belt of British Columbia* (London, 1909), 10, 79, 82.

133 Cole Harris, ed., *The Resettlement of British Columbia: Essays on Colonialism and Geographical Change* (Vancouver: UBC Press, 1997), 231–34.

134 Henry J. Boam, *Twentieth Century Impressions of Canada* (Montreal: Sells, 1914), 763.

135 Ibid., 603.

136 Paul M. Koroscil, "Boosterism and the Settlement Process in the Okanagan Valley, B.C., 1890–1914," *British Columbia. Settlement History* (Kelowna: Big Sage Productions, 2000), 48.

137 PABC, A-1008, Pooley Family Papers, No. 14, Belgian Canadian Fruit Lands Company file; Denby, *op. cit.*, p. 35; Ginette Kurgan- van Hentenryk and J. Laureyssens, *Un Siècle d'investissements belges au Canada* (Bruxelles: Editions de l'Université de Bruxelles, 1986), 24–31.

138 Denby, *op. cit.*, p. 52; Land and Agriculture Company of Canada, *Fruit Farming in the Okanagan Valley, British Columbia* (Winnipeg, 1911), 15; Henry J. Boam, *British Columbia: Its History, People, Commerce, Industries and Resources* (London, 1912), 332.

139 Kurgan-van Hentenryk and Laureyssens, *op. cit.*, 28.

140 Koroscil, "Boosterism and the Settlement Process" ,42–43.

141 R.R. Krueger, "The Physical Basis of the Orchard Industry in British Columbia," *Geographical Bulletin* 20 (1963): 15–38; Kerr, *Okanagan Fruitlands*, 21.

142 Ibid., 44.

143 Ibid., 69.

144 Hilda Cochrane, " Belgian Orchard Syndicate," *Twenty-Sixth Report of the Okanagan Historical Society* (1962), p. 111; Letter to St. Raphaël Society, 24 July 1912, p. 12, cited in Marc Journée, *op. cit.*, p. 50.

145 AMAE, dossier 2669 bis, A-I, "Canada," CL 814/43, Van Rickstal to Hymans, 12 January 1932.

146 A.A. Mackenzie, *Report on the Physical & Financial Conditions of Irrigation Projects in the Vernon and Kelowna Districts* (Vancouver, 1916), I, pp. 25, 46, 56, 66, 74; II, pp. 174–313.

147 William Quigley, "Belgo-Canadian Land Company," *Twenty-Fifth Report of the Okanagan Historical Society* (1961), pp. 140–44; *Echo de la Bourse* [Brussels], 7 September 1920.

148 Denby, *op. cit.*, pp. 53–54.

149 AMAE, dossier 2669 bis, I-B, "Canada," Report of Louis Varlez and Lucien Brunin.

Chapter VII: Language, Religion, and Education

1 *Ottawa Citizen*, 23 October 2004, Report on speech of 22 October.

2 Venini Byrne, *op. cit.*, Felix Lajat to M.A. Harrington, 14 May 1935, p. 223.

3 Lázaro de Aspurz, *La aportacion extrangero a las misiones españoles del patamato regio* (Madrid, 1946), 45–46.

4 E. Sobry, "The West Coast Mission," *Historical Number of the British Columbia Orphans' Friend* (December 1913), p. 67.

5 PABC, Add. Mss. 1267, Letters of G. Donckele to Indian Affairs, 1893–1907.

6 A.D. Fisher, "A Colonial Education System: Historical Changes in Schooling," *Canadian Journal of Anthropology* 2 (1981): 41.

7 Reuben Gold Thwaites, ed., *Early Western Travel, 1748–1846* (Cleveland: Arthur H. Clark, 1905), vol. 29, 239.

8 P.J. De Smet, *Oregon Missions and Travels over the Rocky Mountains* (New York: Edward Dunegan, 1847), 153–54.

9 H.M. Chittenden and A.T. Richardson, eds., *Life, Letters and Travels of Father Pierre-Jean De Smet, S.J., 1801–1873* (New York: Francis P. Harper, 1905), vol. I, 328–29.

10 *Mission de la Congrégation des Missionnaires Oblats de Marie Immaculée* (Paris, 1878), 319.

11 S. Carter, *Lost Harvests* (Montreal: McGill-Queen's University Press, 1990), 209–10.

12 Earle H. Waugh, *Dissonant Worlds, Roger Vandersteene among the Cree* (Waterloo: Wilfrid Laurier University Press, 1996), 32–36, 90–93, 313, 332–35.

13 LAC, MG 15, Laurier Papers, No. 420689, Pascal to Laurier, 18 November 1896.

14 Lucien Léonard, *Un littérateur wallon au Canada* (Namur, s.d.), 60–63.

15 Ibid., 52–53.

16 Donald G. Carlson, "Social and Economic Development of R.M. of Fertile Belt #351" (MA thesis, Sociology, McMaster University, 1934), pp. 15–16; Martin L. Kovacs, "Searching for Land: The First Hungarian Influx into Canada," *Canadian-American Review of Hungarian Studies* 7, no. 1 (1980): 37–43.

17 Jules Pirot, *Contes dau lon èt did près* (Gembloux, 1950), 8–9.

18 J.P. Asselin, *Les Rédemptoristes au Canada* (Montréal, 1981), Tielen to General, 19 November 1883, p. 58; Armand Boni, *De Belgische Redemptoristen in de provincie Quebec, Manitoba en Saskatchewan* (Bruges: De Kinkhoren, 1945).

19 St. Augustine of Canterbury, Brandon's imposing neo-Gothic church, was built with Belgian money, notably the Godt's family fortune.

20 *Ex Occidente Lex – From the West, the Law: The Eastern Catholic Churches under the Tutelage of the Holy See of Rome* (Carteret, NJ: St. Mary's Religious Action Fund, 1979), p. 24.

21 Emilien Tremblay, *Le Père Delaere et l'église ukrainienne du Canada* (Berthierville, 1961), Delaere to Langevin, 12 April 1902, p. 85. Achille Delaere, *Memorandum of the Attempts of Schism and Heresy among the Ruthenians (commonly called Galicians) in the Canadian Northwest* (Winnipeg: West Canada Publishing Co., 1909).

22 APSB, Fonds Langevin, L331132, Delaere to Langevin, 11 April 1904.

23 APSB, Fonds Langevin, L33138, Visit of abbé B. Zoldak, 5 January to 24 September 1904.

24 J.B. Gregorovich, ed., *John Bodrug: Independent Orthodox Church. Memoirs pertaining to the History of a Ukrainian Canadian Church in the years 1903 to 1913* (Toronto: Ukrainian Canadian Research Foundation, 1980), 159. Some of these Ukrainians and their descendants eventually became adherents of the United Church of Canada.

25 Tremblay, *op. cit.*, Delaere to Cardinal Gotti, 15 July 1904, p. 110. George W. Simpson, "Father Delaere. Pioneer Missionary and Founder of Churches," *Saskatchewan History* 1, no, 1 (1950): 7–9.

26 Tremblay, *op. cit.*, pp. 174–80; Rodrigue Théberge, *La Congrégation du Très-Saint Rédempteur* (Ste. Anne de Beaupré, 1978), pp. 373–75; Benjamin J. Smellie, *Visions*

27 Paul Laverdure, *Redemption and Ritual: The Eastern-Rite Redemptorists of North America, 1906–2006* (Yorkton: Redeemer's Voice Press, 2007), pp. 87–89.

28 "The turbulent arrival of Orthodoxy on the Prairies," *Alberta in the 20th Century* (Edmonton: United Western Communications, 1996), V, 168–69.

29 Laverdure, *Redemption and Ritual*, 130.

30 Paul Yuzyk, *The Ukrainians in Manitoba. A Social History* (Toronto: University of Toronto Press, 1953), 71–72.

31 Matteo Sanfilippo, *L'Affermazione del Cattolicisimo nel Nord America* (Vitarbo: SetteCittà, 2003), 253–58.

32 LAC, RG 76, vol. 267, file 244970, McQuaker to Egan, 24 November 1925; *Saskatoon Phoenix*, 30 September 1936, p. 3; ASC, P. 161, f. 94, Grandin to Merry del Val, 24 April 1897, ff. 21/232. communicated by Matteo Sanfilippo.

33 Nancy Christie and Michel Gauvreau, *A Full-Orbed Christianity* (Montreal: McGill-Queen's University Press, 1996), 185–89.

34 Hugh A. Dempsey, *Lethbridge: A Centennial History* (Lethbridge: Historical Society of Alberta, 1985), 43; Hugh A. Dempsey, *The Amazing Death of Calf Shirt and Other Blackfoot Stories* (Saskatoon: Fifth House, 1994), 147; LAC, RG 18, RCMP Papers, vol. 91, file 148, Monthly Report "K" Division, July 1894.

35 Van Tighem Diary, 21 December 1895, communicated by Mary Eggermont-Molenaar.

36 Keith Wilson and James Wyndels, *The Belgians in Manitoba*, p. 55, citing diary entry for 13 March 1931; Terence J. Fay, *A History of Canadian Catholics* (Montreal: McGill-Queen's University Press, 2002), 165.

37 PAA, 7.220, Codex historicus, St. Paul's Church, Lethbridge.

38 AASB, Fonds Langevin, Letterbook I, Langevin to Cardinal Ledochowski, 13 April 1899.

39 Communication from Allen Seager, 7 August 1984.

40 PAA, 75.387, United Church Archives, box UC50, manuscript of address by Miss Canavan, pp. 1, 5, 10, 17, 18.

41 Serge Jaumain and Matteo Sanfilippo, "L'immigrationm belge et l'église catholique au Canada et aux Etats-Unis avant la première guerre mondiale," *Canadian Issues/Thèmes canadiens 18* (1996): 70, 79.

42 ASV, DAC, box 77, file 14, Langevin to Stagni, n.d. [1913]; ASV, DAC, box 131, file 2/3, Langevin to Consistory [1913], ff. 187–99.

43 C.B. Sissons, *Bilingual Schools in Canada* (Toronto, 1917), Appendix III, Pope Benedict XV, *Commisso Divinitus*, 8 September 1916, pp. 222–27.

44 Yvette Brandt, *Memories of Lorne, 1880–1980* (Altona, MB: D.W. Friesen, 1981), 164, 167.

45 Joseph Delmelle, "Les Brabançons de la Montagne Pembina," *Le Folklore Brabançon* 214 (1977): 134.

46 Personnel communication from Annie Boutin, Carlyle, 4 March 2006. Only the widow of Louis Van Hoekelom of the first generation still resided in the community.

47 PASB, Fonds Langevin, L20772, Charles Mahieu to Langevin, 1 May 1911.

48 Wilson and Wyndels, *op, cit.*, Canonical decree of establishment, 9 October 1917, 28–29.

49 Ibid., 53; *Saint Boniface, Manitoba, Canada. Année du Centenaire, 1967* (St. Boniface, 1967), 28–29.

50 MMMN, tape 26, Interview of Camille De Buck, n.d.

51 MHSO, Capuchin Archives, 1939, Document #11, Father Theodosius to Father Raphael, 29 March 1939.

52 MHSO, Capuchin Archives, 1938, Document #6, 1 February 1938.

53 John Sauter, *History of the American College of Louvain, 1857–1898* (Louvain<PUBLISHER?>, 1959).

54 Barry M. Gough, "Father Brabant and the Hesquiat of Vancouver Island," Canadian Catholic Historical Association, *Report*, vol. 50 (1983): 553–68; APF, New Series, vol. 27 (1893), ff. 590–93; Joseph Van den Heyden, *Life and Letters of Father Brabant, A Flemish Missionary Hero* (Louvain; J. Wouters-Ickx, 1920).

55 *Présence Francophone à Victoria, C.B., 1843–1987* (Victoria, BC: Association historique francophone de Victoria, 1987), p. 46.

56 J.M. Hill, "Archbishop Seghers, Pacific coast missionary," CCHA, *Report*, 18 (1951), pp. 15–23; Maurice de Baets, *Mgr Seghers, l'apôtre de l'Alaska* (Poitiers, 1896), *passim*; Sr Mary Annuntiata, "Archbishop Seghers: The Martyred Archbishop of Vancouver Island," *B.C. Historical Quarterly* 14, no.3 (1943): 191–96.

57 Maurice de Baets, *The Apostle of Alaska: Life of the Most Reverend Charles John Seghers* (Peterson,NJ: St. Anthony Guild Press, 1943), 8

58 Charles Moser, *Reminiscences of the West Coast of Vancouver Island* (Victoria, BC: 1926), *passim*.

59 ASV, DAEU, IV, liasse 34, complaints to Sebsatien Martinello (1899), ff. 4–5; Philemon Sabbe and Leon Buyse, *Belgians in America* (Tielt, 1960), 143–44.

60 Archbishop Baudoux was a personal friend of the author. A recent biography is Denise Robillard, is *Maurice Baudoux, 1902-1988* (Québec: Presses de l'Université Laval, 2009).

61 Terence Fay, *op. cit.*, 288–96; Bernard Daly, "The First Reception of the Council," *Mission. Journal of Mission Studies* 10, no. 2 (2003): 214–15.

62 There were three appeals at the district level by Pellant (1892), Bertrand (1909) and Dumas (1916), but the church wanted to recover school rights, not language rights. This was a situation that one legislator, John Williams of Arthur constituency, could not comprehend. *Winnipeg Free Press*, 25 February 1916.

63 Frances Russell, *The Canadian Crucible: Manitoba's Role in Canada's Great Divide* (Winnipeg: Heartland Associates, 2003), 143–86. On continuities and discontinuities relating to ethnicity and religion see George E. Pozzetta, ed., *The Immigrant Religious Experience* (New York: Garland, 1991), *passim*.

64 SHSB, Carton "Belges," "Un journaliste catholique, Monsieur Louis Hacault," *Almanach de l'Action Sociale Catholique*, pp. 125–26.

65 Evelyn Baltessen, "An investigation into how progress and educational directives affect the integrity of a minority group" (typescript, n.d.), p. 4.

66 AASB, Fonds Taché, Dom Paul Benoît to Taché, 21 June 1892; Fonds Langevin, Benoît to Langevin, 1 October 1896.

67 APSB, Fonds Langevin, L-7128-30, Consul General to Langevin, 20 December 1896.

68 Alex Johnson and Andy A. den Otter, *Lethbridge: A Centennial History* (Lethbridge: Historical Society of Alberta, 1985), 52–53, 72.

69 Mary Eggermont-Molenaar and Paul Callens, eds., *Missionaries among Miners, Migrants and Blackfoot* (Calgary: University of Calgary Press, 2007), Leonard Van Tighem's diary entry for 6 April 1893, p. 88.

70 Yvette le Gal, "La restructuration rurale en Province de Saskatchewan: L'éxemple de la paroisse de St-Maurice de Bellegrade (1898–1970)" (thèse de M.A., Université d'Ottawa, 1989), p. 39.

71 René Rottiers, *Soixante-Cinq Années de Luttes. Esquisse historique de l'œuvre de l'ACFC* (Regina: Association Culturelle Franco-Canadienne de la Saskatchewan, 1977), p. 27, translation.

72 AAR, Paroisse de St-Maurice de Bellegarde, 1897–1949, 12 September 1901; 6 September 1902; 3 October 1902; 22 April 1903; 9 June 1903; 11 October 1905; 5 November 1905.

73 As reported in *Manitoba Free Press*, 19 February 1916, during debate of the original provisions.

74 APF, DAC, Falconio to Ledochowski, 29 April 1901, ff. 283–98, translated and communicated by Matteo Sanfilippo; ASV, Fondo Benigni, [1914], 53, f. 226,230.

75 ASV, DAC, Hacault to Sbaretti, 30 November 1907, communicated by Matteo Sanfilippo.

76 Yvette Brandt, *Memories of Lorne*, p. 223.

77 APSB, Fonds Langevin, L-61476-81, Hacault to A. Delmer, 29 July 1907; Louis Hacault, "Les commandements de Dieu et les écoles publiques," *Les cloches de Saint-Boniface*, vol. VI (1907): 258–61; "L'Ecole forcée au Manitoba" *La Vérité* 7, no. 20 (1909), n.p.; *Les cloches de Saint-Boniface*, vol. X (1911), p. 37.

78 PAM, R.A.C. Manning Papers, P. Talbot to Manning, 11 June 1915; *Manitoba Free Press*, 24 July 1914; Cornelius J. Jaenen, "Minority Group Schooling and Canadian National Unity," *Journal of Educational Thought* 7, no. 2 (1973): 90.

79 Charles Newcombe, *Special Report on Bilingual Schools in Manitoba* (Winnipeg: King's Printer, 1916), pp. 1–15.

80 *Report of the Department of Education, 1912–13* (Winnipeg, 1913), p. 123; *Report of the Department of Education, 1915–16* (Winnipeg, 1916), pp. 186–87.

81 *The Manitoba Free Press*, 20 July 1915, 13 January 1916; *Winnipeg Telegram*, 24 February 1916, p. 8; 25 February 1916, p. 8; 11 March 1916, p. 4.

82 Robert Fletcher, "The Language Problem in Manitoba Schools," *Transactions of the Historical and Scientific Society of Manitoba* 3, no. 6 (1951): 53–56.

83 *Report of the Department of Education for the Year ending 30ᵗʰ June 1917* (Winnipeg: King's Printer 1917), p. 55; *Report of the Department of Education for the Year ending 30 June 1918* (Winnipeg: King's Printer, 1918), pp. 51–52; *Report of the Department of Education for the Year ending 30 June 1919* (Winnipeg: King's Printer, 1919), pp. 45–46.

84   *Department of Education Annual Report, 1913*
      (Regina: King's Printer, 1913), Report of
      W.S. Cram, p. 70.

Chapter VIII: Economic, Political and Military Activity

1   AMAE, Personnel 793, I, A. Hart to
      Minister, 10 August 1848; Chamber
      of Commerce to MAE, 20 September
      1848; Chamber of Commerce to MAE,
      19 June 1850.

2   Canada, *Sessional Papers, 1883*, vol. 16,
      no. 12, p. 89.

3   University of British Columbia Archives
      (UBCA), S. Mack Eastman Fonds, box
      1, file 3, "The Congo," p. 8.

4   AMAE, Personnel 1193, III, Convention
      of 23 November 1887.

5   AMAE, Personnel 1193, V. Fernand
      Van Bruyssel.

6   PAM, MG 13, E1, Greenway Papers,
      Van Bruyssel to Greenway, 5 February
      1891.

7   *Recueil Financier* 1 (1893): 311–13.

8   AMAE, dossier 2808, De Vos report, p.
      126.

9   J.E. Vignes, *La vérité sur le Canada* (Paris:
      Union Internationale d'Editions, 1909),
      288.

10   G. Kurgan-Van Hentenryk, "Finance
      and financiers in Belgium, 1880–1940,"
      in Y. Cassis, ed. *Finance and Financiers in
      European History, 1880–1960* (Cambridge:
      Cambridge University Press, 1992), 316–
      35; H. Van der Wee and M. Goossens,
      "Belgium," in R. Cameron et al., eds.
      International Banking, 1870–1914 (London:
      Oxford University Press, 1991), 113–29.

11   *Recueil Financier* (1913): 812.

12   *Moniteur Belge*, 31 March 1905, pp.
      1349–50.

13   AMAE, dossier 2808, VI, undated
      memorandum, 1906.

14   Henry J. Boam, *Twentieth Century
      Impressions of Canada: Its History, People,*

Commerce, Industries, and Resources
(Montreal: Sells, 1914), 603.

15   Ibid., 603.

16   Ibid., 603 which also contains a long list
      of shareholders.

17   His brother, Maurice Pirmez, who
      lived on the family estate of Château
      d'Hansinelle, was a member of the
      Belgian House of Representatives.

18   Foothills Historical Society, *Chaps
      and Chinooks: A History West of Calgary*
      (Calgary: Northwest Printing and
      Lithographing 1976), II, 289.

19   *Annexes au Moniteur Belge*, 8 November
      1913, pp. 817–18; G. Kurgan-van
      Hentenryk and J. Laureyssens, *Un
      siècle d'investissements belges au Canada*
      (Bruxelles: ULB, 1984), 18.

20   AMAE, Consulat de Calgary,
      Correspondence (hereafter CCC),
      Letterbook 4, H. de Burlet to W.H.
      Barker, Merchants Bank of Canada,
      Moose Jaw, 22 April 1919, p. 405.

21   Ibid., H. de Burlet to M. Louis
      Spentincx, Vilvoorde, 22 April 1919,
      pp. 406–7; H. de Burlet to P. Hymans,
      MAE, 14 May 1919, pp. 434–35.

22   AMAE, CCC, Letterbook 5, H. de
      Burlet to City of Prince Albert, 19
      January 1920, pp. 304–5; H. de Burlet
      to City of Vancouver, 26 April 1920, p.
      402; H. de Burlet to Consul L. Ladner,
      Vancouver, 21 May 1920, pp. 433–34.

23   AMAE, CCC, Letterbook 5, H. de
      Burlet to L. Ladner, Vancouver, 24 June
      1920, pp. 460–61.

24   Kurgan and Laureyssens, *op. cit.*, Table
      VII, pp. 32–33.

25   Ibid., p. 43.

26   AMAE, dossier 4403, Goor to Jaspar, 22
      December 1921, 30 May 1922.

27   Leon Dupuis Papers, File: Canada,
      Group VII, Classe 34, Dupuis to R.
      Baird, 30 Novemver 1928; *Vancouver Sun*,
      28 February 1929, p. 1.

28   Leon Dupuis Papers, Charter of
      the Canadian-Belgian Chamber of
      Commerce of Vancouver, Article 1(2).

29   *Lloyd Anversois*, 19 and 20 April 1931;
      Leon Dupuis Papers, file on Canadian-
      Belgian Chamber of Commerce,
      Jean J. Guay, "Facteurs influençant
      l'exportation belge au Canada."

30   Pierre Chartrand, "Le baron Louis
      Empain au Canada: un destin
      contrarié," (Unpublished paper,
      International Colloquium on the
      Belgian Presence in Canada, University
      of Ottawa, October 1999), p. 7.

31   Julie Laureyssens, "Belgian Interests in
      Western Canada," (Unpublished paper
      presented to the Belgium Colloquium,
      2000), p. 5.

32   *Who's Who in Canada, 1980–81* (Toronto:
      University of Toronto Press, 1981),
      1093–94.

33   Julienne Laureyssens, "Growth of
      the Multidivisional Corporation:The
      Genstar Case," *Business History Review*
      56, no. 4 (1982): 519–44.

34   Laureyssens, *op. cit.*, 11–13.

35   Ibid., p. 6; Henri Aubin, *City for Sale*
      (Toronto: James Lorimer 1977), 138,
      202.

36   Laureyssens, *op. cit.*, 7.

37   Kurgan and Laurayssens, *op. cit.*,
      98–116.

38   Ibid., 8–9.

39   William K. Carroll, "Westward Ho?
      The Shifting Geography of Corporate
      Power in Canada," *Journal of Canadian
      Studies* 36, no. 4 (2001): 118–42.
      Only one financial institution had its
      headquarters in the West – the Hong
      Kong Bank of Canada in Vancouver.

40   Wolfgang Sacks, "On the Archaeology
      of the Development Idea," *The Ecologist*
      20 (March/April 1990): 42.

41   MMMN, tape 5, interview with Joe
      Vernander, 1971; David Bercuson,
      "Labour in Winnipeg: The Great War
      and the General Strike" (PhD thesis,
      University of Toronto, 1971); also
      "The Winnipeg General Strike," in R.
      Douglas Francis and Howard Palmer,
      eds., *The Prairie West: Historical Readings*
      (Edmonton: Pica Pica Press, 1985),
      484–10.

42   Thomas Thorner, *A Country Nourished
      on Self-Doubt* (Peterborough: Broadview
      Press, 2003), Petition to Prime Minister
      R.B. Bennett, 30 December 1933, p.
      259.

43   Erhard Pinno, "Temperance and
      Prohibition in Saskatchewan" (MA
      thesis, University of Saskatchewan,
      1971), pp. 20–21.

44   *The Western Prairie*, 2 March 1916.

45   Cheryl K. Warsh, ed., *Drink in Canada:
      Historical Essays* (Montreal: McGill-
      Queen's University Press, 1993), 172–78.

46   Robert A. Campbell, "Sit Down, Shut
      Up and Drink Your Beer," in *Working
      Lives: Vancouver 1886–1986* (Vancouver:
      New Star Books, 1985), 137.

47   Barry Broadfoot, *Ten Lost Years,
      1919–1939* (Toronto: Doubleday, 1973),
      173–74.

48   B.T. Richardson, "High Politics in
      Saskatchewan," *Canadian Forum* 14, no.
      168 (1934): 461–62; Escott Reid, "The
      Saskatchewan Liberal Machine before
      1929," *Canadian Journal of Economics and
      Political Science* 2 (1936): 27–40.

49   John A. Cormie, *Canada and the New
      Canadians* (Toronto: Social Service
      Council of Canada, 1931), 14.

50   For a good account of changing opinions
      in the hierarchy, see Georges-Henri
      Lévesque, o.p., *Crédit Social et Catholicisme*
      (Ottawa: Collège Dominicain, 1936).

51   Author's personal recollection during
      a conversation with a graduate student
      engaged in research on the role of
      women in politics, September 1975.

52   *Edmonton Journal*, 19 December 1938;
      Robert S. Irwin, "The Emergence
      of a Regional Identity: The Peace
      River Country, 1916–46" (PhD thesis,
      University of Alberta, 1995), pp.
      255–58.

53   *Red Deer Advocate*, 24 September 1962;
      Edmonton Journal, 8 December 1972.

54   James B. Wyndels, *Joseph G. Van
      Belleghem: Une biographie* (Trois Rivières:
      Editions du Bien Public, 2002), 52–65.

55   MMMN, tape 28, Camille De Buck.

56 Walter P. Fitzgerald, ed., *The Wheels of Time* (Rivière-Qui-Barre, 1978), 329.

57 Gordon Van Tighem, "My First Job," *Readers' Digest* (December 2004): 24.

58 Verne Clemence, *Saskatchewan's Own People Who Made a Difference* (Calgary: Fifth House, 2004), 39

59 *Deloraine Scans a Century, 1880–1980* (Altona, MB: D.W. Friesen, 1980), 432.

60 As an example of such a community, see Strathmore History Book Committee, *Strathmore: The Village that Moved* (Red Deer: Adviser Graphics, 1986), 554–56.

61 AMAE, dossier 2808, De Vos report [1901], pp. 34–35.

62 John Hewitt, "Canada Beckons" (typescript, 1949), p. 1; Lucie St. André, ed., *Histoire de Girouxville* (Calgary: D.W. Friesen, 1977), 121.

63 Glenbow Archives, Bosmans Fonds, M115, PA 1427, NA 2537.

64 Germany admitted guilt in not respecting Belgian neutrality: "The injustice which we are committing in this fashion will be made good by us as soon as we shall have attained our military objectives." *Belgian Grey Book*, Document No. 20. It was claimed that Belgium had already violated terms of the neutrality agreement by allowing French officers onto its territory, the building of forts by French engineers on its eastern border, and partial mobilization in 1913.

65 Nicole Manuello, "Albert Ier le dernier des rois-soldats," *Jours de France*, 15 March 1985, pp. 2–10.

66 AMAE, CCC, Letterbook 4, H. de Burlet to M. Goor, 20 May 1918, p. 61.

67 *Le Progrès Albertain*, 6 August 1914, p. 5.

68 Jacob Clemens, an uncle of the author, suffered permanent disability as a result of chlorine gas attacks at Ypres.

69 AMAE, CCC, Letterbook 4, Certificate of 27 May 1918, p. 68.

70 Ibid., Letterbook 4, H. de Burlet to Castelein de la Lande, 10 July 1918, p. 127.

71 *Edmonton Bulletin* , 4 August 1915, p. 5.

72 Ibid., Letterbook 3, H. de Burlet to M. Goor, 11 June 1917, p. 246.

73 AMAE, CCC, Letterbook 3, H. de Burlet to M. Goor, 27 February 1917, p. 99.

74 AMAE, CCC, Letterbook 4, H. de Burlet to Joseph Private, Blairmore, 25 April 1918, p. 33; H. de Burlet to M. Goor, 11 May 1918, p. 47.

75 AMAE, CCC, Letterbook 4, H. de Burlet to P. Burns & Co. Ltd., 28 April 1918, p. 28; Ibid., Letterbook 3, H. de Burlet to M. Goor, 3 May 1917, p. 203.

76 LAC, RG 18, A1, vol. 469, file 454, Committee of the Privy Council, 21 August 1914.

77 LAC, RG 24, C1, vol. 769, file HQ 54-21-6-164, Deputy Minister to Napoleon Poirier, 25 October 1919.

78 John Ferri, "Propagandists had huge impact," *Sunday Star* [Toronto], 8 November 1987, p. A16.

79 Beaton Institute, Glace Bay Community Oral History Project, 1982, interview with Sadie Bettens.

80 Author's reminiscences of lengthy talks with Jules Minet, an agricultural mechanic who travelled widely in the Belgian and northern French countryside before the war and during the hostilities.

81 Peter Buitenhuis, *The Great War of Words: British, American and Canadian Propaganda and Fiction, 1914–1933* (Vancouver: University of British Columbia Press, 1987), *passim*.

82 Arthur Lamont, *La Mission belge au Canada* (Montréal, 1914), 6, 75–95, 118–20.

83 Montreal *Herald-Telegraph*, 25 September 1914; *Montreal Daily Star*, 25 September 1914; André Leblanc, "Gustave Francq" (manuscript, n.d.), pp. 17, 55.

84 John H. Archer, *Saskatchewan: A History* (Saskatoon: Western Producer Prairie Books, 1980), 168; *Canadian Annual Review, 1917* (Toronto: CAR, 1918), 758.

85 UBCA, S. Mack Eastman Papers, Correspondence (1912–1915), box 1, file

3, Honorary Secretary to Eastman, 4 May 1915.

86 *Calgary News-Telegram*, 13 January 1915; 3 May 1915.

87 LAC, RG 6/8, Liber 260, Microfilm C-4069.

88 LAC, RG 6/8, Liber 376, Microfilm C-4109.

89 *Belgique-Canada*. 2, no. 5 (1919): 9.

90 *Edmonton Bulletin*, 15 July 1919.

91 AMAE, CCC, Letterbook 5, H. de Burlet to P. Mali, New York, 24 February 1920, p. 346.

92 AMAE, CCC, Letterbook 4, H. de Burlet to M. Goor, 5 March 1919, p. 363.

93 LAC, RG 24, E1, vol. 5196, file 110-G-40, Hugh Keenleyside to Ernest de Selliers, 13 March 1941, Circular of 7 April 1941.

94 LAC, RG 24, E1, vol. 5196, Baron Silvercruys to Norman Robertson, 21 May 1941.

95 LAC, RG 24, E1, vol. 5196, Memorandum of 27 April 1943; Memorandum of 13 May 1943.

96 LAC, RG 27, vol. 997, file 2-114-3, J. K. Houston to M. Wright, 28 July 1944.

97 PABC, Add. Mss. 848, Max Emke Papers, *passim*.

98 Cited from the *Winnipeg Tribune* in Keith Wilson and James B. Wyndels, *The Belgians in Manitoba* (Winnipeg: Peguis, 1976), 47.

CHAPTER IX: ETHNICITY AND CULTURE

1 Keith Wilson and James B. Wyndels, *The Belgians in Manitoba* (Winnipeg: Peguis, 1976), 31.

2 PAM, P5703–P5711, Original documents of Le Club Belge; MMMN, tape 28, Camille De Buck, 1971.

3 LAC, MG 10, G. 1, Microfilm K-137, Varlez-Brunin Report, 1929, L. Varlez to de Roover, 25 September 1929.

4 *The Belgian Club Celebrates Centennial Week: A Salute to Winnipeg* (Winnipeg: National School Services, 1974); Abdolmohammed Kazemipur, "The Model Value of Friendship: Social Networks of Immigrants," *Canadian Ethnic Studies/Etudes ethniques au Canada* (2006): 52.

5 See Chapter III for the context. Also *Les cloches de Saint-Boniface* 9, no. 2 (1910), 14; 10, no. 6 (1911), 82; *Le Manitoba* 47, no. 32 (1918), 4; 49, no. 30 (1920), 4; AASB, Archives paroissiales, Sacré Cœur des Belges, 247-9009.

6 Communication from Jorn De Cock, *De Standaard*, 15 November 2000; Yvette Brandt, ed., *Memories of Lorne, 1880–1980* (Altona, MB: D.W. Friesen, 1981), 148–49; Letter from Brother Omer Beaulieu to Mme Claire Carbonez, 2 April 2001. The community had been founded in Mechelen (Malines) by Msgr Victor Scheppers in 1839. The provincial house was in Kapellen, near Antwerp.

7 Brother Rombaut Obbens, "Les Frères de Notre-Dame de la Miséricorde au Canada: Leur première fondation à Swan Lake, Manitoba" (typescript, n.d.), pp. 1–2.

8 David Jones, "Agricultural Schooling in the Twenties," *BC Studies* 39 (1978): 31–32.

9 Author's interview with George Brandt, Swan Lake, 30 August 1983.

10 Rombaut Obbens, "Les Frères de Notre-Dame de la Miséricorde au Canada," 5.

11 Ibid., idem., p. 7.

12 Danielle de Kegel, "Sport en etniciteit: Volkssporten bij de Nederlands-Vlaams etnische groep in Kanada" (Licentiate thesis, Catholic University of Leuven, 1981).

13 MMMN, tape 28, Camille De Buck, 1971.

14 *Our Van Walleghem Roots* (Altona, MB: D.W. Friesen, 2001), 30.

15 *Our Van Walleghem Roots*, 129.

16 Crowsnest Pass Historical Society, *Crowsnest and its People* (Altona, MB: D.W. Friesen, 1979), 477.

17 [Winnipeg] *Evening Tribune*, 24, 28 July 1934; *Winnipeg Tribune*, 19 February 1938.

18 *Deloraine Scans a Century, 1880–1980* (Altona, MB: D.W. Friesen, 1980), 660.

19 *Gazette van Detroit*, 8 February 1978, p. 8; Roland Renson, Danielle De Kegel and Herman Smulders, "The Folk Roots of Games: Games and Ethnic Identity among Flemish-Canadian Immigrants," *Canadian Journal of the History of Sport* 14, no. 2 (1983): 70; Maria T. Allison, "On the Ethnicity of Ethnic Minorities," *Quest* 31 (1979): 50–56.

20 The best information is found in Joan Magee, *The Belgians in Ontario: A History* (Toronto: Dundurn Press, 1987), 114–32, on sports and games.

21 *Holland, Manitoba, 1877–1967* (Altona, MB: D.W. Friesen, 1967), 120–21.

22 Interview with George and Yvette Brandt, Swan Lake MB, 30 August 1983.

23 *Deloraine Scans a Century, 1880–1980* (Altona, MB: D.W. Friesen 1980), 174–75, 663, 725.

24 G. Karlis and D. Dawson, "Ethnic Maintenance and Recreation: A Case Study," *Journal of Applied Recreation Research* 15, no. 2 (1999): 85–99 as applied to the Greek community.

25 J. Horna, "Leisure Re-Socialization among Immigrants in Canada," *Society and Leisure* 3, no. 1 (1980): 97–110.

26 P. Bolla and D. Dawson, "Meeting the Recreational Needs of Ethnic Communities," *Recreation Canada* (October 1990): 10–15.

27 Claude Fischler, *L'homnivore* (Paris: Odile Jacob, 2001), 66; Enoch Padolsky, "You Are Where You Eat: Ethnicty, Food and Cross-Cultural Spaces," *Canadian Ethnic Studies/Etudes ethniques au Canada* 37, no. 2 (2005): 19–47.

28 Mary Douglas, "Analyser le boire: Une perspective anthropologique spécifique," *Cahiers de sociologie économique et culturelle* 14 (décembre 1999): 68.

29 André Vermeirre, *L'immigration des belges au Québec* (Sillery: Editions du Septentrion, 2001), 93–123; "De Koninck Dynasty," *Le Soleil* (Québec), 25 February 2006.

30 Watson Kirkonnell, *Canadians All* (Ottawa, 1941), 26.

31 Yvette Brandt, ed., *Hutelet Heritage, 1680–1972* (Swan Lake, 1977), 121; *Holland, Manitoba, 1877–1967* (Altona, MB: D.W. Friesen,1967), 125–27; MMMN, tape 5, J. Vermander, 1971.

32 Lucie St. André, ed., *Histoire de Girouxville*, vol. I: *1911–1930* (Altona, MB: D.W. Friesen, 1977), 50.

33 *Calgary Herald*, 4 April 2004.

34 *Le Défenseur du Canada catholique et français*, no. 19 (1910), p. 9; no. 31 (1911), p. 23; no. 34 (1911), p. 19.

35 Communication from Mary Eggermont-Molenaar, Calgary, 9 February 2005.

36 G.P. Baert, "L'émigration belge en Amérique," *Industrie* (April 1958), pp. 226–27; A Verthé, "Gazette van Detroit," *Encyclopedie van de Vlaamse Beweging* (Tielt/Utrecht: 1973), I, pp. 563–64. The *DePere Standard* was published from 1878 to 1907, and *De Volksstem* from 1890 to 1917; Kristine Smets, "Gazette van Detroit and the Belgian American Community, 1907–1921" (MA thesis in History, Kent State University, 1995) not seen.

37 *Le Fanal* 3, no. 14 (1918): 2, 3.

38 *Edmonton Journal*, 25 October 1974.

39 Georges Forestier [Schoeffer], *La Pointe-aux-Rats* (Paris: Plon, 1907).

40 Lucien Léonard, *Un littérateur wallon au Canada: l'abbé Jules-Joseph Pirot* (Namur: Cahiers Wallons, n.d.), 47–50; Jules Pirot to Lucien Maréchal, 14 novembre 1938, p. 55.

41 Berthe de Trémaudan [Gusbin], *Au nord du 53ᵉ: Souvenirs de Berthe de Trémaudan* (Saint-Boniface: Editions du Blé, 1982).

42 Patricia Anne Van Tighem, *The Bear's Embrace: A True Story of Surviving a Grizzly Bear Attack* (Waterville, ME: Wheeler Publishing, 1958).

43 The standard study of this ideology is Michael Hughey, *Civil Religion and Moral*

Order: Theoretical and Historical Dimensions (Westport, CT: Greenwood, 1983). For the Canadian context see Cornelius J. Jaenen, "Minority Group Schooling and Canadian National Unity," *Journal of Canadian Educational Thought* 7, no. 2 (1973): 81–93, 136–37; also "The Public School in Canada: Agency of Integration and Assimilation," *Actes du Congrès International des Sciences de l'Education* (Paris, 1976), I, pp. 203–15.

44 G. Borjas, "Ethnic Enclaves and Assimilation," *Swedish Economic Policy Review* 7 (2000): 82–122; Margaret Walton-Roberts, "Regional Immigration and Dispersal," *Canadian Ethnic Studies/Etudes ethniques au Canada* 27, no. 3 (2005): 14–15.

45 Yvette Brandt, comp., *Memories of Lorne, 1880–1980* (Altona, MB: D.W. Friesen, 1980), 649.

46 Ibid., 132.

47 AASB, Fonds Langevin, Lettres A, Langevin to Charles Caron, 30 September 1899; Langevin to curate of St. François-Xavier, 23 January 1900; Langevin to Cardinal Ledochowski, 13 April 1899.

48 Mathieu published a pamphlet, *Un sujet de méditation, la danse et les bals* (Regina, 1915), p. 31.

49 AS, Pamphlet files, Local History, Gilles Leroy, "Prud'homme."

50 Taped interview of Frank Soulet, August 1980.

51 Yvette Le Gal, "La Restructuration rurale. L'exemple de la paroisee de St-Maurice de Bellegarde" (typescript, n.d.), p. 70.

52 Veronica Strong-Boag, "Pulling in Double Harness, or Hauling a Double Load: Women, Work and Feminism on the Canadian Prairies," *Journal of Canadian Studies* 22, no. 3 (1986): 32–52.

53 Michael Taft, *Discovering Saskatchewan Folklore* (Edmonton, n.p., n.d.), 114–15, 123.

BIBLIOGRAPHY

A. Manuscript Sources

AASB   Archives de l'Archevêché de Saint-Boniface
Fonds Alexandre Taché
Fonds Adélard Langevin
Fonds Dom Benoît/Guéret
Fonds de Paroisses
Prêtres –Correspondance
Religieuses

AAE   Archives of Archdiocese of Edmonton
Fonds Vital Grandin
Fonds Emile Legal

AAR   Archives of Archdiocese of Regina
Parish of St. Maurice de Bellegarde
Colonization and Immigration
Fonds Mathieu
AEG Diocese of Gravelbourg

AAW   Archives of Archdiocese of Winnipeg
Parishes

ADC   Archives of Diocese of Calgary
Anderson Papers

AMAE   Archives du Ministère des Affaires Etrangères, Brussels
2669 bis I-B, "Canada"
2669 bis II, Poursuites judiciaires
2669 bis III, Engagements clandestins
2669 bis IV, Agents d'émigration
2808 Mines/Entreprises diverses, liasses III, IV, VII
2946 Rapports consulaires

2951 Déclarations des émigrants
2954 Transport des émigrants
2955 VIII, Société St-Rapaël
2955 IX, Société de patronage
2955 XII, Abbé Delouche
2958 Canada –Recrutement, liasses 1–10
4093 Rapports consulaires
4346 Renseignements commerciaux, 1921–1925
4387 Statistiques – Port d'Anvers
CCC – Correspondance consulaire, Calgary
Cl B. 392 Visites et échanges
Pers. 793
Pers. 1193 Correspondance Van Bruyssel I–V

APF   Archivum de Propaganda Fide, Rome
Nuova serie, vol. 265

APSB   Archives du Patrimoine, Saint-Boniface
Fonds Taché
Fonds Langevin

AS-R   Archives of Saskatchewan, Regina
Lieutenant-Governor's Office, North-West Territories
Pamphlet file – Local histories
A, B695, Arthur J. Boyer Papers
A, G430, Arséne Godin Papers
R550.52, Lucienne Roberge Papers
R500.62, Famille Dumélie
R500.104, Jules Delanoy Papers
R500.109, Marcel Moor

AS-S   Archives of Saskatchewan, Saskatoon
Department of Agriculture, Land Branch file
M4 Premier Martin Papers

ASV   Archivo Segreto Vaticano, Rome
Delegazione Apostolica – Stati Uniti
Delegazione Apostolica – Canada

Beaton Institute, University College of Cape Breton, Sydney
Tape 2095 – Joe Lothier

BMM   Bibliothèque Municipale de Montréal
Correspondance Curé A. Labelle

British Columbia Sugar Museum, Vancouver
Knight Sugar Company Papers

Canadian Ethnic Studies Research Centre, University of Calgary
    Taped interview – Frank Soulet

Deschatelets Archives, Ottawa
    HEF 3282 Oblate Archives

GAI   Glenbow-Alberta Archives, Calgary
    CPR Colonization Papers
    United Mine Workers of America Papers
    Coal Operators Association Papers
    Western Canadian Collieries, Bellevue Mine Ledger
    Maurice Ingeveld Papers
    Fonds Emile Leblanc
    Fonds Bosmans
    Knight Sugar Company Papers

LAC   Library and Archives Canada, Ottawa
    MG 26-G, Laurier Papers
    MG 28-J, Mackenzie King Papers
    MG 30, Rosenberg Collection
    RG 6, Secretary of State Correspondence
    RG 7, Governor-General's Letterbooks
    RG 9, Militria and Defence Correspondence
    RG 11, Public Works Letterbooks
    RG 13, Justice Department Letterbooks
    RG 15, Interior, Dominion Lands Branch
    RG 17, Agriculture, Immigration/Correspondence/Letterbooks
    RG 18, Royal North West Mounted Police Files
    RG 20, Trade and Commerce
    RG 24, National Defence Registry Files
    RG 25, External Affairs Correspondence
    RG 26, Immigration Statistics
    RG 27, National Selective Service
    RG 30, Canadian National Railways
    RG 76, Immigration Branch Files

MHSO   Multicultural History Society of Ontario, Toronto
    Bel. 2001, Archives of Belgian Capuchins

MMMN   Manitoba Museum of Man and Nature, Winnipeg
    Clipping Files – Bicycle racing; Homing pigeon racing
    Tape 573 – St. Boniface Museum – Bruxelles
    Oral History Project, 1971 Taped interviews:
        Tape 5 – Joe Vermander
        Tape 7 – Walter Van Walleghem
        Tape 28 – Camille De Buck
        Tape 65 – W.J. Van Walleghem
        Tape 75 – William English

Tape 77 – C.A. Bossuyt
Tape 79 – William Danish
Tape 108 – Marcien De Leeuw

PAA   Provincial Archives of Alberta, Edmonton
Attorney General's Papers
Premier's Papers, Files 154, 1498, 1867
Supreme Court of Alberta, Appellate Division
Codex historicus of Lethbridge Parish
United Church Papers
Anglican Church Papers
Clarice Lambert Demers Papers

PABC   Provincial Archives of British Columbia, Victoria
Mining Records, 1861–1900
Pooley Family Papers
Department of Education Papers
Max Emke Papers
Additional Manuscripts

PAM   Provincial Archives of Manitoba, Winnipeg
MG 9, Marie-Anne Roy Papers
MG 12, Archibald Papers
MG 13, Bracken Papers
MG 13, Manning Papers
MG 13, Greenway Papers
MG 13, Norris Papers
P5564, August De Pape Journal
Le Club Belge, Saint-Boniface

PAO   Provincial Archives of Ontario
RG 11, Richard Berne Correspondence

SHSB   Société Historique de Saint-Boniface
Carton "Belges"
Carton "Bruxelles"

SHS   Société Historique de la Saskatchewan, Regina
Dossiers R80: 11,12, 32, 36, 37, 55, 61, 68, 86, 101, 104, 108, 109, 159, 160, 162,165, 169, 173, 176, 180, 184, 263, 265, 270, 277, 519.

UBCA   University of British Columbia Archives, Vancouver
S. Mack Eastman Papers

Léon J. Dupuis Papers, Ganges, BC
File: Canada, Group VII, Classe 34.

B. Government Publications

Alberta. *Report of the Alberta Coal Commission, 1925*. Edmonton, 1926.

Anstey, T.H. *Cent moissons: Direction générale de la recherche. Agriculture Canada, 1886–1986*. Ottawa: Agriculture Canada, 1986.

Asselin, Olivar. *L'émigration belge et française au Canada. Report of an enquiry made during the winter 1911–12*. Ottawa: Imprimerie du Gouvernement, 1913.

Belgium. Affaires Etrangères. *Loi et règlement sur le transport des émigrants*. Bruxelles: Moniteur Belge, 1876.

———. Affaires Etrangères. *Receuil consulaire*. Bruxelles, 1880–1930.

———. Affaires Etrangères. *Le service de renseignements concernant l'émigration*. Bruxelles: P. Weissenbruch, 1888.

Bernier, Thomas Alfred. *Le Manitoba, champ d'immigration*. Ottawa: Imprimerie du Gouvernement, 1886.

Berry, John W., et al. *Multiculturalism and Ethnic Attitudes in Canada*. Ottawa: Supply and Services Canada, 1977.

Bodard, Auguste. *Emigration en Canada: Description du pays. Témoignages et lettres des colons*. Ottawa: n.p., 1892.

British Columbia. *Sessional Papers*. Victoria, 1872–1920.

———. Bureau of Mines. *Special Reports on Coal Mining Explosions*. Victoria: King's Printer, 1918.

Canada. *Canada's International Investment Position, 1926–1954*. Ottawa: Dominion Bureau of Statistics, 1956.

———. *The Canadian Balance of International Payments, 1926 to 1948*. Ottawa: Dominion Bureau of Statistics, 1949.

———. *Sessional Papers*. Ottawa, 1873–1936.

———. Citizenship and Immigration. *Annual Report*. Ottawa, 1930–1965.

———. Foreign Investment Division, Office of Economics. *Foreign Direct Investment in Canada, Selected Years from 1900 to 1945*. Ottawa: Department of Industry, Trade and Commerce. 1970.

———. Foreign Investment Division, Office of Economics. *Foreign Direct Investment in Canada since the Second World War*. Ottawa: Department of Industry, Trade and Commerce, 1970.

———. House of Commons. *Debates*. Ottawa, 1880–1940.

———. Interior. *Les Belges au Manitoba: Lettres authentiques*. Ottawa: Imprimerie de l'Etat, 1894.

———. Interior. *Géographie du Canada et atlas de l'ouest canadien*. Ottawa, 1905, 1910.

———. Interior. *Le guide du colon français, belge et suisse*. Paris: Pernaux, 1894.

———. Interior. *Handbook of Information for Intending Settlers*. Ottawa, 1913.

———. Interior. *Homestead Regulations for North-Western Canada*. Ottawa, 1903.

————. Labour. *Report of the Royal Commission on Coal Mining Disputes on Vancouver Island.* Ottawa: King's Printer, 1913.

————. Manpower and Immigration. *Canadian Immigration and Population Study: "Green Paper."* Ottawa: Information Canada, 1974. 4 vols.

————. Manpower and Immigration. *Three Years in Canada: First report of the longitudinal survey on the economic and social adaptation of immigrants.* Ottawa: Information Canada, 1974.

Canada Year Book, 1948–49. Census 1871–1921.

Canada Year Book, 1957–58. Census 1931–1951.

Chambers, Ernest J. *The Unexploited West.* Ottawa: King's Printer, 1914.

Drapeau, S. *Le guide du colon.* Ottawa: Imprimerie de l'Etat, 1887.

Ellis, J.H. *The Ministry of Agriculture in Manitoba, 1870–1970.* Winnipeg: Department of Agriculture, 1970.

Gagnon, Joseph. *Le Manitoba: Ressources et avantages.* Winnipeg: Ministère de l'Agriculture, 1917.

Morin, J.-B. *En avant la colonisation: Le nord-ouest canadien et ses ressources agricoles.* Ottawa: Imprimerie de l'Etat, 1875.

Restrictive Trade Practices Commission. *Report concerning the Sugar Industry in Western Canada and the proposed merger of Sugar Companies.* Ottawa: Department of Justice, 1987.

Spence, Thomas. *Manitoba et le nord-ouest du Canada, ses ressources et ses avantages pour l'émigrant et le capitaliste.* Ottawa: Imprimerie de l'Etat, 1875.

Stone, Leroy O. *Migration in Canada: Regional Aspects.* Ottawa: Dominion Bureau of Statistics, 1969.

Willems, Gustaaf. *Les Belges au Manitoba: Lettres authentiques.* Ottawa: Imprimerie de l'Etat, 1894.

C. Local and Community Histories

Antler and District History Committee. *Footprints in the Sands of Time.* Altona, MB: D.W. Friesen, 1983.

Boily, Marie-Louise. *Nos braves pionniers en terre manitobaine: Souvenirs de colonisation.* La Broquerie: l'auteur, 1951.

Borgstede, Arlene. *The Black Robe's Vision: A History of St. Albert and District.* St. Albert: St. Albert Historical Society, 1985.

Brandt, Yvette. *Hutlet Heritage, 1680–1972.* Swan Lake: Author, 1977.

————, ed. *Memories of Lorne, 1880–1980.* Altona, MB: D.W. Friesen, 1981.

Campbell, Jessie, ed. *Chatter Chips from Beaver Dam Creek: Castor and her Neighbours, 1909–1974.* Lacombe: Castor Old Timers Association, 1974.

Camrose Canadian. *The Golden Years.* Camrose: the Camrose Canadian, 1955.

Cochrane and Area Historical Society. *Big Hill Country: Cochrane and Area.* Altona, MB: D.W. Friesen, 1977.

Cohoon, W.A. *Jubilee Reminiscences.* Macrorie: Jubilee History Committee, 1957.

Cousins, W.J. *A History of the Crow's Nest Pass.* Lethbridge: Historic Trails Society of Alberta, 1981.

Crowsnest Pass Historical Society. *Crowsnest and its People.* Altona, MB: D.W. Friesen, 1979.

Davidson and District Historical Society. *Halfway Happenings.* Davidson: Davidson and District Historical Society, 1980.

Deloraine History Book Committee. *Deloraine Scans a Century, 1880–1980.* Altona, MB: D.W. Friesen, 1980.

Dempsey, Hugh A., ed. *Lethbridge: A Centennial History.* Lethbridge: Historical Society of Alberta, 1985.

Drumheller Valley Historical Association. *The Hills of Home: Drumheller Valley.* Altona, MB: D.W. Friesen, 1973.

Dugald Women's Institute. *Springfield: First Rural Municipality in Manitoba, 1873–1973.* Altona, MB: D.W. Friesen, 1974.

Duperreault, Marie Anne. *Esquisses canadiennes: Willow Bunch.* Vancouver: Author, 1969.

Eckville District Historical Society. *Homesteads and Happiness.* Eckville, AB: Eckville District Historical Society, 1979.

Fitzgerald, Walter P., ed. *The Wheels of Time: A History of Rivière-Qui-Barre.* Rivière-Qui-Barre: Author, 1978.

Hambley, George H. *Historical Records and Accounts of the Early Pioneers of the District of Swan Lake, Manitoba from its Early Settlement.* Altona, MB: D.W. Friesen, 1950.

Harland, Gordon, et al. *A History of the Rural Municipality of South Norfolk, 1879–1935.* Treherne: Treherne Times, 1939.

Hart, E.J. *Ambition and Reality: The French-Speaking Community of Edmonton, 1795–1935.* Edmonton: Salon d'histoire de la francophonie albertaine, 1980.

Hartney District. *Hartney and District, 1882–1957.* Deloraine: Deloraine Times, 1957.

Hébert, Georges. *Les débuts de Gravelbourg: Son fondateur, ses pionniers, les institutions.* Gravelbourg: l'Auteur, 1965.

Henderson, Alice. *Homesteading in Surprise Valley.* Gladmar: Author, 1970.

History Committee of the R.M. of the Gap. *Builders of a Great Land: History of the R.M. of the Gap No. 39, Ceylon and Hardy.* Altona, MB: D.W. Friesen, 1980.

Holland History Committee. *Holland, Manitoba, 1877–1967.* Altona, MB: D.W. Friesen, 1967.

Jackson, Michael, and Bernard Wilhelm. *Willow Bunch et Bellegarde en Saskatchewan.* Regina: Centre d'Etudes bilingues, 1971.

Laford Historical Committee. *Dreams Become Realities. A History of Laford and Surrounding Areas.* Laford: Laford Historical Committee, 1981.

Manor and District Historical Society. *Memories are Forever.* Altona, MB: D.W. Friesen, 1982.

McCormick, Betty, ed. *Memories of St. Hubert.* Whitewood: Whitewood Herald, 1980.

Meath Park History Committee. *From Bush to Grain: A History of Albertville, Meath Park and District.* Meath Park: Meath Park History Committee, 1984.

Parker, Georgean C. *Proud Beginnings: A Pictorial History of Red Deer.* Red Deer: Advisor Graphics, 1980

Philippot, Aristide. *Cinquante ans de vie paroissiale. Morinville (1891–1941). Fifty Years of Parochial Life.* Edmonton: Editions La Survivance, 1941.

Putnam, Ben, et al. *Fifty Years of Progress: Chiefly the Story of the Pioneers of the Watson District from 1900–1950.* Muenster: St. Peter's Press, 1950.

Radville Book Committee. *Our First 50: A History of the Town of Radville, Saskatchewan and District, 1910–1960.* Weyburn: Weyburn Review, 1960.

Riverside Municipality. *History of the Riverside Municipality, 1879–1967.* Dunrea: Riverside Municipality, 1967.

Robsart Jubilee Committee. *Robsart Pioneers Review the Years.* Robsart: Robsart Jubilee Committee, 1955.

Robson, Irene. *History of Deleau-Bethel District, Centennial Year, 1967.* Deleau: Author, 1967.

Rondeau, Clovis. *La montagne de bois, 1870–1920: Histoire de la Saskatchewan méridionale.* Québec: Action Sociale, 1923.

Roy, Marie-Anna A. *La montagne Pembina au temps des colons.* Winnipeg: Canadian Publishers, 1970.

Sanctuary Community Club. *A Tribute to the Bygone Communities of Saltburn, East Gap, South Dean, Sanctuary and Hamlet.* Elrose: Elrose Review, 1970.

Shipley, Nan. *Road to the Forks: A History of Fort Garry.* Winnipeg: Author, 1970.

St-Amant, Clovis. *Histoire de Notre-Dame de Lorette.* Saint-Boniface: l'Auteur, 1951.

Students of St. Walburg High School. *The St. Walburg Story.* St. Walburg, SK: St. Walburh High School, 1955.

Swan Lake. *The Story of the Early Settlers of the Swan Lake Area.* Swan Lake: n.p., 1970.

Taber History Committee. *From Tank 77 to Taber Today.* Altona, MB: D.W. Friesen, 1977.

Tardif, Emile. *Centenaire de Saint-Albert/Saint Albert Centennial, 1861–1961.* Edmonton: La Survivance Printing, 1961.

Théoret, Anatole E. *Sainte-Rose-du-Lac.* Winnipeg: G.C. Murray, 1948.

Thompson, Muriel L. *New Hope on the Prairies: A History of Stoughton, Heward, Forget, Handsworth Districts.* Weyburn: Weyburn Review, 1955.

Thomson, Marguerite. *Belgian Canadian Builders: DePape-De Roo Families, 1893–1993.* Private printing, 1993.

Weyburn History Book Committee. *As Far as the Eye Can See: Weyburne R.M. 67.* Weyburn: Weyburn R.M. 67 History Book Committee, 1986.

Weyburn New Horizons Book Committee. *In His Hands.* Altona, MB: D.W. Friesen, 1967.

Willis, Alta, et al. *Golden Echoes: History of Galahad and Districts.* Galahad: Galahad History Society, 1908.

Wood Mountain Centennial Committee. *They Came to Wood Mountain.* Wood Mountain: Wood Mountain Centennial Committee, 1967.

Wright, Norman E. *In View of the Turtle Hill.* Deloraine: Deloraine Times, 1951.

Yellow Grass Heritage Committee. *Yellow Grass: Our Prairie Community.* Altona, MB: D.W. Friesen, 1981.

York, Lillian, ed. *Lure of the South Peace: Tales of the Early Pioneers to 1945.* Fort St. John: Alaska Highway Daily News, 1981.

D. Methodology, Concepts, Inventories

Abdolmohammed, Kazemipar. "The Market Value of Friendship; Social Networks of Immigrants." *Canadian Ethnic Studies/Etudes ethniques au Canada* 38, no. 2 (2006): 47–64.

Abridged Guide to the Archives of Catholic Dioceses in Canada. Ottawa: University of Ottawa Press, 1981.

Abu-Laban, Baka, and Brenda Gail Rule. *The Human Sciences: Their Contribution to Society and Future Research Needs.* Edmonton: University of Alberta Press, 1988.

Allen, Richard. *A Region of the Mind: Interpreting the Western Canadian Plains.* Regina: Canadian Plains Research Center, 1973.

Anderson, A.B., and J. S. Frideres. *Ethnicity in Canada: Theoretical Perspectives.* Toronto: Butterworths, 1981.

Anderson, Benedict. *Imagined Communities: Reflections on the Origins and Spread of Nationalism.* London: Verso, 1991.

Artibise, Alan. *Western Canada since 1867: A Select Bibliography and Guide.* Vancouver: University of British Columbia Press, 1978.

Blouet, Brian N., and Mervin P. Lawson, eds. *Images of the Plains: The Role of Human Nature in Settlement.* Lincoln: University of Nebraska Press, 1975.

Briant, P.C. *Ethnic Groups in Canada: A Bibliography of Research, 1959–61.* Ottawa: Department of Citizenship and Immigration, 1962.

British Columbia Centennial Committee. *Ethnic Groups in British Columbia: A Selected Bibliography.* Victoria: Centennial Committee, 1957.

Brye, David L. *European Immigration and Ethnicity in the United States and Canada: A Historical Bibliography.* Santa Barbara: ABC-Clio, 1983.

Cadwallader, M. *Migration and Residential Mobility: Macro and Micro Approaches.* Madison: University of Wisconsin Press, 1992.

Canada. Citizenship and Immigration. *Citizenship, Immigration and Ethnic Groups in Canada: A Bibliography of Research, 1920–58.* Ottawa: Queen's Printer 1960.

———. Secretary of State. *Canadian Ethnic Groups Bibliography.* Ottawa: Information Canada, 1974.

Cook, Terry. "The Canadian West: An Archival Odyssey through the Records of the Department of the Interior." *The Archivist* 12, no. 4 (July–August 1985): 1–4.

Dorge, Lionel. *Introduction à l'étude des Franco-Manitobains: Essai historique et bibliographique.* Saint-Boniface: Société historique de Saint-Boniface, 1973.

Friesen, Gerald, and Barry Potyondi. *A Guide to the Study of Manitoba Local History.* Winnipeg: University of Manitoba Press, 1981.

Frisch, Michael. "The Memory of History." In *A Shared Authority.* Albany: State University of New York Press, 1990.

Gregorovich, A. *Canadian Ethnic Groups Bibliography.* Toronto: Department of Provincial Secretary and Citizenship, 1972.

Hiller, Harry H. *Canadian Society: A Macro Analysis.* Scarborough: Prentice-Hall Canada, 1990.

Hofstede, G.H. *Culture's Consequences: International Differences in Work-Related Values.* Beverley Hills: Sage, 1980.

Hughey, Michael. *Civil Religion and Moral Order: Theoretical and Historical Dimensions.* Westport, CT: Greenwood Press, 1983.

Juteau, Danielle. *L'ethnicité et ses frontières.* Montréal: Presses de l'Université de Montréal, 1999.

Keith, W.J. "Ethnicity, Canada, and Canadian Literature." *Queen's Quarterly* 102, no. 1 (1995): 100–111.

Krotki, Joanne. *Local Histories of Alberta: An Annotated Bibliography.* Edmonton: University of Alberta, Division of East European Studies, 1980.

Kymlicka, Will. *Liberalism, Community, and Culture.* Oxford: Clarendon Press, 1989.

———. *Multicultural Citizenship: A Liberal Theory of Minority Rights.* Oxford: Clarendon Press, 1995.

Kyvig, David E., and Myron Marty. *Nearby History: Exploring the Past Around You.* Nashville: American Association for State and Local History, 1982.

Lambrecht, Kirk N. *The Administration of Dominion Lands, 1870–1930.* Regina: Canadian Plains Research Center, 1991.

Li, Peter S. "Canadian Immigration Policy and Assimilation Theories." In J.A. Fry, ed., *Economy, Class, and Social Reality.* Toronto: Butterworths, 1979.

Morley, Marjorie. *A Bibliography of Manitoba from holdings in the Legislative Library of Manitoba.* Winnipeg: Queen's Printer, 1970.

Ridgeway, Cecilia. *The Dynamics of Small Groups.* New York: St. Martin's Press, 1983.

Robison, Betty. *Bibliography of Population and Immigration.* Hamilton: McMaster University, 1949.

Sacks, Wolfgang. "On the Archeology of the Development Idea." *The Ecologist* 20 (March/April 1990): 40–42.

Saskatchewan. *Index to Source Materials on Ethnic Groups and Women.* Regina: Saskatchewan Archives Office, 1974.

———. *Index to the Immigration Branch Reports ... Sessional Papers, 1876–1906.* Regina: Saskatchewan Archives Office, 1975.

Schrag, C.O. *Radical Reflections and the Origin of the Human Sciences.* Lafayette: Purdue University Press, 1980.

Schultz, John. *Writing about Canada: A Handbook of Modern Canadian History.* Scarborough: Prentice-Hall Canada, 1990.

Seixas, Peter. *Theorizing Historical Consciousness.* Toronto: University of Toronto Press, 2004.

Spry, Irene M., and Bennett McCardle. *The Records of the Department of the Interior and Research Concerning Canada's Western Frontier of Settlement.* Regina: Canadian Plains Research Center, 1993.

Tumin, Melvin M. *Social Stratification: The Forms and Functions of Social Inequality.* Englewood Cliffs, NJ: Prentice-Hall, 1985.

Walinger, R. "Immigrant Enterprise: A Critique and Reformulation." *Theory and Society* 15 (1980): 249–85.

Wardaugh, Robert, ed. *Toward Defining the Prairie Region, Culture, and History.* Winnipeg: University of Manitoba Press, 2001.

Wiesinger, J.P. "Modelling the Agricultural Settlement Process of Southern Manitoba, 1872 to 1891: Some Implications for Settlement Theory." *Prairie Forum* 10 (1985): 83–103.

E. Belgian Background

Anonyme. *L'Immigration au Canada et les perspectives d'avenir offertes aux immigrants.* Louvain-la-Neuve: Université Catholique de Louvain, 1955.

Bockstaele, L., and A. Olivier. *Vestigingsmogdijkheden van landbouwers.* Brugge: Provincaal Comite voor Landbouw, 1955.

Boussart, J. D. "L'exposition universelle et internationale de 1905." *La Vie Liégeoise* 19, no. 6 (1980): 3–18.

Carcan-Chanel, Nicole. *Agents diplomatiques belges et étrangers aux XIXe et XXe siècles.* Bruxelles: Université Libre de Bruxelles, 1968.

Ciceley, Watson. "A Survey of Recent Belgian Population Policy." *Population Studies* 8, no. 2 (1954): 152–87.

Clough, Shepard B. *A History of the Flemish Movement in Belgium.* New York: Octagon Books, 1968.

Communauté Européenne de Charbon et de l'Acier. *Migrations provoquées et problèmes sociaux de mobilité ouvrière.* Liège: Imprimerie H. Vaillant-Carmanne, 1956.

Confédération des Syndicats Chrétiens. *Cent ans de syndicalisme chrétien.* Bruxelles: SOFADI, 1986.

Damas, H. "Les mouvements migratoires: Définition, interprétation, perspective et recherche." *Revue Belge d'Histoire Contemporaine* 12, nos. 1–2 (1981): 195–204.

De Haulleville, A. *Les aptitudes colonisatrices des Belges et la question coloniale en Belgique.* Bruxelles: Schepens, 1898.

De Schryer, Reginald. "The Belgian Revolution and the Emergence of Belgium's Biculturalism." In Arend Lijphart, ed., *Conflict and Coexistence in Belgium.* Berkeley: Institute of International Studies, 1980: 13–33.

Delmelle, Joseph. *L'expansion wallonne hors d'Europe.* Gilly: Institut Jules Destrée, 1967.

Delouche, C. *L'œuvre des émigrants à Anvers: Projet. Rapport.* Anvers: Imprimerie Centrale, 1901.

De Vroede, M. *The Flemish Movement in Belgium.* Antwerp: Flemish Cultural Council, 1975.

d'Haenens, Leen. *Het land de Ahorn: Visies of Canada.* Gand: Academia Press, 1995.

Dumoulin, Michel, and Eddy Stols. *La Belgique à l'étranger aux XIXe et XXe siècles.* Bruxelles: Editions Nauwelaerts, 1987.

Everaert, Jean. "L'émigration en masse." *La Belgique: Société et Cultures depuis 150 ans.* Bruxelles, 1980: 245–47.

Herreboudt, J. *Le Canada au point de vue de l'immigration.* Bruges: Herreboudt & Claeys, 1890.

———. *De l'avenir de nos relations commerciales avec le Canada.* Bruxelles: Auteur, 1892.

Hilden, Patricia. "The Rhetoric and Iconography of Reform: Women Coal Miners in Belgium, 1840–1914." *Historical Journal* 34, no. 2 (1991): 411–36.

Huybrechts, Pierre. *Le commerce extérieur de la Belgique d'après les documents officiels.* Bruxelles: Charles Rozuz, 1895.

Irving, Ronald E.M. *The Flemings and Walloons of Belgium.* London: Minority Rights Group, 1980.

Journée, Marc. "Algemeene achtergronden, profiel, feiten en aspecten van de Belgische emigratie naar Noord Amerika." *De Vlaamse Stam* 23 (1987): 61–72.

———. *Go West! Een verhaal van Vlaamse emigranten naar Canada.* Brugge: Uitgeverij Snoeck, 2006.

Kaiser, Georges. *Au Canada.* Bruxelles: A. Lesigne. 1887.

Kurgan, Ginette, and E. Spelkens. *Two Studies on Emigration through Antwerp to the New World.* Bruxelles: Centre for American Studies, 1976.

Kurgan-van Hentenryk, Ginette. "Aspects de l'émigration belge (1830–1844)." *Bulletin de l'Académie Royale des Sciences d'Outre-Mer* 6 (1964): 1306–1337.

———. "Les activités bancaires de la Société Générale de Belgique à l'étranger de 1900 à 1935." In H. Coppejans-Desmet, ed., *Histoire économique de la Belgique: Traitement des sources et état des questions.* Bruxelles: Archives générales du royaume, 1972: 61–72.

———, ed. *La question social en Belgique et au Canada, XIXe–XXe siècles.* Bruxelles: Editions de l'Université de Bruxelles, 1988.

Laloux, Dominique. *Essai sur l'expansion commerciale belge dans le monde.* Liège: Imprimerie H. Vaillant-Carmanne, 1959.

Landry, Yves, et al. *Les chemins de la migration en Belgique et au Québec, XVIIe–XXe siècles.* Beauport: Publications MNH, 1995.

Lederer, A. "Le rôle des Belges dans le développement des moyens de transport outre-mer." *Bulletin de l'Académie Royale des Sciences d'Outre-Mer,* Suppl. 1 (1980): 65–110.

Lennox. G. *Guide universel de l'émigrant.* Bruxelles: Van Dorslaer-Verbeker, 1885–86, 2 vols.

Lesthaege, Rony. *The Decline of Belgian Fertility, 1890–1970.* Princeton: Princeton University Press, 1977.

Manuel des emigrants. Bruges: Planche Frères, 1892.

McRae, Kenneth D. *Conflict and Compromise in Multilingual Societies: Belgium.* Waterloo: Wilfrid Laurier University Press, 1986.

Moeller, Albert. *A travers le nouveau monde: Etats-Unis et Canada. Notes d'un tourist.* Bruxelles: Goemare, 1911.

Morelli, Anne, ed. *Les émigrants belges.* Bruxelles: EVO, 1998.

Mughan, A. "Accommodation or Diffusion in the Management of Linguistic Conflicts in Belgium." *Political Studies* 31, no. 3 (1983): n.p.

Mussehoot, Dirk. *Wij Gaan Naar Amerika: Vlaamse Landverhuizers naar de Nieuwe Wereld, 1850–1930.* Tielt: Lannoo, 2002.

Nielsen, François. "The Flemish Movement in Belgium after World War II: A Dynamic Analysis." *American Sociological Review* 45 (1950): 76–94.

Oeuvres de l'Archange Raphaël pour la protection des émigrants. Comité d'Anvers. Anvers: Typographie Bellemans Frères, 1891.

Pirotte, J. *Stéréotypes nationaux et préjugés raciaux aux XIXème et XXème siècles: Sources et méthodes pour une approche historique.* Louvain-la-Neuve: Université Catholique de Louvain, 1982.

Pottier, Johan. *Canada Cocktail.* Bruges: Author, 1970.

Renson, Roland, and H. Smulders. "Situatieschets van de volkssporten in Vlaanderen." *Sport* 21 (1978): 167–76.

Rossel, E. "Work Orientations of the Flemish People." *British Journal of Sociology* 30, no. 3 (1979): 362–72.

Ruys, Manu. *The Flemings: A People on the Move, A Nation in Being.* Tielt: Lannoo, 1973.

Stassart, Joseph. *Les avantages et les Inconvénients économiques d'une population stationnaire.* Liège: Faculté de Droit, Université de Liège, 1965.

Stengers, Jean. *Emigration et immigration en Belgique au XIXe et au XXe siècles* Bruxelles: Académie Royale des Sciences d'Outre-Mer, 1978.

———. "Emigration et immigration en Belgique au XIXe et XXe siècles." *Cahiers de Clio* 71 (1982): 7–17.

———. "Les mouvements migratoires en Belgique aux XIXe et XXe siècles." *Les migrations internationales de la fin du XVIIIe siècle à nos jours.* Paris, 1980: 283–317.

Stols, Eddy. "L'émigration des cerveaux." *La Belgique: Société et cultures depuis 150 ans.* Bruxelles: Editions Nauwelaerts, 1980, 248–52.

———. "Kolonisatie en expansie in het dagelijks leven van de hedendaagse tijd (1830–1940)." *Bijdragen tot de Geschiedenis* 3–4 (1981): 237–60.

Van Molle, Leen. *Ieder voor allen. De Belgische Boerenbond, 1890–1990.* Leuven: Kadoc, 1990.

Van Mullem, Josef. *Belgian Emigration to Canada.* Brussels: Ministry of Small Enterprises, 1999.

Vekeman, Gustaaf. *Le Canada: Notes d'un colon.* Sherbrooke: Typographie des Cantons de l'Est, 1884.

———. *Voyages au Canada.* Namur: Boséré, 1885.

Verbist, Pascal-Joseph. *Les belges au Canada.* Turnhout: Antoine Van Genechter, 1872.

Verdoodt, Albert. *Les problèmes des groupes linguistiques en Belgique*. Louvain: Centre de Recherches Sociologiques, 1973.

Verthé, Arthur, M.J. "Some Sociological Aspects of Belgian Emigration." *International Migration Digest* 2, no. 2 (1965): 125–35.

Viger, Denis-Benjamin. *Considèrations relatives à la dernière révolution en Belgique*. Montréal: Cinq-Mars, 1847.

Wilson, T. "Lord Bryce's Investigation into Alleged German Atrocities in Belgium, 1914–1915." *Journal of Contemporary History* 14, no. 3 (1979): 369–84.

Zolberg, Aristide R. "Splitting the Difference, Federalization with Federalism in Belgium." In Milton J. Esman, ed., *Ethnic Conflict in the Western World*. Ithaca, NY: Cornell University Press, 1977: 103–42.

F. Western Canadian Background

Abella, Irving, and David Millar, eds. *The Canadian Worker in the Twentieth Century*. Toronto: Oxford University Press, 1978.

Anderson, Allan. *Remembering the Farm: Memories of Farming, Ranching and Rural Life in Canada. Past and Present*. Toronto: Macmillan, 1977.

Anderson, Frank W. *Canada's Worst Mine Disaster*. Calgary: Frontier Publishing, 1969.

Archer, John B. *Saskatchewan: A History*. Saskatoon: Western Producer Prairie Books, 1980.

Artibise, Alan F. J. *Winnipeg: A Social History of Urban Growth, 1874–1914*. Montreal: McGill-Queen's University Press, 1975.

Avery, Donald. *Dangerous Foreigners: European Immigrant Workers and Labour Radicalism in Canada, 1896–1932*. Toronto: McClelland & Stewart, 1979.

Bercuson, David. *Fools and Wisemen: The Rise and Fall of the One Big Union*. Toronto: McGraw-Hill Ryerson, 1978.

———. "Tragedy at Bellevue: Anatomy of a Mine Disaster." *Labour/Le Travailleur* 3 (1978): 221–31.

Boam, Henry J. *British Columbia – Its History, People, Commerce, Industries and Resources*. London: Sells Limited, 1912.

Breen, David H. *The Canadian Prairie West and the Ranching Frontier, 1874–1924*. Toronto: University of Toronto Press, 1983.

Brennan, J.W. "Wooing the Foreign Vote: Saskatchewan Politics and the Immigrant, 1905–1919." *Prairie Forum* 3, no. 1 (1978): 61–78.

Breton, Raymond. "Institutional Completeness of Ethnic Communities and Personal Relations of Immigrants." *American Journal of Sociology* 70, no. 2 (1964): 193–205.

Burnet, Jean. *Next Year Country: A Study of Social Organization in Alberta*. Toronto: University of Toronto Press, 1951.

Capling, M. Ann. "Drumheller Strike of 1925." *Alberta History* 31, no. 4 (1983): 11–19.

Cavanaugh, Catherine, and Jeremy Mouat, eds. *Making Western Canada: Essays on European Colonization and Settlement*. Toronto: Garamond Press, 1996.

Chapman, George. *Fruit Growing in Manitoba, Saskatchewan, Alberta*. Winnipeg: Country Guide, 1933.

Conway, John. *The West: The History of a Region in Confederation*. Toronto: James Lorimer, 1994.

Cook, Ramsay. *The Dafoe-Sifton Correspondence, 1919–1927*. Winnipeg: Manitoba Record Society, 1966.

Culliton, J.T. *Assisted Emigration and Land Settlement with specific reference to Western Canada*. Montreal: McGill University Economic Studies, 1928.

Daly, George Thomas. *Catholic Problems in Western Canada*. Toronto: Macmillan, 1921,

Danysk, Cecilia. *Hired Hands: Labour and the Development of Prairie Agriculture, 1880–1930*. Toronto: McClelland & Stewart, 1995.

Dawson, Carl A. *Group Settlement: Ethnic Communities in Western Canada*. Toronto: Macmillan, 1936.

Downs, Art. *Pioneer Days in British Columbia*. Surrey: Heritage Publishing, 1979.

Eagle, John. *The Canadian Pacific Railway and the Development of Western Canada, 1896–1914*. Montreal: McGill-Queen's University Press, 1989.

England, John. *The Colonization of Western Canada: A Study of Contemporary Land Settlement (1896–1934)*. Toronto: McClelland & Stewart, 1936.

Fowke, Vernon C. *Canadian Agricultural Policy. The Historical Pattern*. Toronto: University of Toronto Press, 1946.

———. *The National Policy and the Wheat Economy*. Toronto: University of Toronto Press, 1973.

Francis, R. Douglas. *Images of the West: Changing Perceptions of the Canadian Prairies, 1690–1960*. Saskatoon: Western Producer Prairie Books, 1989.

Friesen, Gerald. *The Canadian Prairies: A History*. Toronto: University of Toronto Press, 1984.

Gagan, David P. *Prairie Perspectives*. Toronto: Holt, Rinehart & Winston, 1970.

Gray, James H. *The Winter Years: The Depression on the Prairies*. Toronto: Macmillan, 1966.

Green, Alan G. *Immigration and the Postwar Canadian Economy*. Toronto: Macmillan, 1976.

Hall, David J. *Clifford Sifton*. Vancouver: University of British Columbia Press, 1981–85, 2 vols.

Harney, Robert F. "Boarding and Belonging. Thoughts on Sojourner Institutions." *Urban History Review* 2 (1978): 8–37.

Harris, Cole. *The Resettlement of British Columbia: Essays on Colonialism and Geographic Change*. Vancouver: UBC Press, 1997.

Hawkins, Freda. *Canada and Immigration: Public Policy and Public Concern*. Montreal: McGill-Queen's University Press, 1972.

Hedges, James B. *Building the Canadian West*. Toronto: Macmillan, 1939.

Henson, Tom N. "The Ku Klux Klan in Western Canada." *Alberta History* 25, no. 4 (1977): 1–8.

Higham, C.L., and Robert Thacker, eds. *One West, Two Myths: A Comparative Reader*. Calgary: University of Calgary Press, 2004.

Huel, Raymond. "The Irish-French Conflict in Catholic Episcopal Nominations: The Western Sees and the Struggle for Domination within the Church." *CCHA, Study Sessions* (1975): 51–70.

———. "When a Minority Feels Threatened: The Impetus for French Catholic Organization in Saskatchewan." *Canadian Ethnic Studies/Etudes Ethniques au Canada* 18, no. 3 (1986): 1–16.

Isajiw, Wsevolod W. "The Process of Social Integration: The Canadian Example." *Dalhousie Review* 48 (Winter 1968): 510–20.

Jaenen, Cornelius J. "Le français au Manitoba: Fruit de l'histoire ou d'une contrainte extérieure?" *Langue et Société* 13 (printemps 1984): 3–16.

———. "The Manitoba School Question: An Ethnic Interpretation." In Martin Kovacs, ed., *Ethnic Canadians: Culture and Education*. Regina: Canadian Plains Research Center, 1978: 203–15.

———. "The Public School in Canada: Agency for Integration and Assimilation." *The Contribution of the Fundamental Sciences to Educational Science*. Paris: International Association for the History of Education, 1976: 203–15.

Jones, David, and Ian MacPherson, eds. *Building Beyond the Homestead*. Calgary: University of Calgary Press, 1985.

Killick, C.H.P. *Manitoba Dairying: A Century of Progress*. Winnipeg: Manitoba Dairy Association, 1970.

Leslie, P.M. "The Role of Political Parties in Promoting the Interests of Ethnic Minorities." *Canadian Journal of Political Science* 2, no. 4 (1969): 419–33.

Loewen, Royden. *Ethnic Farm Culture in Western Canada*. Ottawa: Canadian Historical Association, 2002. Ethnic Groups Booklet 29.

MacDonald, Alex. *Cloud-Capped Towers: The Utopian Theme in Saskatchewan History and Culture*. Regina: Canadian Plains Research Center, 2007.

MacGregor, James G. *A History of Alberta*. Edmonton: Hurtig, 1972.

Macleod, R.G. *The North-West Mounted Police and Law Enforcement, 1873–1905*. Toronto: University of Toronto Press, 1976.

Manitoba Dairy Association. *Fifty Years of Dairying in Manitoba*. Winnipeg: Manitoba Dairy Association, 1935.

Marchildon, Gregory P. *The Heavy Hand of History: Interpreting Saskatchewan's Past*. Regina: Canadian Plains Research Center, 2005.

Markle, W. Ward. "The Canadian Experience of Family Immigration." *Migration News* 13 (May/June 1964): 1–4.

McCormick, Veronica. *A Hundred Years in the Dairy Industry, 1867–1967*. Ottawa: Dollio, 1968.

Mitchell, E.B. *In Western Canada before the War: A Study of Communities*. London: John Murray, 1915.

Morin, Rosaire. *L'Immigration au Canada*. Montréal: Action Nationale, 1966.

Morton, Arthur S., and Chester Martin. *History of Prairie Settlement and Dominion Lands Policy*. Toronto: Macmillan, 1938.

Mysyk, Avis. *Manitoba Commercial Market Gardening, 1945–1997: Class, Race and Ethnic Relations*. Regina: Canadian Plains Research Center, 2000.

Norrie, K.H. "The Rate of Settlement of the Canadian Prairies, 1870–1911." *Journal of Economic History* 35, no. 2 (1975): 400–410.

Owram, Douglas. *Promise of Eden: The Canadian Expansionist Movement and the Idea of the West, 1856–1900*. Toronto: University of Toronto Press, 1980.

Palmer, Howard. *Land of the Second Chance: A History of Ethnic Groups in Southern Alberta*. Lethbridge: Lethbridge Herald, 1972.

————, ed. *Immigration and the Rise of Multiculturalism*. Toronto: Copp Clark, 1975.

————, ed. *The Settlement of the West*. Calgary: Comprint, 1977.

————, and Tamara Palmer, eds. *Peoples of Alberta: Portraits of Cultural Diversity*. Saskatoon: Western Producer Prairie Books, 1985.

Potyondi, Barry. *In Palliser's Triangle: Living in the Grasslands, 1850–1930*. Saskatoon: Purich, 1995.

Roberts, Barbara. "Shovelling Out the Mutinous: Political Deportation from Canada before 1936." *Labour/Le Travail* 18 (1986): 77–110.

Robertson, Heather. *Sugar Farmers of Manitoba: The Manitoba Sugar Beet Industry in Story and Picture*. Altona, MB: D.W. Friesen, 1968.

Seager, Allen. "The Pass Strike of 1932." *Alberta History* 25, no. 1 (1977): 1–11.

————. "Socialists and Workers: The Western Canadian Coal Miners, 1900–21." *Labour/Le Travail* 16 (1985): 23–59.

Siemens, Alfred H., ed. *Lower Fraser Valley: Evaluation of a Cultural Landscape*. Vancouver: Tantalus Research, 1968.

Smillie, Benjamin J., ed. *Visions of the New Jerusalem: Religious Settlement on the Prairies*. Edmonton: NeWest Press, 1983.

Stock, Robert. *Monitoring Migration in the Prairie Provinces*. Regina: Canadian Plains Research Center, 1981.

Thomas, Lewis G. *The Canadian West to 1905: A Canadian Sourcebook*. Toronto: Oxford University Press, 1975.

Thompson, John H., and Allen Seager. "Workers, Growers and Monopolists: The Labour Problem in the Alberta Beet Sugar Industry during the 1930s." *Labour/Le Travail* 3 (1978): 153–78.

Vallee, Frank G., et al. "Ethnic Assimilation and Differentiation in Canada." *Canadian Journal of Economics and Political Science* 23, no. 4 (1957): 540–49.

Venini Byrne, M.B. *From the Buffalo to the Cross: A History of the Roman Catholic Diocese of Calgary*. Calgary: Calgary Archives and Historical Publishers, 1979.

Wardaugh, Ronald. *Language and Nationhood: The Canadian Experience*. Vancouver: New Star Books, 1983.

Whiteley, A.S. "The Peopling of the Prairie Provinces of Canada." *American Journal of Sociology* 38 (1932–33): 240–52.

Wilson, J. Donald, ed. *An Imperfect Past. Education and Society in Canadian History.* Vancouver: University of British Columbia Press, 1984.

Woywitka, A.B. "The Drumheller Strike of 1919." *Alberta Historical Review* (Winter 1973): 1–7.

G. Belgians in Canada

Anonyme. "A la mémoire de M. Louis Hacault." *Les Cloches de Saint-Boniface* 20 (1921): 148–49, 169–71.

Anonymous. *Vancouver Island and Its Missions, 1874–1900: Reminiscences of the Rev. A.J. Brabant.* New York: Messenger of the Sacred Heart, 1900.

Anderson, Alan B. *Ethnic Identity Retention in Francophone Communities in Saskatchewan: A Sociological Survey.* Saskatoon: Unité de recherches pour les études canadiennes-françaises,1985.

Anuntiata, Sr. Mary. "Archbishop Seghers: The Martyred Archbishop of Vancouver Island." *B.C. Historical Quarterly* 14, no. 3 (1943): 191–96.

Baudoux, Maurice. "Pour suivre: Le problème des minorités." *Les Cloches de Saint-Boniface* 44 (1945): 131–40.

———. "Radio-Ouest française." *Vie française* 7 (1953): 435–41.

Beaudin, Réjean. "Johan Beetz, un immigrant créatif." *La Revue d'histoire de la Côte-Nord* 13 (novembre 1990): 27–29.

Beetz, Jeannette, and Henry Beetz. *La merveilleuse aventure de Johan Beetz.* Montréal: Editions Leméac, 1977.

Bodson, Pierre. "People of Belgian Origin." In *Encyclopedia Canadiana.* Toronto: Grolier of Canada, 1968: 359–60.

Boni, A. "Pioniers in Canada, De Belgische Redemptoristen in de provincies Quebec, Manitoba en Saskatchewan." *Missiologische monografieen* 4 (1945): 1–278.

Brandt, Yvette. *Hutlet Heritage, 1680–1972.* Swan Lake: Author, 1972.

Breugelmans, René. "Dutch and Flemings in Canada." *Canadian Ethnic Studies/Etudes ethniques au Canada* 2, no. 2 (1970): 84–115.

———. "Integratie, taal – en kulturbewustzijn bi de nederlands-vlaamse etnische groep in Kanada." *Ons Erfdeel* 11, no. 3 (1968): 29–39.

———. "De nederlanders en vlamingen in Kanada – historische premissen." *Ons Erfdeel* 11, no. 1 (1968): 112–24.

———. "Nederlandse en vlaamse bijdragen tot het kanadese level." *Ons Erfdeel* 11, no. 4 (1968): 80–86.

Brouillette, B. "Cultures spécialisées." *Belgique-Canada* (11 mars 1937): 193–95.

Buitenhuis, Peter. *The Great War of Words: British, American and Canadian Propaganda and Fiction, 1914–1933.* Vancouver: University of British Columbia Press, 1987.

Burmeister, Klaus H., ed. *Western Canada 1909: Travel Letters of William Cohnstaedt*. Regina: Canadian Plains Research Center, 1976.

Cantraine, Philippe. "La présence des wallons en Amérique du Nord." In Georges Gauthier Larouche, ed., *450 Ans de Noms de Lieux Français en Amérique du Nord*. Québec: Publications du Québec, 1986: 35–37.

Carbonez-Dejaeger, Claire. "De Belgische aanwezigheid in Canada." *Canadian Journal of Netherlandic Studies* 19, no. 2 (1998): 41–56.

Cochrane, Hilda. "Belgian Orchard Syndicate." *The Twenty-Sixth Report of the Okanagan Historical Society* Vernon, BC: Okanagan Historical Society, 1962): 111.

Dauw, A. "Emigratie naar Noord-Amerika." *Het Land van Nevele* 9, no. 3 (1978): 113–39.

De Baets, Maurice. *Life of the Most Reverend Charles John Seghers*. Peterson, NJ: St. Anthony Guild Press, 1943.

De Buck, Camille. *Le Club Belge: Fifty Years of History*. Winnipeg: n.p., 1955.

de Molinari, Gustave. *Au Canada et aux Montagnes Rocheuses*. Paris: C. Reinwald, 1886.

De Smet, Pierre-Jean. *Oregon Missions and Travels over the Rocky Mountains*. New York: Edward Dunegan, 1847.

De Vocht, Josef. *Eternal Memory: Father Delaere and Canada's Ukrainian Catholic Church*. Yorkton: Redeemer's Voice Press, 2005.

Degh, Linda. *People in the Tobacco Belt: Four Lives*. Ottawa: National Museum of Man, 1975.

Delaere, Achille. *Mémoire sur les tentatives de schisme et d'hérésie au milieu des Ruthènes de l'Ouest canadien*. Québec: Action Sociale, 1908.

Delmelle, Joseph. "Les Brabançons de la Montage Pembina (Manitoba/Canada)." *Le Folklore Brabançon* 214 (1977): 129–38.

Dempsey, Hugh, ed. *The C.P.R. West: The Iron Road, the Making of a Nation*. Vancouver: Douglas & McIntyre, 1984.

Demyttenaere, J. "Schemes for Young Belgian Agriculturalists in Canada." *Migration News* 9, no. 3 (1960): 22–23.

Destrée, R. "Louis Empain et l'industrie." *Art, Vie, Esprit* 41–42 (1976): 13–16.

Drolet, Jean-Claude. "Mgr Eugène Lapointe, initiateur du syndicalisme catholique en Amérique du Nord." *Rapport de la Société canadienne d'histoire de l'église catholique* (1962): 47–56.

Durieux, Marcel. *Un héros malgré lui*. Saint-Boniface: Editions des Plaines, 1986.

Eggermont-Molenaar, Mary, and Paul Callens, eds. *Missionaries among Miners, Migrants and Blackfoot: The Van Tighem Brothers' Diaries, Alberta, 1875–1917*. Calgary: University of Calgary Press, 2007.

Elias, Jacques. "Belgian Emigration to Canada." *Bulletin des Amitiés belgo-canadiennes* 43 (March 1981): n.p.

Forestier, Georges [Schoeffer]. *La Pointe-aux-Rats*. Paris: Plon, 1907.

Foursin, Pierre. *La Colonisation française au Canada: Manitoba–Territoires du Nord-Ouest–Colombie anglaise*. Ottawa: Chamberlin, 1891.

Frémont, Donatien. "Un apôtre de la colonisation française dans l'Ouest canadien: l'abbé Jean Gaire." *Mémoires de la Société Royale du Canada, XLV*, 3ᵉ série, sec. i (1951): 9–14.

———. *Les Français dans l'Ouest canadien*. Winnipeg: Editions de La Liberté, 1959.

Froendt, Antonia H. *The Huguenot-Walloon Tercentenary*. New York: Huguenot Walloon New Netherlands Commission, 1924.

Gaire, Abbé Jean. *Dix Années de missions au grand Nord-Ouest canadien*. Lille: Dom Bosco, 1898.

Gheur, Bernard. *Retour à Calgary*. Paris: ace Editeur, 1985.

Giscard, Gaston. *Dans la Prairie canadienne*. Regina: Canadian Plains Research Center, 1982.

Greening, W.E. "The Belgian Role in Canadian Economic Development." *Canadian Banker* 66, no. 2 (1959): 121–28.

Griffin, Joseph A. *The Contribution of Belgium to the Catholic Church in America (1523–1857)*. Washington, DC: Catholic University of America, 1932.

Griffis, William Elliott. *The Story of the Walloons: At Home, in Lands of Exile and in America*. New York: Houghton, 1923.

Guitard, Michelle. "La Rolanderie." *Saskatchewan History* 30, no. 3 (1977): 110–14.

Gusbin, Berthe. *Au Nord du 53e*. Saint-Boniface: Editions du Blé, 1982.

Hacault, Louis. "Les belges au Canada." *Courrier de Bruxelles*, 27 juillet – 1 août 1890.

———. "Brieven uit Manitoba." *Handelsblad* (Antwerpen), 25, 26 July, 8, 9, 15, 16, 22 August 1890.

———. "Les catholiques de Bruxelles." *Les Cloches de Saint-Boniface* 6 (1907): 228–29.

———. *Les colonies belges et françaises du Manitoba: Notes de Voyage au Canada en 1890*. Bruxelles: Alfred Vromant, 1892.

———. "Les commandements de Dieu et les écoles publiques." *Les Cloches de Saint-Boniface* 6 (1907): 258–61.

Harrington, Lyn. "Ontario's Klondike Gardens." *Farmer's Magazine*, 46, no. 6 (1949): 9, 36, 44.

Herreboudt, J. *Le Canada au point de vue de l'émigration*. Bruges: Herreboudt & Claeys, 1890.

Hill, J.M. "Archbishop Seghers, Pacific Coast Missionary." *Canadian Catholic Historical Association, Report* 18 (1951): 15–23.

Horna, J. "Leisure re-socialization among immigrants in Canada," *Society and Leisure* 3, no. 1. (1980): 97–110.

Huel, Raymond. *L'Association catholique franco-canadienne de la Saskatchewan: un rempart contre l'assimilation culturelle, 1912–34*. Régina: Publications Fransaskoises, 1969.

Huot, Cécile. "Musiciens belges au Québec." *Cahiers canadiens de musique* 8 (1974): 69–77.

Jackson, M.J., and B. Wilhelm. "Willow Bunch et Bellegarde en Saskatchewan." *Vie française* 27, nos. 11–12 (1973): 281–321.

Jaenen, Cornelius J. "Le contexte socio-économique de l'immigration belge au Canada, 1880–1960." In Ginette Kurgan-van Hentenryk, ed., *La question sociale en Belgique et au Canada*. Bruxelles: Editions de l'Université de Bruxelles, 1988: 151–71.

————. "The Belgian Presence in Canada." In Leen d'Haenens, ed., *Images of Canadianness*. Ottawa: University of Ottawa Press, 1998: 67–90.

————. "Belgians." In Paul Robert Magosci, ed., *Encyclopedia of Canada's Peoples*. Toronto: University of Toronto Press, 1999: 257a–270b.

————. "Quelques aspects des activités professionnelles des immigrants belges (XIXe–XXe siècles)." In Serge Jaumain, ed., *Les Immigrants Préférés: Les Belges*. Ottawa: Presses de l'Université d'Ottawa, 1999: 139–58.

Jameson, Sheilagh. "The Story of Trochu." *Alberta Historical Review* 9, no. 4 (1961): 1–9.

Jaumain, Serge, éd. *Le réforme de l'Etat … et après? L'impact des débats institutionnels en Belgique et au Canada*. Bruxelles: Editions de l'Université de Bruxelles, 1997.

Jaumain, Serge. *Les immigrants préférés: Les belges*. Ottawa: Presses de l'Université d'Ottawa, 1999.

Kaiser, Georges. *Au Canada*. Bruxelles: Lesigne, 1897.

Ketels, H. "Possibilités belges au Canada." *Bulletin de l'Association des Licenciés sortis de l'Université de Liège* 4 (1912): 1–3.

Kovacs, Martin. "The Hungarian School Question." In Martin L. Kovacs, ed., *Ethnic Canadians: Culture and Education*. Regina: Canadian Plains Research Center, 1978: 333–58.

Kurgan-van Hentenryk, Ginette, and J. Laureyssens. *Un siècle d'investissements belges au Canada*. Bruxelles: Editions de l'Université de Bruxelles, 1986.

Lalonde, André. "L'Immigration française et belge dans les Prairies canadiennes de 1870–1940." *Perspectives sur la Saskatchewan française*. Regina: Société historique de la Saskatchewan, 1978, n.p.

Land and Agriculture Company of Canada. *Fruit Farming in the Okanagan Valley, British Columbia*. Winnipeg: Bulman Brothers, 1911.

Lapointe, Richard, and Lucille Tessier. *Histoire des franco-canadiens de la Saskatchewan*. Régina: Société historique de la Saskatchewan. 1987.

Laverdure, Paul. *Redemption and Ritual: The Eastern Rite Redemptorists of North America, 1906–2006*. Yorkton: Redeemer's Voice Press, 2007.

Leau, Léopold [Jean de Saugeunay]. *L'aisance qui vient: Vie du colon dans la prairie canadienne*. Paris: Bloud, 1912.

Lecart, G. "Louis Empain au Canada." *Art, Vie, Esprit* 41–42 (1976): 20–21.

Leclerc, Wilbrod. "Le monde des affaires de langue française à Winnipeg de 1870 à 1890." *Cultures du Canada français* 3 (1986): 71–78.

Lefort, F.L. "Les origines de la Chambre de commerce belge et luxembourgeoise au Canada," *Bulletin de la Chambre de Commerce Belge et Luxembourgeoise au Canada*, no. 93 (1984): 3–17.

Lemont, Arthur. *La mission belge au Canada*. Montréal: Chambre de Commerce du District de Montréal, 1914.

Lempereur, Françoise. "Les wallons de l'Amérique du Nord." *Le Guetteur Wallon* 52 (1976): 110–111.

————. *Les wallons d'Amérique du Nord*. Gembloux: Duculot, 1976.

Léonard, Carol. *La Rolanderie*. Régina: Association culturelle franco-canadienne de la Saskatchewan, 1987.

Léonard, Lucien. *Un littérateur wallon au Canada: L'abbé Jules-Joseph Pirot*. Namur: Cahiers Wallons, s.d.

Levasseur, Donald. *Les Oblats de Marie Immaculée dans l'Ouest et dans le Nord du Canada, 1845–1967*. Edmonton: University of Alberta Press, 1995.

Li, Peter S., and Wilfrid B. Denis. "Minority Enclave and Majority Language: The Case of a French Town in Western Canada." *Canadian Ethnic Studies/Etudes Ethniques au Canada* 15, no. 1 (1983): 18–32.

Lillard, Charles, ed. *Mission to Nootka, 1874–1900: Reminiscences of the West Coast of Vancouver Island*. Sidney, BC: Gray's Publishing, 1977.

Linssen, G.C.P. "Limburghers naar Noord Amerika." *Maasgauw* 93 (1974): col. 39–54.

Loudfoot, Raymond. "The Nuyttens of Belgian Town." *Manitoba Pageant* 19, no. 3 (1974): 15–18.

Lubelski-Bernard, Nadine. "Images du Nouveau Monde ramenées par quelques Belges à la fin du XIXe et au début du XXe siècle." In *La Belgique et l'étranger aux XIXe et XXe siècles*. Bruxelles: Nauwelaerts, 1987: 127–46.

Maes, Camillus. "Flemish Franciscan Missionaries in North America, 1674–1738." *Catholic Historical Review* 1 (April 1915): 13–16.

Magee, Joan. *The Belgians in Ontario: A History*. Toronto: Dundurn Press, 1987.

———. "The Canadian Association for the Advancement of Netherlandic Studies: An Overview of the First Decade, 1971–1981." *Canadian Journal of Netherlandic Studies* 3, nos. 1–2 (1982): 3–7.

Malouin, Reine. "Monseigneur Jean Gaire." *Rapport de la Société canadienne d'histoire de l'Eglise catholique* (1964): 85–97.

McGuinness, Robert. "Missionary Journey of Father De Smet." *Alberta Historical Review* 15, no. 2 (1967): 12–19.

Millet, David. "Religion as a Source of Perpetuation of Ethnic Identity." In A. Davia and K. Herman, eds., *Social Space: Canadian Perspectives*. Toronto: New Press, 1971: 1-10.

Moeller, Albert. *A travers le Nouveau Monde: Etats-Unis et Canada. Notes d'un touriste*. Bruxelles: Goemers, 1911.

Mollier, C. *Au pays du ranch*. Montréal: Fides, 1951.

Moser, Charles. *Reminiscences of the West Coast of Vancouver Island*. Victoria: Acme Press, 1926.

Motut, Roger, and Maurice Legros, eds. *Ordinary Heroes: The Journal of a French Pioneer in Alberta by Marcel Durieux*. Edmonton: University of Alberta Press, 1980.

Nordegg, Martin. *The Possibilities of Canada are Truly Great: Memoirs, 1906–1934*. Toronto: Macmillan, 1971.

O'Neill, Joseph. *Diary of a Priest*. Tillsonburg: Author, 1970.

Ouellette, abbé Joseph. *L'Alberta-nord: Région de colonisation*. Edmonton: Le Courrier de l'Ouest, 1909.

Painchaud, Robert. "Les exigences linguistiques dans le recrutement d'un clergé pour l'Ouest canadien, 1818–1920." *Rapport de la Société canadienne d'histoire de l'Eglise catholique* (1975): 43–64.

———. "French Canadian Historiography and French-Canadian Settlement in Western Canada, 1870–1915." *Canadian Historical Review* 54, no. 4 (1978): 447–63.

———. *Le rêve français dans le peuplement de la prairie.* Saint-Boniface: Editions des Plaines, 1987.

Pénisson, Bernard. *Henri d'Hellencourt, un journaliste français au Manitoba (1898–1905).* Saint-Boniface: Editions du Blé, 1986.

Phillips, Paul. *No Power Greater: A Century of Labour in British Columbia.* Vancouver: University of British Columbia Press, 1967.

Puissant, Jean. "Quelques témoignages sur l'émigration hennuyère, 1884–1889." *Académie Royale des Sciences d'Outre-Mer, Bulletin des Séances* 3 (1973): 443–63.

Quigley, William. "Belgo-Canadian Land Company." In *The Twenty-Fifth Report pf the Okanagan Historical Society.* Vernon, B.C.: Okanagan Historical Society, 1961: 140–44.

Reksten, Terry. *The Dunsmuir Saga.* Vancouver: Douglas & McIntyre, 1991.

Renson, Roland, Danielle De Kegel, and Harman Smulders. "The Folk Roots of Games: Games and Ethnic Identity among Flemish-Canadian Immigrants." *Canadian Journal of the History of Sport* 14, no. 2 (1983): 69–79.

Robert, Arthur. "Le Cardinal Mercier à l'Université Laval." *Le Canada français* 3, no. 3 (1919): 200–207.

Robillard, Denise. *Maurice Baudoux, 1902–1988.* Québec: Presses de l'Université Laval, 2009.

Robin, Martin. *Radical Politics and Canadian Labour, 1880–1930.* Montreal: McGill-Queen's University Press, 1968.

Rondeau, Clovis. *La Montagne de Bois. Histoire de la Saskatchewan méridionale.* Québec: Action Sociale, 1923.

Rottiers, René. *Soixante-cinq années de luttes … Esquisse historique de l'œuvre de l'ACFC.* Régina: Association Culturelle Franco-Canadienne de la Saskatchewan, 1977.

Roy, Marie-Anna A. *Les Capucins de Toutes-Aides (Manitoba) et leurs dignes confrères.* Montréal: Editions Franciscaines, 1977.

Rutten, R.P. *L'expérience belge ou leçons pratiques d'action sociale catholique d'après les causeries de Montréal.* Montréal: Godin-Ménard, 1914.

Sabourin, abbé J.A. *L'apostolat chez les Ruthènes au Manitoba.* Québec: Action Sociale, 1911.

St. Stephen, R.M. "Father Gravel, Missionary-Colonizer." *Saskatchewan History* 13, no. 3 (1939): 107–9.

Silverman, P.G. "Aid to the Civil Power: The Nanaimo Coal Miners Strike, 1912–1914." *Canadian Defence Quarterly* 4 (1974): 16–52.

Simpson, George W. "Father Delaere, Pioneer Missionary and Founder of Churches." *Saskatchewan History* 3, no. 1 (1950): 1–16.

Tait, Lyal. *Tobacco in Canada.* Toronto: T.H. Best Printing, 1968.

Tremblay, Emilien. *Le Père Delaere et l'église ukrainienne du Canada*. Berthierville: Imprimerie Bernard, 1961.

Trépanier, Pierre. "La colonie franco-belge de Namur (1871–1881)." *Asticou* 18 (décembre 1977): 14–32.

Trottier, Alice. *Jean-Baptiste Morin: Journal d'un missionnaire-colonisateur, 1890–1897*. Edmonton: Salon d'histoire de la francophonie, s.d.

Van Bruyssel, Ferdinand. *Le Canada. Agriculture. Elevage. Exploitation forestière. Colonisation*. Bruxelles: Weissenbruch, 1895.

———. *Jean Vadeboncoeur et Anne-Marie Lafrance, Canadiens-français*. Paris: Editions de la Revue mondiale, 1934.

Vanderhaeghe, Guy. *Man Descending: Selected Stories by Guy Vanderhaeghe*. Toronto: Macmillan, 1982.

van der Heyden, Joseph. "Life and Letters of Father Brabant, Flemish Missionary Hero." *American College Bulletin (Louvain)* 11, no. 1 (1913): 8–38, 52–69.

———. *Life and Letters of Father Brabant, a Flemish Missionary Hero*. Louvain: Wouters-Ickx, 1920.

Van Tighem, Frank. "Father Leonard Van Tighem, O.M.I." *Alberta Historical Review* 12, no. 1 (1964): 17–21.

Vekeman, Gustaaf. *Canada: Het Groote Noord-Westen*. Ottawa: Government Printing Office, 1882.

———. *Le Canada: Notes d'un Colon*. Sherbrooke: Société Typographique des Cantons de l'Est, 1884.

———. *Eene Reis in Canada of Nuttige Raadgevingen aan de Belgische Landverhuizers*. Sherbrooke: Le Pionnier, 1882.

———. *Guide des Emigrants au Canada et spécialement dans les Cantons de l'Est*. Bruxelles: Loge, 1890.

———. *Lettres d'un Emigrant: ou Voyage au Canada: Suivies d'un appendice sur le Manitoba*, Bruxelles: Loge, 1883.

———. *Voyages au Canada*. Namur: Boséré, 1885.

Verbist, Pascal. *Les Belges au Canada*. Turnhout: Antoine Van Genechten, 1872.

Vermeirre, André. "Un aspect de l'émigration de début du XXe siècle au Québec: H. Biermans." *Canadian Journal of Netherlandic Studies* 4 (1983): 14–19.

———. *Les cinquantes années d'existence de l'Association Belgique-Canada*. Montréal: L'Auteur, 1987.

———. *Hubert Biermans du Congo à Shawinigan*. Sillery: Editions du Septentrion, 2001.

———. *L'immigration des belges au Québec*. Sillery: Editions du Septentrion, 2001.

Verthé, Arthur. *Vlaanderen in de Wereld: Vlamingen in Ontario, Canada*. Brussels: D.A.P. Reinart. 1972.

Waugh, Earle H. *Dissonant Worlds: Roger Vandersteene among the Cree*. Waterloo: Wilfrid Laurier University Press, 1996.

Wilbois, Joseph. *Un pays neuf: L'ouest canadien*. Paris: Valois, 1931.

Wilhelm, Bernard. "Montmartre: Un village en Saskatchewan." *Vie française* 3 (1986): 79–85.

Wilson, Keith, and James B. Wyndels, eds. *The Belgians in Manitoba*. Winnipeg: Peguis, 1976.

Wyndels, James B. *Joseph G. Van Belleghem: A Biography*. Ottawa: J. Merrian Print, 2004.

Zwaenepoel, M. "Kanada en onze landgenoten." *Band en Zuiderkruis* 1 (1963): 15.

H. Theses and Dissertations

Calderwood, William. "The Rise and Fall of the Ku Klux Klan in Saskatchewan." MA, University of Regina, 1968.

Comtois, Robert. "L'expérience migratoire canadienne d'après-guerre, 1946–60." Licence, Université Catholique de Louvain, 1962.

De Kebel, Danielle. "Sport en etniciteit: Volksporten – onderzoek bij de Vlaamse emigranten in Noord Amerika." Licence, Katholieke Universiteit Leuven, 1981.

Dendy, David R.B. "One Huge Orchard: Okanagan Land and Development Companies before the Great War." BA Honours essay, University of Victoria, 1976.

Devos, Julien. "L'émigration belge au Canada: Son influence sur la culture du tabac." Licence, Institut Catholique des Hautes Etudes Commerciales, Bruxelles, 1969.

Goell, Yosef Israel. "Bi-Nationalism and Bi-Lingualism in Three Modern States: A Comparative Study of Canada, Belgium and White South Africa." PhD, Columbia University, 1971.

Den Otter. A.A. "Sir Alexander T. Galt and the Northwest: A Case Study of Entrepreneurialism on the Frontier." PhD, University of Alberta, 1975.

Husaini, Zohra. "Social Networks: A Factor in Immigrant Economic Success." PhD, University of Alberta, 1981.

Irwin, Robert S. "The Emergence of a Regional Identity: The Peace River Country, 1916–46." PhD, University of Alberta, 1995.

Jackson, Wayne. "Ethnicity and Areal Organization among French Canadians in the Peace River District, Alberta." MA, University of Alberta, 1970.

Journée, Marc. "De lokroep van een nieuwe frontier, Belgische emigratie en expansie in Canada, 1880–1940." Licence, Katholieke Universiteit Leuven, 1981.

Karas, Frank. "Labour and Coal in the Crowsnest Pass, 1925–1935." MA, University of Calgary, 1972.

Le Gal, Yvette. "La restructuration rurale en province de Saskatchewan: L'exemple de la paroisse de St-Maurice de Bellegarde." MA, Université d'Ottawa, 1988.

Mabru, Michel. "Les francophones de l'Alberta." Thèse de 3ᵉ cycle, Université de Poitiers, 1978.

Manley, John. "Communism and the Canadian Working Class during the Great Depression: The Workers Unity League, 1930–1936." PhD, Dalhousie University, 1984.

McLeod, Keith. "Education and Assimilation of the New Canadian in the North-West Territories and Saskatchewan, 1885–1934." PhD, University of Toronto, 1975.

McMullen, Charles. "Trade Unions in District 18, 1900–1925: A Case Study." MBA thesis, University of Alberta, 1969.

Milnor, Andrew J. "Agrarian Protest in Saskatchewan, 1929–1948: A Study in Ethnic Politics." PhD, Duke University, 1962.

Moodie, Donald W. "The St. Albert Settlement: A Study in Historical Geography." MA, University of Alberta, 1965.

Painchaud, Robert. "The Catholic Church and the Movement of Francophones to the Canadian Prairies, 1870–1915." PhD, University of Ottawa, 1976.

Palmer, Howard. "Nativism and Ethnic Tolerance in Alberta, 1920–1972." PhD, York University, 1973.

Pinno, Erhard. "Temperance and Prohibition in Saskatchewan." MA, University of Saskatchewan, 1971.

Qureshi, A.S. "Local Variation in Rural Farm Depopulation in Southwestern Saskatchewan." MA, University of Regina, 1977.

Ross, James W.F. "A Static Model of Economic Efficiency in Vegetable Production in Manitoba: An Application of Line Programming." MSc, University of Manitoba, 1969.

Rusak, S.J. "Relations in Education between Bishop Legal and the Alberta Liberal Government, 1905–1920." MEd, University of Alberta, 1966.

Seager, Charles Allen. "A Proletariat in Wild Rose Country: The Alberta Coal Miners, 1905–1945." PhD, York University, 1982.

Smeltzer, M.F. "Saskatchewan Opinions on Immigration from 1925 to 1939." MA, University of Saskatchewan, 1950.

Smets, Kristine. "Gazette van Detroit and the Belgian American Community, 1907–1921." MA, Kent State University, 1995.

Smith, Mathew Elliott. "The Development of a Socialist Opposition: The Case of British Columbia, 1880–1945." PhD, University of North Carolina, Chapel Hill, 1978.

Verdet, Paula. "Interpreting Problems of a Roman Catholic Parish: A French-Canadian Institution and its Bilingual Membership." PhD, University of Chicago, 1959.

I. Typescripts

Baltessen, Evelyn Simoens. "an Investigation into the Progress and Educational Directives Affect the Integrity of a Minority Group." Canadian Studies, University of Manitoba [n.d.].

Bédard, Roméo. "The Colony of Montmartre, 1893–1953" [1953].

Behiels, Maurice, and Laura Behiels. "The Behiels Heritage" [1985].

Boileau, Gilles. "Les Canadiens Français de Rivière-la Paix" [1960].

Chartrand, Pierre. "Le baron Louis Empain au Canada: Un destin contrarié" [1999].

Denis, Anne, and Raymond Murphy. "Schools and the Conservation of the Vertical Mosaic" [1977].

De Roo, Rémi. "The History of the De Pape and De Roo Families in Canada, 1899 to 1978" [1978].

De Trémaudan, Désiré. "Chronologie de Montmartre, Saskatchewan" [1954].

Dickin, George H. "History of Manor" [1955].

Gaire, Jean. "Fondation de St-Raphaël (Cantal) et St-Maurice (Bellegarde)" [1892].

Haegeman, Marcel. "The Belgians of South-Central Manitoba" [1994].

Hewitt, John. "Canada Beckons: A History of the Van De Sompel and De Maertelaere Families" [1999].

Jaenen, Cornelius J. "The Belgian Presence and Interests in Canada" [1999].

———. "Flemish Immigration to Western Canada" [2006].

Jensen, Vincent, S.J. "Manitoba School Question" [1964].

Leblanc, André. Gustave Francq" [n.d.].

Morissette, Pierre. "The French Settlement of Cantal, Bellegarde, Sainte-Antoine, Waucope and Forget" [n.d.]

Obbens, Brother Rombart. "Les Frères de Notre-Dame de la Miséricorde au Canada: Leur première fondation à Swan Lake, MB" [s.d.].

Palmer, Howard. "Interview of Celine Audenart" [1980].

Patterson, H.L. "The Dairy Farm Business" [1945].

Silk [Decock], Nancy. "Tales of the Dump" [n.d.].

Vermeirre, André "Projets d'implantation belge au Canada" [1972].

Wingerter, J. Richard. "Frederick W.J. Haultain: Obstacle to National Understanding" [1972].

INDEX

A

aboriginals. *See* Indians

absorption capacity, 41

acculturation, x–xii

Adam, François, 128–29, 231, 290

Adam, Louis, 89

adaptation, 22–23, 30, 37, 47–48, 75, 129, 131, 162, 235

agricultural ideology, 98–99, 141, 184, 241

agro-business, 87, 96, 209, 257

agronomists, 98–99

Aimé Gyselbrecht & Frères, 14

Albert, Louis, 167, 285

Alberta Company, 24, 167, 179

Alberta Royal Commission on Coal Mining, 159, 172, 294

Alberta Sugar Beet Growers, 137–38

Allen Steamship Lines, 31, 39, 45, 53

American College in Louvain, 148, 174, 184, 197, 332

Americanism, 193

Amerindians. *See* Indians

Anchor Line, 53

Anderson, J.T.M., viii, 116, 257

Anderson, Neville, 173

Anglo-Belgian Treaty, 1862, 210

anglo-conformity, viii, 69, 117, 131, 184, 197, 235, 255, 257, 264

anthracite, 3, 147, 157, 159

Anthracite Coal Company, 157

anticlericalism, xi, 100, 153, 163, 172–74, 260

Anseeuw, Hector, 86

Anseeuw, Joseph, 87

Anseeuw, Tryphoon, 86

Antwerp International Exhibition, 51

aristocrats, 103–4, 105–6, 178–81

Asselin, Olivar, 55, 278, 280

assimilation, xi, 185, 190, 191, 196, 206, 235, 255, 257, 258, 264, 307, 318, 324, 325, 328

atrocities myth, 229, 322

B

Bacchus, Alphonse, 71, 250

Baert, Gerard, 81

Banque de Bruxelles, 212

Banque de Commerce d'Anvers, 170, 213

Banque d'Outre-Mer, 170, 212, 230

Banque Lambert, 217

Bareel, Louis, 21, 22

Bareel, Xavier, 212, 213

Barnard, Edouard, 45

Barre, S.A., 83

Baudoux, Maurice, 111, 114, 196, 197, 198, 222, 223, 259, 288, 300, 326, 331

B.C. Sugar Refining Company, 92

Beernaert, Auguste, 10, 21

Beet Workers' Industrial Union, 136, 137

Behiels, Edward, 115

Behiels, Joseph, 140

Bekaert, 45, 218

Belgian-Canadian Association of British Columbia, 249

Belgian-Canadian Chamber of Commerce, 81

D

dairying, 45, 79, 83–88, 175–76
Davidson, vi, 115, 288, 315
de Baets, Theophil, 89
de Bary, Albert, 212, 213
de Beaudrap, Paul, 104, 105
de Bernard de Fauconsol, Jules, 200
Debleekaere, François, 70
De Buck, Camille, 244, 311, 327
de Burlet, Charles, 178, 212, 275, 277, 294, 302, 304, 305
de Burlet, H., 125, 228
de Burlet, Lucien, 78, 283
De Cock, Richard, 112
De Decker, Constant, 105
De Decker, Ludovic, 178, 180, 212
De Decker, Robert, 213
De Decker, Theophil, 105
De Garro, Paul, 148
de Grelle, Raoul, 177, 181, 213
de Harven, Hélène, 255
Dehon, Léon Jean, 18
De Jardin, Arthur, 135, 179, 181
De Jardin, Fernand, 177, 178, 212, 213
De Jardin, Gaston, 102, 106–7
Delaere, Achille, 188–90, 299, 327, 331, 332
Delanoy, Hector, 125–26, 290
Delbeke, Gustave, 124
Deleau, vi, 44, 69, 75–77, 85, 102, 109, 194, 283, 316
Deleau, Sébastien, 76
De Leeuw, Marcien, 79, 80, 237
Deloraine, vi, 42, 63, 65, 66, 74–76, 99, 102, 110, 111, 112, 113, 126, 157, 194, 205, 224, 244, 246, 312, 315, 317
Delouche, C., 21, 122, 276, 289, 310, 320
de Malherbe, R., 124
Deman, Camille, 130, 290
de Man, Henri, 2, 174, 275, 296
De Meulenaere, O., 6, 274
Demme, R.A., 21, 23
De Molinari, Gustave, 96, 327
d'Empeaus, Dougat, 124
de Nobele, Louis, 237
De Pape, August, 43, 68, 72, 282, 312
De Pape, Charles, 43, 126
De Pape, Clement, 43
deportation, 148, 160, 170, 173, 294, 325

De Roaldes, Georges, 124
De Roo, Francis, 72, 259
De Roo, Rémi, vii, 198, 222, 335
De Roo, Victor, 89
De Saurras, Henri, 103
Desmet, Adile, 123
Desmet, Joseph, 130
De Smet, Pierre-Jean, 185, 298, 327, 330
de Sola, Clarence, 13, 211, 275
Desterbecq, Albert, 16
Destrée, M., 12
De Trémaudan, A., 106
De Trémaudan, Désiré, 287, 335
Devaux, Henri, 151
Devilder, Henri, 181, 213
Devilder, Joseph, 105–6
De Volder, M., 68
De Vos, Robert, 22, 59, 60, 70, 73, 76, 79, 85, 97, 122, 127, 139, 157, 211
De Wetter, Joseph, 142
D'Hearter, Frédéric, 18
d'Hellencourt, Henri, 46, 69, 282, 331
Didion, Marcel, 77
Diedricks, Boniface, 194
Diefenbaker, John, 41, 221
diversification, 97, 106, 119, 180, 209
Dobbelaere, René, 246
Dominion & Temperley Line, 53
Dominion Land Act, 29, 121, 289
Doukhobors, 34, 35, 115, 225
Drapeau, Stanislaus, 48, 279, 314
drought, viii, 8, 20, 25, 36, 40, 43, 57, 74, 75, 89, 90, 96, 97, 107, 108, 109, 112, 113, 116–18, 131, 137, 209, 267, 289
Drumheller, vi, 147, 168–70, 173, 184, 219, 296, 315, 322, 326
dry farming, 97, 110, 123, 144, 285
Dubuc, A.J.H., 22
Duclos, J.E., 192
Duclosville, 192
Dunsmuir, James, 153, 154, 293, 331
Dunsmuir, Robert, 151, 152, 153
Dupuis, Léon, 175, 177, 215, 297, 302, 303, 312
Dutch, xi, 2, 3, 6, 58, 130, 175, 176, 194, 249, 251, 252, 326

Genestar, 216, 217
Gerinrose, Fernand, 108–9, 287
German Development Company, 170
Gheur, Ernest, 171–72, 296
Gibson's Landing, 175
Glaverbel, 217
Glorieux, Medar, 72
Gobert, André, 243, 247
Goblet d'Alviella, Eugène, 4, 273
Godts, Willem, 188
Golden Boy, 88
Goldschmidt, Nicholas, 249
Gouzée, André, 105, 179, 181, 212, 213
Govaerts, Albert, 129
grain trade, 67, 79, 82, 224
Grande Clairière, vi, 54, 59, 64, 66, 74, 75, 76, 99, 100, 108, 194, 204, 283
Grandin, Vital Justin, 121, 185, 309
Grand Trunk Railway, 43, 52, 211, 212
Gravelbourg, vi, 198, 260, 288, 309, 315
Great Depression, 24, 25, 86, 97, 116, 137, 191, 195, 209, 220, 261, 294, 303
grubbers. *See* making land
Gusbin, Berthe, 255, 306, 328

H

Hacault, Antoine, 198, 222
Hacault, Louis, 12, 18, 20, 49, 67, 68, 72, 84, 198, 199, 203, 222, 252, 326, 328
Henry, Gustave, 173, 296
Heynen, Hubert, 191, 194
Hind, Henry Yule, 34, 37, 283
Hoet, Henri, 251
Holland, vi, 43, 46, 71, 73, 88, 126, 204, 246, 250, 251, 315
Holvoet, Ernest, 135
homesteads, 5, 21, 29, 34, 70, 76, 101, 105, 113, 115, 116, 139, 225, 288, 315
horsebreeding, 76, 96, 120, 124, 125, 139, 267, 290
horse ranching, 106, 120, 124–27, 139, 231
Hounjet, Pierre, 114, 286
Hudson Bay Railway, 74, 82, 111, 128, 175, 215
Hudson's Bay Company, 116, 128, 138, 151, 202
Hulot, Etienne, 5, 151, 273, 293

Hungarians, 115, 138, 185, 187–88, 254, 255, 298, 329,
Hutlet, Joseph, 71, 72
Hutterites, 258
Huysmans de Deftal, Baron, 97

I

Icelanders, 34, 35, 83
identities, xi, 125, 184, 194, 203, 220, 223, 225, 235, 245, 258, 264, 265, 267, 297, 303, 333
Immigration Act, 1869, 29, 38, 279
Immigration Act, 1919, 40, 173, 278
Immigration and Colonization Act, 1872, 29
immigration policy, 30, 38–42, 57, 122, 278, 318
imports, 126, 154, 215
Independent Greek Church, 188
Indians, 3, 4, 33, 42, 78, 97, 103, 128, 184, 185–86, 196, 294
Ingeveld, Maurice, 124, 226, 290, 311
institutional completeness, 236
integration, xi, xii, 26, 59, 64, 78, 184, 196, 220, 235, 255, 256, 257–58, 263–67, 307, 324
internal migration. *See* migration patterns
investment, 19, 22, 23, 24, 33, 37, 51, 91, 101, 106, 107, 129, 159, 175, 178, 181, 209–18, 239, 263, 267
irrigation, 39, 97, 122, 123, 127, 130, 132, 133, 135, 137, 167, 178, 179, 181, 290, 298

J

Jacobs, E., 22
Jaenen, Alphonse, 119, 289
Jaenen, Alphonse, Sr., 225
Jaenen, Cornelius, Sr., 107–8
Jaenen, John, 117, 287
Jaumain, Serge, 273, 279, 280, 300, 329
Joseph, Jesse, 19, 210
Journée, Marc, 254, 270, 286, 297, 298, 320, 333

K

Kaiser, Georges, 4, 19, 20, 68, 273, 276, 282, 320, 333
Kaposvar, 187
kermess, 3, 248

Ketels, H., 4, 273, 288, 329
Kimpe, Maurice, 226
King, W.L. Mackenzie, 41, 57, 154, 167, 222,
    291, 295, 311
Klondike gold rush, 50, 149–50, 293
Knight, Jesse W., 132
Knights of Labour, 151
Knight Sugar Company, 126, 132, 133, 291,
    310, 311
Komarno, 189
Kronacher, Paul, 91, 92
Ku Klux Klan, 96, 182, 190, 191, 192, 220,
    323, 333

L

Labelle, Antoine, 20, 46, 276, 310
La Broquerie, 20, 66
Lacombe, Albert, 138, 142, 281
Ladysmith, 154, 155
Land and Agriculture Company of Canada,
    178, 179, 180, 212–14, 298, 329
land speculation, ix, 22, 121, 128, 180, 181,
    209, 211, 212, 214
Langevin, Adélard, 21, 45, 46, 100, 101, 103,
    104, 187, 188, 192, 200, 254, 275, 300,
    301, 307, 309, 310
Langevin, Hector, 45, 54, 280
language, vii, xi, xii, 7, 35, 48, 52, 56, 73, 97,
    122, 141, 142, 160, 173, 174, 183, 185,
    186, 187, 194, 195, 197, 198, 199, 200,
    202–6, 223, 224, 230–32, 236, 239–
    40, 250, 251, 261, 264, 278, 298–302,
    325, 330
Laurent, Octave, 3, 4, 273
Laurier, Wilfrid, 33, 38, 169, 170, 187, 201,
    311
Laurier-Greenway Agreement, 201–3
La Vérendrye Band, 248, 250
Leblanc, Emile, 170, 293, 296, 304, 311
Lebrun, E., 68, 82, 296
Leclercq, Jules, 16, 297
Lecoq, Eugène, 91, 297
LeFloch, Paul, 129, 312
Le Gal, Yvette, 275, 315, 321, 347
Lemieux Act, 181, 309
Lennox, G., 20, 62, 293, 298, 324
Le Rouge le Saunier, Jenny, 265

Lethbridge, 6, 20, 83, 88, 135, 137, 141, 147,
    148, 151, 161, 173, 180–81, 187, 198,
    200, 201, 205, 215, 309, 313, 315, 329
lignite, 3, 124, 125, 126, 171, 306, 308
Lileux, Leonie, 165
Lille, 174, 195, 198
Lobert, Victorine, 179
local newspapers, 188, 241
lockout, 22, 167, 181
Lonay, Alex, 71, 305
Lowe, John, 59, 292, 303

M

Macoun, John, 51, 156, 291
Macoun, W., 104
Maillardville, 189
making land, 85
Manitoba Pole Archery Association, 259
Manitoba School Question, 36, 213, 216
Manitoba Sugar Company, 105
Manor, vi, 33, 56, 59, 116, 120–24, 131, 208,
    225, 239, 329, 349
Maple Creek, vi, 126, 127, 140, 169, 255, 260
Mariapolis, vi, 81, 85, 86, 87, 97
market gardening, 10, 38, 102–4, 106, 189,
    190, 223, 271, 277, 299
Marmette, Joseph, 59, 292
Martin, M., 29
Maufort, Auguste, 177
meat packing, 77, 93, 95
Medecine Hat, 245
Mennonites, 48
Métis, 17, 18, 47, 51, 72, 79, 92, 153, 156, 216,
    291
Mignault, Charles, 97
migration patterns, 24, 56–59, 78, 85, 111,
    114, 115, 122, 125, 154, 158, 182, 328,
    331, 339
military service, 7, 32, 62, 178, 240–42
militia, 47, 65, 169
Millarville, 124
Miners Liberation League, 155
Minet, Jules, 109, 229, 304
Mine Workers' Union of Canada, 155, 158
mining, xi, 7, 22, 23, 82, 85, 121, 135, 147–82,
    190, 191, 192, 209, 212, 216, 218, 219,
    260, 261, 312

women, x, xi, 36, 83, 98, 99, 108, 118–19, 131,
        141, 156, 163, 176, 193, 219, 221, 238,
        246, 261–62, 289, 294, 297, 303, 307,
        318, 320
working class culture, 86, 164, 173–74
work stoppage, 136, 153, 158, 166, 261
World War I, 26, 32, 56, 74, 75, 79, 85, 96,
        119, 125, 129, 134, 135, 155, 160, 168,
        179, 180, 181, 189, 203, 212, 214, 219,
        226–31, 238, 253, 271
World War II, 4, 9, 19, 26, 41, 43, 80, 81, 88,
        89, 97, 107, 126, 137, 180, 195, 216,
        232–33, 219, 244, 245, 250, 252, 255,
        257, 260, 271
Wyndels, Firmin, 80, 241
Wyndels, James B., 80, 254, 333

Y

Yellow Grass, vi, 111, 112, 217
Yellowknife, 221, 223
Yorkton, vi, 188, 189, 190
Ypres, 227, 231, 248, 304
Yukon, 85, 149–50, 197, 221

www.ingramcontent.com/pod-product-compliance
Lightning Source LLC
Chambersburg PA
CBHW050626280326
41932CB00015B/2539